PROVENCE

'the days shot through with the colour
of silvery olives, purple mountains,
yellow sunflowers, black cypresses and
lavender, the nights thrilling,
dry and clear and boiling with stars'

CADOGANguides

Contents

About the authors

Dana Facaros and Michael Pauls lived for eight years in a leaky old farmhouse in southwest France, and now they're back...at least for a while.

About the updater

Jacqueline Chnéour is a freelance translator and researcher. Brought up in Paris and Nice, she moved to England in 1979 to follow a dream, and has lived in London ever since. She has updated or consulted on several guides in the Cadogan France series, including the Paris guide.

Cadogan Guides
Network House, 1 Ariel Way, London W12 7SL
cadoganguides@morrispub.co.uk
www.cadoganguides.com

The Globe Pequot Press
246 Goose Lane, PO Box 480, Guilford,
Connecticut 06437–0480

Copyright © Dana Facaros and Michael Pauls
1992, 1994, 1996, 2000, 2002

Cover and photo essay design by Kicca Tommasi
Book design by Andrew Barker
Cover photographs by John Miller
Maps © Cadogan Guides,
    drawn by Map Creation Ltd
Editorial Director: Vicki Ingle
Series Editor: Linda McQueen
Editor: Christine Stroyan
Indexing: Isobel McLean
Production: Book Production Services

Printed in Italy by Legoprint
A catalogue record for this book is available
    from the British Library
ISBN 1-86011-847-X

The author and publishers have made every effort to ensure the accuracy of the information in this book at the time of going to press. However, they cannot accept any responsibility for any loss, injury or inconvenience resulting from the use of information contained in this guide.

Please help us to keep this guide up to date. We have done our best to ensure that the information in this guide is correct at the time of going to press. But places and facilities are constantly changing, and standards and prices in hotels and restaurants fluctuate. We would be delighted to receive any comments concerning existing entries or omissions. Authors of the best letters will receive a copy of the Cadogan Guide of their choice.

Provence
a photo essay

by John Miller

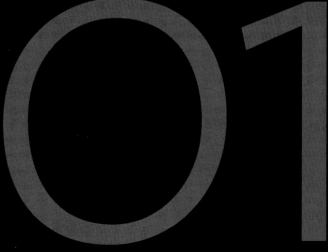

01

The Croix de Provence on
Montagne Ste-Victoire

Avignon

Calanque de Sormiou

Place d'Albertas,
Aix-en-Provence

Café, Aix-en-Provence

Cork oak,
Massif des Maures

Vineyard near Vaison-
la-Romaine

Pâtisserie

The Toulourenc Valley
below Mont Ventoux

Cèpes and olives in
Aix Market

A game of boules

Village overlooking
Mont Venoux

The ruins of Glanum,
St-Rémy-de-Provence
(left and top right)

Abbaye de Sénanque

Gorges du Verdon

Annot Station

Cours Mirabeau,
Aix-en-Provence

Vieux Port, Marseille

Introduction

The sun-drenched landscapes of Provence seduce like few others – the days shot through with the colour of silvery olives, purple mountains, yellow sunflowers, black cypresses and lavender, the nights thrilling, dry and clear and boiling with stars. Vincent Van Gogh, who saw more clearly into the heart of this extravagant world than anyone else, painted these landscapes, and especially those cypresses, as if they were churning and alive, with a lyrical and passionate intensity. Come to the hills around St-Rémy when the mistral is up, and you'll see nature imitating art.

We outsiders have had an on-off love affair with the south of France ever since the Romans colonized it and spent their decline here lounging around their heated pools. Even the medieval popes and cardinals in Avignon succumbed to its worldly temptations, its wines and the scents of the *maquis*, its roses and violets, the droning hum of the cicadas. The painters in the papal court, including some of the greatest artists of the 14th century, lent their radiant Madonnas something of the voluptuous Mediterranean light and colour that would one day inspire Van Gogh and Cézanne, Braque and Picasso, painters whose works have changed the way our eyes see not only the south of France, but the rest of our world as well.

These days, our world has decided on Provence as its possible paradise. Millions come here every year, hoping to catch a glimpse of it, wishing it didn't have so many second homes, holiday flats, trinket shops and traffic jams. To see the region at its best, the delicate question of when to go becomes as crucial as where: in August, the sacred month of French holidays, even the dullest town in Provence can be as frantic as the monkey pit in a zoo. At other times, Provence's essentially classical spirit is easier to grasp – in the lovely countryside around Aix-en-Provence and Cézanne's fetish Montagne Ste-Victoire, or the flame-like peaks of the Alpilles or Cubist tile-roofed *villages perchés* in the Luberon, the cliffs and fjord-like *calanques* off the coast of Marseille, the secret valleys in Mercantour National Park in the Alps, the bullring of Arles and the Roman theatre of Orange, like molten gold in the last rays of the sun. Colourful markets, wild mountains, abandoned Brigadoons and beautifully restored art towns, and restaurants that rival Paris' finest beckon, but perhaps best of all is the leisure in doing as the Romans did and spending the day lounging around the pool, surrounded by perfumed gardens, idly dreaming about what's for lunch. No wonder that Pope Gregory XI, who returned the papacy to Rome in 1377, took one look at the Eternal City and immediately decided to pack his bags to return to the comforts and delights of Avignon. Much to the relief of the Italians, he died before he could go.

A Guide to the Guide

The book opens with a **photo essay** to whet your appetite. The early chapters contain all the background information you need: a **History** of Provence and a brief guide to its **Art and Architecture**; a **Topics** chapter exploring features of Provençal life and culture; **Food and Drink**, introducing the gastronomic specialities of the region and its wines, along with a list of vocabulary that will help you to make sense of the menu; a comprehensive **Travel** chapter which includes details of special-interest

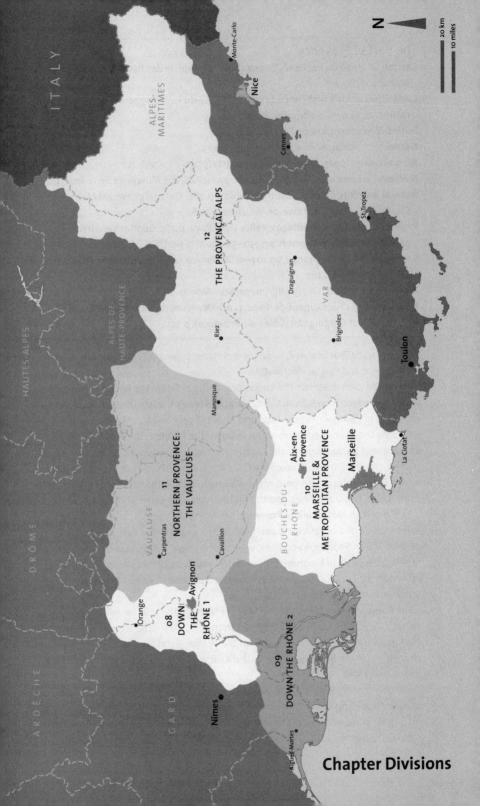

Chapter Divisions

The Best of Provence

Castles: Château du Roi René, Tarascon, p.135; Citadelle des Baux-de-Provence, p.149; Château d'If, p.201.

Curiosities: world's first concrete canoe, Musée du Pays Brignolais, Brignoles, p.298; cathedral, Vaison-la-Romaine, p.262.

Follies: Monument Joseph Sec, Aix, p.217.

Gardens: L'Harmas, northeast of Orange, p.109.

Markets: Arles, pp.155; Apt, p.237; Carpentras, p.251.

Medieval art and architecture: Avignon, pp.114–28; the Abbaye de Sénanque, p.246.

Natural wonders: Grand Canyon du Verdon, p.286; Garagaï chasm on Montagne Ste-Victoire, p.221; Fontaine-de-Vaucluse, p.246.

Regions of picturesque villages: Vallée de la Roya, p.270; Comtat Venaissin, pp.248–64; eastern Luberon, pp.350–52; country north of Draguignan, pp.289–91.

Roman monuments: Orange, pp.107–9; St-Rémy, p.144; Vaison-la-Romaine, p.261; Arles, p.159; Riez, p.287.

Traditional festivals: Gypsy pilgrimage, Stes-Maries-de-la-Mer, p.169.

Wine-touring: Châteauneuf-du-Pape, p.110; Dentelles de Montmirail (Gigondas), p.259; east of Draguignan (Côtes-de-Provence), p.300.

holidays; and a **Practical A–Z**, which covers subjects ranging from climate and health to insurance and tourist information.

The guide then descends the Rhône, beginning in **Down the Rhône 1: Orange to Beaucaire,** which travels from Orange and its Roman theatre through the celebrated vineyards of Châteauneuf-du-Pape and Tavel to lively Avignon, the medieval city of the popes. As the Rhône continues south in **Down the Rhône 2: the Alpilles, Crau and Camargue,** it passes some of the south's most curious natural features: the jagged Alpilles, the rock-strewn plain of the Crau and the marshlands of the Camargue, where Provençal cowboys herd wild bulls and horses. Roman Provence is well represented in St-Rémy and Arles, and the Middle Ages in St-Gilles and Aigues-Mortes.

To the east, in **Metropolitan Provence,** lies Marseille, the metropolis of Provence, set in a coastline of dramatic cliffs and fjord-like *calanques*; here, too, are staid and elegant Aix-en-Provence, and the lovely countryside around Cézanne's Mont Ste-Victoire. Next, in **Northern Provence: the Vaucluse,** comes the heartland of Provence: the Luberon and Mont Ventoux, and pockets of exquisite villages full of artists and refugees from the coast.

The Provençal Alps takes the inland route through the maritime Alps and their secret valleys, difficult of access but worth the trouble for the scenery – Mercantour National Park and the Grand Canyon of the Verdon – and for the art in their medieval chapels. Finally, in **Beaches on the Côte d'Azur** we list the best beaches within reach of inland Provence.

The book concludes with a **Language** chapter supplying some essential basic vocabulary for travelling around; a quick-reference **Glossary** of artistic, architectural and historical terms; and a brief **Chronology** of significant historical events. To enrich your appreciation of the area, there are also some suggestions for **Further Reading**.

History

03

The names of French regions can be maddeningly fluid, and one of the biggest problems with writing a history of Provence is that its boundaries change all the time. The Romans called Gaul's southern coast their dear 'province', their first conquest outside Italy. Specifically, this was the province of Gallia Narbonensis, stretching from Toulouse to Geneva, although its heartland was always the rich coast between Narbonne and Marseille. In the early Middle Ages, Gaul was evolving its linguistic north-south division between the *langue d'oïl* and the *langue d'oc* (two words for saying 'yes', from the Latin *ille* and *hoc*). Provence then came to mean the southern third of what is now France, stretching north to the Dordogne and Lyon.

At the same time, the political boundary of the Rhône river was redefining the terminology, between lands subject to the Holy Roman Emperors and those claimed by the kings of France. 'Provence' came to mean the semi-independent county east of the Rhône, while the rest, as far as Toulouse, came to be known as Languedoc. Today, southerners use the word Occitania (a word only invented in the 18th century) to describe all of the old *langue d'oc*. Old regional names fell out of official use during the Revolution, when France was divided into standardized *départements*. But with the regional autonomy laws passed by the Socialists in 1981, the five *départements* east of the Rhône were formed into the new region of Provence-Côte d'Azur. There, got it?

Prehistory
The First Million Years Or So

It seems that Provence's charms were lost on the earliest inhabitants of the Mediterranean. On the Côte d'Azur, tools and traces of habitation around Monaco go back as far as 1,000,000 BC. To the west, in Languedoc, remains of 'Tautavel Man' date to at least 450,000 BC, and perhaps as far back as 680,000. Someone may have been in Provence through all this, but evidence is rare. Neanderthal Man doesn't turn up till about 60,000 BC. The first evidence of the Neanderthalers' nemesis, that quarrelsome and unlovable species *Homo sapiens*, appears some 20,000 years later.

Neolithic civilization arrived as early as 3500 BC, and endured throughout the region for the next 2,000 years. People knew agriculture and raised sheep, traded for scarce goods, and built dry-stone houses. The Neolithic era left few important monuments: there's an impressive but little-known temple complex at Castellet, near Arles, and some large dolmens in the Massif des Maures. Of succeeding ages we know more about technology than culture and changes in population: the use of copper began about 2000 BC, iron c. 800 BC. In both cases the region was one of the last parts of the Mediterranean basin to catch on.

By this stage, at least, the inhabitants have got a name, even if it is a questionable one applied by later Greek and Roman writers: the people who occupied most of Provence in addition to northwestern Italy were now called the Ligurians. From about 800 BC, they began building their first settled villages, today called by the Latin name *oppidum*, a word you will see often in the south; it even survives in village names

(Oppedette). They were small, fortified villages, usually on a hilltop, built around a religious sanctuary or trading centre. Already, more advanced outsiders were coming to
make deals with the natives: Phoenicians, Etruscans, and most importantly Greeks.
A major event of this same era was the arrival of the Celts, Indo-European cousins of
the Ligurians and Iberians from the north. Beginning in coastal Languedoc in the 8th
century BC, they gradually spread their conquests eastwards until the 4th century at
the expense of the Ligurians. At the same time, Greek merchant activity was turning
into full-scale colonization. The Ionian city-states of Asia Minor had become over-
populated, agriculturally exhausted and politically precarious, and their citizens
sought to reproduce them in new lands. The first was Massalia – Marseille, c. 600 BC.
Soon Massalia was founding colonies of its own: Nice and Hyères were among the
most important. Greek influence over the indigenous peoples was strong from the
start; as with everywhere else they went, they brought the vine (wild stocks were
already present, but the Celts hadn't worked out what to do with them) and the olive,
and also their art. The Celts loved Greek vases, and had metals and other raw materials to offer in return. Increased trade turned some of the native *oppida* into genuine
cities, such as Arles.

300 BC–AD 400
Roman Provincia

From the start, the Greeks were natural allies of the young city of Rome – if only
because they had common enemies. Besides the strong Etruscan federation, occupying the lands in between the two, there were their trade rivals, the Phoenicians
(later Carthaginians), and occasionally the Celts and Ligurians. As Rome gobbled up
Etruria and the rest of Italy, the area became of increasing importance; a fact
Hannibal demonstrated when he marched his armies along the coast towards Italy in
218 BC, with the full support of the Celts (historians still argue over how and where he
got the elephants across the Rhône).

When the Romans took control of Spain in the Second Punic War (206 BC), the
coasts of what they called Gaul became a logical next step. In 125, Roman troops
saved Marseille from a Celtic attack. This time, though, they had come to stay. The
reorganization of the new province – 'Provincia' – was quick and methodical. Domitius
Ahenobarbus, the vanquisher of the Celts, began the great Italy–Spain highway that
bears his name, the Via Domitia, in 121. New cities were founded, most importantly
Aix (122). Dozens of other new foundations followed over the next century, many of
them planned colonies with land grants for veterans of the legions.

The Celts were not through yet, though. Two northern tribes, the Cimbri and
Teutones, mounted a serious invasion of Gaul and Italy in 115. They raided those areas
continuously until 102, when they were destroyed by a Roman army under Marius
near Montagne Ste-Victoire, near Aix. Marius, later populist dictator in Rome, became
a folk hero and the subject of legends ever after (Provençal parents still name their
children after him). Celtic-Ligurian resistance continued intermittently until 14 BC; the

great monument at La Turbie, on the border of Gaul, commemorates the defeat of the last hold-outs in the Alps.

The downfall of Marseille, still the metropolis of Provence and still thoroughly Greek in culture and sympathies, came in 49 BC. Though it had always been famed for its diplomacy, the city made the fatal mistake of supporting Pompey over Julius Caesar in the Roman civil wars. A vengeful Caesar crippled its trade and stripped nearly all its colonies and dependencies. Thereafter, the influence of Marseille gave way to newer, more Romanized towns: Aix, Arles and Fréjus.

Throughout all this, Provence had been easily assimilated into the Roman economy, supplying food and raw materials for the insatiable metropolis. With Caesar's conquest of the rest of Gaul, the Rhône trade route (which had always managed to bring down a little Baltic amber and tin from Cornwall) became a busy river highway and military route. Under the good government and peace bestowed by Augustus (27 BC–AD 14) and his successors, Provence blossomed into an opulence never before seen. The cities, especially those of the Rhône valley, acquired theatres, amphitheatres for the games, aqueducts, bridges and temples. Provence participated in the political and cultural life of the empire, even contributing one of the better emperors, Antoninus Pius (from Nîmes, AD 138–61), only obscure because his reign was so peaceful and prosperous.

Large areas of Roman towns have been excavated at Glanum and Vaison-la-Romaine, and both have turned up a preponderance of wealthy villas. This is the dark side of Roman Provence; from the beginning of Roman rule, wealthy Romans were able to grab much of the land, forming large estates and exploiting the indigenous population. This trend was magnified in the decadent, totalitarian and economically chaotic late empire, when, throughout Roman territory, the few remaining free farmers were forced to sell themselves into virtual serfdom to escape crushing taxes. After AD 200, in fact, everything was going wrong: trade and the cities stagnated while art and culture decayed; and the first of the barbarian raids brought Germans into Provence in the 250s, when they destroyed Glanum.

Constantine, while yet emperor of only the western half of the empire (312–23), often resided at Arles and favoured the city; his baths there were probably the last big Roman building project in Provence. His pro-Christian policy gave the cult its first real influence in Gaul, at least in the cities; under his auspices, the first state-sponsored Church council was held at Arles in 314. Before that Christianity does not seem to have made much of an impression (later, to make up for this, elaborate mythologies were constructed to place Mary Magdalene and other early saints in Provence; see the towns of Saintes-Maries-de-la-Mer and St-Maximin-la-Ste-Baume).

400–930
600 Years of Uninvited Guests

French historians always blame the barbarian invaders of the 5th century for destroying the cities of Provence, as if Teutonic warriors enjoyed pulling down temple colonnades on their days off. In fact, few armies passed through Provence; the

Visigoths, in the early 400s, were the most notable. Though government collapsed in chaos, business went on much as usual, with the Roman landowners (and their new German colleagues) gradually making the transition to feudal nobles. Arles, untouched by the troubles, became the most important city of the west, and briefly the capital, under Constantius III in 412. The weakness of the central power brought some long-due upheavals in the countryside, with guerrillas and vigilante justice against the landlords. The old and new rulers soon found common cause and for a while, a clique of a hundred of the biggest landowners took over administration in Gaul, even declaring one of their own as 'emperor' in Arles (455), with the support of the Visigoths.

The Visigoths soon tired of such games, and assumed total control in 476, the year the Western Empire formally expired. They had to share it, however, with the Ostrogoths, who had established a strong kingdom in Italy and seized all of Provence east of the Rhône – the beginnings of a political boundary that would last in various forms for a thousand years. When the Eastern Empire under Justinian invaded Italy, the Franks were able to snatch the Ostrogoths' half (535). They were never able to hold it effectively, and the area gradually slipped into virtual independence.

The Visigoths kept the western half (now Languedoc), a distant zone of their Spanish kingdom, until the Arab invasion of the early 700s rolled over the Pyrenees. In 719 the Arabs took Narbonne. The next two centuries are as wonderfully confused as anything in prehistory. It's hard to separate fact from legend in, for example, the story of the great Spanish Caliph Abd ar-Rahman, defeated in battle and leaving a magnificent treasure buried somewhere in the Alpilles. Charles Martel, the celebrated Frankish *generalissimo* who stopped the Arab wave at Poitiers in 732, made an expedition to the southern coast in 737–9, brutally sacking Marseille, Avignon and Aix. His mission was hardly a religious crusade – rather taking advantage of the Visigothic defeat to increase Frankish hegemony in the south; the cities of Provence are recorded as petitioning the Arabs at Córdoba to help them keep the nasty Franks out.

The Arabs couldn't help; the climate was too eccentric and the pickings too slim for them to mount a serious effort in Gaul. The nascent Franks gained control everywhere, and the entire coast was absorbed by Charlemagne's father, Pépin the Short, in 759. Under Charlemagne (768–814), Occitania seems to have shared little in the Carolingian revival of trade and culture, and after the break-up of the empire (at the Treaty of Verdun in 843) its misery was complete. The 9th- and 10th-century invasions were the real Dark Age in many parts of Europe. Provence suffered constant and destructive raids by the Normans, the Arabs again (who held the Massif des Maures and St-Tropez until the 970s), and even the Hungarians, who sacked what was left of Nîmes in 924.

930–1000
The Beginnings of the Middle Ages

Even in this sorry period, the foundations were being laid for recovery. Monastic reformers in Charlemagne's time, men such as Benedict of Aniane (in the Hérault), helped start a huge expansion of Church institutions. The Abbey of St-Victor in Marseille took the lead in this, founding hundreds of new monasteries around Occitania; hard-working monks reclaimed land from forests and swamps – later they sat back and enjoyed the rents, while always keeping up the holy work of education and copying books. Pilgrimages became an important activity, especially to Arles (St-Trophime), getting a sleepy and locally bound society moving again and providing an impetus to trade. The Treaty of Verdun (*see* above) had confirmed the Rhône as a boundary, and politically Provence and Languedoc went their separate ways. The Kingdom of Provence (or 'Kingdom of Arles'), proclaimed by a great-grandson of Charlemagne in 879, was little more than a façade for a feudal anarchy. Though Provence was united with the Kingdom of Burgundy in 949, and formally passed to the Holy Roman Empire in 1032, the tapestry of battling barons and shifting local alliances continued without interference from the overlords.

1000–1213
Provençal Medieval Civilization

As elsewhere in Europe, the year 1000 is the rough milestone for the sudden and spectacular development of the medieval world. Towns and villages found the money and energy to build impressive new churches. The end of the foreign raiders made the seas safe for merchants, from Genoa, Pisa and Barcelona mostly, but also a few from Marseille. In 1002, the first written document in Occitan appears. The great pilgrimage to Santiago de Compostela, in Spain, made what was left of the old Roman roads into busy highways once more; along the main southern route the first of the medieval trade fairs appeared, at the new town of St-Gilles-du-Gard.

Things were on the upswing throughout the 11th century, and the trend was given another boost by the Crusades, which began in 1095. With increased prosperity and contact with a wider world, better manners and the rudiments of personal hygiene were not slow to follow. Feudal anarchy began to look quite genteel, maintaining a delicate balance of power, with feudal ties and blood relations keeping the political appetites of rulers from ever really getting out of hand. From the more civilized east, and from nearby Muslim Spain, came new ideas, new technologies and a taste for luxury and art. As an indication of how far Occitania had come, there were the troubadours (*see* pp.59–60), with modern Europe's first lyric poetry. Almost every court of the south was refined enough to welcome and patronize them.

The growing cities began to assert themselves in the 12th century, often achieving a substantial independence in *communes* governed by consuls: Avignon in 1129, Arles in 1132. In the countryside, successive waves of monastic reform spawned a huge number of new institutions: first the movement from Cluny in the 11th century, and in the 12th the Cistercians, who started a score of important monasteries. Efficiently exploiting the lands bequeathed by noblemen made the religious houses rich, and also did much to improve the agricultural economy.

By 1125 the Counts of Barcelona controlled much of Provence south of the Durance. The other leading power in the region, Toulouse, contended with the Catalans for Provence while being overlords of all Languedoc, excepting Carcassonne and Béziers, ruled by the Trencavel family, and Narbonne, with its independent Viscounts. It was a great age for culture, producing not only the troubadours but an impressive display of Romanesque architecture, and an original school of sculpture at Arles. Perhaps the most remarkable phenomenon of the times was a widespread religious tolerance, shared by rulers, the common people and even many among the clergy. Religious dissenters of various persuasions sprang up everywhere. Most of the new sects soon died out, and are little known today – like the extremist 'Petrobrusians' of St-Gilles, who didn't fancy churches, sacraments, relics or priests, and who even had their doubts about the crucifixion of Jesus.

One sect, however, made startling inroads into every sector of society in 11th- and 12th-century Languedoc – the Cathars, or Albigensians. This Manichaean doctrine, obsessed with Good and Evil, had in its upright simplicity a powerful attraction for industrious townspeople and peasants. The Cathars were never a majority in any part of the south; in most places they never made up more than 10 per cent of the population. They might have passed on as only a curious footnote to history, had they not provided the excuse for the biggest and most flagrant land grab of the Middle Ages. The 'Albigensian Crusade', arranged after the 1208 murder of a papal legate, was a cynical marriage of convenience between two old piratical enemies, the papacy and the crown of France. Diplomacy forced King Philip Augustus to disclaim any part in the affair, but nevertheless a big army of knights from the Ile-de-France, led by the redoubtable Simon de Montfort, occupied most of Languedoc, while committing vicious massacres of the heretics everywhere. Montfort won battle after battle and took every town he attacked, save only Beaucaire.

In a last attempt to save their fortunes, Count Raymond VI of Toulouse and King Peter II of Aragon combined to meet the northerners. With an overwhelmingly superior force, they blundered their way to crushing defeat at the Battle of Muret in 1213. Four centuries after the fall of the Carolingian Empire, the French once again had their foothold in the south. Languedoc was finished, its distinctive culture quickly snuffed out.

1213–1542
The Coming of French Rule

Provence was still free, enjoying a prosperous era under its Catalan counts, though still troubled by incessant feudal struggles waged by such local powers as the Seigneurs of Les Baux and Forcalquier. Count Raymond Berenger V (1209–45) was usually strong enough to keep them in check; under him Provence did very well, and developed a constitutional government on the Catalan model. It also managed temporarily to avert French aggression in a roundabout way. In 1246, Raymond Berenger's daughter and heir married Charles of Anjou, St Louis' brother. The ambitious Angevin used Provence as a springboard to create an empire that at its height, in the 1280s, included southern Italy and parts of Greece.

The city of Avignon and its hinterlands, the Comtat Venaissin, loyal possessions of Toulouse, had suffered greatly at the hands of Louis VIII after the Albigensian Crusade. In 1274, Charles and Louis arranged to give the Comtat to the papacy – its discreetly delayed share of the Albigensian booty. In 1309, Pope Clement V, fleeing anarchy in Rome, installed himself at Carpentras in the Comtat. Politically, the popes found Provence a convenient new home and decided to stay – the 'Babylonian Captivity' (as jealous Italians called it) that would last over a century. They soon moved to Avignon, purchasing the city in 1348 and conducting a worldly court that to many seemed a Babylon indeed.

The late 14th century brought hard times to Provence: first the Black Death in 1348, and then political instability under the hapless Queen Jeanne (1343–82). Once more the Seigneurs of Les Baux and their imitators raged over the land, with bands of unscrupulous mercenaries (the *Grandes Compagnies*) to help them ravage town and country. The popes returned to Rome in 1377; they kept control of Avignon and the Comtat, though French-supported anti-popes held Avignon as late as 1403. After 1434 peace had returned and Provence was ruled by Good King René (Count of Provence, and only 'king' from his claim to Sicily, where the Angevins had been replaced by the Aragonese after the 'Sicilian Vespers' revolution of 1282). The 'Good' is equally spurious. René was open-handed to courtiers, and a patron of artists, but his futile dream of recapturing Sicily and Naples led him to wring the last penny out of everyone else.

René's successor, Charles III, lasted only a year and died without an heir (1481), bequeathing Provence to the French crown. It was intended to be a union of equals, maintaining Provençal liberties and institutions. Accepting it as such, the Provençal Estates-General ratified the agreement. The French immediately went back on their word, attempting to govern through royal commissioners. Their attempts to swallow Provence whole had to wait, however, though they were never to cease. Louis XI and Charles XII needed a peaceful Provence as a bridge for their invasions of Italy; the region paid for this, with two destructive invasions in the 1520s and 30s by France's arch-enemy Charles V, Holy Roman Emperor and King of Spain. This era also saw a landmark in the cultural effacement of Occitania, the 1539 Edict of Villars-Cotterets that decreed French to be the official language throughout the kingdom.

1542–1789
The Wars of Religion

Meanwhile, the new Protestant heresy was floating down the Rhône from Calvin's Geneva. The Occitans received it warmly, and soon there were large Protestant communities in all towns. Though this seems a repeat of the Cathar story, the geographical distribution is fascinating – the old Cathar areas in Languedoc were now loyally Catholic, while the orthodox regions of the 1300s now came out strongly for the dissenters. Tolerance was still out of fashion, and the opening round of a pointless half-century of religious wars came with the 1542 massacres in the Luberon mountains. The perpetrator was the Aix *Parlement* (pre-Revolution *parlements* were not parliaments, but powerful judicial bodies appointed by and responsible to the king); the victims mostly Waldensians (Vaudois), pre-Reformation heretics who had migrated to Provence before the union with France, to escape oppression there.

In the open warfare that followed across the south, there were massacres and atrocities enough on both sides. Protestants distinguished themselves by the wholesale destruction of churches and their art (as at St-Gilles); churches were often converted into fortresses. Henry IV's 1598 Edict of Nantes acknowledged Protestant control of certain areas (Orange and Lourmarin in Provence). The French monarchy had been weakened by the wars, but as soon as it recovered new measures were introduced to keep the south in line. Under Cardinal Richelieu in the 1630s, the laws and traditions of local autonomy were swept away; after 1639 the Etats-Généraux of Provence was not allowed to meet until the eve of the Revolution. As insurance, scores of feudal castles (such as Beaucaire and Les Baux) were demolished to eliminate possible points of resistance.

Louis XIV's revocation of the Edict in 1685 caused more troubles. Thousands of Protestants, the south's most productive citizens, simply left; most of the community in Orange went off to colonize new lands in Prussia. Louis' long and oppressive reign continued the impoverishment of the south, despite well-intentioned economic measures by his brilliant minister Colbert. The 18th century witnessed the beginnings of an important textile industry (usually promoted by the remaining Protestants): silk around Nîmes and parts of Provence (where farmers gave up their bedrooms to raise the delicate silkworms in them), and linen and cotton goods in Orange. In the rest of Provence, though, the century told a miserable tale: economic stagnation, deforestation of mountain areas that has still not been entirely repaired today, and plagues. The biggest plague, in 1720, carried off almost half the population of Marseille.

1789–1860
An Unwanted Revolution

The French Revolution was largely a Parisian affair, though southerners often played important roles (the Abbé Sieyès and Mirabeau), while bourgeois delegates from the manufacturing towns fought along with the Girondins in the National Assembly for a respectable, liberal republic. Unfortunately, the winning Jacobin ideology was more centralist and more dedicated to destroying any taint of regional difference than the *ancien régime* had ever dreamed of being. Whatever was left of local rights and privileges was soon decreed out of existence, and when the Revolution divided France into homogenous *départements* in 1790, terms like 'Provence' and 'Languedoc' ceased to have any political meaning.

In 1792 volunteers from Marseille had brought the *Marseillaise* to Paris, while local mobs wrecked hundreds of southern churches and châteaux. Soon, however, the betrayed south became counter-revolutionary. Incidents occurred like the one in

Bédoin, near Carpentras, in 1793: when someone cut down the 'liberty tree', French soldiers burned the town and shot 63 villagers to 'set an example'. The Catalans raised regiments of volunteers against the Revolution. The royalists and the English occupied Toulon after a popular revolt, and were only dislodged by the brilliant tactics of a young commander named Bonaparte in 1793.

The south managed little enthusiasm for Napoleon or his wars. The Emperor called the Provençaux cowards, and said theirs was the only part of France that never gave him a decent regiment. Today the tourist offices promote the 'Route Napoléon', where Napoleon passed through from Elba in 1815 to start the Hundred Days – but he had to sneak along those roads in an Austrian uniform to protect himself from the Provençaux.

After Waterloo, the restored monarchy started off with a grisly White Terror and tried to turn the clock back to 1789. After the Revolution of 1830, the 'July Monarchy' of King Louis Philippe brought significant changes. The old industrious Protestant strain of the south finally got its chance with a Protestant prime minister from Nîmes, François Guizot (1840–8); his liberal policies and his slogan – *enrichissez-vous!* – opened an age where there would be a little Protestant in every Frenchman. Guizot's countrymen were rapidly demanding more; radicalism and anti-clericalism (except in the lower Rhône and Vaucluse) increased throughout the century.

Southerners supported the Revolution of 1848 and the Second Republic, and many areas, especially in the Provençal Alps, put up armed resistance to Louis Napoleon's 1851 coup. Under the Second Empire (1852–70), France picked up yet another territory: Nice and its hinterlands (now the *département* of Alpes-Maritimes), with a mixed population of Provençaux and Italians. This was the price exacted by Napoleon III in 1860 for French aid to Vittorio Emanuele II in Italy's War of Independence.

1860–
Rural Decay and Recovery

The second half of the century saw the beginnings of a national revival in Occitania. While in Languedoc it was political, largely involved with modern France's first agricultural movements, in Provence it tended to be all cultural and apolitical: a linguistic and literary revival bound up with Nobel Prize-winning poet Frédéric Mistral and the cultural group called the Félibrige (*see* pp.55–6), founded in 1854. To counter these advances, the post-1870 Third Republic pursued French cultural oppression to its wildest extremes. History was rewritten to make Occitania seem an eternal part of the 'French nation'. The Occitan languages were lyingly derided as mere *patois*, bastard 'dialects' of French; children were punished for speaking their own language in school, a practice that lasted until the 1970s.

After 1910, economic factors conspired to defeat both the political and cultural aspirations of the Midi; rural depopulation, caused by the break-up of the pre-industrial agricultural society, drained the life out of the villages – and decreased the percentage of people who spoke the native languages. The First World War decimated a generation – go into any village church in the south and look at the war memorial plaques; from a total population of a few hundred, you'll see maybe 30 names of villagers who died for the 'Glory of France'. By 1950, most villages had lost at least half their population; some died out altogether.

After the French débâcle of 1940, Provence found itself under the Vichy government. German occupation came in November 1942, after the American landings in North Africa, provoking the scuttling of the French fleet in Toulon to keep it out of German hands. After 1942, the Resistance was active and effective in the Provençal Alps and the Vaucluse – not to mention Marseille, where the Germans felt constrained to blow up the entire Vieux Port area. Liberation began two months after D-Day, in August 1944. American and French troops hit the beaches around St-Tropez, and in a remarkably successful (and little-noticed) operation they had most of Provence liberated within the following two weeks. In the rugged mountains behind Nice, some bypassed German outposts held out until the end of the war.

The post-war era has brought momentous changes. The overdeveloped, ever more schizophrenic Côte d'Azur has become the heart of Provence – the tail that wags the dog. Besides its resorts, it has the likes of IBM and the techno-paradise of Sophia-Antipolis. Above all, the self-proclaimed 'California of Europe' has money, and will acquire more; in two or three decades it will be the first province in centuries to start telling Paris where to get off. In rural Provence waves of Parisians and foreigners (mostly British) have come looking for the good life and a cheap stone house to fix up. They have brought life to many areas, though the traditional rural side suffers a bit. The increasingly posh Vaucluse has the highest rural crime and suicide rates in France.

The greatest political event of the modern era was the election of the socialist Mitterrand government in 1981, followed by the creation of regional governments across France. Though their powers and budgets are extremely limited, this represents a major turning point, the first reversal of a thousand years of increasing Parisian centralism. Its lasting effects will not be known for decades, perhaps centuries. Already the revival of Occitan language and culture is resuming; indicators include such things as new school courses in the language, and some towns and villages changing the street signs to Provençal.

Politics, quiet in most of the south, can still be primeval in Provence. Jean-Marie Le Pen and his tawdry pack of bigots found their biggest following here, riding a wave of resentment against immigrants that Le Pen himself worked hard to create (although this is a Provençal tradition: there were anti-Italian pogroms in Marseille and other towns in the 1890s). Le Pen's National Front scared the daylights out of the French political class by winning control of four Provençal cities: Toulon, Orange and the gruesome Marseille suburbs of Marignane and Vitrolles. They scored up to 15% of the vote in the mid-1990s and achieved one of their greatest successes in 1998, winning 275 council seats. Since then the party has split and split again, with Le Pen's deputy Bruno Megret, his eldest daughter and his old friend the NF Mayor of Toulon defecting to form a new far-right organization, the National Movement, which itself broke up shortly afterwards in factional battles. The total far-right vote dropped to around 9% in the 1999 European elections, split between the National Movement and the National Front. The splintering and collapse of the far right did not mean that the public opinion it represents had disappeared, but it did perhaps reflect the mood of hope that swept the country in 1998, when the multiracial French football team triumphed in the World Cup, and the second-generation immigrant striker Zinedine Zidane became the new national hero. Unfortunately, however, Le Pen was not down for long – he has a seat in the European Parliament and intends to stand as a candidate in France's presidential elections in 2002.

The other notable Provençal figure in recent years has been Le Pen's arch-enemy, the liberal Marseille industrialist, film star, novelist, rapper, politician, playboy, football club owner and jailbird Bernard Tapie. Tapie became embroiled in scandals involving asset-stripping, tax evasion and game-fixing for his soccer club, L'Olympique de Marseille, the last of which landed him in prison and ended his business career. From chairman of Adidas and Minister for Urban Affairs, to eight months in France's most notorious prison, 'Trampoline Man' Tapie bounced back, using his popular status as an anti-establishment hero and defender of the rights of immigrants to relaunch his acting career, and in 2001 he returned to his old club as sporting director. Watch this space.

Art and Architecture

04

Great art and architecture in Provence coincides neatly with its three periods of prosperity: the Roman, the Middle Ages, and the mid-19th and early 20th centuries, when railways opened up the coast not only to aristocrats, but to artists as well.

Prehistoric and Pre-Roman

Back in the Upper Palaeolithic era, the first known inhabitants of Provence decorated at least one cave, the recently discovered Grotte Cosquer; its awkward submerged entrance in the *calanques* near Marseille suggests that others may have been lost in rising sea levels. Their Neolithic descendants left few but tantalizing traces of their passing: dolmens (there's a good one near **Draguignan**), a few menhirs and a tomb-temple complex at **Castellet**, near Arles. The first shepherds may well have put up the dry-stone, corbel-roofed huts called *bories*, rebuilt since countless times and still a feature of the landscape (especially at the 18th-century Village des Bories outside **Gordes**). In the Iron Age (1800–1500 BC), the Ligurians or their predecessors covered the Vallée des Merveilles under Mont Bégo with extraordinary rock incisions of warriors, bulls, masked figures and inexplicable symbols. The arrival of the Celts around 800 BC coincided with an increase in trade; Greek, Etruscan and Celtic influences can be seen in the artefacts of this age. The Celts had talents for jewellery and ironwork – and a bizarre habit of decapitating enemies and making images of the heads (atavistically surviving in the little grotesque heads that pop up all over Romanesque buildings). The best of the original images and sculptures are in the Musée Granet in **Aix**, the Musée d'Archéologie Méditerranéenne in **Marseille** and the Lapidary Museum of **Avignon**.

Gallo-Roman: 3rd Century BC–4th Century AD

Archaeologically the Greeks are the big disappointment of Provence – the only remains of their towns are bits of wall at **Marseille** and at **St-Blaise** on the Etang de Berre. But what the Romans left behind in their beloved Provincia makes up for the Greeks: the theatre of **Orange**, with the only intact stage building in the West; the amphitheatre and crypto-porticus in **Arles**; the elegant 'Antiques' of **St-Rémy**; the Pont Flavien at **St-Chamas**; the excavated towns at **Vaison-la-Romaine** and **Glanum** (St-Rémy). Thanks to a lingering Celtic influence, Provence was the one province of the Western Roman Empire that developed a definite style of its own, characterized by vigorous barbaric reliefs emboldened by deeply incised outlines. Battle scenes were the most popular subject, or shields and trophies arranged in the exotic, uncouth style you see on the triumphal arches of **Orange** and **Carpentras**, or in the Musée Archéologique in **Arles**.

Roman landowners lived in two-storey stone houses, with their farm buildings forming an enclosed rectangular courtyard known as a *mansio*, the ancestor of the modern Provençal farmhouse, the *mas*.

Early Christian and Dark Ages: 5th–10th Centuries

Very few places had the resources to create any art at all during this period; the meagre attempts were nearly always rebuilt later. The oldest Christian relics are a remarkable sarcophagus from the 2nd century in **Brignoles**, and a large collection of 4th-century sarcophagi in the Musée Archéologique at **Arles**, close to Roman pagan models. Octagonal baptistries from the 5th and 6th centuries survive in **Aix** and **Riez**. Many church crypts are really the foundations of original Dark Age churches.

Romanesque: 11th–14th Centuries

When good times returned in the 11th century, people began to build again, inspired by the ancient buildings they saw around them. There is a great stylistic continuity not only from Roman to Romanesque (rounded arches, barrel vaults, rounded apses), but also in the vigorous, Celtic-inspired decoration of Roman Provence. At the same time, the enduring charm of Romanesque is in its very lack of restrictions and codes, giving architects the freedom to improvise and solve problems in highly original and sophisticated ways. Although parish and monastic churches were usually in the basilican form (invented for Roman law courts, and used in Rome's first churches), masons also created extremely esoteric works, often built as funeral chapels on pre-Christian holy sites: **Notre-Dame-du-Groseau** and **Montmajour** are two in Provence.

Of the four distinct styles of Romanesque that emerged in southern France, the Provençal is the most austere and heaviest, characterized by simple floor plans, thick-set proportions, few if any windows, minimal if any decoration, and façades that are often blank. Churches that could double as fortresses were built along the pirate-plagued coast, most notably the church of **Saintes-Maries-de-la-Mer**. In the mid-12th century, the Cistercians founded three important new abbeys in a sombre and austere style, known as the 'Three Sisters': **Le Thoronet**, **Sénanque** and **Silvacane**. An octagonal dome at the transept crossing is a common feature of more elaborate churches, especially **Avignon** cathedral, the Ancienne-Major in **Marseille**, **Vaison-la-Romaine**, **Le Thor** and **Carpentras** (the ruined original). The finest of the few paintings that survive from this epoch is the 13th-century fresco cycle at the Tour Ferrande, in **Pernes-les-Fontaines**. **Ganagobie** has the only floor mosaics from the period, as well as good sculpture.

In general, churches in the Rhône valley are more ornate, thanks to a talented group of sculptors known as the 'School of Arles'. The wealth of ruins inspired them to adapt Roman forms and decorations to the new religion, complete with triumphal arches, gabled pediments, and Corinthian columns. The saints on the façade of St-Trophime in **Arles** seem direct descendants of Gallo-Roman warriors. Arlésien artists also created the remarkable façade of **St-Gilles-du-Gard**, portraying the New Testament – the true dogma in stone for all to see, perhaps meant as a refutation of the Cathar and other current heresies. Yet other Romanesque sculpture in the area, as at **Vaison-la-Romaine**, seems nothing but heretical.

Gothic and Renaissance: 14th–16th Centuries

Although Gothic elements first appear in Provence in 1150 (the façade of St-Victor in **Marseille**), the style's ogival vaulting and pointy arches belonged to a foreign, northern style that failed to touch southern hearts. The only place where it really found a home was in **Avignon**, when the 14th-century popes summoned architects from the north to design the flamboyant Papal Palace, St-Pierre, the Cloître des Célestines and St-Didier (other isolated examples include the basilica of **St-Maximin-la-Ste-Baume**).

Painting in the south of France took a giant leap forward when the papal court in Avignon hired some of Italy's finest Trecento artists, especially Simone Martini of Siena and Matteo Giovannetti of Viterbo. Their frescoes combined the new Italian naturalism with the courtly, elongated grace of medieval French art to create the fairy-tale style known as International Gothic (*see* **Avignon** and its Petit Palais museum). From International Gothic, and from the precise techniques of the Flemish painters favoured by the last popes, a new local style developed in the early 15th century, the School of Avignon. The school's greatest masters were from the north: the exquisite Enguerrand Quarton (or Charton, *c.* 1415–66) from Laon (**Villeneuve lez Avignon**), and Nicolas Froment (cathedral, **Aix**); also see Aix's church of the Madeleine and the Petit Palais museum in **Avignon**. Their most interesting native contemporaries were a pair of Piedmontese painters, Giovanni Canavesio (*c.* 1430–1500) and Giovanni Baleison (*c.* 1425–95), who would be better known had they not left their charming fresco cycles in remote, out-of-the-way churches up in Provence's alpine valleys, most notably **Notre-Dame-des-Fontaines** in the Roya Valley, and others in the valleys of the Vésubie and Tinée.

This was also the time when King René, the great patron of the artists, built himself a fine chivalric castle in **Tarascon** and had a hand in the evolution of French sculpture when he invited the Italian Renaissance master **Francesco Laurana** (*c.* 1430–1502) to Provence. Laurana, a Dalmatian trained in Tuscany, is best known for his precocious geometrical softening of features and forms, especially in his portrait busts (in St-Didier, **Avignon**; Ancienne-Major, **Marseille**; cathedral, **Aix**).

Despite this promising start, subjugation by the French and the Wars of Religion made the Renaissance a non-event in Provence. The few buildings of the day are imitative, mostly of the heavy, classicizing Roman style, as in the Petit Palais of the Cardinal Legate in Avignon. The best Renaissance building, the once-delightful Château La Tour d'Aigues in the Luberon, is a burnt-out shell today.

The Age of Bad Taste: 17th–18th Centuries

The French prefer to call this their *époque classique*, and even in the poor, benighted south admittedly many fine things were done. Towns laid out elegant squares, fountains and promenades, as in **Pernes-les-Fontaines**, **Aix**, **Barjols**; trees were planted on a grand scale, on market squares and along roads – many (mostly out-of-the-way ones) are still lined with majestic 18th-century avenues of plane trees. **Moustiers** has a collection from its thriving faïence industry of the day (as does **Marseille**'s Musée Cantini). Southerners went ape for organs, gargantuan works sheathed in ornate carved wood.

But nearly everything else is all wrong. People took the lovely churches left to them by their ancestors and tricked them out like cat-houses in pink and purple, and tinkered so much with the architecture that it's often difficult to tell the real age of anything. Aix, the capital of Provence and self-proclaimed arbiter of taste, knocked over its magnificently preserved Roman mausoleum and medieval palace of the Counts of Provence just before the Revolution. Although the 17th- and 18th-century palaces that replaced them lend Aix a distinctive urbanity and ostentation, they are rarely first-rate works of architecture in their own right, but rather eclectic jumbles with touches from Gothic, Renaissance and Baroque style-books.

The one great Baroque sculptor and architect Provence produced, **Pierre Puget** (1620–94), suffered the usual fate of a prophet in his own land. Puget began his career painting ships' figureheads before he went on to study in Rome under Bernini; snubbed at home, he spent much of his career sculpting enormous saints in Genoa, but left his native **Marseille** the striking Vieille-Charité and a handful of sculptures in its Musée des Beaux Arts. In painting, the south produced two virtuoso court painters, Hyacinthe Rigaud and Fragonard, whose portrayals of happily spoiled, rosy-cheeked aristocrats were enough in themselves to provoke a Revolution. The most sincere paintings of the age are the naive *ex votos* in many churches (some of the best are from sailors, as at Notre-Dame de la Garde in **Marseille**). Then there are the works of Avignon native **Claude Joseph-Vernet** (1714–89), a landscape painter best known for his seascapes and ports, in which he showed himself to be one of the first French artists interested in the play of light and water, if in a picturesque manner (Musée Calvet, **Avignon**; Musée des Beaux Arts, **Marseille**).

France's Little Ice Age:
Late 18th–mid-19th Centuries

If the last era lacked vision, taste in the neoclassical/Napoleonic era had all the charm of embalming fluid. The Revolution destroyed more than it built; the wanton devastation of the region's greatest Romanesque art begun in the Wars of Religion was a loss matched only by the mania for selling it off in the next century to the Americans. The greatest monuments of the Napoleonic era include the paintings in many museums by David, Ingres and Hubert Robert, the latter of whom specialized in scenes of melancholy Roman ruins in Provence and Italy, capturing the taste of the day (it was also a great age for cemeteries). **Jacques-Louis David** (1748–1825) deserves special mention as Napoleon's favourite painter, as cold and perfect as ice, who portrayed the Frenchies of his day in kitsch-Roman heroic attitudes and costumes (Musée Granet, **Aix**; Musée Calvet, **Avignon**). David's pupil, **François Marius Granet** (1775–1849), was a native of Aix; although his canvases are run-of-the-mill academic, his watercolours and sketches reveal a poetic observation of nature that became the hallmark of the Provençal school (Musée Granet, **Aix**).

Another current in French painting at the time is represented by **Camille Corot** (1796–1875), a landscape painter of ineffable charm, who made the typical French sojourn in Rome to discover the calm and tranquillity of classical landscapes. Although not a southerner, he spent time in Provence, and his smaller, spontaneous sketches and private portraits that remain here show him off as a precursor of the Impressionists (Musée Calvet, **Avignon**; Musée des Beaux Arts, **Marseille**). In his lifetime, Corot was known for his kindness, and one who benefited the most was **Honoré Daumier** (1808–79), whom Corot supported in his impoverished blind old age. Born in Marseille, Daumier began his career risking jail terms as a political caricaturist for a magazine. But he was also a highly original pre-expressionist painter in the Goya mould, best known for his hypnotic, violently lit scenes based on the inherent tragedy of the human condition – a precursor of Toulouse-Lautrec, Degas and Picasso (Musée des Beaux Arts, **Marseille**).

For the first time, however, there was a reaction to purposeful destruction of the past. Ruskin's contemporary Viollet-le-Duc (1814–79) restored architecture, rather than just writing about it (the walls of **Avignon**). Thanks to the Suez Canal, **Marseille** suddenly had money to burn and tried to revive the past in its own way, with monstrous neo-Byzantine basilicas and the overripe Baroque Palais Longchamp. It also produced **Adolphe Monticelli** (1824–86), perhaps Van Gogh's most important precursor, especially in his technique. Obsessed with light ('*La lumière, c'est le ténor,*' he claimed), Monticelli conveyed its effects with pure unmixed colour applied with hard brushes; subjects dissolve into strokes and blobs of paint (Musée des Beaux Arts and Musée Cantini, **Marseille**).

Revolutions in Seeing: 1850–the Present

A lady once came to look at Matisse's paintings and was horrified to see a woman with a green face. 'Wouldn't it be horrible to see a woman walking down the street with a green face?' she asked him. 'It certainly would!' Matisse agreed. 'Thank God it's only a painting!'

In the 1850 Paris Salon, hanging amongst the stilted historical, religious and mythological academic paintings were three large canvases of everyday, contemporary scenes by **Gustave Courbet** (1819–77). Today it's hard to imagine how audacious his contemporaries found Courbet's new style, which came to be called realism – almost as if it took the invention of photography by Louis Daguerre (1837) to make the eye see what was 'really' there. 'Do what you see, what you want, what you feel,' was Courbet's advice to his pupils. A keen student of luminosity in nature, one thing Courbet felt like doing was painting in the south, where his art revelled in the bright colour and light; his seascapes are awash in atmosphere (Musée des Beaux Arts, **Marseille**).

Courbet's visit and fresh luminous style was a major influence on the 19th-century painters of Provence, especially **Paul Guigou** (1834–71). Born in Villars in the Vaucluse, Guigou sought out the most arid parts of Provence, especially the banks of the Durance, for his subjects, illuminating them with scintillating light and colour. Unable to make a living in the south, he took teaching jobs in the north, where he died at age 37, just as his career began to take off (Musée des Beaux Arts, **Marseille**; Musée Granet, **Aix**).

In the 1860s, physicists made the discovery that colour derives from light, not form. The idea inspired a new kind of art known as Impressionism. Pissarro, Renoir, Manet and company made it their aim to strip Courbet's new-found visual reality of all subjectivity and to simply record on canvas the atmosphere, light and colour the eye saw, all according to the latest scientific theories. The crucial role Provence was to play in modern art came later, in the 1880s, thanks to the careers of the two great postimpressionist painters: Vincent Van Gogh and Paul Cézanne. Not only did they change the history of art, but they produced, albeit in wildly different styles, the most loved images the outside world has of Provence.

A failed Dutch minister, **Vincent Van Gogh** (1853–90) was inspired by the Impressionists and Japanese prints in Paris, but the most astonishing revolution in his art occurred when he moved to Arles in 1888 in search of 'a different light, in the belief that to look at nature under a clearer sky could give us a better idea of the way the Japanese see and draw; finally, I seek a stronger sun'. He responded to the heightened colour and light on such an emotional level that colour came less and less to represent form in his art (as it did for the Impressionists), but instead took on a symbolic value as the only medium Van Gogh found powerful enough to contain his extraordinary moods and visions: 'Instead of trying to reproduce exactly what I have before my eyes, I use colour more arbitrarily so as to express myself more forcibly.' The result was an intense lyricism that has never been equalled, a 'research into the infinite' that ended with suicide. He sold only one painting in his 37 years, and ironically not a single one of the 800 or so canvases he painted around Arles remains in Provence.

Van Gogh's revolutionary liberation of colour from form was taken to an extreme by a group of painters that the critic Louis Vauxcelles nicknamed the **Fauves** ('wild beasts') for the violence of their colours. The Fauves used colour to express moods and rhythms to the detriment of detail and recognizable subject matter. As a movement the Fauves lasted from 1904 until 1908, but in those few years revolutionized centuries of European art. Nearly all the Fauves – André Derain, Matisse, Maurice Vlaminck, Raoul Dufy, Kees Van Dongen – painted in the south, along the Riviera and at La Ciotat, Cassis and L'Estaque. Their work paved the way for expressionism, Cubism and abstractionism – avenues few of the Fauvists themselves ever explored. For after 1908 the collective new vision these young men had shared in the south of France vanished as if they had awoken from a mass hypnosis; all went their separate ways, leaving others to carry their ideas on to their logical conclusions. 'Fauve painting is not everything,' Matisse explained. 'But it is the foundation of everything.'

Unlike Van Gogh, **Paul Cézanne** (1839–1906) was a native of Provence, born in Aix, where fellow schooolmate Emile Zola was his best friend, until Zola published his autobiographical *L'Oeuvre*, which thinly disguised Cézanne as the failed painter Lantier. Cézanne never forgave him, and anyway, compared to poor Van Gogh, Cézanne enjoyed a certain amount of success in his lifetime. His response to Provence was analytical rather than emotional, his interest not so much in depicting what he saw, but in the contradiction between the eye and mind, between the permanence of nature and the ephemeral qualities of light and movement. 'Nature is always the same, but none of it lasts beyond what we perceive,' he wrote. His goal was 'to make Impressionism solid and enduring, like the art of the museums'. His painting went through several distinct periods: a sombre romantic stage (1861–71); an Impressionistic manner, inspired by Pissarro (1872–82); a period of synthesis (1883–95), combining elements of impressionism with an interest in volume, surface planes and the desire to represent perspective by nuances of colour and tonality only; and lastly, his lyric period (1896–1906), where singing rhythms of colour and form are intellectually supported by the basic tenets of Cubism, splitting planes and volumes into prisms to express the tension between seeing and knowing. A handful of his paintings are on display in the Musée Granet in **Aix**.

In 1908, Georges Braque and the Fauvist Dufy went to paint together at L'Estaque in homage to Cézanne. The beginnings of the prismatic splitting of forms are in their respective works, and when the same critic Vauxcelles saw Braque's paintings, he came up with a new name: **Cubism**. In 1912, Braque and Picasso worked together in Sorgues, near Avignon, where they produced canvases that verge on abstraction. **Pablo Picasso** (1881–1973), the 20th century's most endlessly inventive and prolific artist, returned to the south of France for good in 1948. Living here heightened the Mediterranean and pagan aspects of his extraordinarily wide-ranging work; when he felt nostalgic for his native Spain he would attend the bullfights at **Arles** and left a collection of drawings to the town's Musée Réattu.

Although a long list of other 20th-century artists, including Renoir, Matisse and Chagall, settled in the south, like Picasso they usually chose to live on the Côte d'Azur. One exception in Provence is Hungarian-born founder of Op Art and experimenter in kinetic art, Victor Vasarély (1908–97), whose foundation in **Aix-en-Provence** waits to make your eyeballs squirm. Modern architecture has also left most of Provence alone: the one notable exception is Le Corbusier's idealistic Unité d'Habitation in **Marseille** (1952), part of a large housing project that was to consist of a row of rectangular slabs built on stilts. The rest were cancelled by the horrified Marseillais after the first building was finished. Other architects thought it was the future, however, and it's hard to think of any city in the world that has escaped a copy since.

Topics

A Country Calendar

Beyond the glamorous life in the villas and *résidences secondaires*, the cycle of the seasons goes on in the south of France as it has since Hector was a pup. A few crops have changed – silk, madder and a dozen different varieties of wheat have vanished, while flowers and early garden vegetables have become more important. Some corners are warm enough to produce three crops a year.

The calendar begins with two months of repose: *l'ivèr a ges d'ouro*, 'winter has no hours', is an old saying in the country. The mistral howls away, and it snows, sometimes even in Nice. In January the Three Kings are fêted with crown-shaped *brioches* studded with candied fruit. Fattened geese and ducks are turned into *confits* and pigs into sausages and raw ham. In early February the mimosas bloom and olives are squeezed into oil; traditional presses are still used in many villages. Flaky tarts filled with jam or cream are baked for Carnival. By the end of February the almonds burst into lacy bloom.

The real work begins in March, when farmers prune their olives and vines and sow wheat and oats, and plant potatoes and melons. In April two things must be cut: hay and fleece, much of the work done by itinerant sheep shearers who travel from farm to farm. Plums, apricots, cherries and pears spring into blossom; and everyone prays the mistral doesn't blow the flowers and buds off the trees. Good Friday is traditionally celebrated with an *aïoli*, or dried cod and garlic mayonnaise feast; for Easter the first roast lamb of the year is served with a salad of romaine lettuce, fresh onions and hard-boiled eggs. In May the flocks are driven to the greener pastures in the hills, following transhumance trails that date back to the Neolithic era. Early vegetables are abundant in the markets – little green artichokes called *mourre de gat* for omelettes, *fèves* (broad beans), garlic, spring onions and peas.

June brings the wheat harvest, once the most colourful event on the calendar as mountaineers descended by the thousands to provide the labour, fuelled on five meals and a barrel of wine a day. Asparagus, cherries and apricots ripen, and gourmets poke around in the woods for delectable morel mushrooms. The summer solstice and end of the harvest (St John's Day) are given a good old-fashioned Celtic send-off with bonfires and fireworks; the sun itself is said to dance and jump three times over the Alpilles. Almonds are ready to be picked in July, but now and throughout August it's too hot to work except in the early morning. Melons and peaches are everywhere, and the lavender is ready to be cut. The evenings are alive with village fêtes, for this has always been the time to eat, drink and make merry, to hoard strength for hard tasks ahead.

September brings fresh figs, and the rice is ready to be harvested in the Camargue. With the first rains mushrooms begin to poke up in the woods, especially the fragrant *cèpes*; these are tracked down with a relentlessness matched only by the hunters, whose blasting advent is marked by a noticeable decline in birdsong. But the most important event of the month is the *vendanges*, or grape harvest. October, too, is very much occupied with winemaking. The stripped vines turn red, wild boar meat appears in the markets, walnuts and chestnuts are gathered in the hills.

November marks the beginning of a new agricultural year, with the planting of wheat. Cold weather forces the shepherds and their flocks down from the mountains. Olives wait to be picked, and truffle hounds (the picturesque but uncontrollably greedy pigs have been retired) seek out the elusive *rabasso*, the black gold of the Vaucluse.

December brings Christmas, or Calendo in Provençal, a word resulting from an early confusion of Christ's birth with the Roman Calends. On Christmas Eve, *le réveillon*, the grandfather of each family blesses the *cacho-fiô* (a Yule log from a fruit tree) and the youngest in the family lays it in the hearth; a lavish meal of fish and vegetables traditionally followed by thirteen desserts precedes midnight Mass. This being France, the stomach dominates Christmas Day as well: oysters, foie gras, black truffles, stuffed capon, goose with pears, and champagne, by necessity punctuated by frequent 'trous provençaux' – snorts of frozen *marc* that magically make it possible to eat as much as Gargantua. And by New Year's Eve (St-Sylvestre) everyone's digestion has sufficiently recovered to eat it all again.

Mistral and the Félibrige

The attitude of the French to their language was best expressed by Paul Morand's speech upon being admitted to the Académie Française: 'To write in French is to see flowing the waters of a mountain stream, next to which all languages are muddy rivers; it is to live in a crystal palace.' To someone like Morand, master of *pointu* or 'proper' French, with all its mushy slushy vowel sounds, one of the muddiest rivers was *langue d'oc*. Its demise became a priority in the 19th century; after subjugating the south politically and religiously, Paris decided to finish off the job linguistically and decreed French the sole legal language in the schools, military, government and press.

One of the strategies of the *Franchimands* (as the southerners called French speakers) was to divide and conquer: *langue d'oc*, claimed the central Frenchifyers, was actually thousands of dialects and could never constitute a language. Even the southerners admit to seven 'grand dialects' of Occitan, two of which fall into the confines of this book: the Dauphinois of the Alpine valleys and Provençal. But it was in Provence that the reaction to the *Franchimands'* linguistic imperialism took its most curious form – in a sentimental, artificially contrived literary movement called the Félibrige.

According to legend, the idea for the Félibres was 'born of a mother's tear' when the mother of the poet Joseph Roumanille wept because she couldn't understand the French verses of her son. Not long after, on 21 May 1854, at the Château de Font

Ségugne near Avignon, Roumanille, Frédéric Mistral and five other poets proclaimed the formation of a literary school to 'safeguard indefinitely for Provence its language, its colour, its easy liberty, its national honour, and its fine level of intelligence, for such as it is, we like Provence'. It was the 24-year-old Mistral who came up with the name for the school when he quoted a folk rhyme on the Seven Sorrows of Mary from his native village Maillane: *li sètt felibre de la Lèi* – the seven doctors or sages of the law. As 21 May (the day when the sun is in the constellation of the Pleiades, or seven sisters) was the feast day of Santo Estello, the seven-pointed star of the Cathars was adopted as one of the Félibres' symbols. In later years, after Mistral's epic *Miréio* gave the movement its lustre, 21 May would be celebrated with a Grand Félibre Banquet when all the fifty members or Majoraux and their leader, the *capoulié* (Mistral, naturally), would pass around the Coupo Santo, the Félibres' Holy Grail.

The Félibres' greatest moment came in 1904, when Mistral won the Nobel Prize for literature, the only writer in a minority language ever to be awarded a Nobel Prize. Thanks to him and the other Félibres, Provence became conscious and proud of its separate identity; the richness of the language charmed even foreigners like Ezra Pound, who wrote and translated Provençal. But in spite of these successes, the Félibrige best serves as a lesson on how not to revive a language. Today only a few people in their eighties in remote areas still use Provençal as a daily tool, a sorry record compared to the subsequent revivals of Irish, Catalan, Basque, Welsh, and most successful of all, Hebrew. Where did the Félibres go wrong? Not for lack of trying: unlike the courtly troubadours, they purposely wrote in a simple style to appeal to the *paysans*. Slipshod grammar and spelling were codified in Mistral's labour of love, the *Trésor du Félibrige* (a work accused by some of passing off the rustic dialect of Maillane as the last word in Provençal). But the Félibres' biggest mistake was confusing language and time, associating Provençal with folklore and the past, and shunning the necessary political fight with Paris in a romantic illusion that their poetry was powerful enough to revive a dying tongue. Mistral's powerful, mystical evocation of western Provence (the real hero of all his epics) was more of a swansong to a dying culture, not the foundation for a Renaissance of new troubadours.

For nearly everything Mistral celebrated in his poetry was undergoing a sea change – Italians, Corsicans and Spaniards were moving in by the thousands, and helping to build new roads and railroads, while old farming practices, rural customs, traditions, and even villages were rapidly being abandoned. Mistral for all his art, energy, charm and influence could not turn the clock back. He had the unique honour of attending the unveiling of his own statue in Arles – a melancholy recognition that he was dead in his own lifetime.

Hocus Pocus Popes

Filling the lifeless shell of the papal palace in Avignon with the lost trappings of the medieval popes is not an easy task for the imagination. And the more you learn, the harder it gets, for besides all the harlots, speculators, gluttons and cheats that Petrarch railed against, there seems to have been a shocking amount of voodoo. Accusations of sorcery had already sullied the name of one Occitan pope, Sylvester II (Gerbert of the Auvergne), who reigned from 999 to 1003 after studying in the Islamic schools in Toledo, where he acquired a prophetic bronze head that advised him in sticky moments. Even today, his tombstone in St John Lateran sweats and rattles before the death of each pope.

In 1309 the French pope Clement V moved the papacy from Rome to Avignon, then died from eating a plate of ground emeralds (prescribed by his doctor for a stomach ache). He was succeeded by John XXII, a native of Cahors, who owed his election to a magic knife that enchanted the conclave of cardinals. This John was also a famous alchemist, and he filled the papal treasury with gold, while King Philip V gave him a pair of *languiers*, or amulets shaped like serpents' tongues, encrusted with gems that changed colour on contact with poison. They served the pope in good stead, as plenty of rivals in the Church were trying to do him in. The most notable culprits were Clement V's doctor, caught manufacturing a diabolical homunculus, and Hughes Geraud, Bishop of Cahors, who confessed in 1317 that he had tried to assassinate the pope 'by poison and by sorcery with wax images, ashes of spiders and toads, the gall of a pig, and the like substances.' John XXII ordered him burnt at the stake.

The next pope, Benedict XII, spent hundreds of thousands of florins on a new palace, and still had enough gold and precious stones left over to top up his treasury – thanks, it is said, to an elderly woman residing in Avignon's ghetto, who told him where to find the 'treasure of the Jews' buried under her hovel. And in the bitter end, just before the anti-pope Benedict XIII was forced to flee Avignon, he sealed up a secret room in the palace with a cache of solid gold statues, confiding the secret to his friend, the Venetian ambassador. They were never found, although in Mistral's epic *Poème du Rhône*, three Venetian ladies who inherited the secret come to the palace and remove the flagstones that cover up the secret room – only to discover a bottomless abyss.

Marcel Pagnol and the Provençal Mystique

A certain part of Provence's current mystique derives from two of the best-loved French movies in recent years, *Jean de Florette* and *Manon des Sources*, directed by Claude Berri. Not only are both beautifully set in the heart of Provence, but more than that, they stick in the mind like glue: tales of mythic simplicity, of water, of a conspiracy of silence, of revenge. The stories, from *L'Eau des Collines*, were written by

Marcel Pagnol and are based, according to him, on true stories that he heard as a child. The even more recent films, *La Gloire de mon Père* and *La Château de ma Mère*, were based on Pagnol's childhood memories. They evoke a Provençal idyll from the beginning of the century; from the photography alone you can almost smell the wild herbs of the Garrigue baking in the sun.

Yet Marcel Pagnol's role in creating a universal mental image of Provence goes back to the 1930s, when he himself was a pioneer in the then new medium of 'talkies' – in fact, it's impossible to imagine a Pagnol film without sound because most of the time his characters are jawing away non-stop. Now relegated to *cinemathèques* and the occasional late-night movie slot on television, his films, all made on location in Provence's villages, are often difficult to watch for modern viewers, weaned on colour, constantly changing camera angles and scenes, fast-paced dialogue and action. Many families shoot better home videos. Pagnol's photography is bad, the camera angles are boring, and he never uses the slightest cinemagraphic trick, always preferring to 'say' rather than 'show' – it often seems that no one is directing the film at all. Many of Pagnol's ideas were adopted by the *nouvelle vague* directors in the 1960s.

Pagnol was a fervent believer in the power of human speech: for him the word was sacred. He was one of the first playwrights to move on to film because he was delighted to have his actors express themselves in conversational tones – with rich Provençal accents, naturally, and without using the exaggerated voices, gestures and makeup necessary in the theatre or in silent movies. No director before him gave his actors so much freedom. When filming his favourite actor, Raimu, star of *Marius*, *César* and *La Femme du Boulanger*, Pagnol said: 'He's so good that I just let him go on until he's tired of talking or we've run out of film.'

Most importantly, where Mistral and the Félibres failed to reach the masses through atavistic artiness (*see* above), Pagnol succeeded. There is nothing folkloric, stilted or affected in his Provence, but instead a sunny, attractive vision on a human scale and measured to a moral order, where life, as in all Mediterranean lands, revolves around the family. His stories are invariably simple – eternal fables of the human condition, planted in the fragrant soil of the Midi. An often wry sense of humour is never far, even when everything is going wrong. In 1967, French critic Jacques Lourcelles summed up the effect of Pagnol:

> Seeing his films today, one realizes that they are a kind of classic, for which the scenario and creation of characters counted more than anything...His Provence is an immemorial Provence, static, hardly referred to [in the films] but profoundly linked to the destiny of his characters, underemphasized, and yet as present as the landscapes in the best westerns, with which the films of Pagnol are not without affinity. This vanished, non-touristy Provence is without doubt the most interesting feature of Pagnol's classicism.

Troubadours

Lyric poetry in the modern Western world was born around the year 1095 with the rhymes of Count William (1071–1127), grandfather of Eleanor of Aquitaine. William wrote in the courtly language called Old Provençal (or Occitan), although his subject matter was hardly courtly ('Do you know how many times I screwed them?/One hundred and eighty-eight to be precise;/so much so that I almost broke my girth and harness...'). A descendant of the royal house of Aragon, William had Spanish-Arab blood in his lusty veins and had battled against the Moors in Spain on several occasions, but at the same time he found inspiration (for his form, if not his content) from a civilization that was centuries ahead of Christian Europe in culture.

The word troubadour may be derived from the Arabic root for lutenist (trb), and the ideal of courtly love makes its first appearance in the writings of the spiritual Islamic Sufis. The Sufis believed that true understanding could not be expressed in doctrines, but could be suggested obliquely in poetry and fables. Much of what they wrote was love poetry addressed to an ideal if unkind and irrational Muse, whom the poet hopes will reward his merit and devotion with enlightenment and inspiration.

Christians who encountered this poetry in the Crusades converted this ideal Muse into the Virgin, giving birth to the great 12th-century cult of Mary. But in Occitania this mystic strain was reinterpreted in a more worldly fashion by troubadours, whose muses became flesh and blood women, although these darlings were equally unattainable in the literary conventions of courtly love. The lady in question could only be addressed by a pseudonym. She had to be married to someone else. The poet's hopeless suit to her hinged not on his rank, but on his virtue and worthiness. The greatest novelty of all was that this love had to go unrequited.

Art songs of courtly love were known as *cansos*, and rarely translate well, as their merit was in the poet's skill in inventing new forms in his rhyming schemes, metres, melodies and images. But the troubadours wrote many other songs as well, called *sirventes*, which followed established forms but took for their subjects politics, war, miserly patrons, and even satires on courtly love itself.

The golden age of the troubadours began in the 1150s, when the feudal lords of Occitania warred amongst each other with so little success that behind the sound and fury the land enjoyed a rare political stability. Courts indulged in new luxuries and the arts flourished, and troubadours found ready audiences, travelling from castle to castle. One of their great patrons was En Barral, Viscount of Marseille, who was especially fond of the reputedly mad but charming Peire Vidal. Vidal not only wrote of his love for En Barral's beautiful wife, but in a famous incident even went beyond the bounds of convention by stealing a kiss from her while she slept (her husband, who thought it was funny, had to plead with her to forgive him). Vidal travelled widely, especially after the death of En Barral in 1192, and wrote a rare nostalgic poem for the homeland of his lady fair:

With each breath I draw in the air
I feel coming from Provence;
I so love everything from there
that when people speak well of it,
I listen smiling, and with each
word ask for a hundred more,
so much does the hearing please me.

(trans. by Anthony Bonner, in *Songs of the Troubadours*)

Up Your Nose

If nothing else, Provence will make you more aware of that sense we only remember when something stinks. The perfumeries of Grasse will correct this 'scentual' ignorance with a hundred different potions; every *village perché* has shops overflowing with scented soaps, pot-pourris and bundles of *herbes de Provence*; every kitchen emits intoxicating scents of garlic and thyme; every cellar wants you to breathe in the bouquets of its wines. And when you begin to almost crave the more usual French smells of Gauloise butts, *pipi* and *pommes frites*, you discover that this nasal obsession is not only profitable to some, but healthy for all.

Aromathérapie, a name coined in the 1920s for the method of natural healing through fragrances, is taken very seriously in the land where one word, *sentir*, does double duty for 'feel' and 'smell'. French medical students study it, and its prescriptions are covered by the national social security. For as an aromatherapist will tell you, smells play games with your psyche; the nose is hooked up not only to primitive drives like sex and hunger, but also to your emotions and memory. The consequences can be monumental. Just the scent of a madeleine cake dipped in tea was enough to set Proust off to write *Remembrance of Things Past*.

Aromatherapy is really just a fashionable name for old medicine. The Romans had a saying, *Cur moriatur homo, cui salvia crescit in horto?* (Why should he die, who grows sage in his garden?), about a herb still heralded for its youth-giving properties. Essential oils distilled from plants were the secret of Egyptian healing and embalming, and were so powerful that there was a bullish market in 17th-century Europe for mummies, which were boiled down to make medicine.

Essential oils are created by the sun and the most useful aromatic plants grow in hot and dry climates – as in the south of France, the spiritual heartland of aromatherapy. Lavender, the totem plant of the Midi, has been in high demand for its mellow soothing qualities ever since the Romans used it to scent their baths (hence its name from the Latin *lavare*, to wash). Up until the 1900s, nearly every farm in Provence had a small lavender distillery, and you can still find a few kicking about today. Most precious of all is the oil of *lavande fine*, a species that grows only above 3,000 feet on the sunny side of the Alps; 150 pounds of flowers are needed for every pound of oil.

For centuries in Provence, shepherds were regarded as magicians for their plant cures, involving considerable mumbo-jumbo about picking their herbs in certain places and certain times – and indeed, modern analysis has shown that the chemical composition of a herb like thyme varies widely, depending on where it grows and when it's picked. When the sun is in Leo, shepherds make *millepertuis*, or red oil (a sovereign anaesthetic and remedy for burns and wounds), by soaking the flowers of St John's wort in a mixture of white wine and olive oil that has been exposed to the hottest sun. After three days, they boil the wine off, and let the flowers distil for another month; the oil is then sealed into tiny bottles, good for one dose each, to maintain the oil's healing properties.

Still awaiting a fashionable revival are other traditional Provençal cures: baked ground magpie brains for epilepsy, marmot fat for rheumatism, dried fox testicles rubbed on the chest for uterine disease and mouse excrement for bedwetting.

The Village Sociologist

Look up from the lavender fields for a minute, towards the typically picturesque *village perché* on the hills above. It seems a timeless place, where generation after generation of peasants have tilled the soil and lived their simple lives, until modern times came in with tractors, cars and store-bought clothes to spoil the effect. Writers such as Daudet and Giono, living in a time when rapid change was transforming villages and village life, made their careers chronicling the loss of old country ways with a sort of romantic melancholy. City people weren't discouraged, of course. The fantasy that attaches to places like Bonnieux, Les Arcs or Lacoste has a lot to do with this image of a lost rustic paradise. Along with the lavender, it's what draws the tourists, the second-home buyers and the art schools.

This picture isn't entirely false – only nearly so. The romantic point of view can often lead to gross oversimplifications that do the little rural communities of Provence scant justice. If you look closely at a village and its past, you'll most likely find a fascinating story, with as much change and troubles as any big city. One way to do this is to read a lovely book called *Village in the Vaucluse*, written by an American sociologist named Laurence Wylie. In the 1950s, Wylie wangled one of the all-time sweet study grants, allowing him and his family to spend a year in Roussillon (disguised in the book as 'Peyrane') to examine the structure of village society. *Village in the Vaucluse* is hardly a dry sociological text. Wylie poked into every aspect of village life, sitting in at the local school, sifting through the archives (a bag of old papers in the mayor's closet) and gossiping with the old farmers. The result was a book written with considerable understanding and affection, one more like Marcel Pagnol than sociology.

Wylie also took the trouble to explore Roussillon's history, a tale full of ups and downs that makes a perfect illustration of the complexity of village life. In the early 19th century, as Roussillon entered the modern world, it began changing from a largely self-sufficient farming economy. Village women found good money in the exacting work of raising silkworms, while the men raised a new cash crop: madder, used in dying cloth. The Roussillonnais did just fine until the disaster of the 1860s and 70s: silkworm diseases, a terrible winter that destroyed the olive trees, and the phylloxera epidemic that did in the vines. Things picked up again in the 1890s, when the ochre mines came back into production; depending on the market, these have been exploited on and off since Roman times. The First World War shut the mines off from their market in Russia, and carried away all too many of the village's sons, resulting in a steep decline not reversed until the 1950s, when modern farming methods and tourism brought prosperity gradually back.

Along with the changes in the economy there have been correspondingly extreme swings in population. Roussillon has been a boom town many times over the centuries – and bust just as often, as it was in the 50s with half its houses empty and mostly old folks in the rest of them. In the first half of the 19th century, the population increased from 1,195 to 1,568. By 1886 it was back down to 1,213. After the First World War it reached a low point of about 900, and the village has been inching its way back since. Today the population is 1,300 and growing.

This population has always been more complex than just a simple collection of Provençal farmers. Even back in 1896, more than 10 per cent of Roussillon's population was made up of people from elsewhere. In the past, whenever the business cycle favoured a village new people would come from somewhere, and the natives would undoubtedly call them *étrangers*, even if they came from Marseille. In the 1890s Italian immigrants came to try their fortune. More recently it has been the Spanish, many of them Republicans exiled by the Civil War, as well as some Portuguese and a large number of *pieds-noirs*, French settlers chased out of Algeria when that country won its independence. Lately the 'immigrants' have been Parisian, British and American refugees from the rat race.

Another surprise Wylie found is how much internal politics, conflict and mutual dislike a village of a thousand people or so can generate. It's no surprise, really, to anyone who has ever spent time in such a village. Under a seamless veneer of French politeness, you'll always find that most of the inhabitants don't really much care for each other; life can be as intense as any soap opera, though without the glitter. To each, there's always the division between a few families whom one knows and who can be trusted, and *les autres* – those neighbours who are always peeking from behind their curtains, and who might report you to the tax man. Feuds of one sort or another are common – they may be the village's main source of entertainment. In our times these are usually expressed in politics; any French village could provide enough political news and opinions to fill a daily newspaper, if only there were enough people to read it.

Amidst all the change, these feuds sometimes provide the biggest element of stability. Wylie knew of two families in Roussillon that didn't get along, the Jouvauds and the Favres; the family heads were also among the leaders of two rival political parties in the village. Looking through the old records, he found that a Jouvaud had killed a Favre back in 1740, in a dispute that started when the victim led a band dancing the *farandole* (*see* p.91) across a square where Jouvaud had been playing an intense game of *boules*.

In Roussillon, or any other village, there will always be something to talk about. In the anomie of modern life, we may forget just how complex a community of a thousand souls can be. A village is a world in itself, with enough interest and incident to satisfy all but the most jaded. Once they come to know what a rich and intricate place they have moved to, many of the city folk who seek refuge in the village find that this is the biggest attraction of all.

Wide Open Spaces

Gertrude Stein, a great fan of Provence who spent a lot of time in St-Rémy thinking inscrutable thoughts, once dropped a famous line about Oakland, California: 'There's no there there,' she concluded after a brief visit. Take an equally inscrutable modern-day rapper from Oakland out to the exact centre of Provence, around the Lac de Castillon, and you will get a neatly symmetrical opinion. Lac de Castillon, a big artificial lake behind a concrete dam, is a special place, surrounded by wrinkled hills of a grey so immaculately grey that it is hard to see them at all. Outside of a few dam workers and an occasional trendy hang-gliding above, the whole gigantic grey place will be eerily deserted. The Lac de Castillon is nowhere, and all the towns and villages for thirty miles or more in any direction are only variations on the theme. We like to imagine an advert in a London paper: 'Delightful farmhouse half-restored in the heart of the Provençal mountains, near mountain lake; 1½hr from Cannes. Must sell.'

When you visit, take a look at the sort of Frenchman who lives in such a place: no poodles, no shades, no attitudes; even in summer, he may well be wearing a flannel shirt, which under the big moustaches will make him look entirely like one of the jolly Gaulish villagers in Astérix. Some of these are real frontiersmen, rough-edged, self-sufficient types whose lives revolve around hunting, gathering mushrooms and getting in wood for the winter; they grumble laconically in a tongue that is still more Provençal than French.

But we once met a picture-perfect example on the way to Draguignan. He was the baker in a village near the lake, hitch-hiking to the city with a jerry can of petrol to buy a used car (in France one never expects a used car to have any in the tank). His brother had gone off to the Harvard Business School and made it big. The baker, with his degree in cultural anthropology, preferred less stress and yeastier dough; having an assistant allowed him enough time for long scholarly vacations in the darker corners of South America and Asia.

The moral seems to be: rural France provides some of the world's most interesting hitch-hikers. It does, but the point was that the English shibboleth 'the South of

France' is not always what one might expect. The toadstool growth of the Côte d'Azur in the last century has entirely eclipsed the real Provence: lonely expanses of mountain and introverted villages, shepherds who still drive their flocks up to the mountains in summer on the old transhumance paths, and a traditional rural culture that, despite a great loss of population in the last century, is not yet prepared to compromise entirely with the modern world.

One wild snapshot among many sticks in the mind: two Indian chiefs, Iron Tail and Lone Bear, sipping champagne with the Marquis de Baroncelli-Javon (*see* p.172) in 1889, while watching Camargue *gardians* and the cowboys of Buffalo Bill's Wild West Show compare their skills at a Provençal rodeo. The men of two worlds had a great time together, and seemed to understand one another perfectly. One young Sioux, whom the French called Pain Perdu, chose to stay behind in Provence; Frédéric Mistral met him, and thought he might be the reincarnated soul of a troubadour.

Food and Drink

...and south of Valence, Provincia Romana, the Roman Provence, lies beneath the sun. There there is no more any evil, for there the apple will not flourish and the Brussels sprout will not grow at all.

Ford Madox Ford, *Provence*

Eating is a pleasure in the south, where seafood, herbs, fruit and vegetables are often within plucking distance of the kitchen and table. The high quality of these fresh native ingredients demands minimal preparation – Provençal cooking is perhaps the least fussy of any regional French cuisine, and as an added plus neatly fits the modern definition of a healthy diet. For not only is the south a Brussels sprout-free zone, but the artery-hardening delights of the north – the rich creamy sauces, butter, cheese and egg dishes, and mega-calorie desserts – are rare birds in the land of olives, fresh vegetables, apricots and almonds.

Some of the most celebrated restaurants in the world grace the south of France, but there are plenty of stinkers, too. The most tolerable are humble in their mediocrity, while others are oily with pretensions, staffed by folks posing as Grand Dukes and Duchesses fallen on hard times, whose exalted airs are somehow supposed to make their clients feel better about paying an obscene amount of money for the eight *petits pois à la graisse de yak* that the chef has so beautifully arranged on a plate.

Just as intimidating for the hungry traveller are France's much ballyhooed gourmet bibles, whose annual awarding or removing of a star here, a chef's hat there, grade food the way a French teacher grades a *dictée* in school. Woe to the chef who leaves a lump in the sauce when those incognito pedants of the perfect palate are dining, and whose guillotine pens will ruthlessly chop off percentage points from the restaurant's final score. The less attention you pay them, the more you'll enjoy your dinner.

The Cuisine of Provence

Thanks to the trail-blazing work of writers and chefs like Elizabeth David and Roger Vergé, Provençal cooking no longer sends the average Anglo-Saxon into paroxysms of garlic paranoia as it did a hundred years ago. Many traditional dishes actually presage *nouvelle cuisine*, and their success hangs on the quality of the ingredients and fragrant olive oil, like the well-known *ratatouille* – aubergines (eggplant), tomatoes, garlic and courgettes (zucchini) cooked separately to preserve their individual flavour, before being mixed together in olive oil – or *bagna cauda*, a dish of the southern Alps, consisting of raw vegetables dipped in a hot fondue of garlic, anchovies and olive oil.

A favourite **hors d'œuvre** is *tapenade*, a purée of olives, anchovies, olive oil and capers served on toast. The best known starter must be *salade niçoise*, interpreted in a hundred different ways even in Nice, but in general containing most of the following: tomatoes, cucumbers, hard-boiled eggs, black olives, onions, anchovies, artichokes, green peppers, croûtons, green beans, and sometimes tuna and even potatoes. Another dish that tastes best in the summer, *soupe au pistou*, is a thick minestrone served with a fresh basil, garlic and pine-nut sauce similar to Italian *pesto*.

Aïoli Recipe

This typical Provençal mayonnaise is best served with white fish such as cod, or with snails, potatoes or soup.

Ingredients (per person)
1 egg yolk
1 clove of garlic (more if you're a garlic fiend)
extra-virgin olive oil

Using a mortar and pestle, crush the garlic to a paste and add the egg yolks. Begin whipping the mixture with a fork or small whisk while adding good quality (extra-virgin) olive oil, first drop by drop, then in a thin stream as the mayonnaise begins to set. Add salt only once all the oil has been integrated and the mayonnaise formed.

Should the *aïoli* lack substance or the oil separate from the mixture, you can still 'save' your mayonnaise: remove the mixture and add another egg yolk to the clean mortar. Whipping constantly, reintegrate the old *aïoli* mixture and any remaining oil. This operation is called 'reconstituting' the *aïoli*.

Aïoli, a mayonnaise made from garlic, olive oil, lemon juice and egg yolks, served with codfish, snails, potatoes or soup (*see* above), is for many the essence of Provence; Mistral even named his nationalist Provençal magazine after it. In the same spirit Marseille named its magazine *Bouillabaisse*, for its world-famous soup of five to twelve kinds of Mediterranean **fish**, flavoured with saffron; the fish is removed and served with *aïoli* or *rouille*, a sauce of red chilli peppers crushed with garlic, olive oil and the broth. Because good saffron costs money and the fish, especially the gruesome *rascasse* (scorpion fish), are rare, a proper *bouillabaisse* will cost at least €30.

A less expensive but delicious alternative is *bourride*, a soup made from white-fleshed fish served with *aïoli*, or down a gastronomical notch is *baudroie*, a fish soup with vegetables and garlic. A very different kettle of fish is the indigestible favourite, *estocaficada*, salt cod (and salt cod guts) stewed with tomatoes, olives, garlic and *eau-de-vie*. Less adventurous, yet an absolutely delicious dish, is *loup au fenouil*, sea bass grilled over fennel stalks.

Lamb is the most common meat dish; real Provençal lamb (becoming increasingly rare) grazes on herbs and on special salt-marsh grasses from the Camargue and Crau. **Beef** usually comes in the form of a *daube*, slowly stewed in red wine and often served with ravioli. A Provençal cook's prize possession is the *daube* pan, which is never washed, but wiped clean and baked to form a crust that flavours all subsequent stews. **Rabbit**, or *lapin à la provençale*, is simmered in white wine with garlic, mustard, tomatoes and herbs. The more daunting *pieds et paquets* are tripe packages stuffed with garlic, onions and salt pork, traditionally (although rarely in practice) served with calf's or sheep's trotters. Also look for *capoun fassum*, cabbage stuffed with sausage and rice, and *artichauts à la barigoule*, artichokes filled with pork and mushrooms.

Purely **vegetable** dishes, besides ratatouille, include *tian*, a casserole of rice, spring vegetables and grated cheese baked in the oven; *tourta de blea*, a sweet-savoury Swiss chard pie; stuffed courgette (zucchini) flowers; grilled tomatoes with garlic and breadcrumbs (*à la provençale*); and *mesclun*, a salad of dandelion and other green leaves. There aren't many Provençal **cheeses**: *banon*, nutty discs made from goat's, sheep's, or cow's milk, wrapped in chestnut leaves, is perhaps the best known; *poivre d'Ain* is *banon* flavoured with savory; thyme and bay add a nuance to creamy sheep's milk *tomme arlésienne*.

Markets, Picnic Food and Snacks

The food markets in the south of France are justly celebrated for the colour and perfumes of their produce and flowers. They are fun to visit, and become even more interesting if you're cooking or gathering the ingredients for a picnic. In the larger cities food markets take place every day, while smaller towns and villages have markets on one day a week (we've listed all the ones we know in the text), which double as a social occasion for the locals. Most markets finish around noon.

Other good sources for picnic food are the *charcuteries* or *traiteurs*, both of which sell prepared dishes by weight in cartons or tubs. You can also find counters at larger supermarkets. Cities are snack-food wonderlands, with outdoor counters selling pastries, crêpes, pizza slices, *frites*, *croque-monsieurs* (toasted ham and cheese sandwiches) and a wide variety of sandwiches made from baguettes (long thin loaves).

Drink

You can order any kind of drink at any bar or café – except cocktails, unless the place has a certain cosmopolitan *savoir-faire* or stays open into the night. Cafés are also a home from home, places to read the papers, play cards, meet friends, and just unwind, sit back and watch the world go by. You can spend hours over one coffee and no one will try to hurry you along. Prices are listed on the *Tarif des Consommations*: note they are progressively more expensive depending on whether you're served at the bar (*comptoir*), at a table (*la salle*) or outside (*la terrasse*). French coffee is strong and black, but lacklustre next to the aromatic brews of Italy or Spain (you'll notice an improvement in the coffee near their respective frontiers). If you order *un café* you'll get a small black *espresso*; if you want milk, order *un crème*. If you want more than a few drops of caffeine, ask them to make it *grand*. For decaffeinated, the word is *déca*. Some bars offer *cappuccinos*, but again they're only really good near the Italian border; in the summer try a *café frappé* (iced coffee). The French only order *café au lait* (a small coffee topped off with lots of hot milk) when they stop in for breakfast, and if what your hotel offers is expensive or boring, consider joining them. There are baskets of croissants and pastries, and some bars will make you a *tartine beurrée*, baguette with butter. If you want to go native, try the Frenchman's Breakfast of Champions: a *pastis* or two, and five non-filter *Gauloises*. *Chocolat chaud* (hot chocolate) is usually good; if you order *thé* (*au lait*), you'll get an ordinary bag. An *infusion* is a herbal tea – *camomille*, *menthe* (mint), *tilleul* (lime or linden blossom) or *verveine* (verbena). These are kind to the all-precious *foie*, or liver, after you've over-indulged at the table.

Mineral water (*eau minérale*) can be addictive, and comes either sparkling (*gazeuse* or *pétillante*) or still (*non-gazeuse* or *plate*). If you feel run down, Badoit has lots of peppy magnesium in it – it's the current trendy favourite, even though Perrier comes from Languedoc. The usual international corporate soft drinks are available, and all kinds of bottled fruit juices (*jus de fruits*). Some bars also do fresh lemon and orange juices (*citron pressé* or *orange pressée*). The French are fond of fruit syrups – red *grenadine* and ghastly green *diabolo menthe*.

Beer (*bière*) in most bars and cafés is run-of-the-mill big brands from Alsace, Germany and Belgium. Draft (*à la pression*) is cheaper than bottled beer. Nearly all resorts have bars or pubs offering wider selections of drafts, lagers and bottles.

The strong spirit of the Midi comes in a liquid form called *pastis*, first made popular in Marseille as a plague remedy; its name comes from the Latin *passe-sitis*, or thirst quencher. A pale yellow 90% nectar flavoured with anis, vanilla and cinnamon, pastis is drunk as an apéritif before lunch and in rounds after work. The three major brands, Ricard, Pernod and Pastis 51, all taste slightly different; most people drink their '*pastaga*' with lots of water and ice (*glaçons*), which makes it almost palatable. A thimble-sized *pastis* is a *momie*; mixed with *grenadine* it becomes a *tomate*; with *orgeat* (almond and orange-flower syrup) it's a *mauresque*, and a *perroquet* is with mint.

Other popular apéritifs come from Languedoc-Roussillon, including Byrrh 'from the world's largest barrel', a sweet wine mixed with quinine and orange peel, similar to Dubonnet. Spirits include the familiar Cognac and Armagnac brandies, liqueurs and *digestifs* made from walnuts, cherries, pears and herbs (these are a speciality of the Alps), and fiery *marc*, the grape spirit that is the same as Italian *grappa* (but usually better). Many Provençal villages have a special *marc* of their own; the *marc des orangers*, made in spring with orange flowers, is one of the nicest.

Wine

One of the pleasures of travelling in France is drinking great wines for a fraction of what you pay at home, and discovering new ones you've never seen in your local shop. The south holds a special place in the saga of French wines, with a tradition dating back to the Greeks, who are said to have introduced an essential Côtes-du-Rhône grape variety called *syrah*, originally grown in Shiraz, Persia. Nurtured in the Dark and Middle Ages by popes and kings, the vineyards of Provence and nearby Languedoc-Roussillon still produce most of France's wine – certainly most of its plonk, graded only by its alcohol content. Some of Provence's best-known wines grow in the ancient places near the coast, especially its quartet of tiny AOC districts Bellet, Bandol, Cassis and Palette. But the best-known wines of the region come from the Rhône valley, under the general heading of Côtes-du-Rhône, including Châteauneuf-du-Pape, Gigondas, the famous rosé Tavel, and the sweet muscat apéritif Beaumes-de-Venise. Elsewhere, winemakers have made great strides in boosting quality in the past 30 years, recognized in new AOC districts.

Note that restaurants make a good portion of their income from marking up wines to triple or quadruple the retail price. Save money by buying direct from the producers, or *vignerons*. In the text we've included a few addresses for each wine to get you started.

French Menu Reader

Hors-d'œuvre et Soupes (Starters and Soups)

amuse-gueule appetizers
assiette assortie plate of mixed cold hors d'œuvre
bisque shellfish soup
bouillabaisse famous fish soup of Marseille
bouillon broth
charcuterie mixed cold meats, salami, ham, etc.
consommé clear soup
coulis thick sieved sauce
crudités raw vegetable platter
potage thick vegetable soup
tourrain garlic and bread soup
velouté thick smooth soup, often fish or chicken
vol-au-vent puff-pastry case with savoury filling

Poissons et Coquillages (Crustacés) (Fish and Shellfish)

aiglefin little haddock
alose shad
anchois anchovies
anguille eel
bar sea bass
barbue brill
baudroie anglerfish
belons flat oysters
bigorneau winkle
blanchailles whitebait
brème bream
brochet pike
bulot whelk
cabillaud cod
calmar squid

carrelet plaice
colin hake
congre conger eel
coques cockles
coquillages shellfish
coquilles St-Jacques scallops
crevettes grises shrimp
crevettes roses prawns
cuisses de grenouilles frogs' legs
darne slice or steak of fish
daurade sea bream
écrevisse freshwater crayfish
éperlan smelt
escabèche fish fried, marinated and served cold
escargots snails
espadon swordfish
esturgeon sturgeon
flétan halibut
friture deep-fried fish
fruits de mer seafood
gambas giant prawns
gigot de mer a large fish cooked whole
grondin red gurnard
hareng herring
homard Atlantic (Norway) lobster
huîtres oysters
lamproie lamprey
langouste spiny Mediterranean lobster
langoustines Norway lobster (often called Dublin Bay prawns or scampi)
limande lemon sole
lotte monkfish
loup (de mer) sea bass
louvine sea bass (in Aquitaine)
maquereau mackerel
merlan whiting
morue salt cod
moules mussels

If a wine is labelled AOC (*Appellation d'Origine Contrôlée*) it means that the wine comes from a certain defined area and is made from certain varieties of grapes, guaranteeing a standard of quality. *Cru* on the label means vintage; a *grand cru* is a great, noble vintage. Down the list in the vinous hierarchy are those labelled VDQS (*Vin de Qualité Supérieure*), followed by *Vin de Pays* (guaranteed to originate in a certain region), with *Vin Ordinaire* (or *Vin de Table*) at the bottom, which may not send you to seventh heaven but is drinkable and cheap. In a restaurant if you order a *rouge* (red) or *blanc* (white) or *rosé* (pink), this is what you'll get, either by the glass (*un verre*), by the quarter-litre (*un pichet*) or bottle (*une bouteille*). *Brut* is very dry, *sec* dry, *demi-sec* and *moelleux* are sweetish, *doux* sweet, and *méthode champenoise*, sparkling.

oursin sea urchin
pagel sea bream
palourdes clams
petit gris little grey snail
poulpe octopus
praires small clams
raie skate
rascasse scorpion fish
rouget red mullet
saumon salmon
St-Pierre John Dory
sole (meunière) sole (with butter, lemon and parsley)
telline tiny clam
thon tuna
truite trout
truite saumonée salmon trout

Viandes et Volailles (Meat and Poultry)
agneau (de pré-salé) lamb (grazed in fields by the sea)
ailerons chicken wings
aloyau sirloin
andouillette chitterling (tripe) sausage
autruche ostrich
biftek beefsteak
blanc breast or white meat
blanquette stew of white meat, thickened with egg yolk
bœuf beef
boudin blanc sausage of white meat
boudin noir black pudding
brochette meat (or fish) on a skewer
caille quail
canard, caneton duck, duckling
carré the best end of a cutlet or chop
cassoulet haricot bean stew with sausage, duck, goose, etc.
cervelle brains

chair flesh, meat
chapon capon
châteaubriand porterhouse steak
cheval horsemeat
chevreau kid
chorizo spicy Spanish sausage
civet meat (usually game) stew, in wine and blood sauce
cœur heart
confit meat cooked and preserved in its own fat
côte, côtelette chop, cutlet
cou d'oie farci goose neck stuffed with pork, foie gras and truffles
cuisse thigh or leg
dinde, dindon turkey
entrecôte ribsteak
épaule shoulder
estouffade a meat stew marinated, fried and then braised
faisan pheasant
faux-filet sirloin
foie liver
frais de veau veal testicles
fricadelle meatball
gésier gizzard
gibier game
gigot leg of lamb
graisse or gras fat
grillade grilled meat, often a mixed grill
grive thrush
jambon ham
jarret knuckle
langue tongue
lapereau young rabbit
lapin rabbit
lard (lardons) bacon (diced bacon)
lièvre hare
magret/maigret (de canard) breast (of duck)

If you're buying direct from the producer (or a wine co-operative, or *syndicat*, a group of producers), you'll be offered glasses to taste, each wine older than the previous one until you are feeling quite jolly and ready to buy the oldest (and most expensive) vintage. On the other hand, some sell loose wine à la petrol pump, *en vrac*; many *caves* even sell the little plastic barrels to put it in.

Restaurant Basics

Restaurants generally serve between 12 and 2pm and in the evening from 7 to 10pm, with later summer hours; brasseries in the cities don't generally close in the afternoon. Most post menus outside the door so you know what to expect and offer a

manchons duck or goose wings
marcassin young wild boar
merguez spicy red sausage
moelle bone marrow
mouton mutton
museau muzzle
navarin lamb stew with root vegetables
noix de veau (agneau) topside of veal
   (lamb)
oie goose
os bone
perdreau (or perdrix) partridge
petit salé salt pork
pieds trotters
pintade guinea fowl
plat-de-côtes short ribs or rib chops
porc pork
pot au feu meat and vegetables cooked in
   stock
poulet chicken
poussin baby chicken
quenelle poached dumplings made of fish,
   fowl or meat
queue de bœuf oxtail
ris (de veau) sweetbreads (veal)
rognons kidneys
rosbif roast beef
rôti roast
sanglier wild boar
saucisses sausages
saucisson dry sausage, like salami
selle (d'agneau) saddle (of lamb)
steak tartare raw minced beef, often topped
   with a raw egg yolk
suprême de volaille fillet of chicken breast
   and wing
taureau bull's meat
tête (de veau) head (calf's), fatty and usually
   served with a mustardy vinaigrette

tournedos thick round slices of beef fillet
travers de porc spare ribs
tripes tripe
veau veal
venaison venison

Légumes, Herbes, etc.
(Vegetables, herbs, etc.)
ail garlic
aïoli garlic mayonnaise
algue seaweed
aneth dill
anis anis
artichaut artichoke
asperges asparagus
aubergine aubergine (eggplant)
avocat avocado
basilic basil
betterave beetroot
blette Swiss chard
bouquet garni mixed herbs in a little bag
cannelle cinnamon
céleri (-rave) celery (celeriac)
cèpes ceps, wild boletus mushrooms
champignons mushrooms
chanterelles wild yellow mushrooms
chicorée curly endive
chou cabbage
chou-fleur cauliflower
choucroute sauerkraut
ciboulette chives
citrouille pumpkin
clou de girofle clove
cœur de palmier heart of palm
concombre cucumber
cornichons gherkins
courgettes courgettes (zucchini)
cresson watercress
échalote shallot

choice of set-price menus; if prices aren't listed, you can bet it's not because they're a bargain. If you summon up the appetite to eat the biggest meal of the day at noon you'll spend a lot less money, as many restaurants offer special lunch menus – an economical way to experience some of the finer gourmet temples. Some of these offer a set-price gourmet *menu dégustation* – a selection of chef's specialities, which can be a great treat. At the humbler end of the scale, bars and brasseries often serve a simple *plat du jour* (daily special) and the no-choice *formule*, which is more often than not steak and *frites*. Eating *à la carte* anywhere will always be more expensive, in many cases twice as much.

Menus sometimes include the house wine (*vin compris*). If you choose a better wine anywhere, expect a scandalous mark-up; the French wouldn't dream of a

endive chicory (endive)
épinards spinach
estragon tarragon
fenouil fennel
fèves broad (fava) beans
flageolets white beans
fleurs de courgette courgette blossoms
frites chips (French fries)
genièvre juniper
haricots (rouges, blancs) beans (kidney, white)
haricot verts green (French) beans
jardinière with diced garden vegetables
laitue lettuce
laurier bay leaf
lentilles lentils
maïs (épis de) sweetcorn (on the cob)
marjolaine marjoram
menthe mint
mesclun salad of various leaves
morilles morel mushrooms
moutarde mustard
navet turnip
oignons onions
oseille sorrel
panais parsnip
persil parsley
petits pois peas
piment pimento
pissenlits dandelion greens
poireaux leeks
pois chiches chickpeas
pois mange-tout sugar peas or mangetout
poivron sweet pepper (capsicum)
pomme de terre potato
potiron pumpkin
primeurs young vegetables
radis radishes
raifort horseradish

riz rice
romarin rosemary
roquette rocket
safran saffron
salade verte green salad
salsifis salsify
sarriette savory
sarrasin buckwheat
sauge sage
serpolet wild thyme
thym thyme
truffes truffles

Fruits et Noix (Fruit and Nuts)

abricot apricot
amandes almonds
ananas pineapple
banane banana
bigarreau black cherries
brugnon nectarine
cacahouètes peanuts
cassis blackcurrant
cerise cherry
citron lemon
citron vert lime
coco (noix de) coconut
coing quince
dattes dates
figues (de Barbarie) figs (prickly pear)
fraises (des bois) strawberries (wild)
framboises raspberries
fruit de la passion passion fruit
grenade pomegranate
groseilles redcurrants
lavande lavender
mandarine tangerine
mangue mango
marrons chestnuts
mirabelles mirabelle plums

meal without wine, and the arrangement is a simple device to make prices seem lower. If service is included it will say *service compris* or s.c., if not *service non compris* or s.n.c.

French restaurants, especially the cheaper ones, presume everyone has the appetite of Gargantua. A full meal consists of: an apéritif (*pastis*, the national drink of the south, is famous for its hunger-inducing qualities), hors d'œuvre or a starter (typically, soup, pâté, or *charcuterie*), an *entrée* (usually fish, or an omelette), a main course (usually meat, poultry, game or offal, *garni* with vegetables, rice or potatoes), often followed by a green salad (to 'lighten' the stomach), then cheese, dessert, coffee, chocolates and *mignardises* (or petit-fours), and perhaps a *digestif* to round things off. Most people only devour the whole whack on Sunday afternoons, and at other times

mûre (sauvage) mulberry, blackberry
myrtilles bilberries
noisette hazelnut
noix walnuts
noix de cajou cashews
pamplemousse grapefruit
pastèque watermelon
pêche (blanche) peach (white)
pignons pinenuts
poire pear
pomme apple
prune plum
pruneau prune
raisins (secs) grapes (raisins)
reine-claude greengage plums

Desserts
Bavarois mousse or custard in a mould
biscuit biscuit, cracker, cake
bombe ice-cream dessert in a round mould
bonbons sweets, candy
brioche light sweet yeast bread
charlotte sponge fingers and custard
   cream dessert
chausson turnover
clafoutis batter fruit cake
compote stewed fruit
corbeille de fruits basket of fruit
coulis thick fruit sauce
coupe ice cream: a scoop or in cup
crème anglaise egg custard
crème caramel vanilla custard with
   caramel sauce
crème Chantilly sweet whipped cream
crème fraîche slightly sour cream
crème pâtissière thick pastry cream filling
   made with eggs
gâteau cake
gaufre waffle

génoise rich sponge cake
glace ice cream
macarons macaroons
madeleine small sponge cake
miel honey
mignardise same as *petits fours*
œufs à la neige floating island/meringue on a
   bed of custard
pain d'épice gingerbread
parfait frozen mousse
petits fours sweetmeats; tiny cakes and
   pastries
profiteroles choux pastry balls, often filled
   with chocolate or ice cream
sablé shortbread
savarin a filled cake, shaped like a ring
tarte, tartelette tart, little tart
tarte tropézienne sponge cake filled with
   custard and topped with nuts
truffes chocolate truffles
yaourt yoghurt

Fromage (Cheese)
brebis (fromage de) sheep's cheese
cabécou sharp local goat's cheese
chèvre goat's cheese
doux mild
fromage (plateau de) cheese (board)
fromage blanc yoghurty cream cheese
fromage frais a bit like sour cream
fromage sec general name for solid
   cheeses
fort strong

Cooking Terms and Sauces
à point medium steak
bien cuit well-done steak
bleu very rare steak
aigre-doux sweet and sour

condense this feast to a starter, *entrée* or main course, and cheese or dessert. Vegetarians will have a hard time in France, especially if they don't eat fish or eggs, but most establishments will try to accommodate them somehow.

When looking for a restaurant, homing in on the one place crowded with locals is as sound a policy in France as anywhere. Don't overlook hotel restaurants, some of which are absolutely top notch. To avoid disappointment, call ahead in the morning to reserve a table, especially at the smarter restaurants, and especially in the summer. One thing you'll soon notice is that there's a wide choice of ethnic restaurants, mostly North African (a favourite for their economical couscous – spicy meat and vegetables served with a side dish of *harisa*, a hot red pepper sauce on a bed of steamed semolina); Asian (usually Vietnamese, sometimes Chinese, Cambodian or Thai); and

aiguillette thin slice
à l'anglaise boiled
à la bordelaise cooked in wine and diced vegetables (usually)
à la châtelaine with chestnut purée and artichoke hearts
à la grecque cooked in olive oil and lemon
à la jardinière with garden vegetables
à la périgourdine in a truffle and foie gras sauce
à la provençale cooked with tomatoes, garlic and olive oil
allumettes strips of puff pastry
au feu de bois cooked over a wood fire
au four baked
auvergnat with sausage, bacon and cabbage
barquette pastry boat
beignets fritters
béarnaise sauce of egg yolks, shallots and white wine
bordelaise red wine, bone marrow and shallot sauce
broche roasted on a spit
chasseur mushrooms and shallots in white wine
chaud hot
cru raw
diable spicy mustard or green pepper sauce
émincé thinly sliced
en croûte cooked in a pastry crust
en papillote baked in buttered paper
epices spices
farci stuffed
feuilleté flaky pastry
flambé set aflame with alcohol
forestière with bacon and mushrooms
fourré stuffed
frais, fraîche fresh

frappé with crushed ice
frit fried
froid cold
fumé smoked
galantine cooked food served in cold jelly
galette flaky pastry case or pancake
garni with vegetables
(au) gratin topped with browned cheese and breadcrumbs
haché minced
hollandaise a sauce of egg yolks, butter and vinegar
marmite casserole
médaillon round piece
mijoté simmered
mornay cheese sauce
pané breaded
pâte pastry, pasta
pâte brisée shortcrust pastry
pâte à chou choux pastry
pâte feuilletée flaky or puff pastry
paupiette rolled and filled thin slices of fish or meat
parmentier with potatoes
pavé slab
piquant spicy hot
poché poached
pommes allumettes thin chips (fries)
raclette melted cheese with potatoes, onions and pickles
sanglant rare steak
salé salted, spicy
sucré sweet
timbale pie cooked in a dome-shaped mould
tranche slice
vapeur steamed
véronique grape, wine and cream sauce
vinaigrette oil and vinegar dressing

Italian, the latter sometimes combined with a pizzeria, although quality very much depends on geographical proximity to Italy.

Don't expect to find too many of these outside the big cities; country cooking is French only (though often very inventive). But in the cosmopolitan centres, you'll find not only foreign cuisine, but specialities from all over France. There are Breton *crêperies* or *galetteries* (with whole-wheat pancakes), restaurants from Alsace serving *choucroute* (sauerkraut and sausage), Périgord restaurants featuring *foie gras* and truffles, Lyonnaise *haute cuisine* and *les fast foods* offering *basse cuisine* of chips, hot dogs and *croque-monsieurs* and *-mesdames* (toasted cheese sandwiches).

There are still a few traditional French restaurants that would meet the approval of Auguste Escoffier, the legendary chef (and a native of Provence); quite a few serve

Miscellaneous

addition bill (check)
baguette long loaf of bread
beurre butter
carte non-set menu
confiture jam
couteau knife
crème cream
cuillère spoon
formule à €12 €12 set menu
fourchette fork
fromage cheese
huile (d'olive) oil (olive)
lait milk
menu set menu
nouilles noodles
pain bread
œufs eggs
poivre pepper
sel salt
service compris/non compris service
   included/not included
sucre sugar
vinaigre vinegar

Snacks

chips crisps
crêpe thin pancake
croque-madame toasted ham and cheese
   sandwich with fried egg
croque-monsieur toasted ham and cheese
   sandwich
croustade small savoury pastry
frites chips (French fries)
gaufre waffle
jambon ham
pissaladière a kind of pizza with onions,
   anchovies, etc.
sandwich canapé open sandwich

Boissons (Drinks)

bière (pression) beer (draught)
bouteille (demi) bottle (half)
brut very dry
chocolat chaud hot chocolate
café coffee
café au lait white coffee
café express espresso coffee
café filtre filter coffee
café turc Turkish coffee
demi a third of a litre
doux sweet (wine)
eau (minérale, plate ou gazeuse) water
   (mineral, still or sparkling)
eau-de-vie brandy
eau potable drinking water
gazeuse sparkling
glaçons ice cubes
infusion, tisane (verveine, tilleul, menthe)
   herbal tea, (usually either verbena, lime
   flower or mint)
jus juice
lait milk
menthe à l'eau peppermint cordial
moelleux semi-dry
mousseux sparkling (wine)
pastis anis liqueur
pichet pitcher
citron pressé/orange pressée fresh
   lemon/orange juice
pression draught
ratafia home-made liqueur made by
   steeping fruit or green walnuts in alcohol or
   wine
sec dry
sirop d'orange/de citron orange/lemon squash
thé tea
verre glass
vin blanc/rosé/rouge white/rosé/red wine

regional specialities (*see* above, pp.66–8) and many feature *nouvelle cuisine*, which isn't so *nouvelle* any more, and has come under attack by devoted foodies for its expense (only the finest, freshest and rarest ingredients are used), portions (minute compared to usual restaurant helpings, because the object is to feel good, not full), and sheer quackery. For *nouvelle cuisine* is a subtle art, emphasizing the natural flavour and goodness of a carrot by contrasting or complementing it with other flavours and scents; disappointments are inevitable when a chef is more concerned with appearance than taste, or takes a walk on the wild side, combining oysters, kiwis and cashews or some other abomination. But *nouvelle cuisine* has had a strong influence on attitudes towards food in France, and it's hard to imagine anyone going back to smothering everything in a *béchamel* sauce.

Travel

07

Before You Go

A little preparation will help you get much more out of your holiday. Check the Calendar of Events (*see* pp.92–4) to help you decide where you want to be and when, and book accommodation early. If you plan to base yourself in one area, write ahead to the local tourist offices listed in the text for complete lists of self-catering accommodation, hotels and campsites in their areas, or contact one of the many specialist companies in the UK or USA (*see* pp.100–101). For more general information and a complete list of tour operators, contact a French Government Tourist Office or the regional tourist office (*see* p.98).

Useful Websites

There are several excellent websites which provide good information on France and Provence:

www.franceguide.com
www.francetourism.com
www.provencetourism.com
www.provence-tourism.com
www.beyond.fr
www.avignon-et-provence.com
www.provenceweb.fr

Airline Carriers

UK

Air France, t 08450 845 111, *www.airfrance. co.uk.* Daily service to Nice in association with British Midland, and flights to Marseille via Paris.

British Airways, t 0845 7733 377, *www.british-airways.co.uk.* Four flights a day to Nice from Heathrow; three flights a day to Marseille from Gatwick.

British Midland, t 0870 607 0555, *www.flybmi. com.* Two flights a day to Nice from London Heathrow, and flights from other UK airports, including Manchester, Edinburgh, Glasgow and Belfast.

Buzz, t 0870 240 7070, *www.buzzaway.com.* London Stansted to Marseille, with single fares starting from £40.

easyJet, t 0870 600 0000, *www.easyjet.com.* Six flights daily to Nice from Luton and Liverpool airports, with fares starting as low as £39 single if you book well in advance and discounts for booking on the Internet.

Go, t 0845 605 4321, *www.go-fly.com.* Flights from Stanstead to Nice which can be as low as £17.50 single.

USA and Canada

Air Canada, t 888 247 2262, *www.aircanada.ca.* Direct flights to Paris from Montreal and Toronto.

Air France, USA t 800 237 2747, Canada **t** 800 667 2747, *www.airfrance.com.* Regular services to Paris from many cities in the USA and Canada.

American Airlines, t 800 433 7300, *www. im.aa.com.* Flights to Paris from Boston, Chicago, Dallas, JFK and Miami.

Continental, t 800 231 0856, **t** 800 343 9195 (hearing impaired), *www.continental. com.* Flights to Paris from Houston and Newark.

Delta, USA t 800 241 4141, Canada **t** 800 221 1212, *www.delta.com.* Flights to Paris from Atlanta, Boston, Chicago, Cincinnati and Los Angeles International.

Northwest Airlines, t 800 447 4747, *www.nwa. com.* Flights to Paris from Detroit.

United Airlines, t 800 241 6522, *www.ual.com.* Flights to Paris from Chicago, Los Angeles, Miami, New Orleans and Seattle.

Students, Discounts and Special Deals

UK

Besides saving 25% on regular flights, young people under 26 have the choice of flying on special discount charters. Students with the relevant ID cards are eligible for considerable reductions, not only on flights but also on trains and admission fees to museums, concerts and more.

Agencies specializing in student and youth travel can supply ISICs (International Student Identity Cards). Try:

Europe Student Travel, 6 Campden St, London W8, **t** (020) 7727 7647. Caters to non-students as well.

STA, 6 Wright's Lane, London W8 6TA, *www.statravel.com*, **t** (020) 7361 6161. Other

Getting There

By Air

The main **international airports** in the region are at Nice, Marseille and Montpellier. Thanks to the no-frills airlines such as easyJet, Buzz and Go in the UK, prices are becoming more competitive. Shop around and book ahead, especially in the summer and during the Easter holidays, to ensure a seat and save money. It's also worth checking with your travel agent or a major Sunday newspaper for bargains or packages.

There are a number of charters and cheap flights from London to Nice, but from most other points of departure – the rest of the UK, Ireland, North America, Australia, etc. – it's often cheaper to fly to Paris and from there catch a cheap flight or train to the south. There are **domestic flights** on Air France from Orly Airport in Paris to Marseille (every half-hour) and Nice (every hour); sizeable discounts exist if you fly in low 'blue' periods. All services may be less frequent in winter.

branches in the UK include: 117 Euston Rd, London NW1 2SX, Bristol, t (0117) 929 4399; Cambridge, t (01223) 366 966; Manchester, t (0161) 834 0668; Oxford, t (01865) 792 800. Telesales t 08701 600599.

Trailfinders, 194 Kensington High St, London W8 6BD, t (020) 7937 1234, *www.trailfinder.com*.

Usit Campus Travel, 52 Grosvenor Gardens, London SW1 0AG, t (020) 7730 3402, *www.usitcampus.co.uk*; branches at most UK universities, including Bristol, t (0117) 929 2494; Manchester, t (0161) 833 2046; Edinburgh, t (0131) 668 3303; Birmingham, t (0121) 414 1848; Oxford, t (01865) 242 067; Cambridge, t (01223) 324 283.

USA and Canada

If you're resilient, flexible and/or youthful and prepared to shop around for budget deals on stand-bys or even courier flights (you can usually only take hand luggage on the latter), you should be able to get yourself some rock-bottom prices. Check out Airhitch (stand-by tickets), Council Travel (student discounts) or the Yellow Pages for courier companies (Now Voyager is one of the largest in the USA).

For discounted flights, try the small ads in newspaper travel pages (for example, *New York Times*, *Chicago Tribune*, and *Toronto Globe and Mail*). Numerous travel clubs and agencies also specialize in discount fares, but may require you to pay an annual membership fee.

Also *see* the websites at *www.xfares.com* (carry-on luggage only) and *www.smarter living.com*.

Airhitch, 2472 Broadway, Suite 200, New York, NY 10025, t (212) 864 2000, *www.airhitch.org*. Last-minute tickets to Europe from around $170.

Council Travel, 205 East 42nd St, New York, NY 10017, t 800 743 1823, t (212) 822 2700, *www.counciltravel.com*. Major specialists in student and charter flights; branches all over the USA. Can also provide Eurail and Britrail passes.

Last Minute Travel, t 800 527 8646, *www.lastminutetravel.com*.

Nouvelles Frontières, 6 East 46th St, New York, NY 10017, with branches on the West Coast and Canada, t 800 677 0720, t (212) 986 3343, *www.newfrontiers.com*. Discounted scheduled and charter flights on Corsair from LA, Oakland and New York to Paris (from around $400), and non-stop to some French provincial cities. Also offers hotel bookings and packages.

Now Voyager, 74 Varick St, Suite 307, New York, NY 10013, t (212) 431 1616, *www.nowvoyagertravel.com*.

STA, t 800 781 4040, *www.statravel.com*, with branches at most universities and also at 10 Downing St, New York, NY 10014, t (212) 627 3111, and ASUC Building, 2nd Floor, University of California, Berkeley, CA 94720, t (510) 642 3000.

TFI Tours International, 34 West 32nd St, New York, NY 10001, t 800 745 8000, t (212) 736 1140, *www.tfitours.com*.

Travel Cuts, 187 College St, Toronto, Ontario M5T 1P7, t (416) 979 2406. Canada's largest student travel specialists; branches in most provinces.

By Train

Air prices and airport hassles make France's high-speed TGVs (*trains à grande vitesse*) a very attractive alternative. Eurostar trains (t 0990 186 186, *www.eurostar.com*) leave from London Waterloo or Ashford International in Kent, and there are direct connections to Paris (Gare du Nord; 3 hours) and Lille (2 hours). Fares are cheaper if booked at least 7 days in advance and you include a Saturday night away. Check in 20 minutes before departure, or you will not be allowed on to the train.

At Paris, change to Gare de Lyon for a TGV to the south. TGVs shoot along at the average of 170mph when they're not breaking world records, and the journey from Paris Gare de Lyon to Marseille or Montpellier takes only 4½hrs; to Avignon 3½hrs. Some weekday departures require a supplement; all require a seat reservation, which you can make when you buy your ticket or at the station before departure. People under 26 are eligible for a 30% discount on fares if they have an ISIC or other student ID card, and there are also discounts if you're 60 or over, available from major travel agents.

If you plan to take some long train journeys, it may be worth investing in a rail pass. The excellent-value Euro Domino pass entitles EU citizens to unlimited rail travel through France for three–eight days in a month for £99–£198, or £79–£159 for 12–25-year-olds.

There's also the Inter-Rail pass (for European residents of at least six months), which offers 22 days' unlimited travel in Europe (countries are grouped into zones; you pay £129/185 for one zone for under/over the age of 26), plus discounts on trains to cross-Channel ferry terminals and returns on Eurostar from £60. Inter-Rail cards are not valid on trains in the UK.

Passes for North Americans include the France Railpass, which gives three days of unlimited travel throughout the country in a one-month period for $180 (reducing to $146 per person for two people travelling together). The equivalent France Youthpass gives under-26s four days' unlimited travel through France over a two-month period, including reduced rates on Eurostar, for $164. There's also the five-day Rail 'n' Drive pass, giving three days' unlimited rail travel through France and two days' car rental for $175. There are also various Eurail passes valid for 15 days to three months.

Rail Europe, handles bookings for all services, including Eurostar and Motorail, sells rail passes and acts for other continental railway companies. Calls cost 50p a minute. Contact Rail Europe at:

UK: 179 Picadilly, London W1V 0BA, t 08705 848 848, *www.raileurope.co.uk*.

USA: 226 Westchester Ave, White Plains, NY 10064, t 800 438 7245, *www.raileurope.com*.

By Coach

Eurolines offers services from London to Avignon (approx. 18hrs), and Aix and Marseille (20½hrs). There are four services a week and tickets start at £102 return.

Information and bookings: t 08705 143 219, *www.eurolines.co.uk*.

By Car

Taking your car on a Eurotunnel train is the most convenient way of crossing the Channel between the UK and France. It takes only 35mins to get through the tunnel from Folkestone to Calais, and there are up to four departures an hour every day. Tickets cost around £170 for a standard return in low season, rising to around £350 at peak times in the high season, but can drop as low as £139 for a 5-day mini-break. Special-offer day returns (look for them on the website) range from £15–50. The price for all tickets is per car less than 6.5m in length, plus the driver and all passengers. Motorail is a fairly comfortable but much more costly option. There are services from Boulogne and Dieppe to Avignon. Accommodation is compulsory, in a 4-berth (1st-class) or 6-berth (2nd-class) carriage. Linen is provided, along with washing facilities. Be warned that compartments are not segregated by sex.

Eurotunnel: Information and bookings t 08705 353 535, *www.eurotunnel.com*.

Motorail: Contact Rail Europe (t 08705 848 848) or French Motorail (UK t 08702 415 415).

If you prefer the bracing sea air, you've plenty of choice, although changes and mergers may be on the horizon. The shortest ferry crossing from the UK is currently

Dover–Calais with P&O Stena, SeaFrance or Hoverspeed, which offers the fastest crossing at 35mins. P&O Stena also operates Newhaven–Dieppe, P&O Portsmouth has crossings from Portsmouth to Cherbourg and Le Havre; Hoverspeed has a Folkestone–Bologne crossing, and Brittany Ferries operates between Plymouth and Roscoff in Brittany, Portsmouth–Caen and St Malo, and Poole–Cherbourg. Prices vary considerably according to season and demand so it pays to shop around for the best deal. For information and bookings contact:

Brittany Ferries, t 08705 360 360, *www.brittany-ferries.com.*
P&O Stena: t 0870 600 600, *www.posl.com.*
SeaFrance: t 08705 711 711, *www.seafrance.com.*
Hoverspeed: t 08705 240 241, *www.hoverspeed. co.uk.*
P&O Portsmouth: t 0870 242 4999, *www.poportsmouth.com.*

For information on rules and regulations when driving in France, *see* 'Getting Around', below.

Entry Formalities

Passports and Visas

Holders of EU, US, Canadian, Australian and New Zealand passports do not need a visa to enter France for stays of up to three months; most other nationals do.

If you intend to stay longer, the law says you need a *carte de séjour*, a requirement EU citizens can easily get around as passports are rarely stamped. The creeping rise of xenophobic legislation in France as a sop to the extreme right-wing National Front – which has its power base in the south – means that non-EU citizens had best apply for an extended visa before leaving home, a complicated procedure requiring proof of income, etc. You can't get a *carte de séjour* without the visa, and obtaining it is a trial run in the *ennuis* you'll undergo in applying for a *carte de séjour* at your local *mairie*.

Customs

Duty-free allowances have been abolished within the EU. For travellers coming from outside the EU, the duty-free limits are 1 litre of spirits or 2 litres of liquors (port, sherry or champagne), plus 2 litres of wine and 200 cigarettes.

Much larger quantities – up to 10 litres of spirits, 90 litres of wine, 110 litres of beer and 800 cigarettes – bought locally and provided you are travelling between EU countries, can be taken through customs if you can prove that they are for private consumption only.

For more information, US citizens can telephone the US Customs Service, t (202) 354 1000, or see the pamphlet *Know Before You Go* available from *www.customs.gov.* You're not allowed to bring back absinthe or Cuban cigars.

Getting Around

By Train

The SNCF runs an efficient network of trains through all the major cities. Prices have recently gone up but are still reasonable. If you plan on making only a few long hauls the Euro Domino (*see* above) or France Railpass will save you money. Other possible discounts hinge on the exact time of your departure.

For ordinary trains (excluding TGVs and *couchettes*), SNCF has divided the year into *bleue* (blue, off-peak) and *blanche* (white, peak) periods, based on demand: white periods run from Friday noon to midnight, from Sunday 3pm to Monday 10am, and during holidays (all stations give out little calendars).

If you depart in a *période bleue* with a return ticket, travel over 200km and stay at least a Saturday night, you'll get a 25% discount (**Découverte Séjour**). Couples are eligible for a **Découverte à Deux** tariff, which gives a discount of 25% on all trains when travelling together in a blue period.

Anyone over 60 can purchase a **Carte Sénior** (€44), valid for a year and giving 25–50% off individual journeys according to availability, and 25% off train journeys from France to 25 countries in Europe. There is also a **12–25 Carte**, which offers 50% reductions in blue periods and a 25% reduction in white periods for that age group.

Anyone can save money by buying a second-class ticket at least a week to a month in advance (**Découverte J8** or **J30**), the only condition being that you must use it at the designated time on the designated train, with no chance for reimbursement if you miss it.

Tickets must be stamped in the little orange machines by the entrance to the platforms that say *Compostez votre billet* (this puts the date on the ticket, to keep you from using the same one over and over again). Any time you interrupt a journey until another day, you have to re-compost your ticket. Long-distance trains (Trains Corail) have snack trolleys and bar-cafeteria cars; some have play areas for small children.

Nearly every station has large computerized left-luggage lockers (*consignes automatiques*) that spit out a slip with the lock combination when you use them. They take about half-an-hour to puzzle out the first time you use them, so plan accordingly; also note that any recent terrorist activity in France tends to close them down across the board.

SNCF general information: t 08 36 35 35 35 (€0.5/min), *www.sncf.com*. You can book advance tickets from the USA or UK prior to departure on this website, and pay by credit card at an SNCF machine in France.

By Bus

The bus network and extent of services varies from *département* to *département*. The timetable options for anything but travel between the major towns will not be extensive, so check carefully on times of departure and return when heading out to smaller places. Major towns normally call their bus station the *gare routière* – they're most often, but not always, by the railway station. In smaller places, stops can be in slightly surprising spots. They may not be obvious, so ask if you're in any doubt.

The timetable schedules aren't always to be trusted; the tourist office or shopkeepers near the bus stop may have a more accurate instinct for when a bus is likely to appear.

By Car

A car entering France must have its registration and insurance papers. Drivers with a valid licence from an EU country, Canada, the USA or Australia don't need an international licence. If you're coming from the UK or Ireland, the dip of the headlights must be adjusted to the right. Carrying a warning triangle is not mandatory, but advisable and this should be placed 50m behind the car if you have a breakdown.

If you're driving down from the UK, you can either go through or around Paris, a task best tackled on either side of the rush hour, or take the A26 via Rheims and Troyes. The various *autoroutes* will get you south the fastest but be prepared to pay a lot in tolls; the N7 south of Paris takes much longer, but costs nothing and offers great scenery.

Unless you plan to stick to the major cities, a car is unfortunately the only way to see most of Provence. This has its drawbacks: high car rental rates and petrol, and an accident rate double that of the UK (and much higher than the US). Roads are generally excellently maintained, though anything of less status than a departmental route (D-road) may be uncomfortably narrow. Mountain roads are reasonable except in the vertical department of Alpes-Maritimes, where they inevitably follow old mule tracks. Shrines to St Eloi, patron of muleteers, are common here, and a quick prayer is a wise precaution. Blue 'P' signs will infallibly direct you to a village or town's already full car park. Watch out for the tiny signs that indicate which streets are meant for pedestrians only (with complicated schedules in even tinier print); and for Byzantine street parking rules (which would take pages to explain – do as the natives do, and especially be careful about village centres on market days).

Petrol (*essence*) is relatively expensive in France. The cheapest place to buy petrol is at the big supermarkets. Petrol stations keep shop hours (most close Sunday and/or Monday) and are rare in rural areas, so consider your fuel supply while planning any forays into the mountains – especially if you use unleaded (*sans plomb*; diesel is *gazole* or *gasoil*). If you come across a garage with attendants, they will expect a tip for oil, windscreen-cleaning or air.

Speed limits are 130km/80mph on the *autoroutes* (toll motorways); 110km/69mph on dual carriageways (divided highways); 90km/55mph on other roads; 50km/30mph in an 'urbanized area' – as soon as you pass a white sign with a town's name on it and until you pass another sign with the town's name barred. Fines for speeding, payable on the spot, are high, and can be astronomical if you fail a breathalyser test. If you wind up in an **accident**, the procedure is to fill out and sign a *constat amiable*. If your French isn't sufficient to deal with this, hold off until you find

someone to translate for you so you don't accidentally incriminate yourself. If you have a **breakdown** and are a member of a motoring club affiliated with the Touring Club de France, ring the latter; if not, ring the police (**t** 17).

France used to have a rule of giving priority to the right at every intersection. This has largely disappeared, although there may still be intersections, usually in towns, where it applies – these will be marked. Watch out for the *Cédez le passage* (give way) signs and be careful. Generally, as you'd expect, drive on the right, give priority to the main road, and to the left on roundabouts. When you (inevitably) get lost in a town or city, the *toutes directions* or *autres directions* signs are like Get Out of Jail Free cards.

Car Hire

Car hire in France can be an expensive proposition. To save money, look into air and holiday package deals. Prices vary widely from firm to firm: beware the small print about service charges and taxes. It's often cheaper to book through car hire companies in your own country before you go. The minimum age for hiring a car in France is around 21 to 25, and the maximum around 70. If you decide to hire a car once there, local tourist offices can provide information on car hire agencies. Car hire firms are also listed for the larger towns in this book (*see* 'Getting There and Around' sections).

UK

Auto Europe, www.autoeurope.com
Avis, **t** 08705 900 500, **f** 08705 6060 100, www.avis.co.uk
Budget, **t** 08701 565 656, **f** (01442) 280 092, www.budget-international.com/uk
Europcar, **t** 0870 607 5000, **f** (01132) 429 495, www.europcar.com
Hertz, **t** 08705 996 699, **f** (020) 8679 0181, www.hertz.co.uk
Thrifty, **t** 08705 168 238, **f** (01494) 751 601, www.thrifty.co.uk

USA and Canada

Auto Europe, **t** 800 223 5555, **t** (207) 842 2000, www.autoeurope.com
Auto France, **t** 800 572 9655, **t** (201) 934 6994, **f** (201) 934 7501, www.autofrance.com
Avis Rent a Car, **t** 800 331 1084, **t** (516) 222 3000, www.avis.com
Europe by Car, New York, **t** 800 223 1516, **t** (212) 581 3040, **f** (212) 246 1458; California **t** 800 252 9401, **t** (213) 272 0424, **f** (310) 273 9247; www.europebycar.com
Europcar, **t** 800 800 6000, **t** (918) 669 2823, **f** (918) 669 2821, www.europcar.com
Hertz, **t** 800 654 3001, www.hertz.com

By Bicycle

Getting your own bike to France is fairly easy: Air France and British Airways carry them free from Britain, for example. From the USA or Australia, most airlines will carry them as long as they're boxed and are included in your total baggage weight. In all cases, telephone ahead to the relevant airline to check on terms and conditions. On **Eurostar**, you need to pack your bag in a bicycle bag and check it in at least 24 hours before you travel, or wait 24 hours at the other end. Alternatively, Esprit Parcel Service, **t** 08705 850 850, can arrange for your bike to be transported on Eurostar.

The French are keen cyclists and if you haven't brought your own bike the main towns and holiday centres always seem to have at least one shop that hires out bikes – local tourist offices have lists. *Vélo* is the common colloquial word for a *bicyclette*. A *vélo tout terrain*, invariably abbreviated to VTT, is a mountain bike. Be prepared to pay a fairly hefty deposit on a good bike (from around €150). You may want to inquire about insurance against theft. You can also hire bikes from most train stations in major towns; they vary in quality, so check them. The advantage of hiring from a station is that you can drop the bike back off at another, as long as you specify where when you hire it. Rates should be around €8 a day, with a deposit of €45–65 and the yielding of a credit card number. Avoid the busy N roads as far as possible.

Certain French trains (with a bicycle symbol in the timetable) carry bikes for free; otherwise you have to send them as registered luggage and pay a fee of around €6, with delivery guaranteed within five days.

Maps and cycling information are available from the **Fédération Française de Cyclotourisme**, 8 Rue Jean-Marie Jégo, 75013 Paris, t 01 45 80 30 21, *www.ffct.org*, or in Britain from the **Cyclists Touring Club**, Cotterell House, 69 Meadrow, Godalming, Surrey GU7 3HS, t (01483) 417 217, *www.ctc.org.uk*. See also the list of special-interest holiday companies, below.

On Foot

A network of long-distance paths or *Grandes Randonnées*, GRs for short (marked by distinctive red and white signs), take in some of the most beautiful scenery in the south of France. Each GR is described in a *Topoguide*, with maps and details about camping sites, refuges, and so on, available in area bookshops. An English translation covering several GRs in the region, *Walks in Provence*, is available from Stanfords, Long Acre, London WC2, t (020) 7836 1321. Otherwise, the best maps for local excursions, based on ordnance surveys, are put out by the Institut Géographique National (1:50,000 or 1:100,000), available in most French bookshops.

There are 5,000km of marked paths in the Alpes Maritimes alone. Of special interest are: **GR5** from Nice to Aspremont; **GR52** from Menton up to Sospel, the Vallée des Merveilles to St-Dalmas-Valdeblore; **GR52a** and **GR5** through Mercantour National Park, both of which are open only from the end of June to the beginning of October.

In Provence, **GR9** begins in St-Tropez and crosses over the region's most famous mountains: Ste-Baume, Ste-Victoire, the Luberon and Ventoux. **GR4** crosses the Dentelles de Montmirail and Mont Ventoux en route to Grasse; **GR6** crosses from the Alps through the Vaucluse and Alpilles, to Beaucaire and the Pont du Gard before veering north up the river Gard on to its final destination by the Atlantic. **GR42** descends the west bank of the Rhône from near Bagnols-sur-Cèze to Beaucaire.

Most tourist information centres have maps and leaflets on walks in the area.

Special-interest Holidays

There are a number of ways to combine a holiday with study or a special interest. For information, contact the French Centre in London on t (020) 7960 2600; or the Cultural Services of the French Embassy, 23 Cromwell Road, London SW7 2EL, t (020) 7838 2088, or 972 Fifth Ave, New York, NY 10021, t (212) 439 1400. For language courses, also see the Worldwide Classroom site at *www. worldwide.edu*.

In France

Association Cuisine et Tradition, 30 Rue Pierre Euzeby, 13200, Arles, t/f 04 90 49 69 20, *www.cuisineprovencale.com*. Courses in Provençal cuisine, lasting from a meal to a week; includes visits to specialist cheesemakers, bakers, apiaries and vineyards. Also courses in French, English and Japanese.

Association Neige et Merveilles, Hameau de la Minière de Vallauria, 06430 St-Dalmas-de-Tende, t 04 93 04 62 40, f 04 93 04 88 58. Courses in archaeology and restoration; also pony-trekking and guided walks for school groups.

Centre d'Etudes Linguistiques d'Avignon, 16 Rue Sainte Catherine, 84000 Avignon, t 04 74 78 01 31, f 04 90 85 92 01, *www.nrcsa.com*. French courses at all levels.

The **Direction des Antiquités Préhistoriques et Historiques** of each *département* has summer openings for volunteers who are invited to assist at archaeological digs. Write to them in early spring, at 21–23 Bd du Roy René, 13617 Aix-en-Provence.

Institut de Paléontologie Humaine, 1 Rue René Panhard, 75013 Paris, t 01 43 31 62 91, f 01 43 31 22 79. Palaeontology students or fans can spend a minimum of 15 or 30 days excavating caves in southeast France. Address your letter to Professor. Henry de Lumley.

From the UK

Alistair Sawday's Tours, The Home Farm Stables, Barrow Court Lane, Barrow Gurney, Bristol, BS48 3RW, t (01275) 464891, f (01275) 464887, *www.sawdays.co.uk*. Small-group walking tours in Provence with mature, experienced guides who have an in-depth knowledge of the area.

Alternative Travel Group, 69–71 Banbury Rd, Oxford OX2 6PE, **t** (01865) 315 678, **f** (01865) 315 697, *www.atg–oxford.co.uk*. Escorted walking tours in Aix-en-Provence; tailormade cycling holidays; wine tours.

Andante, Grange Cottage, Winterbourne Dauntsey, Salisbury, Wiltshire SP4 6ER, **t** (01980) 610 555, **f** (01980) 610 002, *andante.travel@virgin.net*. Archaeological and historical study tours around Provence led by experts. They are based in Arles, and take in Entremont, Avignon and Orange.

Arblaster and Clarke Wine Tours, Clarke House, Farnham Road, West Liss, Hampshire GU33 6JQ, **t** (01730) 893 344, **f** (01730) 892 88, *www.winetours.co.uk*. Wine and gastronomy tours all over France. The tastings and tours are led by Masters of Wine or journalists.

Artscape Painting Holidays, 85 North Street, Wilton, Salisbury, SP2 0HH, **t** (01702) 743 163. Painting courses in Provence.

Belle France, 15 East St, Rye, East Sussex, TN3 5JZ, **t** (01797) 223777, **f** (01797) 223666, *www.bellefrance.co.uk*. Self-escorted walking and cycling holidays throughout Provence: two-star and up accommodation.

CEI The French Centre, Devonshire House, 164–8 Westminster Bridge Road, London SE1 7RW, **t** (020) 7960 2600, **f** (020) 7960 2601 *www.cei-frenchcentre.com*. Accomodation, jobs and language courses.

The Chain Gang, 4th Floor, 24 Foley St, London W1P 7LA, **t** (020) 7323 1730, **f** (020) 7323 1731, *www.thechaingang.co.uk*. Guided cycling tour through the Luberon and Alpilles to the Rhône Valley and Avignon.

Classic Breakaway, The Courtyard, 2 Woodland Park, Colwyn Bay LL29 7DS, **t** (01492) 532 532, **f** (01492) 535 659, *www.fr-holidaystore.co.uk*. Bespoke holidays for individuals; can also organize golfing and wine tours.

Collineige, 30–32 High Street, Frimley, Surrey **t** (01276) 24262, **f** (01276) 27282, *info@ collineige.com*, *www.collineige.com*. Skiing holidays in winter, hiking and climbing in summer.

Destination Provence, The Travel Centre, 5 Bishopthorpe Rd, York YO23 1NA, **t** (01904) 622 220, **f** (01904) 651 991, *holidays@ destinationprovence.co.uk*, *www.destination*

provence.co.uk. Charmingly run holiday company which organizes tours covering a wide range of interests from walking and cycling, to golf, cookery, painting, gardens, wine and gastronomy tours. Highly recommended.

Elegant Resorts, The Old Palace, Chester, CH1 1RB, **t** (01244) 897 777, **f** (01244) 897 021, *www.elegantresorts.co.uk*. Luxury breaks, including golfing and winter sport tours.

Equitour, **t** (01805) 511 642, **f** (01805) 512 583, *www.peregrineholidays.co.uk/equitour_ home_page.htm*. Riding holidays in the hills of Provence.

Euro Academy, 77a George St, Croydon CR0 1LD, **t** (020) 8686 2363, **f** (020) 8681 8850, *www.euroacademy.co.uk*. French language courses, including a range of activities and sports options in Aix-en-Provence.

Fleur Holidays, **t** (01253) 593 333, **f** (01253) 595 151, *www.fleur-holidays.co.uk*. Camping and walking holidays in Provence.

French Golf Holidays, The Green, Blackmore, Essex CM4 0RT, **t** (01277) 824 100, **f** (01277) 824 222, *www.golf-France.co.uk*. Golfing holidays throughout the south of France.

Headwater Holidays, 146 London Rd, Northwich CW9 5HH, **t** (01606) 813 333, **f** (01606) 813 334, *www.headwater.com*. Weekly and fortnightly cycling and walking tours in Draguignan and the Gorges du Verdon.

InnTravel, Hovingham, York YO62 4JZ, **t** (01653) 629 000, **f** (01653) 628 741, *www.inntravel. co.uk*. Independent walking and cycling holidays – walking notes, maps and luggage transportation provided; also escorted riding holidays for intermediate to experienced riders. They also suggest a range of 'discovery hotels' specially selected for high quality of food, setting and location.

J.M.B. Travel Consultants Ltd, 'Rushwick', Worcester WR2 5SN, **t** (01905) 425 628, **f** (01905) 420219, *www.jmb-travel.co.uk*. Holidays based around the famous Aix-en-Provence music festival; accommodation ranging from pensions to luxury.

LSG Theme Holidays, 201 Main Street, Thornton LE67 1AH, **t** (01509) 231 713, **f** (01509) 230 277. French company offering painting and language courses; cultural discovery; photography; cooking; horse-riding. Mostly two-star accommodation.

Martin Randall, 10 Barley Mow Passage, London W4 4PH, **t** (020) 8742 3355, **f** (020) 8742 7766, *www.martinrandall.com*. Cultural tours of Provence in April and October, all accompanied by specialist lecturers

Peter Deilmann River & Ocean Cruises, 324–5 Regent St, London W1R 5AA, **t** (020) 7436 2931, **f** (020) 7436 2607, *www.peter-deilmann-river-cruises.co.uk*. Week-long river cruises along the Rhône.

Plantagenet Tours, 85 The Grove, Moordown, Bournemouth BH9 2TY, **t/f** (01202) 521 895, *info@plantagenettours.com*, *www.plantagenettours.com*. Cultural tours in Provence in the spring, autumn and at Christmas. Specialist subjects include the Crusades, Roman remains and the troubadours.

Sherpa Expeditions, 131a Heston Rd, Hounslow, Middlesex TW5 0RD, **t** (020) 8577 2717, **f** (020) 8572 9788, *www.sherpa-walking-holidays.co.uk*. Self-guided and escorted walking treks and cycling tours throughout Provence.

Susi Madron's Cycling for Softies, 2 and 4 Birch Polygon, Rusholme, Manchester M14 5HX, **t** (0161) 248 8282, **f** (0161) 248 5140, *www.cycling-for-softies.co.uk*. Rural cycling holidays for every skill level. Based in St-Rémy; staying in comfortable hotels.

Page & Moy, 136–40 London Rd, Leicester LE2 1EN, **t** 08700 106 212, **f** 08700 106 211, *www.page-moy.com*. Eight-day fully escorted tours, also taking in the Côte d'Azur.

Winetrails, Greenways, Vann Lake, Ockley, Dorking RH5 5NT, **t** (01306) 712 111, **f** (01306) 713 504, *www.winetrails.co.uk*. Walks in southern Rhône; cycle trips in the Alpilles; tailormade tours in the vineyards of Châteauneuf-du-Pape.

From the USA

A Touch of France, 660 King George Rd, Fords, NJ 008863, **t** (732) 738 4772, **f** (732) 738 4722, *www.e-francetravel.com*. Tailor-made specialist tours focusing on all aspects of French culture.

Abercrombie & Kent, 1520 Kensington Rd, Oakbrook, IL 60523, **t** 800 323 7308, **f** (630) 954 3324, *www.abercrombiekent.com*. Quality walking, barging and river cruises along the Rhône; plus standard escorted tours throughout the region.

Adventure Center, 1311 63rd St, Suite 200, Emeryville, CA 94608, **t** 800 227 8747, **t** (510) 654 1879, **f** (510) 654 4200, *www.adventurecenter.com*, *tripinfo@adventurecenter.com*. Walking and camping for small groups.

Classic Custom Vacations, **t** 800 221 9748, *www.classiccustomvacations.com*. Customized luxury holiday itineraries.

Dailey-Thorp Travel, 330 West 58th St, Suite 610, New York, NY 10019–1817, **t** (212) 307 1555, **t** 800 998 4677, **f** (212) 974 1420. Visits to the music festival at Aix-en-Provence.

Horizons New England Crafts Programme, P.O. Box 2206, Amherst, MA 01004, **t** (413) 549 2900, **f** (413) 549 5995, *www.horizons-art.org*. Week-long crafts courses in spring and fall in Venasque: painting, fabric printing and photography.

International Curtain Call, 3313 Patricia Av, Los Angeles, CA 90064, **t** (310) 204 4934, **f** (310) 204 4935. Opera and music tours.

Practical A–Z

Climate

Provence has a basically Mediterranean climate, one wafted by winds that give it a special character. The most notorious is the **mistral** (from the Provençal *mistrau*, or master), supposedly sent by northerners jealous of the south's climate – rushing down the Rhône and gusting east as far as Toulon and west to Narbonne. On average the mistral blows 100 to 150 days a year, nearly always in multiples of three, except when it begins at night. It is responsible for the dryness in the air and soil (hence its nickname, *mangio fango*, or mud-eater). Houses in its line of fire are built *pointes en avant*, at an angle, the north side blank and in the shade, protected by cypresses, while on the south side plane trees protect the house from the strong sun. It blows so hard that it can drive people mad: an old law in Provence acquitted a murderer if it could be proved that he killed his victim while the mistral was blowing. But the mistral has its good points: it blows away harmful miasmas and pollution from the Rhône and makes the stars radiantly clear, as alive as in Van Gogh's painting *Starry Night*. Besides the Master, there are twenty-two other winds, most importantly: the **levant**, the east or southeasterly 'Greek' wind which brings much-desired rain; the **pounent**, or west wind; and the suffocatingly hot **sirocco** from Africa.

Rainfall varies widely across the south. The Camargue barely gets 50cm a year, the lowest rainfall in France. In the average year, it rains as much in Nice as Brest (though in one-off downpours, not drizzle) and more in Marseille than Paris. In central Provence it rains less – not at all in the summer, and violently in spring and autumn (up to 13.5cm in an hour), hence the *restanques* or terraces carved in the hills by the farmers to prevent erosion.

Each season has its pros and cons. In January all the tourists are in the Alps. In April and May you can sit outside at restaurants and swim, and within an hour's drive ski at Auron or Isola 2000. By June, the mistral slows down and the resorts begin to fill up; walking is safe in the highest mountains. July and August are bad months, when everything is crowded, temperatures and prices soar, and tempers flare, but it's also the season of the great festivals in Avignon and Aix. Things quieten down considerably once French school holidays end in September. In October the weather is traditionally mild on the coast, although torrential downpours and floods have been known. November is another bad month; the first snows fall in the Alps; elsewhere it rains and many museums, hotels, and restaurants close down. December brings Christmas holiday tourists and the first skiers.

Consulates

UK 24 Av du Prado, 6e, Marseille, **t** 04 91 15 72 10.
USA 12 Bd Paul Peytral, 6e, near the Préfecture, Marseille, **t** 04 91 54 92 00.
Canada 36 Av Montaigne, 75008 Paris, **t** 01 44 43 29 00.
Ireland 4 Rue Rude, 75016 Paris, **t** 01 44 17 67 00.

Crime and the Police

Everyone in Marseille seemed most dishonest. They all tried to swindle me, mostly with complete success.
　　　　Evelyn Waugh

There is a fair chance that you will be had in the south of France, though probably not in Marseille; thieves and pickpockets go for the flashier fish on the Côte d'Azur. Road pirates prey on motorists blocked in traffic, train pirates prowl the overnight compartments looking for handbags and cameras (although the SNCF is now cracking down on this), car bandits just love the ripe pickings in cars parked in isolated scenic areas or tourist car parks (they go for expensive or rental cars, the

Average Temperature Chart in °C (°F) (Avignon)

Jan	Feb	Mar	April	May	June	July	Aug	Sept	Oct	Nov	Dec
7(44)	7(44)	11(52)	15(59)	17(62)	21(70)	23(73)	25(77)	23(73)	16(61)	10(50)	8(45)

latter discernible by their number plates, as most are registered in *département* 51). In the cities, beware the bands of Gypsy children, who push sheets of cardboard in the faces of their victims to distract them as they go through their pockets. Although violence is rare, the moral of the story is to leave anything you'd really miss at home, carry traveller's cheques and insure your property, especially if you're driving. Report thefts to the nearest *gendarmerie*, not a pleasant task but the reward is the bit of paper you need for an insurance claim. If your passport is stolen, contact the police and your nearest consulate for emergency travel documents. Carry photocopies of your passport, driver's licence, etc.; it makes it easier when reporting a loss.

By law, the police in France can stop anyone anywhere and demand an ID; in practice, they only tend to do it to harass minorities, the homeless and scruffy hippy types. If they really don't like the look of you they can salt you away for a long time without any reason.

The drug situation is the same in France as most places in the West: soft and hard drugs are widely available, and the police only make an issue of victimless crime when it suits them (your being a foreigner just may rouse them to action). Smuggling any amount of marijuana into the country can mean a prison term, and there's not much your consulate can or will do about it.

Disabled Travellers

When it comes to providing access for all, France is not exactly in the vanguard of nations, but things are beginning to change. The SNCF, for instance, now publishes a pamphlet, *Guide Pratique du Voyageur à Mobilité Réduite*, covering travel by train for the disabled (all TGVs are equipped) – contact the French Railways office in your country for details. The Channel Tunnel (*see* p.80) is a good way to travel by car since disabled passengers are allowed to stay in their vehicle, and Eurostar gives wheelchair passengers first-class travel for second-class fares. Most ferry companies will offer facilities if contacted in advance.

Vehicles fitted to accommodate wheelchairs or modified for disabled drivers pay reduced tolls on *autoroutes*. An *autoroute* guide for disabled travellers (*Guides des Autoroutes à l'Usage des Personnes à Mobilité Réduite*) is available free from **Ministère des Transports**, Direction des Routes, Service du Contrôle des Autoroutes, La Défense, 92055 Cedex, Paris, **t** 01 40 81 21 22.

The *Gîtes Accessibles aux Personnes Handicapées*, published by Gîtes de France, lists self-catering possibilities (*see* pp.101–2, for their address).

The following organizations provide services for people with disabilities:

France

Association des Paralysés de France, t 01 40 78 69 00. A national organization with an office in each *département*, providing in-depth local information; headquarters are in Paris.

Comité National Français de Liaison pour la Réadaptation des Handicapés, 236b Rue Tolbiac, 75013 Paris, **t** 01 53 80 66 66. Provides information on access, and produces useful guides to various regions in France.

UK

Access Travel, 6 The Hillock, Astley, Lancashire M29 7GW, **t** (01942) 888 844, *info@access-travel.co.uk, www.access-travel. co.uk.* Travel agent for disabled people: special airfares, car hire and wheelchair-accessible *gîtes*.

Chalfont Line Holidays, t (020) 8997 3799, **f** (020) 8991 2982, *www.chalfont-line.co.uk.* Escorted or individual holidays for disabled people.

Holiday Care Service, Imperial Building, Victoria Rd, Horley, Surrey, RH6 7PZ, **t** (01293) 774 535, **f** (01293) 784 647, Minicom **t** (01293) 776 943, *holiday.care@virgin.net, www. holidaycare.org.uk.* Publishes an information sheet on holidays in France (£1).

RADAR (Royal Association for Disability and Rehabilitation), 12 City Forum, 250 City Rd, London EC1V 8AF, **t** (020) 7250 3222, Minicom **t** (020) 7250 4119, *www.radar.org.uk.* Information and books on travel.

USA

Alternative Leisure Co, 165 Middlesex Turnpike, Suite 206, Bedford, MA 01730, **t** (718) 275

0023, *www.alctrips.com*. Organizes vacations abroad for disabled people.

Mobility International USA, PO Box 10767, Eugene, OR 97440, USA, **t/TTY** (541) 343 1284, *www.miusa.org*. Information on international educational exchange programmes and volunteer service overseas for the disabled.

SATH (Society for Accessible Travel and Hospitality), 347 5th Avenue, Suite 610, New York, NY 10016, **t** (212) 557 0027, **f** (212) 725 8253, *www.tenonline.com/sath*. Travel and access information.

Other Useful Contacts

The Able Informer, *www.sasquatch.com/able-info*. International on-line magazine with tips for travelling abroad.

Access Ability, *www.access-ability.co.uk*. Information on travel agencies catering specifically to disabled people.

Access Tourism, *www.accesstourism.com*. Pan-European website with information on hotels, guesthouses, travel agencies and specialist tour operators, etc.

Australian Council for Rehabilitation of the Disabled (ACRODS), PO Box 60, Curtin, ACT 2605, Australia, **t/TTY** (02) 6682 4333, *www.acrod.org.au*. Information and contact numbers for specialist travel agencies.

Disabled Persons Assembly, PO Box 27-254, Wellington 6035, New Zealand, **t** (04) 472 2626, *www.dpa.org.nz*. All-round source for travel information.

Emerging Horizons, *www.emerginghorizons.com*. International on-line travel newsletter for people with disabilities.

Global Access, *www.geocities.com*. On-line network for disabled travellers, with links, archives and information on travel guides for the disabled, etc.

Eating Out

The French tend to eat quite early, often at 12 or 12.30 for lunch, and generally between 7 and 9pm in the evening, with slightly later summer hours for dinner. Brasseries and cafés are flexible and open long hours, but restaurants don't often like serving late. Most restaurants recommended in this book offer a choice of set-price menus; these are often posted outside the door so you know what to

> ### Restaurant Price Categories
> Restaurants have been given a price category, mostly according to the prices of their set menus, to give a rough idea of cost. A la carte will usually be more expensive.
>
> *luxury* over €60
> *expensive* €30–60
> *moderate* €15–30
> *cheap* under €15

expect. If service is included it will say *service compris* or s.c.; if not, *service non compris* (s.n.c.).

For further information about eating in Provence, including local specialities, wines and a menu decoder, *see* the **Food and Drink** chapter, pp.65–76.

Electricity

French electricity is all 220V. British and Irish appliances will need an adapter with two round prongs; North American appliances usually need a transformer as well.

Email and Internet

The old saying that it doesn't pay to be first certainly applies to France with its national computer system, Minitel, which was distributed to every phone subscriber in the 1980s. Next to the Internet it seems a Neanderthal, but its presence considerably slowed French interest in the Internet. This is changing fast: most cities and towns now have cybercafés, and some of the most remarkable websites on the information highway are French.

While most French hotels and institutions will happily give out an email address (and we have included them in the text, along with websites, where relevant), don't rely on this as your only means of communication with them – staff don't always know how to work the system and incoming email is not necessarily checked on a daily basis, although this situation is improving.

Environment

As elsewhere in the Mediterranean, a sad litany of forest fires heads the television news in summer. Especially in Provence, most of the herbs and trees are xerophytes, able to thrive in dry hot conditions on poor rocky soils. Most forests are pine – Aleppo pines in limestone, maritime pines in the Maures and Esterel. Here they often close roads in summer to decrease the chance of fires. Most are caused by twits with matches (you'll be more careful, won't you?), though many fires are deliberately instigated by speculators who burn off protected forests to build more holiday villas and suchlike. Fires often lead to erosion and flooding, though the local governments now do a good job of reforestation. The weird wasteland of Blausasc, in a valley north of Nice (caused by greedy logging in the 1800s), shows what Provence would soon look like if they didn't.

Since the war there has simply been too much money involved for governments to act responsibly when it comes to environmental matters. Paris bureaucrats are as much to blame as local politicians; in public transport, for example, they have insisted on pushing a new TGV route around the coast, bringing even more people down here instead of improving local transport that might cut down on the ferocious traffic they already have. The new route is a monster, cutting across scores of scenic areas and wine regions. Other enemies of the Midi include the army, which has commandeered enormous sections of wilderness (Grand Plan de Canjuers and parts of the Crau) and regularly blows them to smithereens in manœuvres and target practice; the nuclear industry, with France's nuclear research centre at Cadarache and most of its nuclear missiles hidden away on the Plateau de Vaucluse; the *chancre coloré*, a fungus that, like phylloxera, came from the USA (on wooden crates during the Second World War) and now threatens the lovely plane trees of Provence; and finally the truly villainous national electric company, EDF, which once tried to flood the Grand Canyon du Verdon. The one genuine contemporary ecological disaster is the Etang de Berre, now entirely surrounded by the industrial and suburban sprawl of Marseille, a ghastly horror of power pylons, pollution and speculative development. Here too the EDF is involved; heated water, pumped from their giant power plant into the lagoon, is killing off the few remaining fish. Local groups are fighting hard to make them stop.

Festivals

The south of France offers everything from the Cannes Film Festival to the village fête, with a pilgrimage or religious procession, bumper cars, a *pétanque* tournament, a feast (anything from sardines to *cassoulet* to paella) and an all-night dance, sometimes to a local band but often a travelling troupe playing 'Hot Music' or some other electrified cacophony. Bullfights (*see* pp.96–7) play a part in many *fêtes* west of the Rhône. A *bravade* entails pistol or musket-shots; a *corso* is a parade with carts or fabulously decorated floats. St John's Day (24 June) is a big favourite and often features bonfires and fireworks.

At Catalan *festas* you're bound to see the national dance, the *sardana*, a complex, circular dance that alternates 16 long steps with 8 short ones, properly accompanied by a *cobla*, a band of a dozen instruments, some unique to Catalunya. In the southern Rhône valley people still like to celebrate with a *farandole*, a dance in 6/8 time with held hands or a handkerchief, which may be as old as the ancient Greeks. One-man musical accompaniment is provided by a little three-holed flute called a *galoubet* played with left hand, and a *tambourin*, a drum played with the right. Both *farandoles* and flamenco enliven the proceedings of the 24 May pilgrimage at Saintes-Maries-de-la-Mer, by far the best attended of all popular festivities in the south.

Overleaf is a Calendar of Events covering Provence, the Côte d'Azure, and neighbouring Languedoc and Roussillon. Note that dates change every year; for complete listings and precise dates of events, pick up a copy of the annual lists, available in most tourist offices, or consult the Tourist Office website, *www.crt-riviera.fr* (go to 'What's New' and then 'Events').

Health and Emergencies

Ambulance t 15
Police t 17
Fire t 18

France has one of the best healthcare systems in the world. Local hospitals are the place to go in an emergency (*urgence*).

If it's not an emergency, pharmacists are trained to administer first aid and dispense advice for minor problems. In rural areas there is always someone on duty if you ring the bell of a pharmacy; in cities, pharmacies are open on a rota and addresses are posted in their windows and in the local newspaper. Tourist offices can supply lists of local English-speaking doctors.

In France, however you're insured, you pay up front for everything, unless it's an emergency, when you will be billed later. Doctors will give you a brown and white *feuille de soins* with your prescription; take both to the pharmacy and keep the *feuille*, the various medicine stickers (*vignettes*) and prescriptions for insurance purposes at home.

Citizens of the EU should bring an E111 form (available from post offices before you travel), entitling you to the same emergency health services and treatments as French citizens. This means paying up front for medical care and prescriptions, of which 75–80% of the costs are reimbursed a week to 10 days later. In the UK, see the Department of Health website at *www.doh.gov.uk/traveladvice*. You may also wish to take out a travel insurance policy covering medical care (*see* below).

Canadians are usually covered by their provincial health insurance; Americans should check their medical insurance policies.

Insurance

Many of the larger credit card companies will also offer free travel insurance when you use them to book a package holiday or aeroplane/train tickets. Read the small print very carefully, especially if you're travelling with

Calendar of Events

January

Sunday nearest the 17th Fête de St-Marcel, folkdancing and singing at Barjols; every four years Barjols does an ox roast as well (next in 2002)
End of month Monte Carlo rally

February

2 Fête des Chandelles, Marseille
3 Festival of olives and late golden Servan grapes, Valbonne
First week Fête des Oursins, sea-urchin festival, Carry-le-Rouet
10 days at Carnival Feria du Carnaval, Nîmes
Carnival Nice has the most famous festivities in France; there are traditional celebrations during the school break in Prats-de-Mollo
Ash Wednesday Les Paileasses at Cournonterral, a 14th-century parade of boys in straw and turkey feathers, who try to squirt wine on passers-by
End of month Fête de l'Ours, ancient bear festival in Arles-sur-Tech

March

Sunday before Palm Sunday Traditional Carnival in Limoux

April

Maundy Thursday/Good Friday Procession de La Sanch, in Perpignan, Collioure and Arles-sur-Tech
Good Friday–Easter Bullfights in Arles
Easter Flower and sweets fair, Villefranche-de-Conflent
25 Winegrowers' festival, Châteauneuf-du-Pape; Fête de St-Marc, Villeneuve lez Avignon
Last Sunday Fête des Gardians, traditional rodeo in Arles

May

Sunday after the 15th Fête de St-Gens, costumes, pistol shots, etc., at Monteaux
Third Sunday Cherry Festival, Le Luc
Ascension weekend Festival of ochre and colour, Roussillon; International Grand Prix, Monaco
24–25 Gypsy pilgrimage at Saintes-Maries-de-la-Mer
10 days at Pentecost Bullfights at Nîmes; Cavalcade, music festival at Apt

June

June–September Music events in the Arènes, Nîmes; Mirondela des Arts, with folklore, crafts, concerts, etc., Pézenas
1 Cérémonie du St-Vinage, Boulbon
Early June Printemps des Comédiens, theatre festival, Montpellier

expensive equipment (laptops, cameras, etc.). If you're not covered on your credit card, you may want to consider taking out an insurance policy covering theft and losses and offering 100% medical refund and emergency repatriation if necessary; check to see if it covers extra expenses should you get bogged down in airport or train strikes.

Beware that accidents resulting from sports are rarely covered by ordinary insurance.

Money, Banks and the Euro

1 Jan 1999 saw the start of the transition to the **euro**. It became the official currency in France (and 10 other nations of the European Union) and the official exchange rate was set at **1 euro=6.56F**. Euro notes and coins entered into circulation in January 2002, and francs were phased out completely in February 2002. Traveller's cheques are available in euros.

Euros come in denominations of €500, 200, 100, 50, 20, 10 and 5 (banknotes) and €2, €1, 50 cents, 20 cents, 10 cents, 5 cents, 2 cents and 1 cent (coins).

Traveller's cheques are the safest way of carrying money, but the wide acceptance of credit and debit cards and the presence of ATMs (*distributeurs de billets*), even in small villages, make cards a convenient alternative. Visa is the most readily accepted credit card; American Express is often not accepted, however. Smaller hotels and restaurants and bed and breakfasts may not accept cards at all. Some shops and supermarkets experience

---

Last half of June Jazz and chamber music, in Aix; Nuits Musicales, music festival in Uzès
Sunday before St John's Fête de St-Eloi, blessing of the mules at Arles-sur-Tech
23–24 Fête de St-Jean, with processions, Entrevaux; withdancing and fireworks in Perpignan, Céret and Villefranche-de-Conflent
Sunday after the 24th Fête Provençal, with blessings of animals, in Allauch
Late June–early July Festival International de Danse, in Montpellier

July
Last Saturday Folklore festival of St Jean, Les Baux; Fête de la Tradition, Arles
Last Sunday Fête de la Tarasque, Tarascon
July–August Festival of Early Music, Entrevaux; Nuits de l'Empéri, theatre festival in Salon; Festival of Dance, Music and Theatre, Vaison-la-Romaine; Nuits de la Citadelle, music and theatre at Sisteron; Côtes du Roussillon wine festival, Perpignan; Rencontres Internationales d'Eté à la Chartreuse, concerts, dance and theatre at Villeneuve lez Avignon; Joutes Nautiques, Agde
Throughout month Music festival, Carcassonne; Rencontres Internationales de la Photographie, Arles; Festival de la Côte Languedocienne, with concerts in Béziers; Festival de la Sorgue, music, theatre and dance at Fontaine-de-Vaucluse and around

First Sunday Fête de St-Eloi, bullfights and a decorated cart pulled by 40 horses in Châteaurenard
First two weeks Dance Festival, Aix; Folklore Festival, Marseille
Mid-July Jazz festivals in Nice and Toulon; Corso de nuit for Notre-Dame-de-Santé, Carpentras; Soirées Musicales, St-Maximin-la-Ste-Baume; film festival, La Ciotat
14 Fireworks in many places for Bastille Day; Avignon and Carcassonne puts on an excellent shows
Last three weeks Music Festival, Aix; Festival de Radio France, classical music and jazz in Montpellier
Mid-July–mid-Aug International Theatre Festival, Avignon; Festival Pablo Casals, Prades; Festival Passion, operettas, ballet, and music at Carpentras
21–22 Fête de Ste-Madeleine, St-Maximin-la-Ste-Baume
Last two weeks International Jazz Festival, Juan-les-Pins; music festival, Orange; fête in Martigues, with music and dancing; music festival, Béziers; Festival de la Mer, Sète; Rencontres cinématographiques, meet film directors at Prades
Last Sunday Donkey races and village fête, Lacoste
30 Festa Major, processions and distribution of Ste-Tombe's water, Arles-sur-Tech

difficulties reading UK-style magnetic strips (French credit cards now contain a chip, or *puce*, containing ID information), so arm yourself with cash just in case.

Under the Cirrus system, withdrawals in euros can be made from bank and post office ATMs, using your PIN. The specific cards accepted are marked on each machine, and most give instructions in English. Credit card companies charge a fee for cash advances, but rates are often better than those at banks.

In the event of **lost or stolen credit cards**, call the following emergency numbers:

American Express, Paris, **t** 01 47 77 72 00

Barclaycard, **t** (00 44) 1604 230 230 (UK number)

Mastercard, **t** 0800 901 387

Visa (Carte Bleue), Paris, **t** 01 42 77 11 90.

Exchange rates vary, and most banks and *bureaux de change* take a commission of varying proportions. *Bureaux de change* that do nothing but exchange money, hotels and train stations usually have the worst rates or take the heftiest commissions.

For bank opening hours, *see* below.

Opening Hours and National Holidays

Shops: While many shops and supermarkets in Marseille, Nice and other large cities are now open continuously Tues–Sat from 9 or 10am to 7 or 7.30pm, businesses in smaller towns still close down for lunch from 12 or 12.30pm to 2 or 3pm (4pm in summer). There are local exceptions, but

August

All month Music and Dance Festival, Arles; Tournois de Joutes, nautical jousts at Sète, culminating around the 25th

First two weeks Médiévales, jousts and medieval crafts and costumes, Carcassonne; Music and Theatre festival, Gordes

First Tuesday Journées du Terroir, flea markets and bullfights, Sommières

First Sunday Lavender Festival, Digne; Fête de la Madeleine, with parade of flowered carts, Châteaurenard

9 and 11 Fête de St-Laurent, with bullfights, at Eygalières

14–18 Feria at Collioure, with fireworks

15 Village fête and operettas, Le Thor; Feria in Béziers with fireworks, parades, and fountains of wine

Third week Provençal festival with processions, bravades and drama, Séguret

First Sunday after 20th Fête du Traou, dancing and polenta feasts at Tende

Second last Sunday Festival International de Sardane, Catalan dance festival, Céret

Third week Provençal wine festival, Séguret

End of August Bullfights at Béziers; Fête de St-Louis, with historical re-enactment, Aigues-Mortes

29–29 Fête de Notre-Dame-de-Grâce, Maillane

September

First week Fête de Musique in Catalogne, Elne

8 Village fête and pilgrimage to Notre-Dame-des-Fontaines, Brigue

Mid-month Festival du Cinéma Méditerranéen, Montpellier

Third week Feria des Vendanges, bullfights at Nîmes

October

Mid-October Fête-Votive, with Provençal bullfights, at Aigues-Mortes

22 Fête de Ste-Marie-Jacobé, Saintes-Maries-de-la-Mer

Third Sunday Fête du Vin Nouveau, Béziers

November

Last Friday Foire St-Siffrein, with truffle market, Carpentras

Last Sunday Foire des Santons, until Epiphany, at Marseille

December

All month Music festival, Marseille

24 Provençal midnight Mass at Ste-Baume, Séguret and Fontvieille, with shepherds at Allauch (near Marseille); midnight Mass in the Arènes at Nîmes; Fête des Bergers and midnight Mass, Les Baux; torchlight and wake, Séguret nearly everything shuts on Monday, except for grocers and *supermarchés* that open in the afternoon. In many towns, Sunday morning is a big shopping time. Markets (daily in the cities, weekly in villages) are usually open mornings only, although clothes, flea and antiques markets run into the afternoon.

Banks: Banks are generally open 8.30am–12.30pm and 1.30–4pm. They close on Sunday, and most close either on Saturday or Monday as well.

Post Offices: Post offices are open in the cities Monday–Friday 8am–7pm, and Saturdays 8am–noon. In villages, offices may not open until 9am, then break for lunch and close at 4.30 or 5pm.

Museums: Most museums close for lunch, and often all day on Mondays or Tuesdays, and sometimes for all of November or the entire winter. Hours change with the season: longer summer hours begin in May or June and last until the end of September – usually. Most museums close on national holidays. We've done our best to include opening hours in the text, but don't sue us if they're not exactly right. Most museums give discounts on admission (which ranges from €1.5–4.5) if you have a student ID card, or are an EU citizen under 18 or over 65. The third weekend of September is usually reserved for the *Journées du Patrimoine*, when state-owned museums throw open their doors to the public for free. The free (or at least reduced) entry is intended to give everyone a taste of France's national heritage and the weekend's events are very well publicized to ensure a good turn out. Even though queues can spiral around the museums and the hordes have to shuffle past the national treasures, everyone is very cheerful at the thought of a freebie, and nobody seems to mind not seeing very much.

Churches: Churches are usually open all day, or closed all day and only open for Mass. Sometimes notes on the door direct you to the *mairie* or priest's house (*presbytère*), where you can pick up the key. There are often admission fees for cloisters, crypts and special chapels.

National Holidays

On French national holidays, banks, shops, businesses and some museums close, but most restaurants stay open.

1 January New Year's Day
Easter Sunday March or April
Easter Monday March or April
1 May Fête du Travail (Labour Day)
8 May VE Day, Armistice 1945
Ascension Day usually end of May
Pentecost (Whitsun and Monday) beginning of June
14 July Bastille Day
15 August Assumption of the Virgin Mary
1 November All Saints' Day
11 November Remembrance Day (First World War Armistice)
25 December Christmas Day

Post Offices and Telephones

Known as the PTT or *bureaux de poste*, post offices are easily discernible by their sign of a blue bird on a yellow background. Larger post offices are now equipped with special machines for you to weigh and stamp your package, letter or postcard without having to even see a real person. They are surprisingly easy to use and have an English-language option. You can receive letters *poste restante* at any post office; the postal codes in this book should help your mail get there in a timely fashion. To collect it, bring some ID. You can purchase stamps in tobacconists (*tabacs*) as well as post offices.

Nearly all public telephones have switched over from coins to *télécartes*, which you can purchase at any post office or newsstand for €6 for 50 *unités* or €14.5 for 120 *unités*. The French have eliminated area codes, giving everyone a 10-digit telephone number. If **ringing France from abroad**, the international dialling code is 33, and drop the first 'o' of the number. For **international calls** from France, dial 00, wait for the change in the dial tone, then dial the country code (UK 44; US and Canada 1; Ireland 353; Australia 61; New Zealand 64), and then the local code (minus the o for UK numbers) and number. The easiest way to reverse charges is to spend a couple of euros ringing the number and giving your number in France, which is always posted by public phones; alternatively, ring your national operator (for the UK dial 00 33 44; for the USA 00 33 11). For **directory enquiries**, dial t 12, or try your luck and patience on the free, slow, inefficient Minitel electronic directory in every post office.

Racism

Unfortunately in the south of France the forces of bigotry and reaction are strong enough to make racism a serious concern. We've heard some horror stories, especially about Marseille and Nice, where campsites and restaurants suddenly have no places if the colour of your skin doesn't suit the proprietor; the bouncers at clubs will inevitably say it's really the cut of your hair or trousers they find offensive. If any place recommended in this book is guilty of such behaviour, please write and let us know; we will remove it in the next edition, and forward your letter to the regional tourist office and relevant authorities in Paris.

Shopping

Some Provençal villages have more boutiques than year-round residents but their wares are rarely compelling. Traditional handicrafts have all but died out, and attempts to revive them have resulted in little model houses and *santons*, terracotta Christmas crib figures dressed in 18th-century Provençal costumes, usually as artful as the concrete studies of the Seven Dwarfs sold at your neighbourhood garden centre. Every town east of the Rhône has at least one boutique specializing in Provençal skirts, bags, pillows and scarves, printed in intense colours (madder red, sunflower yellow, pine green) with floral, paisley or geometric designs. Block-print fabrics were first made in Provence after Louis XIV, wanting to protect the French silk industry, banned the import of popular Indian prints. Clever entrepreneurs in the papal-owned Comtat Venaissin responded by producing cheap imitations still known today as *indiennes*. The same shops usually sell the other essential bric-à-brac of the south – dried

lavender pot-pourris, sachets of *herbes de Provence* (nothing but thyme and bay leaves), perfumed soaps.

Moustiers has hand-made ceramics, and in Provence at least a million artists wait to sell you their works. Fontaine-de-Vaucluse has a traditional paper and stationery industry; Cogolin specializes in pipes and saxophone-reeds. The sweet of tooth will find western Provence heaven. Nearly every town has its own speciality: candied fruits in Apt, the chocolates and *calissons* (marzipan candies shaped like little boats) of Aix, *berlingots* (mint-flavoured caramels) in Carpentras, and orange-flavoured chocolates called *papalines* in Avignon.

Sport and Leisure Activities

Bullfights

The Roman amphitheatres at Nîmes and Arles had hardly been restored in the early 1800s when they once again became venues for *tauromachie*. Attempts to abolish the sport in the 1900s fell flat when the poet Frédéric Mistral, the self-appointed watchdog of all things Provençal, intervened; and if anything, bullfights are now more popular than ever.

Provence is so long in the tooth that not only does it put on regular bullfights with *picadors* and *matadors*, ultimately derived from the amphitheatres of ancient Rome, but also *courses provençales* (or *courses libres*), which can be traced back to the bull games described by Heliodorus in ancient Thessaly. Played by daring young men dressed in white called *razeteurs*, the sport demands grace, daring and dexterity, especially in leaping over the barriers before a charging bull. The object is to remove a round cockade from between the horns of the bull (or cow) by cutting its ribbons with a blunt razor comb – a sport far more dangerous to the human players than the animals. The animals used for the *courses provençales* are the small, lithe, high-horned breed from the Camargue; good sporty ones retire with fat pensions.

You will see three other types of bullfight advertised. The *corrida*, or traditional Spanish bullfight, is where the bull is put to death. The bullfighters are usually Spanish as well, and the major festivals, or *ferias*, bring some of the top *toreros* to France, although beware that the already expensive tickets tend to be snapped up by touts. A *novillada*, pitting younger bulls against apprentice *toreros* (*novilleros*), is less expensive, but much more likely to be a butchery void of *arte*.

In a *corrida portuguaise* the bullfighter (*rejoneador*) fights from horseback, but doesn't kill the bull.

Canoeing and Kayaking

The **Fédération Française de Canoë-Kayak**, t 01 45 11 08 50, *www.ffck.org*, is the national centre for information. Some of the most dramatic rafting and canoeing in this book is down the Grand Canyon du Verdon, but the journey requires considerable experience and considerable portage. Another disadvantage is that the electric company may be playing with the water. Contact **Verdon Plus**, 4 Allée Louis Gardiol, Riez, t 04 92 77 76 36, f 04 92 77 75 73, for group excursions.

Fishing

You can fish in the sea without a permit as long as your catch is for local consumption; along the Riviera captains offer expeditions for tuna and other denizens of the deep. Freshwater fishing requires an easily obtained permit from a local club; tourist offices can tell you where to find them.

Football

Professional football in Provence is dominated by Marseille Olympique, 1993 winners of the European Cup, who were stripped of their crown following a match-rigging scandal for which their owner, MP Bernard Tapie, was jailed. Since then their international profile has dropped; they remain one of the best teams of France but their glory days in Europe are currently but a memory. Their volatile fans have reacted to this decline by booing and in one case assaulting the players. Following his jail sentence, in 2001 Tapie returned to the club as sporting director.

Gambling

If you're over 21, every big resort along the coast comes equipped with a **casino** ready to take your hard-earned money. Or you can do as the locals do and play for a side of beef, a lamb, or a VCR in a **Loto** in a local café or municipal *salle des fêtes*. Loto is just like bingo, although some of the numbers have names: 11 is *las cambas de ma grand* (my grandmother's legs) and 75, the number of the *département* of Paris, is *los envaïsseurs* (the invaders). Everybody plays the horses, at the bar with the *PMU* (off-track betting) outlet.

Horse-riding

Every tourist office has a list of *centres hippiques* or *centres équestres* that hire out horses. Most offer group excursions, although if you prove yourself an experienced rider you can usually head down the trails on your own. The Camargue, with its many ranches, cowboy traditions and open spaces, is the most popular place to ride, and there are increasing numbers of stables in the Alps for those who want to follow lonesome mountain trails. Most of the posher country inns can also find you a horse.

Pétanque

Like *pastis* and olive oil, *pétanque* is one of the essential ingredients of the Midi, and even the smallest village has a rough, hard court under the plane trees for its practitioners – nearly all male, although women are welcome to join in. Similar to *boules*, the special rules of *pétanque* were according to tradition developed in La Ciotat (*see* p.179). The object is to get your metal ball closest to the marker (*bouchon* or *cochonnet*). Tournaments are frequent and well attended.

Sailing

Most of the resorts along the south coast have sailing schools and boats to hire. Get the complete list from the **Fédération Française de Voile**, 55 Av Kléber, 75084 Paris Cédex 16, t 01 44 05 81 00, *www.ffvoile.org*.

Skiing

If the weather ever decides to settle down to what's expected of it (in 1990–1 Nice had as much snow as some of the Alps), you can do as in California: ski in the morning and bake on the beach in the afternoon. The biggest resorts in the Alpes-Maritimes are Isola 2000, Auron and Valberg, and closest to Nice,

Gréolières-les-Neiges. For the Alpes-Maritimes, contact the **Comité Régional de Tourisme Provence Alpes Côte d'Azur**, C.M.C.I., Espace Colbert, 2 Rue Henri Barbusse, 13241 Marseille, **t** 04 91 39 38 00, **f** 04 91 56 66 61, *www.crt-paca.fr*.

Walking

See 'Getting Around', p.84.

Water Sports and Beaches

In 1763, the consumptive English writer and doctor Tobias 'Smelfungus' Smollett tried something for his health that shocked the doctors in Nice: he went bathing in the sea. Most extraordinary of all, it made him feel better, and he recommended that people follow his example, though it would be difficult for women 'unless they laid aside all regards to decorum' – as they so often do in the most fashionable resorts along the Riviera. For the best, if scarcely less indecorous, beaches, see p.304.

Time

France is 1 hour ahead of GMT, 6 hours ahead of US Eastern Standard Time, 9 ahead of Pacific Coast Time and 9 hours behind Sydney. Summer time (daylight-saving time) begins and ends on the same dates as in Britain (end of March and end of October). The question of summer time is under review in France, but in the meantime will continue unchanged at least until 2002.

Tourist Information

French Government Tourist Offices Abroad

Australia: 25 Bligh St, Level 22, NSW 2000 Sydney, **t** (02) 9231 5244, **f** (02) 9221 8682.
Canada: 1981 Av McGill College, No.490, Montreal, PQ H3A 2W9, **t** (514) 288 4264, **f** (514) 845 4868, *mfrance@attcanada.net*.
Ireland: 10 Suffolk St, Dublin 1, **t** (01) 679 0813, **f** (01) 679 0814, *frenchtouristoffice@tinet.ie*.
UK: 178 Piccadilly, London W1V OAL, **t** 0906 824 4123 (calls charged at 60p/min), *info@mdlf.co.uk*, *www.franceguide.com*.

USA: 444 Madison Av, New York, NY 10022, **t** (410) 286 8310, **f** (212) 838 7855, *info@francetourism.com*, *www.francetourism.com*.
676 N. Michigan Av, Chicago, IL 60611, **t** (312) 751 7800, **f** (312) 337 63 39, *fgto@mcs.net*.
9454 Wilshire Bd, Suite 715, Beverly Hills, CA 90212, **t** (310) 271 6665, **f** (310) 276 2835, *fgto@gte.net*
For some more useful websites to help plan your holiday, see p.78.

Regional and Local Tourist Offices

Contact the regional tourist office for Provence at:
Comité Régional de Tourisme Provence-Alpes-Côte d'Azur, Les Docks, 10 Place de la Joliette, Atrium 10.5, BP 46214, F-13567 Marseille cedex 02, **t** 04 91 56 47 00, **f** 04 91 56 47 01, *information@crt-paca.fr*, *www.crt-paca.fr*.

Every city and town, and most villages, have a tourist information office, usually called a *syndicat d'Initiative* or an *office de tourisme* or even a *maison de tourisme*. In smaller villages this service is provided by the town hall (*mairie*). They distribute free maps and town plans, hotel, camping and self-catering accommodation lists for their area, and can inform you on sporting events, leisure activities, wine estates open for visits, and festivals. Addresses and telephone numbers are listed in the text, and if you write to them they'll post you their booklets to help you plan your holiday before you leave.

Where to Stay

Hotels

In the south of France you can find some of the most splendid hotels in Europe and some genuine scruffy fleabags of dubious clientele, with the majority of establishments falling somewhere between. Like most countries in Europe, the tourist authorities grade them by their facilities (not by charm or location) with stars from four (or four with an L for luxury – a bit confusing, so in the text luxury places are given five stars) to one, and there are even some cheap but adequate places undignified by any stars at all.

We would have liked to put the exact prices in the text, but almost every establishment has a wide range of rooms and prices – a very useful and logical way of doing things, once you're used to it. In some hotels, every single room has its own personality and the difference in quality and price can be enormous; a large room with antique furniture, a television or a balcony over the sea and a complete bathroom will cost much more than a poky back room in the same hotel, with a window overlooking a car park, no antiques, and the WC down the hall. Some proprietors will drag out a sort of menu for you to choose the level of price and facilities you would like. Most two-star hotel rooms have their own showers and WCs; most one-stars offer rooms with or without. Hotels with **no stars** are not necessarily dives; their owners probably never bothered filling out a form for the tourist authorities. Prices are usually the same as one-star places.

Standards vary so widely that it's impossible to be more precise, but we can add a few more generalizations. **Single rooms** are relatively rare, and usually two-thirds the price of a double, and rarely will a hotelier give you a discount if only doubles are available (again, because each room has its own price); on the other hand, if there are three or four of you, **triples** or **quads** or adding extra beds to a double room is usually cheaper than staying in two rooms. Flowered wallpaper, usually beige, comes in all rooms with no extra charge – it's an essential part of the French experience. **Breakfast** (usually coffee, a croissant, bread and jam for €5 or €6) is nearly always optional: you'll do as well for less in a bar. As usual rates rise in the busy season (holidays and summer, and in the winter around ski resorts), when many hotels with restaurants will require that you take **half board** (*demi-pension* – breakfast and a set lunch or dinner). At worst the food will be boring, and it can be monotonous eating in the same place every night when there are

so many tempting restaurants around. In the off-season board requirements vanish into thin air. Many hotel restaurants are superb and described in the text, and non-residents are welcome.

Your holiday will be much sweeter if you **book ahead**. The few reasonably priced rooms are snapped up very early across the board. July and August are the only really impossible months; otherwise it usually isn't too difficult to find something. Phoning a day or two ahead is always a good policy, although beware that hotels will only confirm a room with the receipt of a cheque covering the first night (although many now take a credit card number). Tourist offices have complete lists of accommodation in their given areas or even *département*, which come in handy during the peak season; many will even call around and book a room for you on the spot for free or a nominal fee.

Chain hotels (Sofitel, Formula One, etc.) are in most cities, but always dreary and geared to the business traveller more than the tourist, so you won't find them in this book. Don't confuse chains with the various **umbrella organizations** like *Logis et Auberges de France*, *Relais du silence*, or the prestigious *Relais et Châteaux* which promote and guarantee the quality of independently owned hotels and their restaurants. Many are recommended in the text. Larger tourist offices usually stock their booklets, or you can pick them up before you leave from the French National Tourist Office. If you plan to do a lot of driving, you may want to pick the English translation of the French truckers' bible, *Les Routiers*, an annual guide with maps listing reasonably priced lodgings and food along the highways and byways of France (£7.99 from Routiers Ltd, 188–90 Earl's Court Rd, London SW5 9QT, **t** (020) 7370 5113).

Bed and breakfast: In rural areas, there are plenty of opportunities for a stay in a private home or farm. *Chambres d'hôtes*, in the tourist office brochures, are listed separately from hotels with the various *gîtes* (*see* below). Some are connected to restaurants, others to wine estates or a château; prices tend to be moderate to inexpensive. Also try B&B France, 95 Bell St, Henley-on-Thames, Oxon RG9 1XS, **t** (01491) 578 803, **f** (01491) 410 806, *bookings@ bedbreak.demon.co.uk, www.bedbreak.com*

Hotel Price Ranges

Note: Prices listed here and elsewhere in this book are for a double room.

luxury €230 and over
expensive €90–230
moderate €60–90
inexpensive €30–60
cheap under €30

Self-catering Holiday Operators

In the UK

Allez France, 27 West St, Storrington, West Sussex RH20 4DZ, **t** (01903) 748 100, **f** (01903) 745 044, *www.allezfrance.com*. A wide variety of accommodation, from cottages to châteaux.

Angel Travel, 34 High St, Borough Green, Sevenoaks TN15 8BJ, **t** (01732) 884 109, **f** (01732) 883 221, *www.angel-travel-uk.com*. Villas, *gîtes* and flats.

The Apartment Service, 5–6 Francis Grove, London SW19 4DT, **t** (020) 8944 1444, **f** (020) 8944 6744, *res@apartment.co.uk*, *www.apartment.co.uk*. Selected apartment accommodation in cities for long or short stays.

Bowhills, Mayhill Farm, Swanmore, Southampton SO32 2QW, **t** (01489) 877627, **f** (01489) 877 872, *www.bowhill.co.uk*. Luxury villas, farmhouses, mostly with swimming pools.

Brittany Ferries, The Brittany Centre, Wharf Rd, Portsmouth PO2 8RU, **t** 08705 360 360, **f** (01705) 873 237, *www.brittany-ferries.com*.

The official *Gîtes de France* representative in the UK.

Destination Provence, The Travel Centre, 5 Bishopthorpe Rd, York YO23 1NA, **t** (01904) 622 220, **f** (01904) 651 991, *holidays@ destinationprovence.co.uk*, *www.destination provence.co.uk*. Villas and flats in Provence. Highly recommended.

Dominique's Villas, 13 Park House, 140 Battersea Park Rd, London SW11 4NB, **t** (020) 7738 8772, **f** (020) 7498 6014, *dom.villas@ btinternet*. Large villas and châteaux with pools in Provence and the Côte; phone for brochure.

French Life Holidays, Kelly House, Kelly Street, Horsforth, Leeds LS18 4AW, **t** (0113) 239 0077, **f** (0113) 258 4211, *www.frenchlife. co.uk*. Apartments and *gîtes* throughout Provence.

French Villa Centre, 175 Selsdon Park Rd, South Croydon CR2 8JJ, **t** (020) 8651 1231, **f** (020) 8651 4920, *www.french-villa-centre.com*. *Gîtes, villages de vacances*, and coastal villas in the Var and Vaucluse.

InnTravel, Hovingham, York YO62 4JZ, **t** (01653) 628 811, **f** (01653) 628 741, *www.inntravel. co.uk*. Apartments with pools.

International Chapters, 47–51 St John's Wood High St, London NW8 7NJ, **t** (020) 7722 0722,

(catalogue £13.99); or in France, 6 Rue de l'Europe, 95470 Fosses, **t** 01 34 68 83 15 (catalogue €13.50).

Youth Hostels, *Gîtes d'étape* and *Refuges*

Most cities and resort areas have **youth hostels** (*auberges de jeunesse*) which offer simple dormitory accommodation and breakfast to people of any age for around €6–10.5 a night. Most offer kitchen facilities as well, or inexpensive meals. They are the best deal going for people travelling on their own; for people travelling together a one-star hotel can be just as cheap. Another down-side is that many are in the most ungodly locations – in the suburbs where the last bus goes by at 7pm, or miles from any transport at all in the country. In the summer the only way to be sure of a room is to arrive early in the day. Most require a Youth Hostels Association membership card, which you can usually

purchase on the spot, although regulations say you should buy them in your home country (UK: from YHA, 14 Southampton Street, London WC2, **t** 0870 870 8808; USA: from AYH, P.O. Box 37613, Washington DC 20013, **t** (202) 737 2333; Canada: from CHA, 75 Nicholas Street, Ottawa, Ont K1N79, **t** (613) 235 2595; Australia: from AYHA, 11 Rawson Place, opposite Central Station, Sydney, New South Wales 2010, **t** (02) 9281 9111).

Another option in cities is the single-sex **dormitories** for young workers (*Foyers de jeunes travailleurs et de jeunes travailleuses*) which will rent out individual rooms if any are available, for slightly more than a youth hostel.

A *gîte d'étape* is a simple shelter with bunk beds and a rudimentary kitchen set up by a village along GR walking paths or a scenic bike route. Again, lists are available for each *département*; the detailed maps listed under 'Getting Around' (*see* p.84) mark them as well.

f (020) 7722 9140, *www.villa-rentals.com*.
A wide range of farmhouses, châteaux
and villas.

LSG Theme Holidays, 201 Main St, Thornton,
Coalville LE67 1AH, t (01509) 231 713, f (01509)
230 277. Seaside *gîtes*.

Meon Villas, Meon House, College St,
Petersfield GU32 3JN, t (01730) 268 411,
f (01730) 230 399, *www.meontravel.co.uk*.
Villas with pools.

Unicorn Holidays, 2 Place Farm,
Wheathampstead AL4 8SB, t (01582) 834
400, f (01582) 831 133. Fly-drive and tailor-
made holidays to château-hotels.

Vacances en Campagne, Bignor, Pulborough,
West Sussex RH20 1QD, t (01798) 869 433,
f (01798) 869 381, *www.indiv-travellers.com*.
Farmhouses, villas and *gîtes*.

VFB Holidays, Normandy House, High St,
Cheltenham GL50 3FB, t (01242) 240 339,
f (01242) 570 340, *www.vfbhols.co.uk*. A good
range of accommodation from rustic *gîtes* to
luxurious farmhouses.

In the USA and Canada

At Home Abroad, 405 East 56th St, Apt 6H,
New York, NY 10022–2466, t (212) 421 9165,
f (212) 752 1591, *athomeabroad@aol.com*.
Châteaux and farmhouses.

Doorways Ltd., P.O. Box 151, Bryn Mawr, PA
19010 3105, t (610) 520 0806, t 800 261 4460,
f (610) 520 0807, *www.villavacations.com*.
Villas and farm apartments in Provence.

Families Abroad, 194 Riverside Drive, New York,
NY 10025, t (212) 787 2434, (718) 768 6185,
f (212) 799 8734. Sabbatical and vacation
rentals, apartments, villas and chateaux in
Provence, the Alps-Maritimes and the
French Riviera.

Hideaways International, 767 Islington St,
Portsmouth NH 03801, t (603) 430 4433,
www.hideaways.com. Farmhouses and
châteaux.

Overseas Connections, Long Wharf
Promenade, P.O. Box 2600, Sag Harbor, NY
11963, t (516) 725 9308, 725 1805, f (516) 725
5825, *www.overseasvillas.com*. Villas and
apartments.

Vacances Provençales, 1425 Bayview Ave, Suite
204, Toronto, Ontario M4G 3A9, t 800 263
7152, f (416) 322 0706. Moderate–luxury
villas, country homes, chalets and apartments in Provence.

Villas of Distinction, P.O. Box 55, Armonk, NY
10504, t (914) 273 3331, t 800 289 0900,
f (914) 273 3184, *www.villasofdistinction.com*.
Private villas, cottages and chateaux mainly
in Provence.

In the mountains similar rough shelters along
the GR paths are called *refuges*, most of them
open summer only. Both charge around €6–7.5
a night.

Camping

Camping is very popular, especially among
the French themselves, and there's at least
one campsite in every town, often an inexpensive, no-frills place run by the town itself
(*camping municipal*). Other campsites are
graded with stars like hotels from four to one:
at the top of the line you can expect lots of
trees and grass, hot showers, a pool or beach,
sports facilities, and a grocer's, bar and/or
restaurant, and on the coast, prices rather
similar to one-star hotels (although these, of
course, never have all the extras). You'll find
more living space inland. If you want to camp
outside official sites, it's imperative to ask
permission from the landowner first, or risk a
furious farmer, his dog and perhaps the police.

Tourist offices have complete lists of campsites in their regions, or if you plan to move
around a lot pick up a *Guide officiel
camping/caravaning*, available in French bookshops. A number of UK holiday firms book
camping holidays and offer discounts on
Channel ferries: Canvas Holidays, t (01383) 644
000; Eurocamp Travel, t (01606) 787 878;
Keycamp Holidays, t 0870 7000 123.

Gîtes de France and Other Self-catering Accommodation

Provence offers a vast range of self-catering:
inexpensive farm cottages, history-laden
châteaux with gourmet frills, flats in modern
beach resorts or even on board canal boats.
The **Fédération Nationale des Gîtes de France**
is a French government service offering
inexpensive accommodation by the week in
rural areas. Lists with photos arranged by
département are available from the Maison
des Gîtes de France, 35 Rue de Godot de

Mauroy, 75439 Paris Cedex 09, or in the UK from Brittany Ferries, the official **Gîtes de France** rep: Brittany Ferries, The Brittany Centre, Wharf Rd, Portsmouth PO2 8RU, t 08705 360 360.

If you want to stay in châteaux, request the *Chambres d'hôtes et Gîtes de prestige*. Prices range from €150 to €400 a week.

Other options are advertised in the Sunday papers or contact one of the firms listed above. The accommodation they offer will nearly always be more comfortable and costly than a *gîte*, but the discounts that holiday firms can offer on the ferries, plane tickets, or car rental can make up for the price difference.

Down the Rhône 1:
Orange to Beaucaire

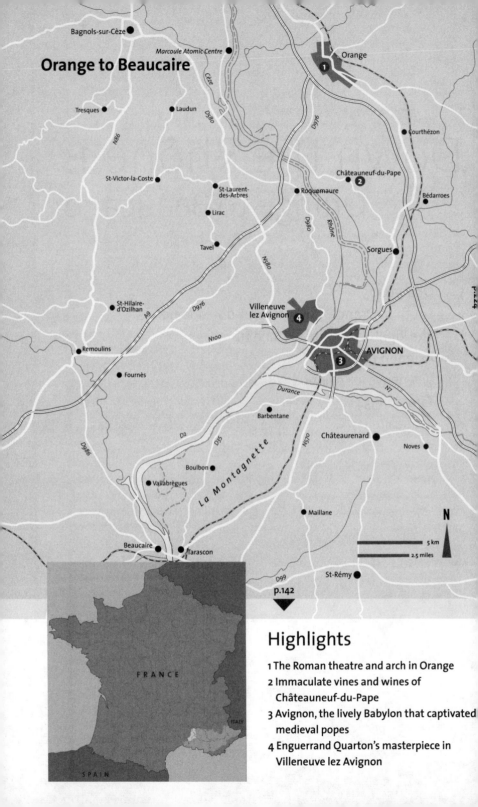

Orange to Beaucaire

Bagnols-sur-Cèze

Marcoule Atomic Centre

Orange

Cèze

Tresques

Laudun

D580

Courthézon

D976

N86

Châteauneuf-du-Pape

St-Victor-la-Coste

St-Laurent-des-Arbres

Roquemaure

Bédarroes

Lirac

D980

Rhône

Tavel

Sorgues

N580

p.124

St-Hilaire-d'Ozilhan

D976

Villeneuve lez Avignon

AVIGNON

N9

N100

Remoulins

Fournès

Durance

N7

Barbentane

D2

D35

Châteaurenard

Noves

N570

D986

Boulbon

Vallabrègues

La Montagnette

Maillane

N

Beaucaire

Tarascon

5 km

2.5 miles

D99

p.142

St-Rémy

FRANCE

ITALY

SPAIN

Highlights

1 The Roman theatre and arch in Orange
2 Immaculate vines and wines of Châteauneuf-du-Pape
3 Avignon, the lively Babylon that captivated medieval popes
4 Enguerrand Quarton's masterpiece in Villeneuve lez Avignon

Despite Frédéric Mistral's best efforts in the epic 1896 *Poème du Rhône*, this is not a lyrical river, neither fair of face nor full of grace. Its nickname *malabar*, the strongman, describes it well: deep and swift-flowing with muscular currents, its banks like bulging biceps, its secret depths hosting legendary man-eating monsters such as the Tarasque and Drac. For the Rhône is a Saturday's child and has to work for a living: after serving the industries and nuclear plants to the north, it does it all again in Provence, at France's biggest centre for the processing of nuclear waste, Marcoule, at the hydroelectric plant and Satanic mills of Avignon's industrial quarter, and at the paper mills near Tarascon.

Historically, most of the Rhône's traffic has come south with the current, ferrying the blond barbarians, the eaters of *frites* and drinkers of beer, down to the sultry Mediterranean. The river also divided the spoils: Provence, on the east bank, owed allegiance to the emperor and pope; Languedoc, on the west, belonged to the kingdom of France after the Albigensian Crusade. Rhône boatmen called the banks not port and starboard, but Empire and Kingdom. On the empire's side are Orange, with its famous Roman theatre; Châteauneuf-du-Pape and Avignon, where 14th-century popes spent what Petrarch called their 'Babylonian exile'; and Tarascon, favoured home of Provence's Good King René.

Orange

There seems to have been a settlement of some kind around the hill of St-Eutrope in prehistoric times, and the city dates its chronicles from 35 BC – enough time for all imaginable Oranges to have come and gone.

The present incarnation must be one of the sadder ones, a miasmic provincial town with a few cosy corners among the prevailing drabness. Fate, or the lack of a bypass road, has made its streets a kind of Le Mans for heavy lorries, fouling the air, menacing pedestrians and coating the old houses with a sooty film. Nevertheless, there are two ancient monuments unmatched in France, and some surprises besides. You'll probably like it best on a Sunday, when the law bans trucks from the road.

History

Rome took good care of its soldiers; keeping its word by them was one secret of the Empire's success. Nine years after Julius Caesar's death, many veterans of the Second Gallic Legion were ready for their promised retirement. The pattern was already set. Rome would establish a colony for them in the lands they had conquered, often replacing a native village they had destroyed; the veterans farmed their allocated lands, and could look forward to real wealth in their declining years as the colony grew into a town. The colony that became Orange was called Colonia Julia Secundanorum Arausio. Exceedingly prosperous throughout Roman times, Orange survived the Visigothic conquest in 412; it was the site of two Church councils in the following decades. The chronicles are largely blank from then until the mid 12th century, when the city's feudal lord was Raimbaut d'Orange, troubadour and patron of troubadours. Even then, history was on the back burner; the city and its hinterlands were often put in hock to pay Raimbaut's debts, while he presided over the most brilliant of Provençal courts. He died in 1173, at the age of only 29, and Orange passed to the Counts of Baux.

In the 14th century it was a thriving place, with a municipal charter and even a university. In 1530 the city became the property of the German House of Nassau, just in time for the Reformation and the most unusual page of the city's history, an odd chance that would let Orange lend its colour to the Dutch, the Northern Irish, the Orange Free State and Orange, New Jersey. The Nassaus declared for Protestantism, and Orange rapidly became the dissenters' chief stronghold in Provence, a home for thousands of refugees and a thorn in the side of arch-Catholic Avignon, just to the south. Soon after, William of Nassau – William of Orange – became the first *stadhouder* of the United Provinces and led the fight for Dutch independence. Orange held fast through all the troubles of the Wars of Religion, and came out of it a Dutch possession, giving its name to the Netherlands' present-day royal family.

Maurice of Nassau, in the early 17th century, did Orange a bad turn by destroying most of its ancient ruins, using their stone for the new wall he was building against the French. It didn't keep them out for long. In 1672, during one of his frequent wars against the Dutch, Louis XIV seized the city and demolished its wall and castle.

Getting There and Around

The **train** station on Av Frédéric Mistral has direct connections to Paris, Avignon, Arles, Marseille, Nice and Cannes.

Buses depart from Cours Portoules, t 04 90 34 15 59, several times a day for Carpentras, Vaison-la-Romaine and Avignon, and three times daily for Séguret.

Hire a **bike** at Picca, 544 Av de Verdun, t 04 90 51 69 53.

Tourist Information

Tourist office: 5 Cours Aristide Briand, t 04 90 34 70 88, f 04 90 34 99 62, orangetourisme@hotmail.com, www.office detourismefree.fr or www.provence-orange. com. Open April–Sept Mon–Sat 9–7 and Sun 10–6, Oct–Mar Mon–Sat 10–1 and 2–5. There's another office opposite the Théâtre Antique.

Market Day

Thursday morning on Cours Aristide Briand.

Where to Stay and Eat

Orange ⌂ **84100**

★★★**Arène**, Place de Langes, t 04 90 11 40 40, f 04 90 11 40 45, www.avignon-et-provence.com (*moderate*). Pleasant, with a good restaurant, on a quiet square where you can't hear the lorries. *Closed Nov.*

★★**St-Florent**, 4 Rue du Mazeau, t 04 90 34 18 53, f 04 90 51 17 25, stflorent@yahoo.fr (*inexpensive*). A decent budget choice, all rooms with bath and TV. *Closed Dec.*

★★**Clarine Orange-Centre**, 4 Rue Caristie, t 04 90 34 10 07, f 04 90 34 89 76, finneman@wanadoo.fr (*inexpensive*). As above; near the theatre.

For lunch, try one of the restaurants on Rue du Pont Neuf or Place Sylvian.

Le Yaka, Place Sylvian, t 04 90 34 70 03 (*moderate–cheap*). A pretty place with appetizing menus. *Closed Tues eve, Wed and Nov.*

Le Pigraillet, Colline St-Eutrope, t 04 90 34 44 25. In a wooded park overlooking the Rhône, this is an unforgettable place to spend a warm summer's night; clients may use the swimming pool before eating, for a fee. *Closed Sun eve and Mon.*

French rule, particularly after the revocation of the Edict of Nantes in 1685 (*see* p.41), was a disaster; Orange, like many other town in the south, lost many of its best citizens. The city has never really recovered, but it earns a fair living today from industry, and from the army and air force bases that make it one of the most important military centres in France. Electing a National Front mayor didn't help it either.

The Best-preserved Theatre of Antiquity

t 04 90 51 17 60; open daily 9–6.30 in summer, 9–12 and 1.30–5 in winter; guided tours t 04 90 11 02 31; adm; ticket also valid for Musée Municipal.

The architects of the **Théâtre Antique** might be distressed to hear it, but these days the most impressive part of this huge structure is its back wall. 'The best wall in my kingdom,' Louis XIV is said to have called it. If the old prints in the municipal museum are accurate, this rugged, elegant, sandstone cliff facing Place des Frères-Mounet was originally adorned with low, temple-like façades. In its present state, it resembles a typical Florentine Renaissance palace, without the windows. The classically minded architects of the 15th century all travelled in Provence, and perhaps this stately relic of Rome at its best had a hidden influence that would have made its architects proud.

Built in the early 1st century AD, the theatre is a testimony to the culture and wealth of Arausio. Like the Colosseum in Rome, it even had a massive awning (*velum*), a contraption of canvas and beams that could be raised to cover most of the 9,000 spectators. All over the Mediterranean, theatres fell into disuse in the cultural degradation of the late Empire. This one was probably already abandoned when it burned down in the 4th or 5th century. In the Middle Ages, other buildings grew up over the ruins; old prints show the semicircular tiers of seats (*cavea*) half-filled in and covered with ramshackle houses.

The site is typical for a Roman theatre, backed into the hill of St-Eutrope, where the banks of seats could be built on the slope. These have been almost completely restored. Since 1869, Orange has used the theatre for a summer festival called *Les Chorégies*. Mistral and the Félibres (*see* pp.55–6) were active in its early years, when Greek and Roman plays were often on the bill; today contemporary drama and opera are more common.

Unlike Greek theatres, which always opened to a grand view behind the stage, those of the Romans featured large stage buildings, serious architectural compositions of columns, arches and sculptured friezes. This is what the great exterior wall is supporting; Orange's stage building (115ft high) is one of two complete specimens that remain to us (the other is at Aspendos in Turkey), although the fragments of its decoration are mostly in the municipal museum across the street. A statue of Augustus remains, in the centre, over an inscription honouring the people of Arausio and welcoming them to the show. Outside the theatre, foundations of a temple have been excavated, along with a semicircular ruin that may have been a nymphaeum or a gymnasium.

Musée Municipal

*t 04 90 51 18 24; open daily 9.30–7 in summer, 9–12 and 1.30–5.30
in winter; adm; ticket also valid for the Roman Theatre.*

Save some time for this bulging curiosity shop, directly opposite the theatre on
Place des Frères-Mounet; it is one of the most fascinating town museums in
Provence. As expected, the main rooms are given over to Roman art, including an
exceptional frieze of satyrs and Amazons from the theatre. The *plan cadastral* (land
survey) is unique: a stone tablet engraved with property records for the broad Roman
grid of farmland between Orange and Montélimar. The first pieces of it were discovered in 1856, though no one guessed what they were until the rest turned up,
between 1927 and 1954; since then they have been a great aid to scholars in filling in
some of the everyday details of Roman life and law.

Climbing the stairs into the upper levels of the museum, you'll pass rooms of Dutch
portraits and relics of Nassau rule, and a collection of works by the Welsh Impression-
ist Frank Brangwyn (who was, in fact, born in Bruges): heroic compositions among
wharves and factories, along with some lovely country scenes. The most unexpected
exhibit is the **Salle des Wetter**, a remarkable relic of the Industrial Revolution in
France. The Wetters were a family of mid 18th-century industrialists who produced
indiennes, printed cotton cloth much in demand at the time. They commissioned an
artist named G. M. Rossett, to paint a record of their business; this he did (1764) in
incredible detail, on five huge, colourful, naïve canvases, showing every aspect of the
making of *indiennes*, from the stevedores unloading the cotton on the docks to the
shy, serious factory girls in the great hall – the Wetters were among the first in France
to stumble on the factory system, and employed over 500 people.

Old Orange and the Triumphal Arch

Touring old Orange does not handsomely reward the visitor. You can walk up the hill
of **St-Eutrope** for a view over the town and a look at the foundations of the castle
destroyed by the French; in the city centre, there is only an utterly pathetic cathedral,
begun in 529 over a Temple of Diana and rebuilt to death between 1561 and 1809. One
thing Orange does have is original street names – sometimes unintentionally hilar-
ious ones, like the *Impasse du Parlement*.

Rue Victor-Hugo, roughly following the route of the ancient Roman main street,
leads to Orange's other Roman attraction. The **Triumphal Arch**, built around AD 20,
celebrates the conquests of the Second Gallic Legion with outlandish, almost abstract
scenes of battling Romans and Celts. This is the epitome of the Provençal-Roman
style: excellent, careful reliefs, especially in the upper frieze, portraying a naval battle,
though with a touch of Celto-Ligurian strangeness in the details. Odd oval shields are
a prominent feature, decorated with heraldic devices and thunderbolts. Seemingly
random symbols at the upper left – a whip, a pitcher, something that looks like a
bishop's crozier, and others – are in fact symbols of animal sacrifice and marine attrib-
utes (the 'crozier' is the prow of a ship). On the sides of the arch are heaps of arms –
'triumphs' – that were to influence the militaristic art fostered by rulers such as

Emperor Charles V in the Renaissance. Little more than half a century before this arch was built, Orange was still Rome's wild frontier, and art such as this evokes it vividly. Note the standards the legionaries are carrying: not the Roman eagle, but a boar.

When frontier days returned to Orange, in the Middle Ages, the arch was expanded into a castle by Raymond of Baux – typical of that haughty family. It is said that Raymond arranged it so that the battle reliefs would be a wall of his dining hall; we have his arrogance to thank for their relatively good state of preservation.

Around Orange: Sérignan-du-Comtat and the 'Virgil of Insects'

Eight kilometres northeast of Orange on the D976, you can pay your respects to the great entomologist, botanist, scientist and poet Jean-Henri Fabre (1823–1915). Born into poverty, the largely self-taught Fabre qualified as a *lycée* teacher of sciences in Avignon, only to be fired in 1870 for explicitly describing the sex life of flowers to a night class of spinsters. Left without means, he borrowed money from his friend John Stuart Mill and settled in Orange for nine years, cranking out books on popular science on the average of one every four months – he was to produce over a hundred in total. He made enough in royalties to pay back his debts and in 1879 to buy an abandoned property in Sérignan that he called **L'Harmas**, the 'fallow land' (*t 04 90 70 00 44; generally open Mon and Wed–Sat 9–11.30 and 2–6, to 5 in winter, but ring ahead to make sure; adm*). Fabre walled in the garden and planted a thousand species of flower and herb, letting them run wild to create the perfect environment for his true passion: observing insects. Over the years he wrote 10 volumes of *Souvenirs entomologiques*, works of such beauty that he was twice nominated for the Nobel Prize for literature. The Japanese, in particular, are huge fans; recent reissues of Fabre's books in Japan (1991) have sold over a million copies.

L'Harmas was purchased by the state in 1922, and has been left as it was during Fabre's life: you can see his curious apparatus for observing insects, his collections of fossils, shells, rocks, insects, plants, eggs, coins and bones (including some human bones, chewed on by cannibals – *not* found locally, mind), letters from Darwin and his harmonium, which he would play to accompany the lullabies and songs he wrote in Provençal. Most extraordinary of all is the display of a selection of his 700 watercolours of the fungi of the Vaucluse, so real that you can hardly believe they are only two-dimensional. The village has erected a statue to Fabre, magnifying glass in hand, in front of the convex Baroque façade of the parish church, and you can visit his grave in the village cemetery with its Latin inscriptions, one from Seneca: 'Those who we believe lost have been sent in advance.'

Where to Stay and Eat

Sérignan-du-Comtat ✉ 84830

***Hostellerie du Vieux Château, Route de Ste-Cécile, t 04 90 70 05 58, f 04 90 70 05 62 (*expensive–moderate*). On the edge of the village, this grand old place has only seven rooms, but they're all you could ask for in the way of comfort and quiet; there's a pool and restaurant. *Closed Feb and 2 weeks in Nov; restaurant closed Mon lunch in season.*

Vieille Auberge La Vénus, t 04 90 70 08 48 (*moderate*). Here you will get a plate of salmon ravioli and duck marinated in Gigondas (*see* p.259) for a reasonable price. *Closed Sat lunch and Sun eve.*

South of Orange: Châteauneuf-du-Pape

Je veux vous chanter, mes amis,
Ce vieux Châteauneuf que j'ai mis
Pour vous seuls en bouteille:
Il va faire merveille!

Quand de ce vin nous serons gris,
Vénus applaudira nos ris:
Je prends à témoin Lise,
La chose est bien permise!

(My friends, I want to sing you/Of this old Châteauneuf that I've bottled just for you/
It will work miracles!/For when this wine makes us tipsy/Venus will crown our mirth/
I take Lise as my witness/No one will mind if I do!)

Pope John XXII's drinking song

Wine: Châteauneuf-du-Pape

An inspiration to both popes and lovers, Châteauneuf-du-Pape's reputation has remained strong through the ages; to safeguard it, in 1923 its growers agreed to the guarantees and controls that formed the basis for France's modern *Appellation d'Origine* laws.

Several factors combine to give the wine its unique character: the alluvial red clay and pebbly soil, brought down by a Rhône glacier in the ice age; the mistral, which chases away the clouds and haze, letting the sun hit the grapes like an X-ray gun; and the wide palette of 13 varieties of grape that each winemaker can choose from: grenache, syrah, cinsault, mourvèdre, terret noir, vaccarèse, counoise and muscardin for the reds; and clairette, bourboulenc, roussane, picpoul and picardan for the whites, 30 years ago dismissed as mere novelties and today celebrated as some of Provence's top wines – pale blond, with greenish highlights and a fresh, floral bouquet.

Because of the complex blends that give Châteauneuf its voluptuous qualities, the grapes are sorted by hand –unique among southern wines. The end result must have the highest alcoholic minimum of any great French wine (12.5%), a level achieved by spacing the vines a good 6–7ft apart to soak up the maximum amount of sun, and from the heat-absorbing pebbles underneath the vines that keep the grapes toasty after dark. Light, soft and fast to mature, Châteauneuf-du-Pape red can be enjoyed much earlier than its Rhône rivals (often in three years), and only gets better the longer you can bear to wait.

In its home town, the wine is not exactly hard to find; even in the cellars it's not cheap, though, as many of the *cuvées* of the late 1980s and early 90s are superb, if difficult to get hold of. The tourist office distributes a map of the vineyards: perhaps

You'll begin to understand why Châteauneuf's wines are so expensive when you pass through the vineyards between Orange and Avignon. Blink, and you'll miss them. This pocket-sized wine region, tucked between the outskirts of Avignon and Orange, has become one of the most prosperous corners of France; every available square inch is covered with vines of a rare beauty, so immaculately precise and luxuriant they resemble bonsai trees. Such good fortune is not without its disadvantages.

Châteauneuf-du-Pape, the very attractive village that gives the wine its name, has not resisted the temptation to become the Midi's foremost oenological tourist trap; along the main street there are few grocers or boutiques, but plenty of wine shops. In places it is hard to see the buildings for the signs, advertising other shops or the wine-makers' estates in the hinterlands.

Legend has it that one of the first things Clement V did on leaving Rome was to inspect his vineyards north of Avignon. In 1316 his successor John XXII, a celebrated imbiber, went one better by building a castle here, which the Avignon popes used as a summer residence – a 14th-century Castel Gandolfo. Sacked by the Protestants in the Wars of Religion, it was finally blown up by the retreating Germans in 1944; two

the best known of the many excellent wineries that welcome visitors are **Château La Nerthe, t** 04 90 83 70 11, with its fascinating ancient cellars, and the vaulted cellars of **Château de la Gardine, t** 04 90 83 73 20.

In Bédarrides, the vineyards of **Domaine du Vieux Télégraphe**, 3 Route de Châteauneuf, **t** 04 90 33 00 31, occupy a rugged promontory topped by a tower once used for optic telegraphic experiments; the 1993 and 95 reds and whites are excellent buys.

The three finest estates are in a class of their own and have such highly individual styles as to be unmistakable even tasted blind. **Le Clos des Papes, t** 04 90 83 70 13, is run by the highly intelligent and innovative Paul Vincent Avril. Avril is alone in employing humidifiers in his cellar to alleviate the drying effects of the mistral wind in particular and the heat in general. As a consequence, his wines have the best defined fruit of the region and are the most elegant. With age, Avril's Châteauneuf-du-Pape can taste like expensive claret.

The wines of **Château de Beaucastel**, in Courthézon, **t** 04 90 70 41 00, have been consistently among the top wines of the appellation – in particular, the superb 1994 red, and a very classy 1991 white.

The most extraordinary source of Châteauneuf-du-Pape and possibly one of the country's most interesting wines is made by Emmanuel Raynaud at **Château Rayas**. His wines are a must for all keen wine lovers: they are the product of a bygone era – wines of incredible concentration and depth with the capacity to age for 20 years or more. Wines such as these are increasingly rare in an age when technology, which has helped to ensure that most wine is well made, also means that too many are sound but mediocre.

Tourist Information

Tourist office: Place du Portail, **t** 04 90 83 71 08, **f** 04 90 83 50 34, *tourisme-chato9-pape@ wanadoo.fr, http://perso.wanadoo.fr/ot- chato9-pape. Open summer Mon–Sat 9–1 and 2–7, Sun 10–1 and 2–6; winter Mon–Sat 9–12.30 and 2–6.*

Market Day

Friday morning, Av des Bosquets.

Festivals

July, *Floraisons musicales*, music festival. August, *Fête de la Véraison*, local town festival.

Where to Stay and Eat

Châteauneuf-du-Pape ✉ **84230**
★★★★Château des Fines Roches, 2km south on the D17, **t** 04 90 83 70 23, **f** 04 90 83 78 42, *finesroches@enprovence.com, www. chateau-neuf-du-pape.enprovence.com/ finesroches (expensive)*. The château is an imposing but entirely fake crenellated castle (19th-century vintage) with gardens, set among the vineyards south of Châteauneuf. It's elegant and quite expensive; the kitchen

shines in seafood dishes and elaborate desserts. *Closed Sun eve and Mon and Tues lunch out of season.*

★★★La Sommellerie, D17 towards Roquemaure, **t** 04 90 83 50 00, **f** 04 90 83 51 85, *la-sommellerie@wanadoo.fr (moderate)*. A peaceful place to sleep, in a restored 18th-century sheepfold, with rooms overlooking the pool or vines. The restaurant (*expensive*), presided over by Pierre Paumel, *Maître cuisinier de France*, serves delicately perfumed Provençal dishes and fish trucked up daily from the coast. Don't miss his reproductions of Van Gogh's paintings – in spun suga. *Closed Sun eve, Mon and Nov–Mar.*

La Mère Germaine, Place de la Fontaine, **t** 04 90 83 54 37, **f** 04 90 83 50 27, *resa@ lamergermaine.com, www.lamergermaine. com (inexpensive)*. It's difficult to imagine how such a sweet old hotel-restaurant could survive in a tourist trap like Châteauneuf-du-Pape. There are fine rooms decorated with antiques, while the restaurant (*expensive*) serves tantalizing dishes such as *millefeuille de morue fraîche* and the succulent *galet de Châteauneuf-du-Pape*. The adjacent brasserie offers a cheap *plat du jour* and dessert. *Closed Tues eves and Wed, and Feb.*

crenellated walls still stand. Even if you don't like ruins or crowds, brave the hordes anyway to see the huge plain below you, and the Rhône muscling away on its way south to Avignon; wait till dusk if you can, for a magnificent sunset. Down on the plain, on the road to Avignon, you can taste chocolate if you're bored with wine (Castelain, **t** 04 90 83 54 71).

The Right Bank of the Rhône, through Rosé-tinted Glasses

Once you cross the Rhône into the Gard, the land takes on a more arid and austere profile, its knobby limestone hills and cliffs softened by crowns of silver olives and the green pinstripes of vines, especially in the riverbend north of Villeneuve along the D976. The landmark here is **Roquemaure**, where Pope Clement V died his peculiar death (*see* p.57) in its ruined castle, although it's not his ghost who haunts it, but that of a lovely but leprous queen who was quarantined in the tower. After she died, Rhône boatmen would see her on summer nights, flitting along the bank, dressed in white and sparkling with jewels. Roquemaure's church of St-Jean Baptiste, opened by

Wine: Tavel and Lirac

The sun-soaked, limestone pebbly hills on the right bank of the Rhône are as celebrated for their rosés as Châteauneuf-du-Pape is for its reds and whites. Tavel has the longest pedigree, a wine beloved of kings since the 13th century, when Philippe le Bel declared: 'It isn't good wine unless it's Tavel.' By the 1930s, the vine stocks – grenache, cinsault, bourboulenc, carignan and red clairette – were so old that Tavel nearly went the way of the dodo. Since revived to the tune of 825 healthy hectares, the French have once again crowned it as king of the rosés, the universal, harmonious summer wine that goes with everything from red meat to seafood. Be warned, however, that Tavel may be a little strong in alcohol to less acclimatized, non-French constitutions. Some growers add syrah and mourvèdre to give their Tavels extra body and colour, including the two best-known producers in the village, whom you can visit by ringing ahead: the de Bez family at the **Château d'Aquéria, t** 04 66 50 04 56, **f** 04 66 50 18 46, and the prize-winning **Domaine la Mordorée, t** 04 66 50 00 75, **f** 04 66 50 47 39, where the talented Christophe Delorme also bottles a potent red Côtes-du-Rhône, Lirac and Châteauneuf-du-Pape.

The Lirac district begins 3km to the north of Tavel and encompasses four *communes* – Roquemaure, Lirac, St-Laurent-des-Arbres and St-Geniès-de-Comolas. Its pebbly hills are similar to Tavel, and the appellation differs in the addition of two grape varieties – white ugni and maccabéo – and the fact that everything doesn't come up rosé: Lirac is making a name for its fruity whites, with a fragrance reminiscent of the wild flowers of the nearby garrigue, and for its well-structured reds. Both 1993 and 1994 were fine years and can be sampled weekdays by appointment at **Domaine Duseigneur**, St-Laurent-des-Arbres, **t** 04 66 50 02 57, **f** 04 66 50 43 57, and at **Château St-Roch**, Roquemaure, **t** 04 66 82 82 59, **f** 04 66 82 83 00.

Where to Stay and Eat

Roquemaure ✉ 30150

★★★Château de Cubières, Route d'Avignon, **t** 04 66 82 64 28, **f** 04 66 90 21 20 (*moderate*). Large gardens, swimming pool and old-fashioned rooms combine to make a restful stay in this 18th-century hotel; the annexe has modern, but equally stylish, rooms. The restaurant (*moderate*), independent of the hotel, **t** 04 66 82 89 33, is excellent, serving French classics, including tasty roast pigeon with figs and prunes. *Closed Sun eve, Mon, Feb and Oct.*

★★★Hostellerie de Varenne, Sauveterre, **t** 04 66 82 59 45, **f** 04 66 82 84 83, *hostellerie. varenne@wanadoo.fr, www.avignon-et-provence.com/hotels/varenne (expensive). An 18th-century building set in a beautiful park with enormous trees; dine on seasonal specialities, a good range of seafood and helpful wine suggestions. *Closed Wed out of season and two weeks in Nov and Feb.*

★★Clement V, Route de Nîmes, **t** 04 66 82 67 58, **f** 04 66 82 84 66, *hotel.clement@ wanadoo.fr (inexpensive)*. An excellent, moderately priced alternative, with a pool. *Closed Nov–mid-Mar.*

Tavel ✉ 30126

★★★Auberge du Tavel, Voie Romaine, **t** 04 66 50 03 41, **f** 04 66 50 24 44, *romaine@ net-up.com, www.auberge-de-tavel.com (moderate)*. Charming, quiet, well-equipped rooms and a good restaurant (*expensive–moderate*). *Closed Tues & Wed out of season.*

La Louisia, St-Laurent-des-Arbres, on the N580, **t** 04 66 50 20 60 (*moderate*). Try the *gâteau de rascasse à l'américaine. Closed Sun eve, Mon and the first half of Sept.*

Clement V in 1329, has sheltered since 1868 the relics of a certain St Valentine, whom it celebrates with a Festival of Lovers in 19th-century costume (Terni, in Umbria, which enshrines the relics of its third bishop Valentine in a basilica and celebrates his feast day on 14 February, would be surprised to learn this). The church also houses a superb organ of 1680, built for the Cordeliers in Avignon and transferred here in 1800, which still has all of its original pipes.

The D976 continues west to the charming little village of **Tavel**, a place just as haunted – by wine fiends slaking their thirst on the pale ruby blood of the earth. **Lirac**, 2km north, is even smaller; a pretty kilometre's walk to the west of the village leads to the **Sainte-Baume**, a cave holy since time immemorial, where a statue of the Virgin was discovered in 1647; a hermitage was built on the outside of the cave chapel.

North, little **St-Laurent-des-Arbres** was owned by the medieval bishops of Avignon, and has a fortified Romanesque church built in 1150, a tower and a castle keep.

Avignon

Avignon has known more passions and art and power than any town in Provence, a mixture of excitement whipped to a frenzy by the mistral. But even the master of winds has never caused as much trouble as the papal court, a vortex of mischief that ruled Avignon for centuries, trailing violence, corruption and debauchery in its wake. 'In Paris one quarrels, in Avignon one kills,' wrote Hugo. In Avignon, Petrarch's platonic, courtly love for Laura was an aberration. 'Blood is hot there,' wrote an anonymous writer in the 17th century, 'and the most serious occupation in the land is the search for pleasure...even most of the husbands are accommodating in love, and allow their wives the same freedoms they enjoy themselves.'

Avignon still has a twinkle in its eye; it is alive and ebullient, and has been one of France's most innovative cities ever since the Italian Renaissance filtered through here to the rest of Europe. As the cultural and publishing centre of the south, it rocked the cradle of the Félibrige, the Provençal literary movement (*see* pp.55–6), and since the war it has been the stage for Europe's most exciting theatre festival. Charming it is not but, as an old Provençal proverb puts it: *Quau se lèvo d'Avignoun, se lèvo de la resoun* – 'He who takes leave of Avignon takes leave of his senses.'

History

Rome, anno Domini 1303. Anarchy reigns: popular riots, regular visits from foreign armies, and clans waging medieval gang war in the streets, turning the tombs of the Caesars into urban fortresses. The papacy, though in the thick of it all, usually kept the papal person himself in places like Viterbo and Anagni for safety's sake – as it had the arrogant intriguer Boniface VIII, now fresh in his grave. Boniface's arch-enemy, Philip the Fair of France, had just bribed the conclave to elect a Frenchman, Clement V. Philip also suggested that the new pope flee the inferno of Rome for the safer havens of the Comtat Venaissin in Provence – and Clement didn't have to be asked twice.

Getting There and Around

By Air
Avignon's airport is at Caumont, **t** 04 90 81 51 51.

By Train
The train station is outside the Porte de la République. Central bookings **t** 08 36 35 35 35. Avignon is on the Paris–Marseille TGV line, and has frequent links to Arles, Montpellier, Nîmes, Orange, Toulon and Carcassonne.

By Bus
The *gare routière* is also outside the Porte de la République, next to the train station (Bd St-Roch, **t** 04 90 82 07 35). There are plenty of daily buses to Carpentras, Cavaillon, St-Rémy and Orange, four to Arles, five to Nîmes, one early morning run to Nice, Aix and Cannes (along with six others to Aix), three for Marseille and Salon, six for Fontaine-de-Vaucluse, and some services to the Pont du Gard, Uzès, Châteaurenard, Châteauneuf-du-Pape and Tarascon. For Villeneuve lez Avignon, take city bus no.11 from in front of the post office (buy tickets on board).

By Boat
Travellers of yore always approached Avignon by boat, a thrill still possible on the **tourist excursion boat** *Le Cygne* from Beaucaire, **t** 04 66 59 35 62, or with a **lunch or dinner cruise** on *Le Miréio*, based at Allées de l'Oulle, **t** 04 90 85 62 25, **f** 04 90 85 61 14, *www.avignon-et-provence.com/mireio*; the food is delicious and an afternoon's exploration of Arles is included in the price. You can also spend a week on the Rhône and Saône on the *Princesse de Provence* (*April–Nov*), **t** 04 78 39 13 06. In July and August, the **Bateau-Bus** makes regular trips between Avignon and Villeneuve, starting from the Allées de l'Oulle. There are several other cruise boats; the tourist office has full information.

Car and Bike Hire
Inexpensive car hire firms are **VEO**, 51 Av Pierre Sémard, **t** 04 90 87 53 43, and **SIXT** Locagest, 3 Av Saint Ruf, **t** 04 90 86 06 61. Bike hire shops in Avignon are: **Aymard**, 80 Rue Guillaume Puy, **t** 04 90 86 32 49; **Richard Masson**, Place Pie, **t** 04 90 82 32 19; and **Transhumance** (for all-terrain and mountain bikes), located in the main tourist office (summer only), **t** 04 90 27 92 61.

Tourist Information

Tourist office: The helpful office is at 41 Cours Jean Jaurès, **t** 04 32 74 32 74, **f** 04 90 82 95 03, *information@ot-avignon.fr*, *www.ot-avignon.fr* or *www.avignon-tourisme.com*. *Open April–Sept Mon–Sat 9–6; July Mon–Sat 10–8, Sun 10–5; Oct–Mar Mon–Fri 9–6, Sat 9–1 and 2–5, Sun 10–12*. There's another office in Espace St-Bénezet (*open April–Oct daily 10–7*).

Post office: Cours Président Kennedy, just inside the Porte de la République, near the train station.

Market Days
Tuesday–Sunday, covered market at Les Halles in Place Pie; Saturday and Sunday, food in Place Crillon; flower market Saturday morning and flea market Sunday morning in Place des Carmes; Saturday and Sunday morning, travelling market at Rampart St-Michel.

Festivals
In 1947, Jean Vilar with his Théâtre National Populaire founded the **Avignon Festival**, with the aim of bringing theatre to the masses. It is now rated among the top international theatre festivals in Europe, and Avignon overflows in July and August with performances by the Théâtre National in the Palais des Papes, and by others throughout the city; the cinemas host films from all over the world, and there are concerts in churches. The **Maison Jean Vilar** (8 Rue de Mons, **t** 04 90 86 59 64) is the nerve centre and hosts exhibitions, films, and lectures the rest of the year. For festival bookings and information, contact the **Bureau du Festival d'Avignon**, 8 bis Rue de Mons, Avignon 84000, **t** 04 90 27 66 50. During the festival, Avignon's squares and streets overflow with fringe (or 'Off') performers. To receive the Off programme, write to Avignon Public Off., BP5 75521 Paris Cedex 11, or call **t** 01 48 05 01 19.

Otherwise, there seems to be some sort of festivity every month, whether it's a Passion for horses (the *Cheval Passion*, Jan), Baroque art (April), a Triathlon (May) or, of course, fireworks on 14 July. The fortnightly broadsheet *Rendez-Vous*, from the tourist office, is an exhaustive map of what exactly's going on.

Shopping

Pâtisseries, especially around Rue Joseph Vernet, sell Avignon's gourmand speciality, *papalines*, made of fine chocolate and a liqueur, *d'Origan du Comtat*, distilled from 60 herbs picked from the slopes of Mont Ventoux and said to be a sure cure for cholera. You will find all the regional specialities: *fruits confits d'Apt, berlingots de Carpentras, melon de Cavaillon, nougat de Sault, truffe de Carpentras et du Tricastin*, garlic, olives, honey, pastis, goat's cheese, *fougasse*, and the omnipresent *herbes de Provence*. If you're not going to Aix, don't fail to buy some delicious, diamond-shaped almond *calissons d'Aix* here.

There are also essential oils, *santons*, bold Provençal fabrics, local pottery and soaps. Behind the Hôtel de Ville, in Place des Puits-de-Bœufs, the **Maison des Pays de Vaucluse**, t 04 90 85 55 24, has a large display of regional products and crafts, but best of all is to browse at the markets (*see* above).

Where to Stay

Avignon ✉ 84000

Avignon gets full to the brim in July and August: it's imperative to book ahead, and many places raise their rates. Note that there are other choices just across the river in Villeneuve (*see* p.129), and a huge number of chain hotels in all price ranges spread around the suburbs and major road entrances.

The Avignon area also has a large number of *gîtes* and rooms in private homes, some on the idyllic Ile de la Barthelasse. For one of these, contact the **Service des Meublés de Tourisme en Vaucluse**, 21 Rue Collège de la Croix, t 04 90 80 47 17, f 04 90 86 86 08.

****Hôtel d'Europe**, 12 Place Crillon, t 04 90 14 76 76, f 04 90 14 76 71, *reservations@hotel-d-europe.fr* (*luxury–expensive*). Oldest, and classically formal, with Louis XV furnishings, this was built in the 16th century and converted to an inn in the late 18th century. Napoleon stayed here, as did the eloping Robert Browning and Elizabeth Barrett.

****Cloître Saint-Louis**, 20 Rue du Portail Boquier, t 04 90 27 55 55, f 04 90 82 24 01, *hotel@cloitre-saint-louis.com* (*expensive*). Built in 1589 as part of a Jesuit school of theology, the beautiful cloister is an island of tranquillity. Rooms are austerely modern; meals are served under the portico or by the rooftop swimming pool.

****La Ferme Jamet**, Chemin de Rhodes (off Pont Daladier), t 04 90 86 88 35, f 04 90 86 17 72, semja@club-internet.fr (*expensive*). A 16th-century farmhouse on the Ile de la Barthelasse, this *ferme* has rooms ranging from traditional Provençal in style to a Gypsy caravan, around a tennis court and a pool. *Closed Nov–Easter.*

***Hôtel du Palais des Papes**, 1 Rue Gérard Philippe, t 04 90 86 04 13, f 04 90 27 91 17, *www.hotel-avignon.com* (*expensive–moderate*). Has the best views of the Palace, modern soundproofed rooms and air-con.

***Hôtel d'Angleterre**, 29 Bd Raspail, t 04 90 86 34 31, f 04 90 86 86 74, *info@hoteldangleterre.fr* (*inexpensive*). A friendly simple place. *Closed Jan* .

***Saint-Roch**, 9 Rue Mérindol, t 04 90 16 50 00, f 04 90 82 78 30 (*inexpensive*). Quieter, with a delightful garden, just outside the walls of Porte St-Roch.

Mignon, 12 Rue Joseph Vernet, t 04 90 82 17 30, f 04 90 85 78 46, *hotel.mignon@wanadoo.fr* (*inexpensive*). Bright and charming, with small but modern rooms.

Splendid, 17 Rue A. Perdiguier, t 04 90 86 14 46, f 04 90 85 38 55 (*inexpensive*). It doesn't quite live up to its name, but it is cheap.

Ile de la Barthelasse has four **campsites**, one of which, **La Bagatelle**, t 04 90 86 30 39, f 04 90 27 16 23, has dormitory rooms in summer.

Eating Out

Hiely-Lucullus, 5 Rue de la République, t 04 90 86 17 07 (*expensive–moderate*). Avignon's gourmet bastion for the past 60 years is a resolutely old-fashioned place with a 1st-floor dining room. The kitchen never disappoints, with its *tourte* of quail and foie gras and a legendary *cassoulet de moules aux épinards*, accompanied by Châteauneuf-du-Pape or Tavel. *Closed Tues and Wed lunch in low season, and last 2 weeks June.*

La Fourchette, 17 Rue Racine, t 04 90 85 20 93 (*moderate*). Hiély-Lucullus' less expensive sister restaurant serves as good for less; a choice of 12 desserts and wine by the carafe. *Closed Sat, Sun and end of Aug.*

Le Bain Marie, 5 Rue Pétramale, t 04 90 85 21 37 (*moderate*). A popular place serving traditional French fare. *Closed Sat lunch and Sun.*

Entrée des Artistes, Place des Carmes, t 04 90 82 46 90 (*moderate*). Located in a quiet square. *Closed Sat and Sun.*

Rose au Petit Bedon, 70 Rue Joseph Vernet, t 04 90 82 33 98 (*moderate*). An Avignon institution for well-prepared dishes seldom found elsewhere, like *lotte au Gigondas*, angler-fish cooked in wine. *Closed Sun and Mon Nov–Mar; Sun & Mon lunch April–Oct.*

Le Tournesol, 64 Rue Bonneterie, t 04 90 14 00 31 (*cheap*). Polynesian dishes. *Closed Sun and Aug.*

Izmir, 72 Place des Corps Saints, t 04 90 82 66 90 (*moderate*). Döner kebab or full Turkish dinners.

Woolloomoolloo, 16 bis Rue des Teinturiers, t 04 90 85 28 44 (*moderate*). Go global with a feast of 'world cuisine' and live music.

Terre de Saveur, Rue St-Michel, t 04 90 86 68 72 (*cheap*). For lunch try this vegetarian-orientated place, with plenty of omelettes and pasta dishes, many with wild mushrooms. *Closed Sun, Mon and 15–31 Aug.*

Around Avignon

If your pockets are deep enough, within easy driving distance of Avignon are three exceptional hotel-restaurants.

****Le Jardin des Frênes**, 645 Av les Vertes-Rives, 84140 Montfavet (5km east on the N107), t 04 90 31 17 93, f 04 90 23 95 03, contact@hostellerie-les-frenes.com, www.lesfrenes.com (*luxury–expensive*). A Relais & Châteaux member, its buildings set around a beautiful garden and pool; antiques furnish the rooms. The food, with imaginative delights like salmon with truffles in a sweet and sour sauce, is as marvellous as the setting. *Closed Nov–Mar.*

****Hostellerie Hermitage-Meissonnier**, 30 Av de Verdun, 30133 Les Angles (4km west on D900), t 04 90 25 41 68, f 04 90 25 11 68, meissonnier.michel@wanadoo.fr, www.avignon-et-provence.com (*moderate*). Sixteen luxurious rooms and a glorious restaurant (*expensive–moderate*) specializing in Provençal cuisine of the highest order – even the tomatoes taste better here, especially in the lovely garden. *Closed first 2 weeks in Mar; restaurant closed Sun eve, Mon, and Tues lunch out of season.*

*****Auberge de Cassagne**, 450 Allée de Cassagne, 84130 Le Pontet (5km north on the N7), t 04 90 31 04 18, f 04 90 32 25 09, cassagne@wanadoo.fr, www.valrugues-cassagne.com (*expensive; restaurant luxury*). Pool, tennis courts, sauna and gym, and access to a golf course. The food and wine cellar are perfect. *Closed Jan.*

Entertainment and Nightlife

Outside the Festival

Théâtre du Chêne Noir, 8 Rue Ste-Catherine, t 04 90 82 40 57. One of Provence's most talented theatre companies; their range covers the classics to the avant-garde.

Théâtre des Carmes, 6 Place des Carmes, t 04 90 82 20 47. Avignon's oldest permanent company performs in the restored Gothic cloister of the Eglise des Carmes.

AJMI, 4 Rue Escalier Ste-Anne, t 04 90 86 08 61. A jazz club with live music every Thurs at 9pm (membership cards available at door).

Cinemas

Cinéma Utopia, 4 Rue Escalier Ste-Anne, t 04 90 82 65 36. Old and new films in v.o.

Pathé Palace, 38 Cours Jean-Jaurès, t 08 36 68 22 88.

Cinéma Vox, 22 Place de l'Horloge, t 04 80 82 03 61.

Bars and Clubs

Pub Z, 58 Rue Bonneterie, t 04 90 85 42 84. With rock music and a bar decked out in black and white stripes.

Le Yucatan, 46 Bd St-Roch, t 04 90 27 00 84. Disco near the station.

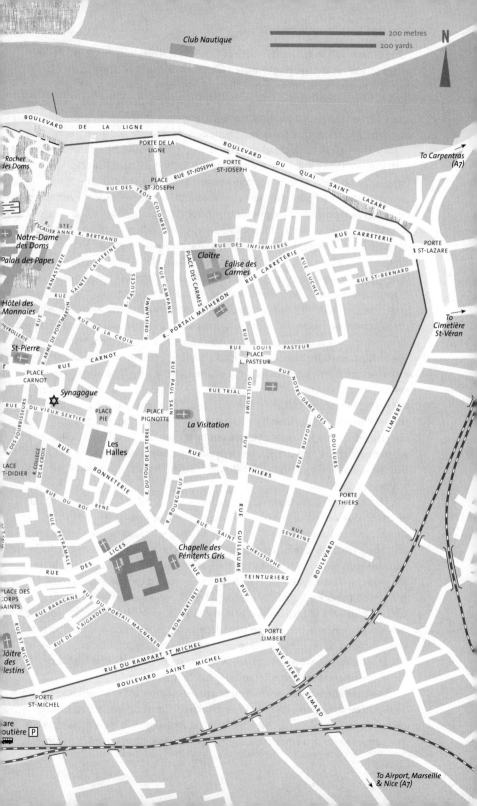

The Church had picked up this piece of Provence real estate as its spoils after the Albigensian Crusade (*see* p.39). Isolated within it was the little city-republic of Avignon, belonging to the Angevin counts of Provence – old papal allies, who welcomed their illustrious visitor. Clement V always intended to return to Rome, but when he died the French cardinals elected a former archbishop of Avignon, John XXII (1316–34), who moved the Curia into his old episcopal palace and greatly enriched the papacy (through alchemy, it was rumoured: *see* p.57). Although he enlarged the palace with the proceeds, it still wasn't roomy enough for his successor, Benedict XII (1334–42), who replaced it with another palace, or for Clement VI (1342–52), who added another. It seemed that the popes meant to stay forever, especially after 1348, when Clement purchased Avignon outright from the young Angevin Countess of Provence, Jeanne I of Naples, for the sale price of 80,000 florins and an absolution for her possible involvement in the suspicious strangulation of her husband.

Meanwhile, all the profits that the 14th-century papal machine generated – from tithes, the sale of indulgences, pardons and offices, and the visits of pilgrims – went to Avignon instead of Rome. Overcrowding, debauchery, dirt, luxury, plague, blackmail and crime came with the deal, troubles exacerbated by papal tolerance that admitted outcasts from everywhere else into Avignon, as long as they could pay. Such refugees included not only common criminals but also Jews and, during the Schism, heretics. The Italians, mortified at losing their cash cow during this 'Babylonian captivity', expressed their self-righteous indignation through the long-time Avignon resident Petrarch: 'Avignon is the hell of living people, the thoroughfare of vice, the sewers of the earth... Prostitutes swarm on the papal beds.' Yet these same popes summoned the best Trecento artists from Italy, especially from Siena, who perfected in Avignon the elegant, courtly, fairy-tale style of painting known as International Gothic. And when he wasn't being outraged, Petrarch wrote incomparable love sonnets to his beloved Laura, a mysterious figure believed to have been an ancestress of the Marquis de Sade.

In 1377, Avignon's population rose to 30,000 souls, a third of them under religious orders. In that year, St Catherine of Siena convinced the seventh Avignon pope, Gregory XI, to return to Rome. The pope came, he saw, he sickened, but before he could pack his bags to return to Avignon, he died. The Roman mob seized their chance and physically forced the cardinals to elect an Italian pope who would re-establish the papacy in Rome. When the French cardinals escaped the Romans' clutches, they sparked off the Great Schism by electing a French antipope, Clement VII, and went back to Avignon. A Church council, held in Pisa 30 years later to resolve the conflict, only ended in the election of yet a third pope. In 1403 the French went over to the Rome faction and sent in an army to persuade Avignon's second antipope, Benedict XIII, to leave for his native Catalunya – where he spent the rest of his life bitterly raining anathemas and excommunications on all and sundry.

When the Church finally decided on one pope, Avignon and the Comtat Venaissin settled in for three and a half centuries of relaxed rule by cardinal legates, under whom the debauchery and violence continued, although on a more modest level. The party really ended when the Comtat Venaissin was incorporated into France during the Revolution in a blood rite of atrocities and the destruction of centuries of art and architecture.

But even as part of France, Avignon has maintained its lively international character. Publishers who first set up shop with the popes stayed on under the cardinal legates, beyond the bounds of French censorship (there were 20 in town before the Revolution); in the 1850s they took on a new life publishing the works of the Félibrige. In 1946 actor Jean Vilar founded the Avignon Festival of Theatre and Film, the liveliest and most popular event on the entire Provençal calendar.

The Famous Half-Bridge

From the Rhône, Avignon is a brave two-tiered sight: in front rise the sheer cliffs of the **Rocher des Doms**, inhabited since Neolithic times, and behind it the sheer man-made cliffs of the Palais des Papes, the same colour as the rock and almost as haphazard a pile. The ensemble includes the **walls** that the popes wrapped around Avignon: bijou, toothsome garden walls ever since Viollet-le-Duc recrenellated them and filled in the moat in 1860.

From the walls, four arches of a bridge leapfrog into the Rhône, sidle up to a water-bound, two-storey Romanesque chapel (the lower half is dedicated to St Nicholas, patron of the Rhône boatmen) and then stop abruptly mid-river, long before reaching Villeneuve lez Avignon on the distant bank. This is the famous **Pont St-Bénezet**, or simply the Pont d'Avignon, begun in 1185 (**t** *04 90 85 60 16; open daily April–Oct 9–7, Nov–Mar 9.30–5.45; adm*). It was built at a time when all bridges were the work of either devils or saints; in this case a shepherd boy named Bénézet, obeying the mandates of heaven, single-handedly laid the huge foundation stones. Originally 22 arches and half a mile long, the bridge enriched Avignon with its tolls: its presence was a major factor in the popes' decision to live here. In 1660 the Avignonnais got tired of the constant repairs it demanded, however, and abandoned it to the monsters of the Rhône.

And did they ever '*danse, tout en rond*' on their bridge, as the nursery song would have it? No, the historians say, although they may well have danced *under* it on the mid-river **Ile de la Barthelasse**, formerly a hunting reserve and headquarters for many of Avignon's prostitutes and thieves. It was here that in later years the Avignonnais came for Sunday picnics. The Félibres liked to bring pretty 'Félibresses' here to recite poetry. In the summer, people still come to cool off in its Olympic-size pool.

The Palais des Papes

t 04 90 27 50 74, www.palais-des-papes.com; open daily April–Oct 9–7, to 8pm July–Sept; Nov–Mar 9.30–5.45, to 9pm during Festival; adm. Last ticket 45mins before closing time. Optional audio guide in English.

For a curious sensation, park directly under the popes' palace and take the lift up to the traffic-free **Place du Palais**. Once crowded with houses, the square was cleared by antipope Benedict XIII to emphasize the message of the palace's vertical, impregnable walls: 'you would think it was an Asiatic tyrant's citadel rather than the abode of the vicar of the God of peace,' wrote Mérimée. But the life of a 14th-century pope justified paranoia. What is less obvious is that the life of a 14th-century pope and his cardinals, courtiers, mistresses and toadies was also extremely luxurious. The palace was spared destruction in the Revolution only to end up serving as a prison and a barracks, and until 1920 its bored residents amused themselves by chipping off frescoes to sell to tourists, so that on most of the walls the only remaining decoration is an extraordinary variety of masons' marks.

The entrance is up the steps, in the centre of Clement VI's façade.

Old Palace: Ground Floor

After crossing the **Cour d'Honneur**, the great courtyard dividing Benedict XII's stern Cistercian Palais Vieux (1334–42) from Clement VI's flamboyant Palais Neuf (1342–52), the tour begins in the **Jesus Hall**, so called for its decorative monograms of Christ. Once used to house the pope's treasure and account books, it now contains a hoard of maps, views of old Avignon and curios, such as a pair of 17th-century bell-ringing figures (*jacquemarts*). The most valuable loot was stored behind walls 10ft thick in the windowless bowels of the **Angels' Tower**, its ceiling supported by a single stone pillar like an enormous palm tree.

Next is the **Consistory**, where the cardinals met and received ambassadors; as its lavish frescoes and ceiling burned in 1413, it now displays 19th-century pictures of Avignon's popes and Simone Martini's fresco of the *Virgin of Humility*, detached from the cathedral porch in 1960. Under the fresco, the restorers found Martini's *sinopia*, or initial line sketch, etched in the stone. As an artist could only paint a small patch of fresh, wet plaster a day, such *sinopie* were essential to maintain the composition, and these, as is often the case in Italy, give a clearer idea of the painter's intent than the damaged fresco itself. There are traces of *sinopie in situ* in the **Chapelle St-Jean**, dedicated to both Johns, the Baptist and the Evangelist. Matteo Giovannetti of Viterbo, a *trecento* charmer who left the bulk of his work in Avignon, did the frescoes for Clement VI: saints floating overhead in starry blue landscapes (recall that at the time ultramarine blue paint was even more expensive than gold). On one wall, John's head is served to Herod at table, as if in a restaurant.

Old Palace: First Floor

The tour continues to the first floor and the banqueting hall, or **Grand Tinel**, hung with 18th-century Gobelin tapestries. Although big enough for a football pitch, the Grand Tinel was too small to hold all the cardinal-electors who would gather in a conclave 10 days after a pope's death. Masons were brought in to accommodate them: the arches at the far end were knocked down to give the cardinals more room to manœuvre (in both senses of the word), while the doors and windows were bricked up to keep them from bringing in more food and endlessly prolonging the conclave. The trick always worked, for the appetites of the 14th-century Curia were Pantagruelian – the adjacent **Upper Kitchen** boasts a pyramidal chimney that could easily handle a roast elephant, or the menu of Clement VI's coronation feast: 1,023 sheep, 118 cows, 101 calves, 914 kids, 60 pigs, 10,471 hens, 1,446 geese and 300 pike, topped off by 46,856 cheeses and 50,000 tarts, all consumed by just 3,000 guests – some 16 tarts per person, with a few thousand left over for the pope's midnight snack. Off the Grand Tinel, more delightful frescoes by Matteo Giovannetti decorate the **Chapelle St-Martial**, celebrating the French saint who came from the same Limousin village as Benedict XII.

The New Palace

The tour continues from the Grand Tinel to the pope's **Antechamber**, where he would hold private audiences, and then on to the **Pope's Bedroom** in the Tower of Angels, a room covered with murals of spiralling foliage, birds and birdcages. It leads directly into the New Palace and the most delightful room in the entire palace, the **Chambre du Cerf**, Clement VI's study, where he would come 'to seek the freedom of forgetting he was pope'. In 1343 he had Matteo Giovannetti (probably) lead a group of French painters in depicting outdoor scenes of hunting, fishing and peach-picking that not only quickened the papal gastric juices, but expressed what was then a revolutionary new interest in the natural world, where flowers and foliage were drawn from observation rather than copying a 'source'.

The arrows direct you next to the **Sacristy**, crowded with statues of kings, queens and bishops escaped from Gargantua's chessboard, followed by Clement VI's **Great Chapel**, longer even than the Grand Tinel and just as empty, though the altar has recently been reconstructed. The **Robing Room** off the chapel contains casts of the Avignon popes' tombs. Revolutionaries bashed most of the figures that once adorned the elaborate **Chapel Gate**; through the bay window in front of this, the pope would bless and give indulgences to pilgrims. A grand stair leads down to the flamboyant **Great Audience Hall**, where a band of Matteo Giovannetti's *Prophets* remain intact, along with outline sketches of a *Crucifixion* that would have been splendid if it had ever been completed.

Around the Palace: Notre-Dame-des-Doms

Before spray paint, the posterity-minded had to record their passing with family emblems. None did it better than the family of the Borghese pope, Paul V; his nephew, legate in Avignon, produced the striking 1619 **Hôtel des Monnaies**, or mint, just across from the Palais des Papes, where reliefs of the Borghese dragon and eagle prance in garlands of fruit salad.

To the left of the palace is Avignon's cathedral, **Notre-Dame-des-Doms**, built in 1150, its landmark square bell tower ridiculously dwarfed by a massive gilt statue of the Virgin added in 1859, an unsuccessful attempt to make the church stand out next to the overwhelming papal pile. The interior has been fuzzily Baroqued like a soft-centre chocolate, but it's worth focusing on the good bits: the dome at the crossing, with an octagonal drum pierced by light, the masterpiece of this typically Provençal conceit; the 11th- or 12th-century marble bishop's chair in the choir; and in a chapel next to the sacristy, now the **Trésor** (*adm*), the flamboyant *Tomb of John XXII* (d. 1334) by English sculptor Hugh Wilfred, mutilated in the Revolution and restored in the 19th century with a spare effigy of a bishop on top to replace the smashed pope.

Next to the cathedral, ramps lead up to the oasis of the **Rocher des Doms**, now a garden enjoying panoramic views from the Rhône below to Mont Ventoux rising to the northeast. Peacocks squawk and preen in trees so crippled by the mistral they need crutches; you can tell the hour with your own shadow on a sundial called the *cadran solaire annalemmatique*, and admire a statue dedicated to an Armenian refugee named Jean Althen who 'introduced the cultivation of madder to the Midi' (don't laugh; used for making dark-blue dyes, madder was once the south's most important cash crop).

Musée du Petit Palais

t 04 90 86 44 58; open June–Sept daily 10–1 and 2–6, otherwise Wed–Mon 9.30–1 and 2–5.30; adm.

Overlooking the Rhône at the end of the Place des Papes stands the **Petit Palais**, built in 1318 and modified in 1474 to suit the tastes of Cardinal Legate Giuliano della Rovere – one day to become Michelangelo's patron and nemesis as Pope Julius II. In 1958 the Petit Palais became a museum to hold all the medieval works remaining in Avignon.

Although the scale of the Petit Palais can be daunting, it contains rare treats from the dawn of the Renaissance by artists hailing for the most part from Siena or Florence. But Avignon gets its say as well: the sculptures and pretty courtly frescoes from the 12th to the 14th centuries in the first two rooms demonstrate the city's role in creating and diffusing the late International Gothic style. The third room contains some fascinating fragments of the 35ft, eight-storey **Tomb of Cardinal Jean de Lagrange** (1389), which stood in Avignon's church of St-Martial before the Revolution. One bit that survived was the *transi*, or relief, of the decomposing corpse that occupied the lowest level of the tomb and was carved with morbid anatomical exactitude. Such *memento mori* would soon become popular in northern France, always used to contrast the handsome effigy of the deceased while alive. The mouldering Cardinal Lagrange is one of the earliest, perhaps the prototype of the genre.

The next six rooms glow with the gold backgrounds (the better to show up in dim churches) of 14th- and early 15th-century Italian painting. Nearly all depict the Virgin and Child, a reflection of the cult of Mariolatry and chivalric ideals of womanhood that began where the troubadours left off. Although the subject matter is repetitive, it makes it easy to trace the medieval revolution in art and seeing, back in the good old days when art was content merely to imitate nature and not try to outdo her. The iconic, Byzantine flatness of the earliest paintings (see especially Paolo Veneziano's *Virgin* of 1340, remarkably never restored in its 660 years) begins to give way to a more natural depiction of space, composition and human form after the innovations of Giotto in Italy (see especially Taddeo Gaddi, Pseudo Jacopino di Francesco, Lorenzo Monaco and Gherardo Starnina). Meanwhile, Sienese artists, following the lead of the great Duccio di Buoninsegna, took up a more elegant, stylized line and richer colours (see Simone Martini and the many works by Taddeo di Bartolo).

The taste of Avignon's popes for Sienese art made the latter the strongest influence in the International Gothic style forged at the papal court (Room 8), a style which the Sienese kept at long after the Florentines had moved on to new things – see Giovanni di Paolo's *Nativity* (1470), or Pietro di Domenico da Montepulciano's kinky *Vierge de Miséricorde* (1420), a delicate portrayal of a congregation sheltered under the Virgin's mantle while a band of flagellants whip themselves. Bridal chests (*cassoni*) were often used to illustrate cautionary tales for women: in Room 9 see Domenico de Michelino's *cassone* panels of 1450 on the story of Suzanna and the Elders.

Renaissance Gems, Sacred and Profane

Beyond the *salon de repos* hangs the museum's best-known work, Botticelli's *Virgin and Child*, a tender, lyrical painting of his youth inspired by his (and Leonardo da Vinci's) master, Verrocchio. The next few rooms offer nothing as striking until Room 15 and its four delightful narrative panels from bridal chests (*c.* 1510) by the Maestro dei Cassoni Campana. This unknown master's meticulous, miniaturist style is as rare as the subject of his cautionary tale: *The Minotaur*, beginning with Queen Pasiphae of Crete's love for a white bull, resulting in the birth of the Minotaur. The third panel shows Ariadne and her ball of twine and Theseus slaying the Minotaur in an exquisite circular labyrinth. The sacred equivalent of the *cassoni* is in Room 16b: the *Sacra Conversazione* by Venetian Vittore Carpaccio, lyrical master of charm, colour and incidental detail. Such 'sacred conversations' portray the Virgin and saints meditating together on matters sublime to the accompaniment of angelic music. To this, Carpaccio has added a landscape dominated by a natural rock bridge, where episodes from the lives of SS. Jerome, Augustine and Paul the Hermit take place.

Lastly, Rooms 17–19 are devoted to works by French artists in Avignon, who after 1440 formed one of the most important schools of French Renaissance art. Influenced by the realism of Flemish oil painting (introduced to Avignon by Benedict XIII) and the almost abstract, decorative lines of the Italians, it concentrates on strong, simple images, as in the altarpiece *Virgin and Child between Two Saints* (1450), by the school's greatest master, Enguerrand Quarton, with a pair of luminous shutters with SS. Michael and Catherine on the reverse by Jossé Lieferinxe. Or take two works by an accomplished but unknown hand: the striking *Jacob's Dream* and the lyrical *Adoration of the Child* (*c.* 1500), where the well-dressed donor seems to have stumbled unexpectedly onto the divine mystery.

Place de l'Horloge and Quartier des Fusteries

Just below the Place du Palais, an antique carousel spins gaily in the lively centre of old Avignon, **Place de l'Horloge**, site of the old Roman forum, now full of buskers and holiday layabouts. The timepiece of its name is in the 1363 tower of the Hôtel de Ville; this originally belonged to a Benedictine monastery on the site, but was secularized with a clock and two *jacquemarts* who sound the hours. They aren't the only archaic figures here: many first-time visitors do a double take when they notice the windows on the east side of the square, filled with trompe-l'œil paintings of historic personages who all are linked in some way to the city.

Behind the Hôtel de Ville lies the **Quartier des Fusteries**, named after the wood merchants and carpenters who had their workshops here in the Middle Ages. These were replaced in the 18th century with *hôtels particuliers*: in one, the **Maison aux Ballons** (with little iron balloons on the window sills) at 18 Rue St-Etienne, Joseph de Montgolfier discovered the principle of balloon flight in 1782 when he noticed how his shirt, drying by the fire, puffed up and floated in the hot air. From the Quartier des Fusteries, the steep picturesque lanes of the **Quartier de la Balance** wind back up to the Place du Palais.

Off Place de l'Horloge and Rue St-Agricol, Rue du Collège-du-Roure leads to the fine mid-15th-century **Palais du Roure**, marked by a flamboyant gate topped with intertwining mulberry branches in memory of the Taverne de Mûrier that it replaced. Equally flamboyant was the 19th-century descendant of the Florentine family who built it, the Félibre poet Marquis Baroncelli-Javon, who preferred to spend his time as a cowboy in the Camargue and lent this town house to Mistral as a headquarters for his Provençal-language journal *Aïoli*. It now houses a study centre and exhibits on the language (*t 04 90 80 80 88; free guided tours Tues at 3pm, and by appointment*). Rue St-Agricol is named after the recently restored Gothic church of **St-Agricol** (1326); its treasure is the *Doni Retable*, a rare Provençal work from the Renaissance. At No.19 is the **Librairie Roumanille**, founded in 1855 by the Avignon poet Joseph Roumanille, father of the Félibrige (*see* p.55). The bookshop published the movement's first masterpiece, Mistral's epic *Miréio* (1859), and continues to put out books in Provençal, while Avignon's literati chum around in the shop's atmospheric 19th-century salon.

Museums: Vouland, Calvet, Requien, Lapidaire and Mont de Piété

At the end of Rue St-Agricol curves Rue Joseph Vernet, lined with 18th-century *hôtels particuliers*, antiques shops, pricey restaurants and cafés. The kind of overly ornate, spindly furniture, porcelains and knick-knacks that originally embellished these mansions is on display nearby in Rue Victor Hugo's **Musée Louis Vouland** (*t 04 90 86 03 79; open May–Oct Tues–Sat 10–12 and 2–6, otherwise 2–6; adm*).

More exciting are the contents of the handsome Hôtel de Villeneuve-Martignan, at 65 Rue Joseph Vernet, first opened to the public as a 'cabinet of curiosities' in the late 18th century by collector Esprit Calvet. Now the **Musée Calvet** (*t 04 90 86 33 84; open Wed–Mon 10–1 and 2–6; adm*) and recently reopened after a long restoration, it offers something for every taste: 6,000 pieces of wrought iron, Greek sculpture, 18th-century seascapes by Avignon native Joseph Vernet and paintings of ruins by Hubert Robert and Panini, mummies, a portrait of Diane de Baroncelli (grandmother of the Marquis de Sade), a bust of a boy by Renaissance sculptor Desiderio da Settignano, tapestries, prehistoric statue-steles, dizzy kitsch paintings of nude men (David's *Mort de Bara* and Horace Vernet's *Mazeppa and the Wolves*), as well as an excellent collection of 19th- and 20th-century paintings by Corot, Guigou, Soutine, Daumier, Dufy, Morisot, Utrillo, Seurat, Toulouse-Lautrec, Vlaminck and Rouault. For all that, the best part of this museum may be the building itself, a light and airy palace from the Age of Enlightenment that complements perfectly the soft, romanticized landscapes and portraits on the walls.

Adjacent to the Calvet museum, the **Musée Requien** is Avignon's fuddy-duddy natural history collection (*t 04 90 82 43 51; open Tues–Sat 9–12 and 2–6*), where an 81lb beaver found in the Sorgue steals the show. Lastly, at 27 Rue de la République, in the chilly 17th-century chapel of a Jesuit College, are the sculptures of the **Musée Lapidaire** (*Museum of Stone-Carving; t 04 90 86 33 84; open Wed–Mon 10–1 and 2–6; adm*). It's worth popping in for the 2nd-century BC (or Merovingian) man-eating *Tarasque de Noves*, each hand gripping the head of a Gaul, while an arm dangles from its greedy jaws; for the statues of Gallic warriors, looking much nattier in their mail than Asterix; or for the unlabelled masks in petal-like hoods. There is good Renaissance sculpture as well, but the best is in the nearby church of **St-Didier** (1359), just to the north in Place St-Didier: Francesco Laurana's polychrome reredos of Christ bearing the Cross, called *Notre-Dame du Spasme* for the spasm of pain on Mary's face; it was one of the first Renaissance sculptures to reach France, executed for Good King René in 1478. Opposite, in the first chapel on the left, are Florentine frescoes *c.* 1360, uncovered in 1952.

More 14th-century frescoes have recently been restored opposite the church in the **Livrée de Ceccano**, now the town library. Nearby, at 5 Rue Laboureur, the treasures of a serious art collector named Jean Angladon-Dubrujeaud have been opened to the public as Avignon's newest museum, the **Fondation Angladon-Dubrujeaud** (*t 04 90 82 29 03; open July–Sept Tues–Sun 1–6, Oct–June Wed–Sun 1–6pm; adm*). These include Renaissance and Art Deco furniture, bronzes and African art, but the main reason for coming is a fine assortment of modern painting never before seen: works by Modigliani, Picasso, Manet, Degas and Cézanne, as well as the only Van Gogh on display in Provence, called *Les Wagons de chemin de fer*.

The **Musée du Mont de Piété** (*6 Rue Saluces, t 04 90 86 53 12; open Mon–Fri 8.30–12 and 1.30–5*), the oldest pawnbroker's in France, now houses not only the town archives but the *conditions des soies*, or silk conditioning, once the wealth of Avignon.

The Eastern Quarters

From Place St-Didier, Rue du Roi René is lined with chiselled palaces, one built on the site of the church of Ste-Claire (No.22), where Petrarch first saw his Laura on Good Friday 1327. ('It was the day when the sun darkened, as God Himself vanished into death, when I was taken,' he wrote.) Laura died, probably of the plague, in 1348, and was buried nearby in the Franciscan **Couvent des Cordeliers**, by the corner of Rue des Lices and Rue des Teinturiers; only the Gothic bell tower survived the fury of the Revolution. In 1533 a humanist from Lyon claimed to have found Laura's tomb in the church, and such was Petrarch's reputation that François I made a special trip to Avignon to see it.

Rue des Teinturiers, the most picturesque street in Avignon, was named after the dyers and textile-makers who powered their machines on water wheels in the Sorgue, two of which survive. Shaded by ancient plane trees, crossed by little bridges, it is a pleasant place to dawdle over a beer or dinner; it's hard to believe this Sorgue is the same stream that comes bursting like a bomb out of that other Petrarchan shrine, the Fontaine de Vaucluse (*see* pp.246–7).

Rue des Teinturiers turns into Rue Bonneterie on its way to Avignon's shopping district and Place Pie, home of the ugly-duckling new **market** (Les Halles), although the produce inside is fit for a swan.

Another evocative street, Rue du Vieux Sextier, once the site of the Jewish Ghetto, is the address of Avignon's 19th-century synagogue, while just beyond Place Carnot, **St-Pierre**'s flamboyant façade boasts a set of beautifully carved walnut doors (1551). Facing St-Pierre, Avignon's cosiest museum, **Musée Théodore Aubanel** (*t 04 90 86 35 02; private, free visits on request*), is dedicated to printing in Avignon, and to the romantic poet and Félibre Théodore Aubanel, whose family still owns one of Avignon's oldest publishing houses.

From Place St-Pierre, Rue Carnot continues to another charming square, the Place des Carmes, dominated by the 14th-century **Eglise des Carmes** (Church of the White Friars), Avignon's biggest church, with a pretty cloister refurbished as a Festival venue.

Visitors in the last century would continue from here along Rue Carreterie, out of the city gate and down the Lyon road to the **Cimetière St-Véran**, a romantic, shady park where John Stuart Mill and his wife Harriet are buried. Harriet died at the Hôtel d'Europe in 1858, a loss so devastating for the philosopher of utilitarianism that he lived in a house by the cemetery until he himself died in 1873. Another celebrated tomb belongs to Maurille de Sombreuil, who became a heroine during the Revolution when, to save the life of her father, the governor of the Invalides, she drank a goblet of human blood. Contemporaries noted that she always ordered white wine with her meals after that.

Villeneuve lez Avignon

In 586, on Puy Andaon, the rock that dominates Villeneuve lez Avignon, a Visigoth princess-hermit named Casarie died in the odour of sanctity (holiness smells like crushed violets, apparently). In the 10th century, Benedictines built the abbey of St-André to shelter her bones and lodge pilgrims on the route to Compostela. St-André grew to become one of the mightiest monasteries in the south of France, and in 1226, when Louis VIII besieged pro-Albigensian Avignon, the abbot offered the king co-sovereignty of the abbey in exchange for royal privileges. And so what was once an abbey town became a frontier fortress of the king of France, a new town (*ville neuve*) and a heavily fortified one, in case the pope over the river should start feeling frisky.

But Villeneuve was soon invaded in another way; wanton, squalid Avignon didn't suit all tastes, and the pope gave permission to his cardinals who liked it not-so-hot to retreat across the Rhône into princely *livrées cardinalices* (palaces euphemistically 'freed' from their original owners by the Curia). Though a dormitory suburb these days, Villeneuve still maintains a separate peace, with well-fed cats snoozing in the sun, leisurely afternoons at the *pétanque* court and some amazing works of art.

Getting There

Bus no.11 runs every 30mins from the train station or Porte de l'Oulle in Avignon to Villeneuve.

Tourist Information

Tourist office: Place Charles-David, **t** 04 90 25 61 33, **f** 04 90 25 91 55, *villeneuve.les.avignon. tourisme@wanadoo.fr, www.villeneuve-lez-avignon.com*. Place Charles David is also the best place to **park**. In summer, there is an office on Rue de la République, near the Chartreuse. *Open July Mon–Fri 10–7, Sat and Sun 10–1 and 2.30–7; Aug daily 9–12.30 and 2–6; Sept–June Mon–Sat 9–12.30 and 2–6*. **Note** that everything except the Chartreuse is **closed** on Tuesdays and in February.

Market Days

Thursday on Place Charles-David and Saturday morning on Place Jean-Jaurès. On Saturday morning there's also a flea market.

Where to Stay and Eat

Villeneuve lez Avignon ✉ 30400

Villeneuve makes an attractive alternative to Avignon, and has some notable lodgings

****Le Prieuré**, Place du Chapître, **t** 04 90 15 90 15, **f** 04 90 25 45 39, *leprieure@relais chateaux.fr, www.leprieure.fr (expensive)*. Exquisite and centrally located, Le Prieuré gives you the option of sleeping in the 14th-century *livrée*, where the rooms are furnished with antiques, or in the more comfortable annexe by the swimming pool; gardens, tennis and a remarkable restaurant that does delightful things with seafood and truffles. *Closed Nov–mid-Mar*.

****La Magnaneraie**, 37 Rue Camp-de-Bataille, **t** 04 90 25 11 11, **f** 04 90 25 46 37, *www.avignon-et-provence.com/ lamagnaneraie (expensive)*. Choose between the old-fashioned rooms in a former silk-worm nursery, or another modern annexe; it too has a pool, gardens and Le Prieuré's rival for the best restaurant in town.

***L'Atelier**, 5 Rue de la Foire, **t** 04 90 25 01 84, **f** 04 90 25 80 06, *hotel-latelier@libertysurf.fr (moderate–inexpensive)*. For a less expensive sojourn into history, a charming 16th-century building with a walled garden in the centre of town. *Closed Nov*.

***Les Cèdres**, 39 Bd Pasteur, **t** 04 90 25 43 92, **f** 04 90 25 14 66 *(inexpensive)*. Built in the 17th century and named after its ancient cedars, with a pool and a bungalow annexe. *Closed Nov–Mar*.

Les Jardins de la Livrée, 4 bis Rue Camp de Bataille, **t** 04 90 26 05 05, **f** 04 90 25 37 78 *(moderate)*. One of several old buildings in Villeneuve that have been beautifully restored as *chambres d'hôtes*; with a walled garden, pool and parking. The restaurant is good too. *Closed Sun eve and Mon in winter*.

Foyer UCJG YMCA, 7 bis Chemin de la Justice, **t** 04 90 25 46 20, **f** 04 90 25 30 64. Cheapest of all, with superb views of the Rhône and a pool to boot.

Aubertin, 1 Rue de l'Hôpital, **t** 04 90 25 94 84 *(expensive)*. You'll have to book ahead to get a table at this intimate place under the porticoes. *Closed Sun, and Mon lunch in winter, and last 2 weeks in Aug*.

La Maison, 1 Rue Montée du Fort St-André, **t** 04 90 25 20 81 *(moderate)*. An old favourite, with a traditional menu and friendly service. *Closed Wed and Aug*.

Around Town

In 1307, when Philip the Fair ratified the deal that made Villeneuve royal property, he ordered that a citadel should be built on the approach to Pont St-Bénezet and named after guess who. As times grew more perilous, this bright white **Tour Philippe-le-Bel** (*t 04 32 70 08 57; open April–Sept 10–12.30 and 3–7, Oct–Mar 10–12 and 2–5.30; 15 June–15 Sept open daily, otherwise closed Mon; closed Feb*) was made higher to keep out the riffraff, and from its terrace, reached by a superb winding stair, it offers splendid views of Avignon, Mont Ventoux and, on a clear day, the Alpilles.

From here, Montée de la Tour leads up to the 14th-century **Collégiale Notre-Dame**, once the chapel of a *livrée* and now Villeneuve's parish church. From Villeneuve's Chartreuse (Charterhouse) it has inherited an elaborate marble altar of 1745, and it contains a copy of Enguerrand Quarton's famous *Pietà de Villeneuve lez Avignon* (the original is in the Louvre). However, the church's most famous work, a beaming, swivel-hipped, polychrome ivory statue of the Virgin, carved in Paris out of an elephant's tusk *c.* 1320, has been removed to safer quarters in the nearby **Musée Pierre-de-Luxembourg** (*t 04 90 27 49 66; same hours as Tour Philippe-le-Bel; adm*), housed in yet another *livrée*.

The museum's other prize is the masterpiece of the Avignon school: Enguerrand Quarton's 1454 *Couronnement de la Vierge*, one of the greatest works of 15th-century French painting, commissioned for the Chartreuse (*see* below). Unusually, it portrays God the Father and God the Son as twins, clothed in sumptuous crimson and gold, like the Virgin herself, whose fine sculptural features were perhaps inspired by the ivory Virgin. Around these central figures the painting evokes the spiritual route travelled by the Carthusians through vigilant prayer, to purify the world and reconcile it to God. St Bruno, founder of the Order, saints, kings and commoners are present, hierarchically arranged, while the landscape encompasses heaven, hell, Rome and Jerusalem, and local touches like Montagne Ste-Victoire and the cliffs of the Estaque.

Other notable works in the museum include a curious 14th-century *double-faced Virgin*, the 'Eve' face evoking original sin and the 'Mary' face human redemption; Simon de Châlon's 1552 *Entombment*; and, amid the uninspired 17th-century fluff, Philippe de Champaigne's *Visitation*.

La Chartreuse and Fort St-André

From the museum, take Rue de la République up to No.53, the **Livrée de la Thurroye**, the best-preserved in Villeneuve; a cardinal would maintain a household of 100 or so people here. Further up the street and up the scale rises what was the largest and wealthiest charterhouse in France, the **Chartreuse du Val de Bénédiction** (*open daily April–Sept 9–6.30, Oct–Mar 9.30–5.30; adm*). This began as the *livrée* of Etienne Aubert who, upon his election to the papacy in 1352 as Innocent VI, deeded his palace to the Carthusians for a monastery. For 450 years it was expanded and rebuilt, acquired immense estates on either side of the Rhône from kings and popes, accumulated a precious library, two more cloisters and various works of art, and in general lived high on the hog by the usual Carthusian standards. In 1792, the Revolution forced the monks out, and the Chartreuse was sold in 17 lots; squatters took over the cells and outsiders feared to enter the cloisters after dark. Now repurchased and beautifully restored, the buildings house the CNES (the *Centre National des Écritures du Spectacles*), where playwrights and others are given grants to work in peace and quiet in some of the former cells; it hosts seminars, exhibitions and performances, especially during the Avignon festival.

Still, the sensation that lingers in the Charterhouse is one of vast silences and austerity, the hallmark of an order where conversation was limited (originally) to one hour a week; monks who disobeyed the rule of prayer, work and silence ended up in one of the seven prison cells around the laundry in the Great Cloister – each with a cleverly arranged window on the prison chapel altar. Explanations (in English) throughout offer an in-depth view of Carthusian life: one cell has been furnished as it originally was. Pierre Boulez discovered that the dining hall, or **Tinel**, has some of the finest acoustics in France, designed so that all could hear the monk who read aloud during meals. In the Tinel's chapel are ruined 14th-century frescoes by Matteo Giovannetti and his school: originally their work covered the walls of the huge **church**, now bare except for their masons' marks and minus its apse, which collapsed. The star attraction here is **Innocent VI's tomb**, with an alabaster effigy under a fine Gothic baldachin. Innocent was solemnly reburied here in 1960: a hundred years ago the tomb was used as a rabbit hutch. Popes who took the name Innocent have tended to suffer similar posthumous indignities: the great Innocent III was found stark naked in Perugia cathedral, a victim of poisoned slippers, while the corpse of Innocent X – the last of the series – was dumped in a tool shed in St Peter's.

Gazing down into the Charterhouse from the summit of Puy Andaon are the formidable bleached walls of **Fort St-André**, built by the French kings around the old abbey in the 1360s, not only to stare down the pope over the river but to defend French turf during the heyday of the *Grandes Compagnies* (bands of unemployed mercenaries who pillaged the countryside and held towns to ransom). The two round towers afford a famous vantage point over Avignon; the southwestern tower is called the Tour des Masques (sorcerers' tower), although no one remembers why. Jumbly ruins are all that remain of the once splendid abbey of St-André, amid beautiful Italian gardens – sumptuous in the springtime – restored and presided over by Roseline Bacou, a former curator at the Louvre.

Between Avignon and Tarascon: La Montagnette

Just south of Avignon and the confluence of the Durance, the Rhône curves to accommodate La Montagnette, a micro-region that is still something of a best-kept secret, close to the tourist fleshpots of Provence and yet distant in spirit, self-contained and serene. The Montagnette itself is a striking, 10km-long outcrop of white stone, isolated from its sisters in the Alpilles and surrounded by orchards, a bijou landscape that **Barbentane** fits into like an old shoe – a friendly old town that so loved its *farandole* that a man who could not dance it would not be considered a fit husband. It is still defended by the 14th-century Tour Angelica, its medieval gates and, near the church, the arcaded Renaissance Maison des Chevaliers. Outside the walls, the château (*t 04 90 95 51 07; open Easter–Oct daily 10–12 and 2–6, rest of the year Sun only; adm*) was built in 1674, not for defence but for pleasure, by the Marquis de Barbentane, the king's ambassador to Tuscany. It would not look out of place in the Ile de France: the furnishings are Louis XV and Louis XVI, but the builder's Italian tastes permeate the other decoration. The enormous plane trees in the garden were brought over from Turkey by an earlier marquis in the 1670s.

On the D35 south of Barbentane, **Boulbon** was known as Bourbon until 1792, when the guillotine cut into the name's popularity. Still defended by its fairy-tale

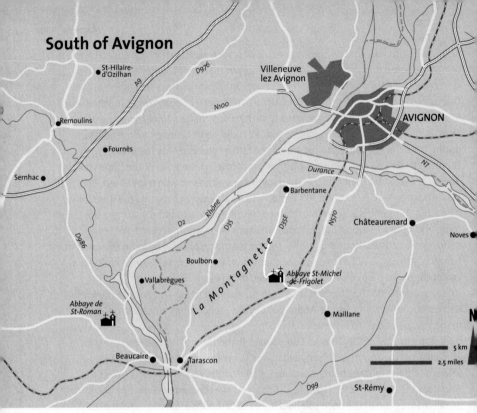

St-Hilaire-d'Ozilhan

Villeneuve
lez Avignon

AVIGNON

Remoulins

Fournès

Durance

Sernhac

Barbentane

Châteaurenard

Noves

Boulbon

Abbaye St-Michel
-de-Frigolet

Vallabrègues

La Montagnette

Abbaye de
St-Roman

Maillane

Beaucaire

Tarascon

St-Rémy

5 km

2.5 miles

10th-century walls built dramatically into and onto the rocky escarpment overlooking the Rhône, Boulbon is known for its unique 1 June *cérémonie du St-Vinage*, in honour of its patron saint Marcellin: the men of the village each bring a full bottle of wine to the saint's Romanesque chapel and hear the Gospel in Provençal, after which the wine is blessed and God is toasted with a mighty swig. The bottle is then corked and for the rest of the year the blessed wine is used as a sovereign remedy for grave illnesses.

Leaving Barbentane on the D35E will bring you to the **Abbaye St-Michel-de-Frigolet**, founded around the year 1000 (**t** *04 90 95 70 07; guided tours by a monk 1 May–31 Dec Mon–Fri 2.30pm, Sun 4pm; all year by appointment for groups of 10 or more*). The word *Frigolet* comes from the Provençal *férigoulo*, or thyme, a healthy, invigorating herb that scents the air of La Montagnette. The monks of Montmajour (*see* p.152), ener-vated by the swamps, would come up here for a cure – some of it in the form of a liqueur called *Le Frigolet*, still distilled and on sale at the monastery. It may also have an effect on sterility: in 1632, Anne of Austria, barren after 20 years of marriage, prayed in the Romanesque chapel of the Conception Immaculée for a son, and soon after gave the world Louis XIV. In gratitude, the queen sent the sumptuous gilt *boiseries* that frame 14 turgid Mignards. Another celebrity to pass through was the young Frédéric Mistral, who attended an improvised school here, where lessons were bartered for food; the stories and customs of these hills were to become a powerful source of inspiration.

The Petite Crau

East of Barbentane and the Montagnette, **Châteaurenard** is one of Provence's main wholesale fruit and vegetable markets, a big bustling place under its plane trees. It lords over the rich verdant plain of the **Petite Crau**, a large marshland drained by the Romans, planted with market gardens and orchards of cherries and apricots, and protected from the huffing and puffing of the mistral by hedgerows and poplars – nothing at all like the rocky waste of the 'big' Crau (*see* p.165). Two proud towers on Châteaurenard's hill are all that remain of the castle that first belonged to Reinardus, a friend and ally of Charles Martel, who was killed below its walls fighting the Saracens; his wife Emma took over the command and fought bravely, keeping the enemy at bay, then died of a broken heart. Her ghost haunts the **Tour du Griffon**, with great views over the Luberon and Alpilles and containing the Musée d'Histoire Locale au Château (**t** *04 90 90 11 59; open June–Sept 10–12 and 2–6, closed Fri and Sat am; Oct–May 3–5, closed Fri*). Five kilometres east of Châteaurenard, **Noves** claims to have been the home, or summer residence, of Petrarch's Laura: you can see her supposed house, and a gate she might have passed through.

In 1830, Mistral was born in **Maillane**, southwest of Châteaurenard, and spent as much time as possible there until he died in 1914. It's been bypassed by the main routes, leaving a quaint, dusty nowhere with two old-fashioned bars in the square, dogs sleeping in the middle of the streets, and a *tabac* selling keychains sporting Mistral's mug – the only noticeable effort by the locals to cash in on their Nobel

Where to Stay and Eat

Barbentane ✉ 13570

Castel Mouisson, at the foot of the Montagnette in Quartier Castel Mouisson, **t 04 90 95 51 17, **f** 04 90 95 67 63, *contact@hotelcastelmouisson.com*, *www.hotel-castelmouisson.com* (*inexpensive*). A typical Provençal hotel, with a pool and tennis, and bikes to borrow. *Closed mid-Oct–mid-Mar.*

St-Jean, 1 Le Cours, **t/f** 04 90 95 50 44, *gg@hotelsaintjean.com* (*inexpensive*). Decent rooms in the centre and a restaurant with good, substantial fare (*moderate–cheap*). *Open all year; restaurant closed Sun eve and Mon.*

Hostellerie de Frigolet, St-Michel-de-Frigolet, **t** 04 90 90 52 70, **f** 04 90 95 75 22, *www.frigolet.com* (*inexpensive*). Run by the Prémontrés monks, with 36 rooms for guaranteed quiet retreats for a day or two, or even a month; book through the Service Hostellerie, Abbaye St-Michel-de-Frigolet, 13150 Tarascon.

Châteaurenard ✉ 13160

Les Glycines, 14 Av Victor Hugo, **t 04 90 94 10 66, **f** 04 90 94 78 10 (*inexpensive*). A simple and reasonably priced base, with an average restaurant (*moderate*). *Restaurant closed Mon.*

Noves ✉ 13550

****Auberge de Noves, 2km northwest on the D28, **t** 04 90 24 28 28, **f** 04 90 24 28 00, *message@aubergedenoves.com* or *resa@aubergedenoves.com*, *www.aubergedenoves.com* (*luxury*). A superb *bastide* in a 15-hectare forest, converted three generations ago by the Lalleman family into one of the most prestigious Provençal hotels (Relais & Châteaux). Lovely, air-conditioned rooms, endowed with every creature comfort; tennis and pool in the grounds, riding and golf nearby. The restaurant is a serious gastronomic temple, serving a seductive mix of regional and traditional dishes matched with a superb wine cellar. *Restaurant closed Mon & Tues lunch out of season.*

Prize-slinging hero (he *does* look like Buffalo Bill). The house the master Félibre had built after 1876 is now the Musée Mistral (*t 04 90 95 74 06; open Mon–Thurs 8–12 and 2–6, Fri and Sat 8–12; adm*) – don't mistake it for the rotting concrete Centre F. Mistral, which is something else. Preserved as it was the day he died in 1914, it is 'as sympathetic and as cosy as a coffin,' as James Pope-Hennessy described it.

The guide, a sinewy cockerel of a man, won't let you in until the tour begins, and then his high-speed spiel won't be stopped. If you do interrupt, he will forget where he is and have to start from the beginning again. No concessions if you only speak English. Mistral's tomb, in the ghastly, gravelly graveyard over the road, is modelled after the Pavillon de la Reine Jeanne at Les Baux, and decorated with a seven-pointed star and other Félibre symbols. If you can, leave Maillane southwards by the D27, and travel over beautiful fields and streams.

Tarascon

Few towns in Provence are as determinedly unglamorous as Tarascon. Most of the houses are not only unrestored, but cry out for a lick of paint; garages outnumber craft shops; even the poodles look like real dogs instead of topiary hedges. Meanwhile, the rival fairy-tale castles of Tarascon and Beaucaire muse at each other across the Rhône like the embodiments of a bicommunal Walter Mitty daydream, reminders of heroism, romance, international markets, man-eating monsters and Alphonse Daudet's buffoonish antihero Tartarin, who never told a lie but, under the hot sun, was prone to imagine things. Provençal nationalists accuse Daudet (a native of Nîmes) of creating a stereotype that only heightened Paris' already smug attitude towards the Midi, to which Daudet replied that 'All Frenchmen have in them a touch of Tarascon.'

Tarascon and St Martha

All centuries have quirks that seem quaint to later generations: tulip-bulb speculation in the 18th, ladies' bustles in the 19th, muzak in the 20th. In the 11th and 12th centuries, it was a mania for the bodily parts of saints, a fad so passionate that a sure candidate for the inner circle, such as St Francis, had bodyguards from Assisi in his dying days to prevent rival towns from kidnapping him. If it had no fresh relics, every town with a saintly legend attached to it began digging for bones; and in Tarascon, *voilà*, in 1187 they just happened to stumble across the relics of St Martha. The pious 9th-century legend told how she found Tarascon bedevilled by a Tarasque, a man-eating amphibian whose ancestors are portrayed in Celtic sculpture chomping on human heads. Martha neatly tidied away the monster by showing it a Cross, lassoing it with her girdle, then ordering it to the bottom of the Rhône, never to return.

The new-found relics attracted so many pilgrims that the 12th-century **Collégiale Ste-Marthe** was enlarged in the 13th and 16th centuries into a curious Romanesque-Gothic hybrid. The church was badly bombed in the Second World War, but even worse mischief had been done earlier in the Revolution, when the great south portal

Getting There and Around

By Train
Nearly every east–west train from Provence to Languedoc stops in Tarascon.

By Bus
Buses run regularly between Beaucaire, Tarascon, Nîmes and Avignon (t 04 66 29 27 29); other lines, from Tarascon station, go to Arles, Boulbon, St-Rémy and Cavaillon (t 04 90 93 74 90).

Tourist Information

Tourist office: 59 Rue des Halles, t 04 90 91 03 52, f 04 90 91 22 96, tourisme@tarascon.org, www.tarascon.org. Open April–Sept Mon–Sat 9–12.30 and 2–6, Sun 10–12; Oct–Mar Mon–Fri 9–12.30 and 2–6.

Market Day
Tuesday morning, Place Verdun.

Festivals
Nowadays the *Fêtes de la Tarasque* take place for five days around St John's Day (24 June), and include bonfires, costumes, bull-fights, cavalcades, dances, opera (the *Miréio* of course), and – yes – someone dressed up like Tartarin. On 5 Jan, there's the arrival of the Three Kings procession.

Where to Stay and Eat

Tarascon ✉ 13150

★★★Hôtel Mazets des Roches, Route de Fontvieille, t 04 90 91 34 89, f 04 90 43 53 29, *mazets-des-roches@wanadoo.fr* (*moderate*). Comfort and quiet, modern, air-conditioned rooms set in a large park of tall pines, with a restaurant, pool, tennis courts and bike rentals. *Closed Nov–mid-Mar; restaurant closed Thurs and Sat lunch.*

★★★De Provence, 7 Bd Victor Hugo, t 04 90 91 06 43, f 04 90 43 58 13, hoteldeprovence@faxvia.net (*moderate*). A *hôtel particulier* in the centre with big rooms, big baths and colour TV.

★★Le Terminus, Place Colonel Berrurier, t 04 90 91 18 95, f 04 90 91 08 00 (*inexpensive–cheap*). With a restaurant offering 16 different starters and 10 main dishes. *Closed mid-Feb–mid-March.*

Auberge de la Jeunesse, 31 Bd Gambetta, t 04 90 91 04 08, f 04 90 91 54 17, *tarascon@fuaj.org* (*cheap*). Guests can take advantage of the hostel's inexpensive bike hire. Victuals are cheap, if not *cordon bleu. Closed mid-Dec–Feb.*

of 1197 was shorn of its sculptures. Nowadays, the chapels of the attractive five-aisled Gothic nave are filled with the lukewarm efforts of Mignard and Parrocel, masters of the Baroque fruitcake style, while in the crypt (part of the original 1197 church) there's a king-sized statue of Martha from 1400, and the slightly later and much more refined *Effigy of Jean de Cossa*, Seneschal of Provence, which is attributed to Francesco Laurana.

Château de Tarascon

t 04 90 91 01 93; open April–Sept daily 9–7, Oct–Mar daily 9–12 and 2–5; adm.

Rooted in a limestone rock over the Rhône, Tarascon's château gleams like white satin between the sun and the water, a storybook feudal castle with crenellations and moat, named after the one character in Tarascon's history actually rounded out in flesh and blood. Good King René earned the 'Good' in his name for his good appetite and fondness for the good things of life, as well as for having the good sense not to let troubles or sorrows, of which he had many, get under his skin. He spent the last decade of his life (1471–80) surrounded by poets and artists in Tarascon, in this castle begun in 1401 by his father, Louis II of Anjou. After René's death and Provence's annexation to France, it underwent the usual conversion into a prison.

While the exterior is all business, the interior was designed with the good taste of René in mind – flamboyant and elegant, and now eloquently empty except for ten 17th-century tapestries on the Life of Scipio and a collection of 18th-century pharmaceutical pots. In the courtyard there are busts of the king and his second wife, Jeanne de Laval; here and there, sculptural titbits and faded ceiling panels offer clues to the original decoration. Graffiti by British sailors imprisoned here between 1754 and 1778 recall the castle's later use. Taking in the precipitous views from the top, you can see why no one ever tried to sneak up on it; or why, during the Revolution, Tarascon never needed to invest in a guillotine.

Elsewhere around Town

Perhaps because they haven't been prettified to death as in some Provençal towns, the streets of Tarascon, lined with rose, lemon and ochre houses with pots of geraniums in the windows and laundry flapping in the breeze, make it a delightful place to wander around. The main **Rue des Halles** is still covered by medieval arcades. Halfway up it from the tourist office you'll find the Franciscan **Cloître des Cordeliers** (1450s), now only open for special exhibitions (*t 04 90 91 38 71; open 10–12 and 2–5.30*). At the top of Rue des Halles stands the handsome **Hôtel de Ville** (1648) – compare it with Beaucaire's, built 30 years later; the ceilings and original consuls' stalls are still intact. Near here, at 39 Rue Proudhon, the **Musée Souleiado** (*t 04 90 91 08 80; open May–Sept daily 10–6, Oct–April Tues–Sat 10–12 and 2–5*) is run by Souleiado (Provençal for 'sunray piercing through clouds'), France's leading manufacturer of block-printed textiles. Founded here in 1938 by Charles Deméry in the hopes of reviving a 200-year-old Tarascon industry, the museum holds 40,000 18th-century fruitwood blocks – still the basis for all the company's patterns. Brought back to fashion in the 1950s on such diverse backs as Bardot's and Picasso's, Souleiado's colour-drenched prints can be purchased in the nearby shop, or in the many boutiques in the south of France.

Lastly, there's the so-called **House of Tartarin**, across from a Fiat garage at 55 bis Bd Itam (*t 04 90 91 05 08; open April–Sept Mon–Sat 10–12 and 2–7, Oct–Mar Mon–Sat 10–12 and 1.30–5, closed Sun and mid-Dec–mid-Mar; adm*). The modern Tarasconnais say they have forgiven Daudet for making them ridiculous, for in the age of Tourist Man he has also made them famous. Daudet claimed that the character of Tartarin was derived from his cousin, a big-game hunter whom Daudet accompanied on a lion hunt in Algeria, but there's another version: in the original story, published as a newspaper serial, Tartarin was named Barbarin after an old Tarasconnais family – the head of which had rejected the author's suit for the hand of his daughter. The family threatened to sue if Daudet used their name in his novel, so he changed it to the fictional Tartarin, then got his own back by making the whole town the butt of his jokes. In the house are mementoes from the three Tartarin novels, and photos from the plays and films. The garden has been planted to fit the books' exotic flora and baobab tree, where Tartarin held court with his tall tales.

Also on display is the famous **Tarasque**, a moustachioed armadillo covered with red spikes. Scholars argue whether the monster is named after the town or vice versa; when King René founded the *Jeux et Courses de la Tarasque* in 1474, it was given a thick carapace to hide the men that made it walk, while fireworks blasted out of its nostrils and the people sang '*Lagadigadèu, la Tarasco, Lagadigadèu!*', or 'Let her pass, the Tarasque, let her dance.'

Beaucaire

Beaucaire can match Tarascon's stories tit for tat. It, too, was plagued by a river monster, called the Drac – a dragon in some versions, or a handsome young man – who liked to stroll invisibly through Beaucaire, before luring his victims into the Rhône by holding a bright jewel just below the surface. When the Drac became a father, he kidnapped a washerwoman to nurse his baby for seven years, during which time the woman learned how to see him when he was invisible. Years later, during one of his prowls through Beaucaire she saw him and greeted him loudly. He was so mortified that he was never seen again, although like the Tarasque he makes an annual reappearance by proxy, the first weekend in June. Beaucaire was also the setting of one of the most charming medieval romances: of Aucassin, son of the count of Beaucaire, and his 'sweet sister friend' Nicolette, daughter of the king of Carthage, whom Aucassin loved so dizzily that he fell off his horse and dislocated his shoulder, among other adventures.

Tourist Information

Tourist office: 24 Cours Gambetta, **t** 04 66 59 26 57, **f** 04 66 59 68 51, *info@ot-beaucaire.fr*, *www.ot-beaucaire.fr. Open summer Mon–Fri 8.45–12 and 2–7, Sat 9.30–12.30 and 3–6, Sun 10–12.30; winter Mon–Fri 8.45–12 and 2–6.*

Market Days

Thursday and Sunday mornings, Place de la Mairie and Cours Gambetta. In July and August, Friday evening, there's a market along the canal (7–11pm) with local produce, crafts, flea market and entertainments.

Where to Stay and Eat

Beaucaire ✉ 30300
★★★Les Doctrinaires, Quai Général de Gaulle, **t** 04 66 59 23 70, **f** 04 66 59 22 26, *www.archimix.com/web/doctrinaires/* (*inexpensive; restaurant moderate*). Home of the Doctrinaire fathers of Avignon before the Revolution, now metamorphosed into a fetching, old-fashioned hostelry. Half board is obligatory in season, but eating 'in', in the pretty courtyard, is pleasant. *Closed Sat lunch.*

★★★Robinson, 2km north on the Route de Remoulins, **t** 04 66 59 21 32, **f** 04 66 59 00 03, *contact@hotel.robinson.fr* (*inexpensive*). Thirty rooms set in acres and acres of countryside, with pool, tennis, playground etc. and a restaurant (*moderate*). *Closed Feb.*

Napoléon, 4 Place Frédéric-Mistral, **t** 04 66 59 05 17 (*cheap*). Comfortable rooms with bath in the centre. In 1793, Napoleon, while still unknown, visited the fair and wrote a little booklet called *Supper at Beaucaire*, a dialogue of merchants on the subject of Federalism.

For a real escape, hire a **houseboat** and make the leisurely loop down the Rhône–Sète canal to the Camargue, west to Aigues-Mortes and up the Languedoc canal past St-Gilles to Beaucaire. Try **Connoisseur Cruisers**, 14 Quai de la Paix, **t** 04 66 59 46 08, **f** 04 66 59 27 19.

But in those days Beaucaire was on everyone's lips. It was here, in 1208, that a local squire assassinated Pope Innocent III's legate, who had come to demand stricter measures against the Cathars. It gave Innocent the excuse he needed to launch the Albigensian Crusade against Beaucaire's overlords in Toulouse, and all their lands in Languedoc. In 1216, when the war was in full swing, Raymond VII, the son of the count of Toulouse, recaptured the town from its French occupiers, who took refuge in the castle. As soon as word reached Simon de Montfort, he set off in person to succour his stranded men and to teach Beaucaire a lesson, besieging the town walls, while his troops took up the fight from inside the castle, so that Beaucaire was sandwiched in a double attack. The siege lasted 13 weeks before the troops in the castle ran out of food and surrendered and Simon de Montfort had to admit to one of his very few defeats. In gratitude, Raymond VI granted Beaucaire the right to hold a duty-free fair. But five years later the town was gobbled up by France along with the rest of Languedoc, and lost all its rights and freedoms.

In 1464, Louis XI, eager to win Beaucaire to his side, restored its freedoms and fair franchise; soon its *Foire de la Ste-Madeleine* became one of the biggest in western Europe. For 10 days in July, merchants from all over the Mediterranean, Germany and England would wheel and deal in the wooden booths of the *pré*, a vast meadow on the banks of the Rhône; by the 18th century, when the fair was at its height, Beaucaire (with a population of 8,000) attracted some 300,000 traders, as well as acrobats, prostitutes, pickpockets and sweethearts, who came to buy each other rings of spun glass as a symbol of love's fragile beauty. So much money changed hands that Beaucaire earned as much in a week as Marseille did in a year. The loss of Beaucaire's duty-free privileges just after Napoleon lost at Waterloo put an end to the fair, and since then Beaucaire has had to make do with traffic on the Rhône and Rhône–Sète Canal (now the town's marina), its quarries and its wine, ranging from good table plonk to the more illustrious AOC Costière du Gard. But if you come in the spring, you can try one last legacy of the great fair in Beaucaire: *pastissoun*, patties filled with preserved fruits, introduced by merchants from the Levant.

The Château and Historic Centre

Louis XI's restoration of Beaucaire's rights paid off for a later Louis (XIII); in 1632, when the château was besieged by the troops of the king's rebellious brother, Gaston d'Orléans, the loyal citizens forced them out. To prevent further mishaps, Richelieu ordered Beaucaire's castle razed to the ground. But after demolishing the south wall, the shell was left to fall into ruins romantic enough for an illustration to *Aucassin and Nicolette*, a fitting background to **Les Aigles de Beaucaire** (*t 04 66 59 26 72; Easter–Nov hourly between the following times: Mar, Sept, Oct and Nov 2.30–4.30; April, May and June 2–5; July–Aug Thurs–Tues 3–6; adm*), displays of the falconer's art in Roman costume. There are sweeping views of the Rhône and the old fair grounds, the Champ de Foire, from the 80ft **Tour Polygonale**. In the castle gardens below, the **Musée Auguste Jacquet** (*t 04 66 59 47 61; open April–Oct 10–12 and 2.15–6.45, Nov–Mar 10.15–12 and 2–5.15, closed Tues and hols; adm*) has finds from Roman Beaucaire (then clumsily called Ugernum), including a fine statue of Jupiter on his throne, and another of the lusty Priapus found in a villa. There's a geological collection, popular arts, and advertising posters and mementoes from the fair, when thousands of brightly coloured cloths swung over the streets, each bearing a merchant's name, his home address and his address in Beaucaire; it was the only way in the vast, polyglot throng to find anyone.

From the château, arrows point the way to the venerable **Place de la République**, shaded by giant plane trees, and the grand, elegant Baroque **church of Notre-Dame-des-Pommiers** (1744), which perhaps more than anything proves how many annual visitors this town once expected. It replaced a much smaller Romanesque church, but conserves, on its exterior transept wall (facing Rue Charlier), a superb 12th-century **frieze**, depicting Passion scenes in the same strong, lively relief as at St-Gilles-du-Gard. The stately French classical **Hôtel de Ville** (1683) in Place G. Clemenceau was designed by Jacques Cubiol and bestowed on Beaucaire by Louis XIV, who wanted to provide it with a monument worthy of its importance: note Louis' sun symbols on the façade, the town's coat of arms set in the Collar of St Michael (the French equivalent of the Order of the Garter – Beaucaire was the only town in France awarded the honour), and Beaucaire's motto: 'Renowned for its Fair, Illustrious for its Fidelity'. The other *hôtels* you can't stay in aren't anywhere near as magnificent. If it's a holiday, there's likely to be some dramatic bull follies in the **Arènes**: a hundred bulls are brought in for the *Estivales*, a week-long recreation of the medieval market and other celebrations in late July. Beaucaire's *razeteurs* have the reputation as the most daring of them all: statues of Clairon and Goya, the bulls that gave them the best sport, greet visitors respectively by the Rhône bridge and in Place Jean-Jaurès.

Around Beaucaire: Roman Wine and Roads, and Troglodyte Monks

The outskirts of Beaucaire are home to two new yet old attractions. **Le Vieux Mas**, 8km south on the Route de Fourques (*t* 04 66 59 60 13; open April–Sept daily 10–7; Oct–Mar Wed, Sat and Sun 10–12.30 and 1.30–6; adm), is a living evocation of a Provençal farmhouse at the turn of the last century, with a working blacksmith and other craftsmen, farm animals and regional products. The **Mas Gallo Romain des Tourelles**, 4km southwest at 4294 Route de Bellegarde (*t* 04 66 59 19 72; open April–Oct daily 2–6; July and Aug Mon–Sat 10–12 and 2–7, Sun 2–7; Nov–Easter Sat 2–6), is more original: since 1909 archaeologists have been working on the 210-acre vineyard of Château des Tourelles (owned by the Durands for 250 years), excavating a huge 1st-century AD agricultural estate that produced olives, wheat and wine, complete with a pottery factory capable of producing 4,000 amphorae a day. The current Durand in charge, Hervé, became so fascinated with the digs that, together with the National Centre for Scientific Research, he has recreated a Gallo-Roman winery – during the harvest you can watch the grapes being gathered and pressed in the old Roman way and later see the wine bottled, or rather amphora-ed, in jars from 5 to 1,000 litres, wrapped in straw to keep them from breaking in transit. You can taste and buy the result, although there's no way of knowing how close it comes to the stuff quaffed by Nero and Co. – the Romans added lime, egg whites, plaster, clay, mushroom ashes and pig blood to 'improve' their wines, and Durand does not.

Beaucaire's Roman incarnation, Ugernum, made its living transferring goods (including its wine) along the Roman 'superhighway', the **Via Domitia** that linked Rome to Spain. An 8km stretch of this has come through in remarkably good nick, especially in a place known as **Les Bornes Milliaires** (take the D999 1km northwest past the train tracks, turn left and continue for 800m, following the Enclos d'Argent lane). Nowhere else along the route have the milestones survived so well: these three, on the 13th mile between Nîmes and Ugernum, were erected by Augustus, Tiberius and Antoninus Pius.

In the same area, the unique and vaguely spooky **Abbaye Troglodytique Saint-Roman**, 4km up the D999 (*t 04 66 59 52 26; open April–June daily 10–6, July and Aug daily 10–6.30, Oct–Mar Sat and Sun 2–5; adm*), was founded in a cave in the perilous 5th century and laboriously carved out of the living rock. It was mentioned in the chronicles in 1363, when Pope Urban V made it a *studium*, a school open even to the poorest children, but by 1537 it had lost its importance and was engulfed in the construction of a fortress. When the fortress in turn lost its importance in the 19th century and was destroyed, the abbey was rediscovered: the chapel, with its remarkable abbot's chair; the subterranean cells; the water cisterns and wine press; and 150 rock-cut tombs in the necropolis on the upper terrace, from where the dead monks had better views than the live ones down below.

Northeast of Beaucaire, **Valabrègues**, 'the most Provençal town of Languedoc', was cut off from the rest of the Gard when the Rhône changed its bed. Surrounded by clumps of osier, it makes its living from wicker and basketry: learn all about it in the Musée de la Vannerie (*t 04 66 59 48 14; open Easter–Oct Wed–Sun 3–7; adm*).

Down the Rhône 2:
The Alpilles, Crau and Camargue

10

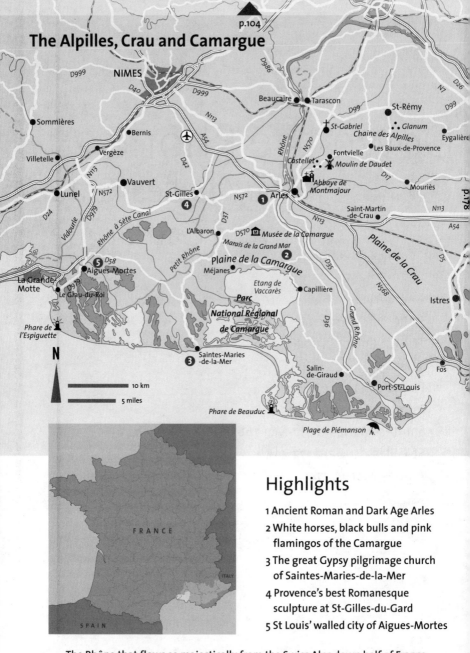

The Alpilles, Crau and Camargue

p.104

NIMES

Sommières

Bernis

Villetelle

Vergèze

Vauvert

Lunel

St-Gilles

L'Albaron

Méjanes

La Grande Motte

Le Grau-du-Roi

Aigues-Mortes

Phare de l'Espiguette

Beaucaire • Tarascon

St-Rémy

St-Gabriel

Glanum

Chaine des Alpilles

Eygalière

Fontvieille

Les Baux-de-Provence

Castellet

Moulin de Daudet

Abbaye de Montmajour

Mouriès

Arles

Saint-Martin-de-Crau

Musée de la Camargue

Marais de la Grand Mar

Plaine de la Crau

plaine de la Camargue

Etang de Vaccarès

Capillière

Istres

Parc National Régional de Camargue

Saintes-Maries-de-la-Mer

Salin-de-Giraud

Fos

Port-St-Louis

Phare de Beauduc

Plage de Piémanson

N

10 km

5 miles

FRANCE

ITALY

SPAIN

Highlights

1 Ancient Roman and Dark Age Arles
2 White horses, black bulls and pink flamingos of the Camargue
3 The great Gypsy pilgrimage church of Saintes-Maries-de-la-Mer
4 Provence's best Romanesque sculpture at St-Gilles-du-Gard
5 St Louis' walled city of Aigues-Mortes

The Rhône that flows so majestically from the Swiss Alps down half of France comes to a rather messy end in the Camargue, dithering indecisively through a delta of swamps, salt pans and sand dunes. And yet if all the chapters of this book had to compete in a talent show, this would be the one to beat. It has wild bulls, horses and pink flamingos; it has the cowboys, Gypsies and the fancy dress of the Arlésiennes; it has Roman ruins, the best Romanesque art and the most romantic stories, worthy of Sir Walter Scott; it has the sharpest mountains, a plain so uncanny that it took a myth to explain it and the mistral-whipped landscapes painted by Van Gogh; and it has the biggest bullring, France's only AOC hay (from Arles) and all the aluminium ore you could ask for.

St-Rémy-de-Provence

Enclosed by a garland of boulevards lined with plane trees, St-Rémy's tranquillity has attracted its share of the famous. Nostradamus was born here, Gertrude Stein spent years here, Charles Gounod stayed here while writing his opera based on Mistral's *Mireille*, and Princess Caroline of Monaco drops in for discreet visits (St-Rémy used to belong to the family). Vincent Van Gogh spent his tragic last year in St-Rémy's asylum, which was commandeered to hold interned Germans in the First World War – the one who got Van Gogh's room was Albert Schweitzer.

Nowadays, St-Rémy is home to a good many artists, and there are always exhibitions going on. The newest attraction is the bizarre-looking organ in the **church of St-Martin** on Bd Marceau. Built only in 1983, it is said to be one of the finest in the world; the Organ Festival in August pulls out all the stops, as do the Saturday afternoon concerts in summer and autumn.

Older attractions are two fine Renaissance palaces, both around Place Flavier, behind the church one street to the north. The **Hôtel Mistral de Mondragon** (1550) contains the **Musée des Alpilles** (*t 04 90 92 68 24; open Mar–Dec daily 10–12 and 2–5, longer hours in summer; adm*), local folk life and arts, with a special section on Nostradamus; the **Hôtel de Sade** has a small but interesting **Musée Archéologique** (*t 04 90 92 64 04; open daily July and Aug 10–12 and 2–7, the rest of the year 10–12 and 2–5; adm; guided tours in French every hour; combined ticket with Glanum and Musée des Alpilles available*). St-Rémy is the medieval successor to the abandoned Roman town of Glanum (*see* below); finds on display here include architectural fragments, statues and reliefs of deities from Hermes to the Phrygian god Attis, and Roman glass and jewellery.

The Grimaldi representative in St-Rémy lived in the beautiful 18th-century **Hôtel Estrine**, in Rue Estrine, now the **Centre d'Art Présence Vincent Van Gogh** (*t 04 90 92 34 72; open April–Dec Tues–Sun 10.30–12.30 and 2.30–6.30; adm*), where you'll find a permanent exhibition of photos and documents, plus a film on Van Gogh's life, as well as changing exhibitions of classic and contemporary art.

Other places to visit in the centre include the **Parfumerie Artisanale** at 34 Boulevard Mirabeau, with a display of scents, classic bottles, and others dating back 3,000 years; and the 12th-century **Chapelle Notre-Dame de Pitié Donation Prassinos**, near the tourist office on Avenue Durand Maillane (*t 04 90 92 35 13; open Mar–Dec daily 2–6, July and Aug 11–1 and 3–7; adm*), containing 11 *Peintures du Supplice* painted for the chapel by Greek painter Mario Prassinos, long-time resident of nearby Eygalières, as well as a video on the artist and displays of some of 105 works he donated to the French government in 1985.

Getting Around

By Bus

Although there are no trains, St-Rémy is a crossroads, surrounded by several big towns; consequently the bus service is slightly better than in most places. All leave from Place de la République, across from the church. There's at least one a day to Arles, Tarascon, Cavaillon and Aix; more to Avignon. You can easily walk to Les Antiques (*see* below) and Glanum, but buses from St-Rémy to Les Baux are rare and inconvenient. The latter is better connected to Arles, with four or five buses a day, stopping at Fontvieille.

By Bike

The Alpilles are not too steep for cycling in most places; the tourist office in St-Rémy has a list of bike-hire firms. You might enjoy a tour around the southern slopes of the Alpilles, near St-Rémy, looking for the spots where Van Gogh painted many of his famous landscapes (inaccessible July–Sept).

Tourist Information

Tourist office: Place Jean-Jaurès, on the way to Les Antiques, t 04 90 92 05 22, f 04 90 92 38 52, *www.saintremy-de-provence.com*. *Open mid-June–mid-Sept Mon–Sat 9–12 and 2–7, Sun 9–12; mid-Sept–mid-June Mon–Sat 9–12 and 2–6*.

Market Day

Wednesday morning.

Where to Stay and Eat

St-Rémy ✉ 13210

St-Rémy gets heaps of tourists, and consequently has a wide choice of places to stay; it makes a convenient base for visiting the Alpilles and the Camargue. Most places to stay are on the outskirts.

****Le Vallon de Valrugues, Chemin de Canto Cigalo, t 04 90 92 04 40, f 04 90 92 44 01, *vallon.valrugues@wanadoo.fr*, *www.valrugues-cassagne.com* (*expensive*).

Les Antiques, and Van Gogh's Asylum

The Romans had a habit of building monuments and impressive mausoleums on the outskirts of their towns, along the main roads. Just a 15-minute walk from the centre of St-Rémy, south on the D5, stand two of the most remarkable Roman relics in France. They were here long before the D5, of course; originally they decorated the end of the Roman road from Arles to Glanum, the ruins of which lie just across the D5. The **Triumphal Arch**, probably built in the reign of Augustus, was one of the first to be erected in Provence. Its elegant form and marble columns show the Greek sensibility of the artists, far different from the strange Celtic-influenced arches of Orange and Carpentras. In the Middle Ages it inspired the creators of St-Trophime in Arles. Evidently, someone long ago carted off the top for building stone; the slanted tile roof is an 18th-century addition to protect what was actually left.

Next to it, the so-called **Mausoleum** was really a memorial to Caesar and Augustus, erected by their descendants in the early 1st century AD. There is nothing else quite like this anywhere, and it is one of the best-preserved Roman monuments. The form is certainly original: a narrow four-faced arch on a solid plinth, surmounted by a cylinder of columns and a pointed roof, 56ft above the ground; inside are statues of Caesar and Augustus. The **reliefs** on the base are excellent work: mythological scenes including a *battle with Amazons*, a *battle of Greeks and Trojans* and a *boar hunt*. At the top of the arch, you can make out a pair of winged spirits holding a civic crown of laurel – Augustus' symbol for his new political order.

Waiting to spoil you with lovely Provençal-style rooms, pool, sauna, Jacuzzi, putting green and delicious meals (including lots of seafood and truffles, in season) in the palatial restaurant serving the best gourmet feasts in town.

****Château des Alpilles**, D31, **t** 04 90 92 03 33, **f** 04 90 92 45 17, *chateau.alpilles@ wanadoo.fr* (*expensive*). Outside the busy one-way rush of traffic round the centre, yet just a few steps out of town, in a park of trees (some rare), and with a tennis court and pool. It's all mirrors, period furniture (19th century) and creature comforts; the restaurant is for hotel guests only. *Closed mid-Nov–mid-Feb; restaurant closed Wed.*

***Castellet des Alpilles**, 6 Place Mireille, **t** 04 90 92 07 21, **f** 04 90 92 52 03, *hotel. castel.alpilles@wanadoo.fr* (*moderate– inexpensive*). An old country mansion with pretty rooms and a lovely terrace under a century-old cedar. *Closed Nov–Easter.*

Villa Glanum, 46 Av Van Gogh, **t** 04 90 92 03 59, **f** 04 90 92 00 08, *villa.glanum@ wanadoo.fr* (*inexpensive*). Near the ruins, this has some surprising amenities for an inexpensive hotel: a pool and garden. *Closed Nov–mid-Mar.*

****Du Cheval Blanc**, 6 Av Fauconnet, **t** 04 90 92 09 28, **f** 04 90 92 69 05 (*inexpensive*). Be warned, the centre is noisy, but if you want to look out onto the *place* as you wake, try this place. The owners are cheerful and it has a garage. *Closed Jan.*

La Maison Jaune, 15 Rue Carnot, **t** 04 90 92 56 14 (*expensive*). For dining in central St-Rémy, you won't do better than the panoramic terrace here, especially if you plump for the menu of Provençal specialities. *Closed Sun eve and Mon in winter, Jan and Feb.*

L'Assiette de Marie, 1 Rue Jaume Roux, **t** 04 90 92 32 14 (*moderate*). Vegetarians (and others) will find joy here; try the home-made pasta. Good wine list. *Closed Tues in winter and Mon lunch.*

Le Bistrot des Alpilles, 15 Bd Mirabeau, **t** 04 90 92 09 17 (*moderate*). Fresh pasta, great desserts and a pleasant terrace. *Closed Sun.*

Just across the road from Les Antiques, a shady path leads to the **monastery of St-Paul-de-Mausole** (*t 04 90 92 77 00; open April–Oct Mon–Fri 9.30–7, Sat and Sun 10.30–7; Nov–Mar daily 10.30–1 and 1.30–5; adm*), in a beautiful setting with gardens all around. Founded in the 10th century, the complex includes a simple Romanesque church and a cloister. In 1810 the monastery buildings were purchased for use as a private hospital. This is the place Vincent Van Gogh chose as a refuge from the troubles of life in the outside world, in May 1890, not long after he chopped off the ear. He spent a year here, the most intense and original period of his career, painting as if possessed – 150 canvases and over 100 drawings, including many of his most famous works, such as *Nuit étoilée* (*Starry Night*) and *Les Blés Jaunes* (*Cornfield and Cypress Trees*). The blueish mountains in the background of this work and many others are the Alpilles. Appropriately enough, the patients and staff of the hospital have taken a keen interest in art therapy: you can see the results on the walls of the lovely cloister, as well as some interesting carved capitals.

Van Gogh painted the impressive Greco-Roman quarries (*La Carrière de St-Rémy*) just down the road, writing that they resembled a Japanese drawing. In the midst of the quarries, excavated out of the rock, the **Mas de la Pyramide** (*open daily 9–12 and 2–5, to 7pm in summer; adm*) is one of the oldest farmhouses in the region – it dates at least from the 8th century. It contains typical Provençal furnishings and a collection of 19th-century farm tools.

Glanum

Glanum began as a Celtic settlement – a proper town, really, under a heavy cultural influence from the Greeks at nearby Marseille. The Romans under Marius snatched it around 100 BC, but not until the great prosperity of the Augustan Empire did the city begin to bloom. Almost all of the ruins visible today (as well as Les Antiques) date from this period. In a prelude to the fall of the Empire, the Franks and Alemanni ranged throughout Gaul in the 250s and 260s. In one of their last hurrahs before the recovering Roman legions drove them out, they sacked Glanum in 270. After that, the townspeople relocated to a healthier and safer site, today's St-Rémy; silt washed down from the Alpilles gradually covered the city and it passed out of memory until the 19th century, when some accidental finds alerted archaeologists to its presence. Excavations began in 1921, and have since uncovered a fascinating cross section of Glanum, including its Forum.

More than Vaison-la-Romaine or anywhere else in France, this is the place to really feel at home in the Roman world. But you'll have to work for it; only the foundations remain, and recreating Glanum will require a bit of imagination (see the museum in the Hôtel de Sade first). From the entrance, to the left are the **Maison des Antes** and the **Maison d'Atys**, two typical wealthy homes built around peristyle courtyards. The latter had apparently been transformed into a sanctuary of Cybele and Attis; this cult was one of the most popular of the mystery religions imported from the east in Imperial times.

Across the street are remains of a fountain and the **thermae** (baths), with mosaics, a *palestra* (exercise yard) and a *piscina* (pool). Next door is a building with an exedra that was probably a temple; altars to Silenus were found inside. In this part of the street the **sewers** have been uncovered. The **forum** wasn't very impressive, by the standards of most Roman towns, and it is hard to make anything out today from the confusion of buildings from various ages that have been excavated. Beyond it, to the right, are foundations of temples; to the left are bases of another fountain and a monument. The street closes at a **gate** from Hellenistic times that was retained as the city expanded outside the original walls. Also retained was the **nymphaeum** beyond it, to the left; these decorated fountains were a common feature of Greek cities, built to allow travellers to refresh and clean up before entering the town.

The Chaîne des Alpilles

The ruins were nice, but there is an even greater treat ahead. The five twisting kilometres of the D5 that take you from Les Antiques into the heart of the Alpilles are, in fact, one of the greatest sensual experiences Provence can offer. Van Gogh and cypresses, lushness and flowers are left behind; in a matter of minutes the road has brought you to another world. This world, incredibly, is at most 16km across, and a stone's throw from the swamps of the Camargue and the sea. It is made of thin, cool breezes and brilliant light; its colours are white and deep green – almost exclusively – in an astringent landscape of limestone crags and patches of scrubby *maquis*.

Les Baux-de-Provence

A l'asard, Bauthezar! ('Kill 'em at random, Balthazar!')
Battle cry of the Seigneurs des Baux

From as early as 3000 BC, this exotic massif attracted residents. The Alpilles are full of caves, many of which were once inhabited. The Ligurians took advantage of its natural defences to found an important *oppidum* at Les Baux, a steep barren plateau in the centre of the massif, 11km from St-Rémy. In the Middle Ages, this made the perfect setting for the most feared and celebrated of Provence's noble clans. The Seigneurs des Baux are first heard of in the 10th century. 'A race of eaglets, vassals never', as their slogan went, they never acknowledged the authority of the French king, the emperors, or anyone else, and their impregnable crag in the Alpilles allowed them to get away with it. They claimed to be descended from Balthazar, one of the magi at Bethlehem, and put the Christmas star on their feudal escutcheon.

The symbol was never a harbinger of glad tidings to their neighbours, however, for during the next two centuries the lords of Baux waged incessant warfare on all comers, and occasionally on each other, gradually becoming a real power in Provence. They did it with flair, and the chronicles are full of good stories about them: one seigneur once besieged the castle of his pregnant niece and sent sappers to undermine her bedchamber. And they met memorable ends: one was stabbed to death by his wife, another flayed alive when he fell into the hands of his enemies. All the while, the family headquarters at Les Baux maintained a polished court where troubadours

Tourist Information

Les Baux ✉ **13520**: Impasse du Château, t 04 90 54 34 39, f 04 90 54 51 15, *tourisme@lesbauxdeprovence.com*, *www.lesbauxdeprovence.com*. *Open summer daily 9–7, winter daily 9–6.*
Fontvieille ✉ **13990**: 5 Rue M. Honorat, t 04 90 54 67 49, f 04 90 54 69 82, *ot.fontvieille@visitprovence,com*, *www.fontvieille-provence.com*. *Open Mon–Sat 9–12 and 2–6.*

Market Days
Fontvieille: Monday and Friday.

Where to Stay and Eat

Les Baux ✉ 13520
Les Baux, with its tourist hordes, isn't the most desirable place to stop over – and you'll have to pay a lot for the privilege.
★★★★**Oustau de Baumanière**, Route d'Arles, t 04 90 54 33 07, f 04 90 54 40 46, *contact@oustaudebaumaniere.com*, *www.oustaudebaumaniere.com* (*expensive*). In magical surroundings in the Val d'Enfer, this is a restored farmhouse with all the amenities, along with a highly rated restaurant (two Michelin stars) and a spectacular terrace view. There are sumptuous desserts and a formidable wine list (over 100,000 bottles) of Provençal treasures (*luxury*). *Closed Jan and Feb.*
★★★★**La Cabro d'Or**, D27, t 04 90 54 33 21, f 04 90 54 45 98, *contact@lacabrodor.com*, *www.lacabrodor.com* (*expensive*). This charming place has recently undergone a complete rehab and offers similar facilities to L'Oustau de Baumanière for kinder prices, as well as the expertise of a chef trained with Ducasse and Robouchon. *Closed Mon and Tues lunch in winter.*
★★★**Mas d'Aigret**, literally cut into the rocks just below Les Baux (east on the D27), t 04 90 54 20 00, f 04 90 54 44 00, *contact@masdaigret.com*, *www.masdaigret.com* (*expensive–moderate*). Some rooms have great views, others open onto the gardens; other rooms (*chambres troglodytes*) are

were always welcome. It ended with a bang in 1372, when an even nastier fellow took over: Raymond de Turenne, a distant relation who was also a nephew of Pope Gregory IX. Taking advantage of confused times in the reign of Queen Jeanne, this ambitious and bloodthirsty intriguer found enough support, and enough foreign mercenaries, to bring full-scale civil war to Provence, bringing it the same kind of misery to which the rest of France had become accustomed in the Hundred Years' War.

When the last heir of Les Baux died in 1426, the possessions of the house were incorporated into the County of Provence. That isn't quite the end of the story; in the 16th century Les Baux began to thrive once more, first under Anne of Montmorency, who rebuilt the Seigneurs' castle in the best Renaissance taste, and later under the Manvilles, who inherited it and made it a Protestant stronghold in the Wars of Religion. Cardinal Richelieu finally put this eternal troublespot to rest in 1632, demolishing the castle and sending the owners the bill for the job. Until the Revolution, the remains of Les Baux were, like St-Rémy, in the hands of the Grimaldis of Monaco.

After the demolition, the village that surrounded the castle of Les Baux almost disappeared; Prosper Mérimée, in the 1830s, reported only a few beggars living among its ruins. But Provençal writers kept the place from being forgotten, men such as Mistral (born at Maillane, near St-Rémy) and Alphonse Daudet, whose famous windmill is just over the Alpilles (*see* below). In the last 50 years, Les Baux has become the second-biggest tourist attraction in France after the Mont St-Michel. The village below the castle has been rebuilt and repopulated in the worst way, and whatever spark of glamour survives in this tremendous ruin, you will have to run the gauntlet

---

actually hewn from the rock face. There is a pool, and attention to every detail.

★★★Mas de L'Oulivié, t 04 90 54 35 78, **f** 04 90 54 44 31, *contact@masdeloulivie.com* (*expensive*). A modern hotel built in traditional Provençal style among the olive groves and lavender fields. Lunch is served around a landscaped pool. Elegant, comfortable, with attentive service and care. *Closed mid-Nov–mid-Mar.*

★★Hostellerie de la Reine Jeanne, t 04 90 54 32 06, **f** 04 90 54 32 33 (*inexpensive; restaurant moderate*). In the village itself and relatively cheap, with a bird's-eye view. *Closed Nov–mid-Dec.*

Fontvieille ✉ 13990

★★★★La Régalido, 118 Rue Mistral, **t** 04 90 54 60 22, **f** 04 90 54 64 29, *la-regalido@wanadoo.fr, www.relaischateaux.com/regalido* (*expensive*). A luxurious Relais & Châteaux hotel in a restored mill with lovely gardens, and a restaurant that is a little temple of *haute cuisine* with prices to match, serving *agneau des Alpilles* or a

special menu entirely dedicated to the olive. *Closed Jan–mid-Feb; restaurant closed Mon, Tues lunch and Sat lunch.*

★★★Le Val Majour, 22 Route d'Arles, **t** 04 90 54 62 33, **f** 04 90 54 61 67, *contact@hotel-valmajour.com, www.hotel-majour.com* (*moderate–inexpensive*). Well-furnished quiet rooms, with a pool and tennis, and a restaurant next door, giving 10% discount to hotel residents.

★★Hôtel de la Tour, 3 Rue des Plumelets, **t** 04 90 54 72 21 (*inexpensive*). Budget rooms, with a pool. *Closed Nov–mid-Mar* .

★Chez Bernard, 6 Cours M. Bellon, **t** 04 90 54 70 35, **f** 04 90 54 68 59 (*inexpensive*).

La Cuisine du Planet, 144 Grand Rue, **t** 04 90 54 63 97 (*moderate*). An excellent three-course summer menu and great desserts.

Le Homard, 29 Route du Nord, **t** 04 90 54 75 34. Appetizing home cooking; no lobster, but *terrine de poisson, filet de rascasse* and *cassoulet* feature on the menus (*moderate*), washed down with local Coteaux des Baux wines. Be sure to reserve. *Closed mid-Nov–mid-Feb.*

of shops peddling trinkets, knick-knackery, scowling dolls, herbs, *santons* and soaps to reach it.

The first sight to greet you as you trudge up from the car park is an elegant carved Renaissance fireplace, open to the sky and standing next to a souvenir shop. Walk a bit further, bearing right, and you will come to the **Musée des Santons** on Place Louis Jou, which you could give a miss. Up the street, past the ramparts, is the **Porte d'Eyguères**, which until the 18th century was the only entrance to the city.

Up the Rue de la Calade you will come to the Place de l'Eglise, where the 16th-century **Hôtel des Porcelet** has now become the **Musée Yves Brayer** (*t 04 90 54 36 99; open daily April–Sept 10–12.30 and 2–6.30, Oct–Mar 10–12.30 and 2–5.30, closed Jan–mid-Feb; adm*). Brayer (1907–90), a respected figurative painter, left his major works here, pictures of Spain and Italy as well as Provence; you can get a preview of his work in the 17th-century **Chapelle des Pénitents Blancs** opposite, where he frescoed scenes of a shepherds' Christmas (*same hours as museum*). **St-Vincent**, in the same square, dates from the 12th and 16th centuries. This is probably the coolest and least crowded place in Les Baux; there's a Cistercian nave, and stained glass by Max Ingrand (1955) donated by Prince Rainier of Monaco. The domed turret with gargoyles on the south side is a *Lanterne des Morts*, a rare medieval survival: whenever anyone died in Les Baux, it would be announced by a flame.

Also in the village are the **Hôtel Jean de Brion** and the **Hôtel de Manville**, on the Grand' Rue. The first houses the **Fondation Louis Jou** (*visit by appointment only, t 04 90 54 34 17; adm*), containing Jou's engravings, as well as pre-20th-century ones, engravings by Dürer, Rembrandt and Goya and early books. The second is the Hôtel de Ville. Both these and the Hôtel des Porcelet date from the architectural development of the 16th century, before the castle was destroyed.

Next, to the **Citadel** (*t 04 90 54 55 56; open 9–6.30, to 8.30pm July and Aug, to 5pm in winter; adm*), and a new museum to keep the tramping tourists from the thing itself. The **Musée d'Histoire des Baux** is perfectly nice, with illustrations and archaeological finds as well as models in glass cases, to give you an overview, or to save you the walk over the site outside if the mistral's blowing.

When you see Les Baux itself, the ambience changes abruptly – a rocky chaos surrealistically decorated with fragments of once-imposing buildings. The path leads through this 'Ville Morte' (on the left are remains of the hospital and the chapelle Saint-Blaise, where you can watch a slide show on the olive tree) to the tip of the plateau, where there is a monument to Provençal poet Charlon Rieu, and a grand view over the Alpilles.

Turning back, the path climbs up to the **château** itself, with bits of towers and walls everywhere, including the apse of a Gothic chapel cut out of the rock, and the long eastern wall that survived Richelieu's explosives, dotted with finely carved windows. What looks like a monolithic honeycomb is really a 13th-century pigeonry. Medieval siege engines have been reconstructed to add something of the spirit of the gangsters who built the place. The only intact part is the **donjon**, a rather treacherous climb to the top for a bird's-eye view over the site. Locals say the best time to see it is with a blanket, under a starry night.

Wine: Coteaux des Baux-en-Provence

The AOC wine of the Alpilles is rosé, like most of Provence's vintages, but in recent years the reds of Les Baux have made a quantum jump in quality and attracted the most attention. This relatively new appellation comes under the heading of Coteaux d'Aix-en-Provence, and a majority of its growers are good environmentalists dedicated to growing grapes free from artificial fertilizers, pesticides and herbicides; the grapes that grow into it include grenache, cabernet-sauvignon, syrah, cinsault, carignan and counoise.

A good source is the charming **Domaine de La Vallongue**, in Eygalières, t 04 90 95 91 70, which uses traditional methods to create organic wines: fresh, fruity, fragrant rosés and intense reds, hinting at vanilla and spice; every year between 1985 and 1990 was a happy success, as were 1993 and 94. **Domaine Hauvette**, in St-Rémy, t 04 90 92 03 90, is a tiny estate, but one of the few vineyards in the region both owned and run by a woman, Dominique Hauvette, whose wines (also organic) have a warm, velvety quality, especially the 1990.

In Les Baux itself, at the foot of the cliffs, visitors can take a didactic nature walk through the vines of **Mas Ste-Berthe**, t 04 90 54 39 01, and learn all about the grapes, some of which (ugni blanc, sauvignon and grenache blanc) go into the white wine. The sombre red, especially the 1990, is excellent and is still reasonably priced.

An Infernal Valley and a Blonde Sorceress

Beneath Les Baux, on the western side, the **Pavillon de la Reine Jeanne** has nothing to do with the famous queen, but is a pretty Renaissance garden folly of 1581. The road that passes it will take you in another 3km to the **Val d'Enfer**, the wildest corner of the Alpilles, a weird landscape of eroded limestone, caves and quarries. One thing the Alpilles has a lot of is aluminium ore – bauxite – a useless mineral until the process for smelting it was discovered in the 19th century. Now there are bauxite mines all over southern Provence; those to be seen here are exhausted, but Jean Cocteau took advantage of the landscape to shoot part of his last film, *Testament d'Orphée*. Today the quarries host one of Les Baux's big attractions, the **Cathédrale d'Images** (t 04 90 54 38 65; open daily Mar–Sept 10–7, Oct–Feb 10–6; adm), a slick show where 30 projectors bounce giant pictures over the walls; the theme of the show changes annually.

Off the D27A, near the crossroads for Les Baux, the **Col de la Vayède** holds scanty remains of the pre-Roman *oppidum*; the lines of the walls can be traced in some places, and there are bits of wall and no fewer than three necropolises, with small niches carved into the rock to hold the ashes of the deceased. On the side of the hill facing the D27A, you can climb up a dirt path to see the mysterious relief called the **Trémaïé**. Neatly carved on a smoothed rock face are three figures and an effaced Latin inscription. It seems to be a Roman funeral monument, but local legend has it that the figures represent Marius, his wife and a blonde Celtic sorceress named Marthe who helped Marius in his campaigns against the Teutones. Another relief, less well preserved, can be seen a few hundred metres to the south. Finally, for hikers, there is the GR6 trail, which traverses the best parts of the Alpilles from east to west. It passes right through Les Baux.

St-Gabriel and Fontvieille

The eastern half of the Alpilles is the more scenic, and, if you're heading in that direction, lonely roads like the D78 and D24 make worthwhile detours that won't take you more than a few kilometres out of the way; **Eygalières**, on the D24B, is a lovely village with a ruined castle.

Along the western fringes of the Alpilles, on the D33, you will pass the canal port of Ernaginum, later called St-Gabriel, which flourished from Roman times until the Middle Ages. You won't see anything; the drying-up of the old canal doomed the city to a slow death, and Ernaginum has disappeared more completely than any ancient city of Provence, leaving only the impressive 12th-century **church of St-Gabriel** standing alone in open fields. There is little to see inside and it's never open anyhow; the real interest is one of the finest Romanesque façades in the Midi. Very consciously imitating Roman architecture, it shows a stately portal with a triangular pediment, flanked by Corinthian columns. There are excellent sculpted reliefs on and above the tympanum: an *Annunciation*, *Daniel in the Lions' Den* and *Adam and Eve*, apparently just realizing they have no clothes on. Above it, a small Italianate rose window is surrounded by figures of the four Evangelists.

From here, the only village on the way to Arles is **Fontvieille**, best known for the **Moulin de Daudet**, south on the D33, a rare survivor among the hundreds of windmills that once embellished every hill top of southern Provence. Alphonse Daudet never really lived here, but his *Lettres de mon moulin*, a collection of sentimental tales of the dying life of rural Provence in the late 19th century, is still popular across France today. The windmill has become a museum to Daudet, with photographs and documents. It has a huge car park where coaches like fridges on wheels disgorge cooled tourists, and local driving instructors take their pupils to practise. Two kilometres further south, there are sections of two Roman **aqueducts** that served Arles, along with vestiges of a **Roman mill**, unique in Europe. This huge installation was a serious precursor to the Industrial Revolution, using the flow of the water to power 16 separate mills along a stretch of canal over a kilometre long; nothing like it has been found anywhere else. There's no tourist tack, not even a railing. Give Daudet a miss for this.

The Hypogeum of Castellet

On the D17, at the crossroads with the D82, you will find a very ruined castle that once belonged to the counts of Provence. The surrounding area, a low, flat-topped hill called Castellet, contains one of the most unusual and least-known Neolithic monuments in France. The **Hypogeum** consists of four covered avenues, carefully carved out of the rock or earth, under tumuli that have long since disappeared. They were made as collective tombs about 3500 BC or later by the Ligurians or their predecessors, and probably also served as a kind of temple. Many have carvings, cup-marks and sun-symbols, inside or near their openings. The sites are not marked, and you may have to scramble and scout to find their narrow, trapezoidal entrances in the undergrowth. All are within 200 yards of the D17, three south of the road and one north.

From Castellet you'll see another hill, the **Montagne de Cordes**, about half a kilometre to the south. Like Castellet, this was an island in Neolithic times. Nearby Montmajour (*see* below) was a third. The Cordes is private property and you'll need permission from the owner (in the farmhouse on the slopes) to see another remarkable tomb-temple. The **Grotte des Fées** is also known as the 'Epée de Roland'; the tapering 230ft tunnel has two small side chambers that give it the shape of a sword.

Abbaye de Montmajour

Just before Arles, the D17 passes one of the most important monasteries of medieval Provence. Founded in the 10th century, on what was then almost an island amidst the swamps, this Benedictine abbey was devoted to reclaiming the land, a monumental labour that would take centuries to complete. By the 14th century, the monastery had grown exceedingly wealthy, a real prize for the Avignon popes, who gained control of it and farmed it out, along with its revenues, to friends and relations. Under such absentee abbots, it languished thereafter, and its great church was never completed. To give some idea of its later decadence, an attempt to reform it in 1639 included importing new monks; the old crew refused to go and sacked the abbey before they were chased out by royal troops.

Montmajour became a national property not in the Revolution, but five years earlier. The 1786 'Affair of the Diamond Necklace' was a famous swindle that involved both Marie Antoinette and the great charlatan Cagliostro. One of the principal players was Montmajour's abbot, the Cardinal de Rohan; he got caught, and all his property, including the abbey, was confiscated. The abbey did service as a farmhouse, and its church as a barn, before restorations began in 1907. Consequently, there isn't much to see.

At the church entrance you'll notice the piers, built into the adjacent wall of the cloister, that would have supported the nave had it been completed. The interior is austere and empty, but gives a good idea of the state of Provençal architecture c. 1200, in transition from Romanesque to Gothic. The most interesting part is the **lower church**, a crypt with an unusual plan, including a long, narrow nave and a circular enclosure under the high altar, with radiating chapels behind it; its purpose has not been explained.

The **cloister** has some fanciful sculptural decoration; see if you can find the camel. Around the back of the church, you'll see a number of tombs cut out of the rock; these are a mystery too, and may predate the abbey. The mighty 85ft **donjon** was built in the 1360s for defence, in that terrible age when the lords of Les Baux and a dozen other hoodlums were tearing up the neighbourhood; next to it, the tiny chapel of **St-Pierre** (usually closed) was the original abbey church, built on the spot where St Trophime of Arles (*see* below) had his hermitage.

Ste-Croix

A few hundred yards behind the apse of the church, in the middle of a farm, stands what was the abbey's funeral chapel, **Ste-Croix**. Don't miss it, even though you'll have to walk through the farmyard muck (it's visible from the road, near a barn). Few buildings show so convincingly the architectural sophistication of the Romanesque as this small work of the late 11th century, a central-plan chapel with apses along three sidesand an elegant lantern on top. Some complex geometry and a mastery of proportions went into this simple but perfect form, based on the Golden Section. Too much decoration would be superfluous, and there is only a discreet carved floral frieze along the cornice, along with Moorish-style interlocking arches.

Arles

Like Nîmes, Arles has enough intact antiquities to call itself the 'Rome of France'; unlike Nîmes, it lingered in the post-Roman limelight for another thousand years, producing enough saints for every month on the calendar – Trophimus, Hilarius, Césaire and Genès are some of the more famous. Pilgrims flocked here for a whiff of their odour of sanctity, and asked on their deathbeds to be buried in the holy ground of the Alyscamps. Nowadays, Arles holds the distinction of being the largest *commune* in France, ten times larger than Paris, embracing 750 square kilometres of the Camargue and Crau plains; it has given the world the rhythms of the Gypsy Kings and the pungent joys of *saucisson d'Arles*, France's finest donkey-meat sausage.

Henry James wrote: 'As a city Arles quite misses its effect in every way: and if it is a charming place, as I think it is, I can hardly tell the reason why.' Modern Arles, sitting amidst its ruins, is still somehow charming, in spite of a general scruffiness that seems more intentional than natural. For all the tourists it gets, no town could seem less touristy; a noxious paper mill across the Rhône wafts its stink over the comfortably-at-heel old quarters, while grass grows up between the pavement cracks around the Roman ruins and medieval palaces. Unhappily, Jeanne Calment, born here in 1876, who met Van Gogh as a young girl and was for a long while the oldest person in the world, died in 1997. The city's pride in her longevity continues though, and the way to her grave is clearly marked in the cemetery at Trinquetaille.

History

In 1975 the remains of a Celto-Ligurian settlement were uncovered near the Boulevard des Lices. It's hard to imagine what its builders thought in the 6th century BC, when Greek traders from Marseille arrived and began to haggle over prices. We know at least that the Greeks were pleased, and over the years they established the site as their principal 'counter' for dealings with the Ligurians, calling it Arelate ('near sleeping waters' or, less poetically, 'bog town'). Business picked up considerably after Marius' legionaries made Arelate a seaport by digging a canal to Fos (104 BC). In 49 BC the populace, tired of getting bum deals from the wily Greeks, readily gave Caesar the boats he needed to punish and conquer Marseille for siding with Pompey. In return,

Getting Around

By Train

The train station is on the northern edge of town, on Avenue Paulin Talabot. Arles has frequent connections to Paris, Marseille, Montpellier, Nîmes, Aix-en-Provence, and to all the towns along the main line to Spain.

There are also frequent services to Avignon and Tarascon, and a less frequent service to Orange.

By Bus

The *gare routière* is just across the street from the train station, **t** 04 90 49 38 01. There are about five daily buses to Albaron and Stes-Maries-de-la-Mer in the Camargue, two to Tarascon, seven to Salon, Aix and Marseille, five to Avignon, six to Nîmes and two to St-Gilles, among other destinations; in July and August there are services to Aigues-Mortes.

(Before you hurry into Arles from here, step over the road for a minute to the bank of the Rhône and admire the city on the bend of the river; an unlikely spot for an unparalleled view.)

By Taxi

For a taxi day or night, call **t** 04 90 96 90 03 (Jardin d'Eté, Bd des Lices).

Car Hire

Europcar, t 04 90 93 23 24, **f** 04 90 96 18 99, and **Hertz, t** 04 90 96 75 23, **f** 04 90 93 21 95, are both on Av Victor Hugo.

Bike Hire

Hire a bike at the train station, at **Dall'Oppio,** Rue Portagnel, **t** 04 90 96 46 83 (*Mar–Oct*), or **Peugeot,** 15 Rue du Pont, **t** 04 90 96 03 77.

Tourist Information

Tourist offices: Bd des Lices, next to Hôtel Jules César, **t** 04 90 18 41 20, **f** 04 90 18 41 29, ot-arles@visitprovence.com, *www.arles.org. Open summer daily 9–6.45; winter Mon–Sat 9–5.45, Sun 10.30–2.30.* There's another office in the train station, **t** 04 90 49 36 90.

Post office: 5 Bd des Lices, **t** 04 90 18 41 00.

If you intend to see more than two of Arles' monuments and museums, stop at the tourist office to purchase the €12 **global ticket** to save money (you can also pick one up at any of the museums). The office also sells tickets for the 2hr **Van Gogh tours** of sites associated with the artist (*departing every Tues and Fri at 5pm, 1 July–30 Sept, in French only*).

Market Days

Saturday, Bd des Lices and Bd Georges-Clémenceau. Wednesday, Bd Émile Combes.

Arles was rewarded the spoils and received a population boost with a colony of veterans from the Sixth Legion. Most important of all, it got all the business that had previously gone through Greek Marseille. A bridge of boats was built over the Rhône, and the Colonia Julia Paterna Arelate Sextanorum was known far and wide for its powerful maritime corporations, called *utriculares* from their rafts that floated on inflated bladders.

At the crossroads of Rome's trading route between Italy and Spain and the Rhône, Arles grew rapidly, each century adding more splendid monuments – a theatre, temples, a circus, an amphitheatre, at least two triumphal arches and a basilica. Constantine built himself a grand palace and baths as big as Caracalla's in Rome. In AD 395, Emperor Honorius made it the capital of the 'Three Gauls' – France, Britain and Spain – and as late as 418 it was recorded that 'Arles is so fortunately placed, its commerce is so active and merchants come in such numbers that all the products of the universe are channelled there: the riches of the Orient, perfumes of Arabia, delicacies of Assyria...'

Arles was one of the last cities to fall to the Visigoths, only to become their capital in 476. The Franks inherited it in 536, and Saracen raids were frequent. But on the whole,

On the first Wednesday of every month there is a *foire à la brocante* on Bd des Lices.

Festivals and Annual Events

Arles does its best to keep its visitors entertained. The free broadsheet *Farandole* gives details of everything from theatre, concerts, fairs and exhibitions to local basketball results.

Easter is celebrated by a **Feria Pascale**, with four days of bullfights, most of them Spanish *corridas* (for ticket reservations for Arènes events, call **t** 04 90 96 03 70, **f** 04 90 46 64 31). On 24 June, **St John's Day**, there are typical Arlésien dances in costume around bonfires, and the distribution of blessed bread.

July is the busiest month, with a festival of music, dance and drama, the **Cocarde d'Or** bullfights, and the **Rencontres Internationales de la Photographie**, with shows and workshops, held in the Théâtre Antique. At the end of August there's the **Festival du Film Peplum**.

The last bullfights of the year, on the second Sunday in September, coincide with the **Prémices du Riz**, or rice harvest.

Shopping

L'Arlésienne, 12 Rue du Président-Wilson, **t** 04 90 93 28 05. Traditional clothes for women.
Arlys, 35 Rue Voltaire, **t** 04 90 96 45 89. Provençal fabrics and *santons*.

Cabane Soleil, 15 Rue du Quatre Septembre, **t** 04 90 96 07 34. Enchanting locally made puppets, as well as other modern curiosities in metal and wood.
Camille, 15 Bd Georges-Clemenceau, **t** 04 90 96 04 94. Authentic *gardian* costumes.
Les Olivades, 2 Rue Jean Jaurès, **t** 04 90 96 22 17. Colourful Provençal fabrics.
Puyricard, 5 Rue Dulau, **t** 04 90 93 46 91. Buy your *calissons d'Aix*, or come just to see the crystallized fruits, marzipan models, chocolates and other bright goodies stacked like small sugared mountains.

Any good butcher will sell you spicy donkey-filled *saucisson d'Arles*.

Where to Stay

Arles ✉ 13200

Arles offers relief for the budget-bruised traveller and charges less for more than you'll get in cities like Avignon or Aix.

If you arrive without a reservation, the tourist office has a room-finding service for a small fee.

Expensive

★★★★**Jules César** (locally known as *Chez Jules*), Bd des Lices, **t** 04 90 52 52 52, **f** 04 90 52 52 53, *julescesar2@hotel-julescesar.com*. The luxurious grand-daddy of hotels in Arles,

the Dark Ages were not so dark in Arles; from 879 to 1036 it served as the capital of Provence–Burgundy (the so-called 'Kingdom of Arles'), a vast territory that stretched all the way to Lorraine. Most importantly, Arles was a centre of power for Christianity. Several major Church councils convened here, including one back in 314 that condemned the heresy of Donatism (the quite reasonable belief that sacraments administered by bad priests had no value). Arles' cathedral of St-Trophime became the most important church in Provence; in 597 its bishop, St Virgil, consecrated St Augustine as first Bishop of Canterbury, and as late as 1178, Emperor Frederick Barbarossa was crowned King of Arles at its altar. After a busy career in the 11th and 12th centuries as a Crusader port and pilgrimage destination, the city's special history ended in 1239 when Raymond Bérenger, Count of Provence, evicted Arles' imperial viceroy. As the city declined even the sea abandoned it, leaving the former port stranded between marshes and the rocky plain of the Crau, compressed in a time capsule of Roman monuments and ancient customs.

With the improved communications of the 19th century, Arles slowly resurfaced. The Roman amphitheatre was restored. The city's women, celebrated for their beautiful Attic features, inspired Daudet's story *L'Arlésienne* (1866) and Bizet's occupying a former Dominican monastery with a Caesar-ish temple porch tacked on. The rooms are vast, air conditioned and furnished with Provençal pieces; the pool is heated and the gardens beautiful. *Closed Nov–23 Dec; restaurant closed Mon and Sat lunch.*

★★★★Nord Pinus, Place du Forum, t 04 90 93 44 44, f 04 90 93 34 00, *info@nord-pinus. com, www.nord-pinus.com*. Look out for the columns from a Roman temple embedded in its façade. Once the favourite of the Félibres, poets and literati like Stendhal, Mérimée and Henry James, it now draws the top matadors and wealthy aficionados. The premises are comfortable and full of heavy dark furniture, bullfighting posters, trophies and the mounted heads of famous bulls; weekend hunts in the Camargue and private boat excursions to the beach are some of its offerings. *Restaurant closed Wed.*

★★★D'Arlatan, 26 Rue du Sauvage, t 04 90 93 56 66, f 04 90 49 68 45, *hotel-arlatan@ provnet.fr, www.hotel-arlatan.fr*. Near the lively Place du Forum, this is the former 12th–18th-century home of the Comtes d'Arlatan. After a warm welcome, wait for the lift standing on glass over Roman excavations; the house was built over part of the Constantine basilica, and in 1988 a Roman drain and a statue plinth from the 1st

century BC were uncovered. If you're alone and can do without a TV and your own bathroom, ask for room 38: a single bed for half the price, located in a converted chapel overlooking the courtyard with a fountain; a cherub flies at the head of the bed.

★★★Du Forum, 10 Place du Forum, t 04 90 93 48 95, f 04 90 93 90 00, *resa@hotelduforum. com*. In another old house; it may have less charm but it does have a swimming pool. *Closed Nov–Feb.*

★★★Auberge La Fenière, Raphèle-les-Arles ✉ 13280, 5km east of Arles on the N453; t 04 90 98 47 44, f 04 90 98 48 39, *lafeniere.com@provnet.fr, www.lafeniere. com*. An attractive, ivy-covered inn on the edge of the Crau; nice rooms, some with air conditioning, and a restaurant (*moderate*) with an outdoor terrace which offers Camarguaise beef, duck with olives or salmon roulades. *Closed Wed out of season.*

Inexpensive

★★St-Trophime, 16 Rue de la Calade, t 04 90 96 88 38, f 04 90 96 92 19. In an old house with a central courtyard. *Closed mid-Nov–Jan.*

★★Le Calendal, 22 Place Pomme, t 04 90 96 11 89, f 04 90 96 05 84, *contact@lecalendal. com*. Rooms overlook a garden with palms.

★★Hôtel du Musée, 11 Rue du Grand-Prieuré, t 04 90 93 88 88, f 04 90 49 98 15. An

opera (1872). Its furniture makers invented what has become the traditional south Provençal style, more elegantly rococo than the heavy pieces of northern Provence. The Félibres made much of the city for the striking costumes the women continued to wear, for its bullfights and for its *farandole*, a dance in 6/4 time dating back at least to the Middle Ages.

The Arles of Van Gogh

Vincent Van Gogh was a fervent admirer of Daudet, and it may well have been his stories that first brought him to Arles in February 1888. To his surprise, the city was blanketed with snow – a very rare occurrence and, in a way, an omen. When the snow melted it revealed an Arles made mean and ugly by new embankments along the Rhône, cutting the city off from its lifeblood (previously the flooding of the river had fertilized the countryside, like the Nile in Egypt). At the same time, a new railway line was being installed by workers brought in from Belgium and housed in cheap tickytacky buildings. Arles had never looked shabbier. But Van Gogh stayed, found a room to rent in a poor neighbourhood by the station, and painted the shabby Arles around him – the *Café de nuit* with its hallucinogenic lightbulb, *La Maison jaune* and *Le Pont* attractive converted 17th-century residence opposite the Musée Réattu. Quiet, subtly chic and above all friendly, the hotel epitomizes all Arles has to offer.

There are plenty of inexpensive hotels on the streets toward the train station.

Gauguin, 5 Place Voltaire, **t 04 90 96 14 35, **f** 04 90 18 98 87, *hotelgauguin@wanadoo.fr*. Simple but tidy rooms just south of Place Lamartine, some with balconies.

*France, 3 Place Lamartine, **t** 04 90 96 01 24, **f** 04 90 96 90 87. Also good, and slightly less expensive.

*Terminus et Van Gogh, 5 Place Lamartine, **t/f** 04 90 96 12 32. Bright and welcoming.

Auberge de Jeunesse, 20 Rue du Maréchal Foch, **t** 04 90 96 18 25, **f** 04 90 96 31 26. Get the bus from Place Lamartine. *Closed 20 Dec–5 Feb.*

Eating Out

Lou Marquès, Jules César hotel (*see* above), **t** 04 90 52 52 52, **f** 04 90 52 52 53 (*expensive*). Arles' elegant citadel of traditional *haute cuisine*, featuring dishes such as *croustillant de Saint-Pierre* and *carré d'agneau* with artichokes, and an excellent wine cellar.

Le Jardin de Manon, 14 Av des Alyscamps, **t** 04 90 93 38 68 (*moderate*). For lunch after a walk through the Alyscamps; *cuisine*

provençale on a pretty terrace out back. *Closed Wed.*

Vitamine, 16 Rue du Docteur Fanton, **t** 04 90 93 77 36 (*cheap*). This vegetarian eatery offers a welcome injection of greenery: 50 different salads for bargain prices.

For something different you could arrange a day course in **Provençal cuisine** (*Mar–Oct*), run by Erick Vedel, its high priest, and his polyglot American wife Madeleine (**t/f** 04 90 49 69 20).

Entertainment and Nightlife

The most sociable bars in Arles are in Place du Forum; for lazy watching-the-world-go-by, go for a chair in Place Voltaire or Bd des Lices.

Le Méjan/Actes Sud, Quai Marx-Dormoy, **t** 08 36 68 47 07. The liveliest place in Arles after dark; a complex that includes a book and record shop, art gallery, concerts, three cinemas showing films in their original language (v.o.), and a bar and restaurant where you can eat cheaply.

Cargo de Nuit, 7 Av Sadi Carnot, **t** 04 90 45 55 99. Live music and a philosophy night (*open till 5am Thurs–Sat*).

Le Femina, 7 Bd Emile Zola. Recommended bar.

Le Krystal, at Moulès, **t** 04 90 98 32 40. Disco.

de Langlois (part of a ghastly irrigation project) – with colours so intense in their chromatic contrasts they seem to come from somewhere over the rainbow.

Van Gogh's dream was to found an art colony in Arles, similar to the one in Pont Aven in Brittany. He begged his overbearing friend Gauguin to join him, but when Gauguin finally arrived in October he found little to like in Arles, dashing Van Gogh's hopes. The tension between the two men reached such a pitch in December that the overwrought Van Gogh went over the edge and confronted Gauguin in the street with a razor. Gauguin stared him down and Van Gogh, despising himself, went back to his room, cut off his own ear and gave it to a prostitute. Arles was scandalized, and breathed a sigh of relief when Van Gogh voluntarily committed himself to the local hospital, the Hôtel Dieu.

In May 1889 he left for the hospital in St-Rémy. Van Gogh's output in Arles was prodigious (from February 1888 to May 1889 he painted 300 canvases), but not a single painting remains in the city today. His admirers, looking for the places he painted, have just as little to see: the famous bridge, yellow house and café were destroyed in the Second World War or afterwards; only the clock in the Bar Alcazar in Place Lamartine remains as Van Gogh painted it (in *Café de nuit*), along with some of the ancient plane trees around the Alyscamps. To make up for its belated appreciation of the mad, lonely genius who sojourned here, Arles has converted the Hôtel Dieu (which Van Gogh also painted) into a multimedia gallery, the Espace Van Gogh, displaying the works of others.

The Arènes and Théâtre Antique

Despite the pictures in children's history books, Rome was ruined not so much by tribes of horrid Vandals, but by the latter-day Romans themselves, who regarded the baths, theatres and temples they inherited as their private stone quarries. The same holds true of Arles' great monuments, except for the amphitheatre, **Les Arènes** (*t 04 90 96 03 70; open daily Nov–Feb 10–5, Mar–April and Oct 9–6, May–Sept 9–7*), all of 10ft wider than its rival in Nîmes. As enormous as it is, the amphitheatre originally stood another arcade higher and was clad in marble; as with most public buildings in the Roman Empire, no expense was spared on its comforts. A huge awning operated by sailors protected the audience from the sun and rain, and fountains scented with lavender and burning saffron helped cover up the stink of blood spilled by the gladiators and wild animals below. This temple of death survived in good repair because it came in handy. Its walls were tricked out with towers by Saracen occupiers and used as a fortress (like the theatres of Rome), and from the Middle Ages on it sheltered a poor, crime-ridden neighbourhood with two churches and 200 houses, built from stones prised off the amphitheatre's third storey. These were cleared away in 1825, leaving the amphitheatre free for bullfights and still able to pack in 12,000 spectators. The first was held in 1830, to celebrate the capture of Algiers.

A different fate was in store for the **Théâtre Antique** (*same hours as Arènes*), just south of the Arènes: in the 5th century, in a fury usually reserved for pagan temples, Christian fanatics pulled it apart stone by stone. A shame, because the fragments of fine sculpture they left in the rubble suggest that the theatre, once capable of seating 12,000, was much more lavish than the one in Orange. Of the stage, only two tall Corinthian columns survived; they were nicknamed 'the two widows', after being pressed into service as gibbets in the 17th and 18th centuries. The most famous statue of Roman Provence, the *Venus of Arles*, lay buried at their feet until she was dug up in 1651 and presented to Louis XIV to adorn the gardens of Versailles. Tiers of seats have been rebuilt for modern performances and costume pageants, most of which take place in July.

South of the theatre runs the **Boulevard des Lices** ('of the lists'), where large cafés under the plane trees provide ringside seats for the rollicking Saturday and monthly Wednesday morning markets. Since the 17th century, the Boulevard has been the favourite promenade of the Arlésiens, where visitors like Van Gogh would go on Sunday to see the women dressed in their best costumes. On either side of the street are the **Jardin d'Eté** (with a bust of Van Gogh) and **Jardin d'Hiver** (where the 5th-century BC *oppidum* was uncovered). Just north of the Boulevard, off Rue du Président Wilson, the old Hôtel Dieu has been converted into the **Espace Van Gogh**, which also contains the town's library; it's worth a look inside for the lovely, colourful courtyard, restored to look just as it did when Van Gogh painted it. Here, as elsewhere around Arles, the town has put up reproductions of his works all over the place.

Place de la République: St-Trophime

From Boulevard des Lices, Rue Jean Jaurès (the Roman *cardo*) leads to the harmonious **Place de la République**, an attractive square on the Roman model, with a fountain built around a granite **obelisk** that once stood in the *spina* (or barrier) of the circus. Overlooking this pagan sun needle is one of the chief glories of Provençal Romanesque, the **cathedral of St-Trophime**.

The original church, built by St Hilaire in the 5th century and dedicated to St Stephen, was rebuilt at the end of the 11th century, and the great **Portal** added in the next – one of the best-preserved ensembles of Romanesque sculpture in the Midi. Inspired by the triumphal arches of Glanum and Orange, its reliefs describe the Last Judgement, mixing the versions of the Apocalypse and Gospel of Matthew. As angels blast away on their trumpets, the triumphant Christ sits in majesty in the tympanum, accompanied by the symbols of the four Evangelists, the 12 Apostles, and a gospel choir of 18 pairs of angels. On the left side, St Michael weighs each soul, separating the good from evil for their just deserts in the afterlife – the fortunate in their long robes are delivered into the bosoms of Abraham, Isaac and Jacob, while the damned, naked and bound like a chain gang, are led off in a conga-line to hell: as in all great Romanesque art, the figures on this portal seem to dance to an inner, cosmic rhythm. The large saints set back in the columned recesses below are, from left to right: Bartholomew, James the Minor, Trophime as bishop, John the Evangelist, Peter (over the man-eating lions), Paul, Andrew, Stephen (being stoned), James the Major and Philip. Van Gogh found it admirable but 'so cruel, so monstrous, like a Chinese nightmare, that even this beautiful example of so good a style seems to me to belong to another world and I am glad not to belong to it...'

After the sumptuous portal, the spartan nudity of the long, narrow nave is as striking as its unusual height. Aubusson tapestries from the 17th century hang across the top, and there are several palaeochristian sarcophagi along the sides. The best decoration, however, is by a Dutchman named Finsonius, who came down to Arles in 1610. Like Van Gogh, he stayed, mesmerized by the light and colour, and met a bad end, drowning in the icy Rhône in 1642. St-Trophime has three of his paintings: in the crossing, a beautiful *Annunciation* (1610), the *Stoning of St Stephen* over the triumphal arch in the nave and, on the right, a singular *Adoration of the Magi*, with nightmare architecture and animals in attendance.

The Cloister

Same opening hours as the Arènes (see above) – but come around midday if you want to see the sculptures at their best.

Around the corner in Rue du Cloître is the entrance to St-Trophime's cloister. No other cloister in Provence is as richly and harmoniously sculpted as this, carved in the 12th and 14th centuries by the masters of St-Gilles. Because Arles was as anti-

Revolutionary as a town could be, this masterpiece was spared the wanton vandalism that destroyed so much elsewhere.

The north gallery is the oldest, supported by two monumental pillars adorned with statues; *St Peter* and *St Trophime* on the northwest are masterpieces of the classically influenced Arles school – even the foliage in the borders has a certain Corinthian air. The capitals in the Romanesque north and east galleries are carved with scenes from the New Testament, their figures moving to the same wonderful rhythms as those on the portal. The capitals of the more severe Gothic gallery to the south are elaborately carved with the life of St Trophime, while on the west the capitals closely resemble the south gallery of Montmajour's cloister (*see* p.152): note the Magdalene kissing Christ's feet and St Martha with her Tarasque.

Hôtel de Ville and the Cryptoportiques

Sharing Place de la République with the church of St-Trophime is Arles' palatial **Hôtel de Ville**, built in 1675 after plans by Hardouin-Mansart, architect of the Hall of Mirrors at Versailles; here, his virtuoso signature is in the remarkable flat vaulting of the vestibule. Facing the inner courtyard are remnants of older civic buildings: sections of the 12th–15th-century palace of the *podestats* (or prefects of the Holy Roman Emperor), and the town hall of 1500, with a Roman tympanum and bell tower modelled after the mausoleum of Glanum.

Just around the corner on Rue Balze is the cryptoporticus of the forum, the **Cryptoportiques** (*same hours as the Arènes; adm*), entered through a long-unused Jesuit church, with an unusual wooden vaulted ceiling and a huge wooden Baroque retable that covers the entire apse. With the ramparts, this cryptoporticus was the first large construction of the Roman colony. Forming three sides of a rectangle measuring 289 by 192ft, these subterreanean barrel-vaulted double galleries of the 1st century BC were built as foundations for the monumental Forum above. You can see a model of the Forum's original appearance in the Musée de l'Arles Antique; like the Imperial Fora in Rome, this one was built all at once, as a unified architectural grouping, consisting of a rectangle of colonnades for public business and a temple in the centre. No one knows for sure what other purpose a cryptoporticus may have served – for storage, or perhaps, as on Rome's Palatine Hill, for cool promenades. During the last war the galleries came in handy as an air-raid shelter.

The Muséon Arlaten

29 Rue de la République, t 04 90 96 08 23; open April–May and Sept 9.30–12.30 and 2–6, June–Aug 9.30–1 and 2–6.30, Oct–Mar 9.30–12.30 and 2–5; Oct–June closed Mon; adm.

The indefatigable Frédéric Mistral began his collection of ethnographic items from Provence in 1896; in 1904, when he won the Nobel Prize, he used the money to purchase the 16th-century Hôtel de Castellane-Laval to house his **Muséon Arlaten**. Mistral's aim was to record the details of everyday life in Provence for future generations. The evolution of the traditional Arlésienne costume, one of Mistral's obsessions, is thoroughly documented, with adjustments made to match fashion changes in Paris. The wearing of it declined along with the use of the Provençal language, in spite of the poet's folklore parades (the 'Festivals of Virgins') in Arles' theatre and his pronouncements that the costume 'in the shadowy transition of the centuries, lets us see a lightning flash of beauty!' Nowadays, the female museum attendents here are the last Arlésiennes to wear the traditional costume, as they sit crocheting by the windows and gossiping (not in Provençal, but French).

Most memorable and strange are the life-size dioramas: a Christmas dinner at a *mas*, with a table groaning with wax food; a reed-thatched *cabane des gardiens*; and a visit to a new mother and her infant. The curious gifts of salt, a match, an egg and bread brought by the visitors symbolize the hope that the baby may grow to be (in the same order) wise, straight, full and good. The gallery of rituals has a prickly Tarasque retired from the procession at Tarascon, and a lock of golden hair discovered in a medieval tomb at Les Baux. One room is dedicated to the Félibrige, and another to Mistral himself, with the great man's cradle under glass.

In the courtyard, a section of the Forum was uncovered, complete with an **exedra** cut with 10 niches for statues. To the north of the Muséon Arlaten, the café-filled **Place du Forum** is the centre of modern life in Arles, watched over helplessly by a **statue of Frédéric Mistral**, moustachioed and goateed like his near-double, Buffalo Bill. Mistral himself attended its unveiling in 1909, thanking his admirers, but regretting that they made him look as if he were waiting for a train.

Constantine's Baths and the Réattu Museum

From the Place de la République, Rue de l'Hôtel de Ville leads north to the ruins of Constantine's palace, of which only part of the baths, or **Les Thermes de Constantin**, remain (*same hours as the Arènes; adm*). Across the street stood the Priory of the Knights of Malta, built in the 14th century. The knights, who came from all over Europe, were divided into eight *langues* (tongues), and this was the local headquarters of the *Langue de Provence*; the façade with gargoyles facing the river gives the best idea of its original appearance. After the Revolution, an academic painter named Jacques Réattu purchased the priory and his daughter made it into the **Musée Réattu** (*Rue du Grand Prieuré, t 04 90 49 38 34; same hours as the Arènes; adm*). Besides Réattu's own contributions, there are works by Théodore Rousseau, followers of Lorrain and Salvator Rosa, and one painting so marvellously, indescribably awful that it deserves a museum to itself: Antoine Rospal's portrait of himself and his family.

In 1972 the museum was jolted awake with a donation of 57 drawings from Picasso, in gratitude for the many bullfights he enjoyed in Arles. Nearly all date from January 1971 and constitute a running dialogue the artist held with himself on some of his favourite subjects – harlequins, men, women, the artist and his model – and, more unusually, a Tarasque. Other Picassos in the museum include a beautiful portrait of his mother, Maria, from the 1920s, donated by his widow, and a sculpture of a woman with a violin. There are more recent works by César (a compacted motorbike) and Pol Bury (the bizarre *monument horizontal no.3*, with 12,000 magnetized steel balls demonically clicking away on a table), and upstairs an gallery devoted to photography.

The Alyscamps

A 10min walk from the centre; follow Rue E. Fassin, the first street south of the Boulevard des Lices, eastwards. Same opening hours as the Arènes; adm.

One of the most prestigious necropolises of the Middle Ages, the Alyscamps owed its fame to the legend of St Trophime, a cousin of the proto-martyr St Stephen who became a disciple of St Paul. Paul sent Trophime to convert Gaul, and medieval hagiographers later confused him with a 2nd- or 3rd-century Bishop of Arles of the same name. The story has it that Trophime arrived in Arles in the year 46 and held secret meetings with his new converts in the lonesome Roman cemetery of Alyscamps (believed to be a corruption of *Elisii Campi*, or Elysian Fields), which according to Roman custom was built outside the city walls, along the Via Aurelia. Trophime eventually attracted quite a following, and before he died he gave a special blessing to the Alyscamps; Christ himself attended the ceremony and left behind a stone imprint of his knee.

Burial in such holy ground was so desirable that bodies sealed in barrels with their burial fee attached were floated down the Rhône to Arles. Some rascals in Beaucaire took to robbing the dead of their coins as they floated downstream, but they were found out when the barrels miraculously returned upstream to the scene of the crime. At its greatest extent, the necropolis stretched for one and a half miles and contained 19 chapels and several thousand tombs, many of them packed five bodies deep. Dante mentions it in the *The Divine Comedy* (IX, 112), and it makes an appearance in numerous *chansons de geste*. Ariosto wrote how Charlemagne's peers, cut down at Roncevalles, were flown here and buried by angels.

The Alyscamps' mystique began to decline in 1152, when the relics of St Trophime were transferred to the cathedral. Grave robbers pillaged the tombs and the most beautiful sarcophagi were given away as presents to Renaissance potentates. Under Louis Napoleon, the Alyscamps itself was dismembered by a railroad, a canal, factories and a housing estate, leaving only one romantic, melancholy lane lined with empty, mostly plain sarcophagi. Little holes of mysterious purpose are carved into the stone of many of them, similar to holes in other tombs from the megalithic era; they may have held tiny oil lamps. Of the 19 chapels, all that remains is a 15th-century chapel that now serves as the ticket booth, along with the recently restored Romanesque **St-Honorat** at the far end. Its two-storey octagonal tower still stands, rebuilt in the 12th century by the monks of St-Victor in Marseille; in the apse are three Carolingian sarcophagi.

Musée de l'Arles Antique

t 04 90 18 88 88; open daily Mar–Oct 9–7, Nov–Feb 10–5; adm.

Arles' newest museum, at Presqu'île du Cirque Romain, Avenue de la 1ère D. F. L., has been erected in an eerie wasteland slightly out of town, opposite the Palais des Congrès (follow the Boulevard des Lices to its western end, and pass under the motorway); in front of the museum you'll see foundations of the curve of Arles'

Roman circus. This shiny modern building houses the collected contents of several of Arles' old museums. Though the ancient works themselves are not especially noteworthy, the detailed explanations (in French) and especially the brilliant architectural models bring the Roman city back to life in a way that few museums anywhere can match. Here you'll see how the Roman sailors wired up the sailcloth awning to shade the amphitheatre, how the city centre – the Forum and temples – looked to the man in the street, how the army engineers made the floating bridge over the Rhône, and much more.

Amongst the exhibits are the pagan statues and sarcophagi of the former Musée d'Art Païen. Nearly everything here was made in the Arles region, with the exception of the beautiful white marble *Hippolytus and Phaedra sarcophagus* (2nd or 3rd century AD), with its hunting scenes. Two exceptional mosaics brought in from nearby Roman villas show the rape of Europa and Orpheus enchanting the wild beasts; there's a graceful but damaged dancing girl, and a headless statue of Mithras, the god of the Legionnaires, his torso decorated with signs of the Zodiac entwined by a serpent.

The large statue of Augustus was found in the theatre, as was the *Venus of Arles*, represented here by a copy made before Louis XIV had it 'restored'. Although a fairly chaste specimen as marble love goddesses go, she earned from Théodore Aubanel the most ham-handedly erotic of all Félibre poems:

Laisso ti pèd toumba la raubo qu'à tis ancò
S'envertouio, mudant tout ço qu'as de plus bèu:
Abandouno toun ventre i pountoun dóu soulèu!
Coume l'èurre s'aganto à la rusco d'un aubre,
Laisso din mi brassado estregne en plen toun maubre:
Laisso ma bouco ardènto e mi det tremoulant
Courre amouros pertout sus toun cadabre blanc!

(Throw to your feet the robe that around your hips/hangs, hiding all that is most beautiful about you:/Abandon your stomach to the kisses of the sun!/As ivy entwines the bark of a tree,/Let me in my embraces clasp all of your marble;/Let my ardent mouth and burning fingers/run lovingly over your body so white!)

Mothers in Arles use this armless Venus for their own ends. They bring their children to see her and warn: 'The same thing will happen to you if you keep biting your nails!'

Also here are the contents of the former Musée d'Art Chrétien, the best collection of 4th-century Christian sarcophagi of any museum. Carved by Arlésien sculptors between the years 330 and 395, these remarkably preserved tombs make a fascinating documentary of the newly victorious faith; as their pagan ancestors carved scenes from mythology, so these early Christians spared no expense to decorate their last resting places on earth with scenes from the Old and New Testaments. Nearly every figure of importance wears a Roman toga; on the *sarcophage de Trinquetaille*, discovered in 1974, the Three Magi sport Phrygian bonnets.

Plaine de la Crau

Hercules, after completing his Tenth Labour, the theft of the cattle of Geryon, passed through Provence with the booty on his way home to Greece. He had some trouble with the native Ligurians, who apparently tried to pinch the cows. One thing led to another, and before long the big fellow found himself in single-handed battle with the entire nation. As they advanced across the marshy plain, Hercules, armed only with his club, got down on his knees in despair at having nothing to throw at them. Zeus took pity on him and sent down a shower of stones, with which the hero soon put the Ligurians to flight. This was an unaccountably important story in the mythology of the Greeks. They and the Romans put the Hercules of this battle in the sky; the northern constellation we know as Hercules, they called *Engonasis*, the 'kneeler'.

The carpet of stones Zeus sent are still there for all to see, on the weird wasteland called the **Crau**, which stretches from Arles to the Etang de Berre, between the Camargue and the Alpilles. The ancients found it fascinating, and many Greek and Roman writers attempted to explain it; Aristotle, a hopeless bird-brain at anything involving natural science, said the stones were formed by volcanoes, and 'rolled down naturally' to the low plain. In fact, the rounded stones are alluvial deposits from the Durance, from long ago when the river followed this path into the Rhône delta.

The empty, wind-blown Crau is a major element of the Provençal mystique; Mistral, for example, dragged his poor Mireille across it before she met her sad end. Today it does its best to keep up a romantic appearance. Over 100,000 sheep make their winter home here, nibbling the tufts of grass between the stones before migrating in the old-fashioned way up to the Provençal Alps in May or June; the stone shepherd huts are still one of the few features of the Crau. The French, unfortunately, have been trying to make it disappear. Most of the northern part has been reclaimed for farmland. The rest is crisscrossed with railways, canals and roads, and decorated with army firing ranges and the gigantic Istres military airport; there's even a dynamite plant.

There are no good roads over the unspoiled parts of the Crau, and the only village, **St-Martin-de-Crau**, is a dismal spot, but you can still see something of the original effect along the N568 (for Fos and Marseille) and the N113 (for Salon), both east of Arles.

Into the Camargue

To its handful of inhabitants, the Camargue was the *isclo*, the 'island' between the two branches of the Rhône. The river's course has taken many different forms over the millennia, and the present one, with its two arms, has created a vast marshland – France's salt cellar, its greatest treasure-house of waterfowl and the home of some of its most exotic landscapes. The two branches, the Grand and Petit Rhônes, really build separate deltas, leaving the space in between a soupy battleground where land and sea slowly struggle for mastery.

Getting Around

Due to its proximity, Arles is the traditional jumping-off point for the Camargue.

By Train and Bus

The only public transport to the centre of the Camargue begins at the *gare routière* in Arles: one or two **buses** a day each to Stes-Maries-de-la-Mer (via Albaron) and Salin-de-Giraud. St-Gilles has regular bus connections to Nîmes (five a day), a few to Arles and one to Lunel. There are also one or two SNCF **trains** to St-Gilles from Arles.

On Foot, Horseback and by Bike and Jeep

Remember that the Camargue is really quite small – it's never more than 40km from Arles to the coast. A serious hiker could see the whole thing in three days. It is perfect country for cycling, and there are a few places in Stes-Maries-de-la-Mer to rent some wheels. Horses are even more popular; there are many places to hire one, including **L'Etrier**, at l'Etang de l'Estagel (**t** 04 66 01 36 76).

Destination Camargue, **t** 04 90 96 94 44, organizes day and half-day trips into the Camargue by jeep, from March for individuals and all year for groups.

By Boat

This is another possibility: **Blue-Line** (**t** 04 66 87 22 66) and other firms in St-Gilles rent boats fit for a few days' trip through the Petite Camargue. At Stes-Maries-de-la-Mer and St-Gilles there are excursion boats that make short cruises around the Camargue.

Where to Stay and Eat

Almost all of the accommodation in the area is in Stes-Maries-de-la-Mer (*see* below). But if you want to stay in the eastern or central parts of the Camargue, away from the tourists, there are some possibilities.

Albaron ✉ 13123

★★Le Flamant Rose, **t** 04 90 97 10 18, **f** 04 90 97 12 47 (*inexpensive*). A simple Logis de France open all year with menus (*moderate*) including a *salade de fruits de mer* and stewed beef cowboy style – *bœuf à la gardian*. Closed Tues in summer, Wed in winter.

Salin-de-Giraud ✉ 13129

Amidst its vast salt pans, Salin-de-Giraud doesn't even dream of attracting tourists.

★La Camargue, Bd de la Camargue, **t** 04 42 86 88 52, **f** 04 42 86 83 95 (*inexpensive*). The only place to stay in town, simple and basic. *Closed Nov–Easter.*

Le Saladelle, 4 Av des Arènes, **t** 04 42 86 83 87 (*moderate–cheap*). The family-favourite restaurant, with a wide choice on the menus, including spicey *bœuf à la gardian*, chops and fish. Of course, there are shakers of the local speciality on every table – all you can eat. *Closed Sat and Oct–Mar.*

With its unique coastline and wild expanses, the Camargue provides a soothing antithesis to the more crowded areas of the region. It is also ideal for outdoor activities: hiking, climbing, diving, surfing and horse-riding (*see* 'Getting Around', for details).

History

Ancient writers recorded the people of the Camargue hunting boar in the swamp forests and actually raking fish out of the mud; besides remarking on its curiosities, the Greeks and Romans left it entirely alone. In the early Middle Ages, however, at least four monastic colonies were founded on the edges of the Camargue, not only to reclaim land but to collect that most precious of medieval commodities, salt. In this inhospitable country, these colonies disappeared long ago; the most important was the Abbey of Psalmody, which became quite a power in Provence. Today only scant ruins can be seen, on a farm still called Psalmody, north of Aigues-Mortes in the region called the Petite Camargue, west of the Petit Rhône.

By the 17th century, the monks gave way to cowboys (*gardians*), who created large ranches to exploit the two totem animals of the Camargue: the native black longhorn cattle that thrive on salt grass and have always been the preferred stock for Provençal bullfights, and the beautiful white horse, believed to have been introduced by the Arabs back in the Dark Ages. A true cowboy culture grew up, a romantic image dear to the Provençaux, and especially to Provençal writers like Mistral.

There are still a few score *gardians* in the Camargue today, keeping up the old traditions. Big changes have come to the swampland in the last century. For a while, the French threatened to dispose rationally of this land altogether, with dikes and drainage schemes turning large areas into salt pans and rice fields. Fortunately, nature societies secured the creation of a wildlife reserve around the heart of the Camargue in 1928, and the government made a Regional Park of the area in 1970.

Flora and Fauna

First and most spectacularly, there are the flamingos (*flamants roses*), a symbol of the Camargue; several thousand of them nest around the southern lagoons. Probably no place in the Mediterranean has a wider variety of aquatic birds: lots of ducks, grebes, cormorants, curlews and ibis. The little egret is a common sight, though they spend the winter in Africa, as does the avocet, which looks like an aquatic magpie. There are also many purple herons, conspicuously striped on the head and breast. Not all are water birds; you may see an eagle or a majestic red kite (*milan royal*).

Deforestation in favour of ranches destroyed most of the natural habitat for land animals, but there are still boars, beavers and blue frogs. Trees are rare, although there are umbrella pines and scrubby, pink-flowered tamarisks. Common plants include the purple-flowered *saladelle* and the *salicorne*, which grows in tough clumps. Among the fauna, we nearly forgot the most important – the hard-drilling, inescapable Camargue mosquito; make her the prime consideration when you visit.

The Musée de la Camargue

t 04 90 97 10 82; open April–Sept daily 9.15–5.45, July and Aug daily 9.15–6.45, Oct–Mar Wed–Mon 10.15–4.45; adm.

It was an inspiration on the part of the Regional Park management, creating this museum in what not long ago was a working Camargue cattle and sheep ranch, the **Mas du Pont de Rousty**, 9km southwest of Arles on the D570. The buildings are well restored and documented, giving a feeling of what life was like on the *mas* a century ago. There are special exhibitions on the *gardians*, on the fickle Rhône (you'll learn that 400,000 years ago it flowed past Nîmes), on Mistral's *Miréio*, and other subjects. Outside, there are marked nature trails leading into the surrounding swampy plain, the **Marais de la Grande Mar**. About 4km beyond the museum on the D570, little **Albaron** was one of the first inhabited centres of the Camargue; a stout medieval tower survives, built to guard Arles from any attack or pirate raid up the Petit Rhône.

The Etang de Vaccarès

For all of us lazy motor tourists, the way to see the best of the Camargue is to take the D37, a left turn 4km south of the museum. After another 4km, a side road leads to the **Domaine de Méjanes**, with horse-riding and canoes; on summer weekends the *gardians* put on shows of cowboy know-how, and occasionally bullfights. Call ahead, **t** 04 90 97 10 62, for information. Further on, the D37 skirts the edges of the **Etang de Vaccarès**, the biggest of the lagoons and centre of the Camargue wildlife reserve. In some places, you can see flocks of nesting flamingos year round. A side road, the D36B, leads down to Salin-de-Giraud, passing the **Centre d'Information la Capelière** (**t** *04 90 97 00 97; open April–Sept daily 9–1 and 2–6, Oct–Mar Wed–Mon 9–1 and 2–5,*), with exhibits on flora and fauna and guided nature walks around the lagoon.

The scenery changes abruptly at **Salin-de-Giraud**, a 19th-century industrial village that was devoted to the largest saltworks in Europe: a staggering 110 square km network of pans, annually producing 800,000 tonnes of salt. There's another nature centre on the D36, **La Palissade** (**t** *04 42 86 81 28; open daily 9–5*), with white horses, bulls, audiovisuals, a small aquarium, walks etc., and information on the flamingo-filled Etang de Grande-Palun. The *salins* are barred from the Mediterranean by one of the longest and emptiest beaches in France, the **Plage de Piémanson** at the mouth of the Grand Rhône; the current is a bit treacherous for swimming. To get away from it all, head west of Salin for the **Plage de Beauduc** (signposted), where you'll find a couple of places that grill the day's catch.

With good local maps, determined swamp fans can hike the 40km or so to Stes-Maries-de-la-Mer in summer, through the most unspoiled parts of the Camargue; a sea wall, the **Digue de la Mer**, provides a crossing around the lagoons, and the only hazards are secluded beaches that have been taken over by bands of *naturistes*. You might even make it over to the Camargue's forest, **Bois des Rièges**, on a large island at the southern end of the Etang de Vaccarès. Though officially off limits, as part of the nature reserve, it can sometimes be reached on foot in summer. Be careful though; this is the home of the Camargue's Abominable Snowman, the *Bête de Vaccarès*, a mysterious part-human creature first sighted in the 15th century.

Saintes-Maries-de-la-Mer

Set among the low sand dunes, lively Saintes-Maries-de-la-Mer has an open-armed approach to visitors that long predates any interest in the Camargue and its ecological balance. For this is one of Provence's holiest places, and if you come out of season you may still sense the dream-like, insular remoteness that made it the stuff of legend.

The pious story behind it all was promoted to the hilt by the medieval Church: after Christ was crucified, his Jewish detractors took a boat without sails or oars and loaded it with three Marys – Mary Salome (mother of the apostles James and John), Mary Jacobe, the Virgin's sister, and Mary Magdalene – Martha and her resurrected brother Lazarus, St Maximin and St Sidonius. As this so-called Boat of Bethany drifted

Getting Around

By Bus

There are at least two buses daily from Arles (55mins; t 04 90 96 36 25). In July and August there are direct services to Aigues-Mortes and Montpellier (t 04 67 92 01 43) and others to St-Gilles and Nîmes (t 04 66 29 52 00).

By Boat

From the end of March to September the paddle steamer *Tiki III*, t 04 90 97 81 68, offers hour-long cruises on the Petit Rhône.

On Horseback

Go for a ride – the best way of exploring the trails (the tourist office has a list of stables, some offering tours for beginners).

By Jeep and Bike

Camargue Safaris is one of many firms offering jeep tours of the Camargue, t 04 90 97 86 93. Hire a bike from **Le Vélociste**, Av de la République, t 04 90 97 83 26 (*open Sept–June*).

Tourist Information

Tourist office: 5 Av Van Gogh, t 04 90 97 82 55, f 04 90 97 71 15, *saintes-maries@ enprovence.com, www.saintesmariesdelamer. com*. Open daily July–Aug 9–8, April–June and Sept 9–7, Mar and Oct 9–6, Jan–Feb and Nov–Dec daily 9–5.

Market Days

Monday and Friday mornings.

Festivals

The *Pèlerinage des Gitans* is held on 24–25 May. The Gypsies began making the pilgrimage in numbers in the mid-19th century. In 1935, thanks to the intervention of the Marquis de Baroncelli, 24 May was especially set aside as St Sarah's day. Although the famous all-night candle vigil by her statue has been abolished by some bureaucratic killjoys, her statue is still symbolically carried to the sea by a procession of Gypsies, *gardians* and costumed Arlésiennes, where in imitation of ancient rain-making ceremonies the statue is sprinkled with sea water while all are blessed by the bishop.

Afterwards, the beaches and streets are alive with music and flamenco, *farandoles*, horse races and bullfights, attended by as many tourists as Gypsies.

The whole ceremony happens again, with considerably fewer Gypsies and tourists, on the Sunday nearest 22 October for Mary Salome.

Where to Stay

Saintes-Maries-de-la-Mer ✉ 13460

There are a lot of choices in Saintes-Maries-de-la-Mer, but if you don't book during the summer or pilgrimages, you'll have to join the crowd on the beach.

off shore, Sarah, the black Egyptian servant of Mary Salome and Mary Jacobe, wept so grievously that Mary Salome tossed her cloak on the water, so that Sarah was able to walk across on it and join them. The boat took them to the Camargue, to this spot, where the elderly Mary Salome, Mary Jacobe and Sarah built an oratory, while their younger companions went to spread the Gospel, live in caves and tame Tarasques. In 1448, during the reign of Good King René (who was always pinched for money), the supposed relics of the two Marys were discovered, greatly boosting the local pilgrim trade. Saintes-Maries became, as Mistral called it, the 'Mecca of Provence'.

A few facts blazed the trail for the legend's ready acceptance. In the 4th century, a Roman writer described a settlement on this site called *Oppidum priscum Ra*. This lent its name to the first Christian church, Notre-Dame-de-Ratis, built over the site of a spring of fresh water – where a Gallo-Roman temple had been dedicated to three sea goddesses. *Ratis* was taken to mean raft (*radeau*), hence the connection not only with the Boat of Bethany but to ancient Egypt, where in the *Book of the Dead* the deceased

★★★**Mas du Clarousset**, Route de Cacharel, 7km north on the D85A, t 04 90 97 81 66, f 04 90 97 88 59 (*expensive*). Small and pink, with a fresh, simple décor. Each room has a private terrace, and there are extras – horses to ride, a pool, jeep excursions and Gypsy music evenings in the excellent restaurants. *Closed mid-Nov–mid-Dec.*

★★★★**Le Pont des Bannes**, 3km north on the D570, t 04 90 97 81 09, f 04 90 97 89 28, *le.pont.des.bannes@wanadoo.fr* (*expensive*). You can sleep comfortably in a *cabane de gardian* here; there's also a pool, garden and stables for the total Camargue experience.

★★★**Le Mas Sainte-Hélène**, Chemin Bas-des-Launes, t 04 90 97 83 29, f 04 90 97 89 28, *le.pont.des.bannes@wanadoo.fr* (*moderate*). The Pont des Bannes' annexe, spread out along an islet in the Etang des Launes, which lets you get eye to eye with the pink flamingos on its waterside terraces.

★**Le Delta**, Place Mireille, t 04 90 97 81 12, f 04 90 97 72 85 (*inexpensive*). Good value for the price.

Eating Out

This is the place to try *bœuf gardian*, or bull stewed in red wine with lots of garlic; *bouriroun*, an omelette made with elvers from the Vaccarès; *salade de téllines*, made of tiny shellfish with garlic mayonnaise; and *poutargue*, Camargue caviar made from red mullet eggs.

Le Brûleur de Loups, Av Léon Gambetta, t 04 90 97 83 31 (*moderate*). Elegant, with a terrace overlooking the beach and more delights from the sea, like a seafood mix in white Châteauneuf-du-Pape. *Closed mid-Nov–Mar.*

Hostellerie du Pont de Gau, 4km north on the Route d'Arles, t 04 90 97 81 53 (*moderate*). Jolly Provençal décor and a delicious *pot-au-feu de la mer*. *Closed Jan–mid-Feb.*

Le Mangio Fango, Route d'Arles, t 04 90 97 80 56 (*moderate*). Seafood-lovers should get a table on Le Mangio Fango's skeeter-free patio; excellent Camargue bull stew, too.

Activities and Entertainment

There are other entertainments in Saintes-Maries-de-la-Mer: in the summer, nightly *Courses Camargues* in the bullring, guitars and buskers in the streets, and miles of white sand beaches, including a *plage naturiste* 6km to the east.

At Pont de Gau, 4km north, there's a **Centre d'Information du P.N.R.C.** (t 04 90 97 86 32; open summer 9–6, winter 9.30–5, closed Fri Oct–Mar), and a **Parc Ornithologique** (t 04 90 97 82 62; open April–Sept 9–sunset, Oct–Mar 10–sunset; adm), a very friendly company offering walks through the marshlands and aviaries frequented by some 200 species of birds, including some rare ones.

sails in a boat without oar or sail, but with the image of Ra. Even the name Mary had a familiar ring to Provence's early Christians; not only for its resemblance to the word for mother (*Matre*) but to Marius, a local cult figure after his defeat of the Teutones, who was advised by the blonde sibyl Marthe (as pictured at Les Baux; *see* p.150). Today, Saintes-Maries-de-la-Mer is best known for the pilgrimage of Mary Jacobe on 24 and 25 May. This attracts Gypsies from all over the world, who have canonized her servant Sarah as their patron saint. The reason seems to owe something to yet another coincidence – the discovery of the relics coincided with a great convergence of Gypsies in Provence in the 1440s, some of whom wandered up from North Africa and Spain, while others crossed into Europe by way of Greece and the Balkans. The Gypsies, however, claim that Sarah was not Egyptian at all, but one of their own, Sarah-la-Kâli ('the black', but also recalling the Hindu goddess Kali), who met the Boat of Bethany here and was the first of their tribe to be converted to Christianity. The Church obliged by 'discovering' the bones of Sarah in 1496.

The Church

In 869, during the construction of a new church to replace the 6th-century oratory 'built' by the two Marys, the Saracens swooped down in a surprise raid and carried off the archbishop of Arles, who just happened to be down to inspect the work. The pirates demanded a high ransom in silver, swords and slaves for their hostage, and were dismayed when the bishop died on them – dismayed, but not so put out as to risk losing the ransom. They tied the bishop's corpse in all its vestments to a throne and made off with the loot before the Christians realized the hostage was dead.

With the threat of similar shenanigans, stones were shipped down from Arles at great expense to rebuild the church in 1130. The result is, along with St-Victor in Marseille, the most impressive fortified church in Provence: a crenellated ship with loopholes for windows in a small pond of white villas with orange roofs. Inside, along the gloomy nave, are wells that supplied the church-fortress in times of siege; pilgrims still bottle the water to ensure their protection by St Sarah. In the second chapel on the left, near the model of the Boat of Bethany that is carried in the procession to the sea, is the polished rock 'pillow' of the saints, discovered with their bones in 1448.

The capitals supporting the blind arches of the raised choir are finely sculpted in the style of St-Trophime. Under the choir is the **crypt**, where the relics and statue of St Sarah in her seven robes are kept; the statue has been kissed so often that the black paint has come off in patches. Here, too, is a *taurobolium*, or relief of a bull-slaying from an ancient Mithraeum, the bits scratched away long ago by women who used the dust to concoct fertility potions, along with photos and *ex votos* left by the Gypsies. From April to mid-November, you can take a stroll below the **bell tower** (*t 04 90 97 87 60; open 10–12.30 and 2–6*), with views stretching across the Camargue that take on a magic glow at sunset.

This roof walk circles the lavish **upper chapel** (*usually closed*), dedicated to St Michael, which in times of need served as a donjon. The coffer holding the relics of the Marys is kept here, except during the arcane *deus ex machina* rites unique to this church: during feast days the coffer is slowly lowered through a door over the altar after the singing of a special hymn, *Les Saintes de Provence*; the pilgrimage ends to the tune of *Adieu aux Saintes*, as the relics are slowly raised back into the chapel. In the 18th century this hocus-pocus had a reputation for curing madness, combined with the shock therapy of stripping the afflicted naked and throwing them in the sea. When Mistral attended the pilgrimage as a young man, a beautiful girl from Beaucaire abandoned by her fiancé dramatically flung herself across the altar just as the relics were being lowered, praying for the return of her lover. The girl made a considerable impression on Mistral and became the basis for his heroine Mireille, who arrives in Saintes-Maries-de-la-Mer to make a similar prayer and dies of too much sun and love in the upper chapel of this church, while the congregation in the lower church, like the chorus in a Greek tragedy, accuses the holy Marys: *Reino de Paradis, mestresso/De la Planuro d'amaresso* ('Queens of Paradise, mistresses/of the plain of bitterness').

Around Saintes-Maries-de-la-Mer

Mireille, in statue form at least, lives on in the main square north of the church, while to the south in Rue Victor-Hugo the **Musée Baroncelli** is devoted to zoology, archaeology and folklore. It is named after the Camargue's secular saint, the Félibre Marquis Folco de Baroncelli-Javon (1869–1943), a descendant of a Florentine merchant family in Avignon, who abandoned all at the age of 21 to live the life of a *gardian*. Baroncelli spent the next 60 years herding bulls, writing poetry and doing all he could to maintain the Camargue and its customs intact. Although he was by trade a cowboy, his heart was with the American Indians and other oppressed minorities; Chief Sitting Bull, visiting France with Buffalo Bill and his Wild West Show, smoked the peace pipe with the Marquis and named him 'Faithful Bird'.

St-Gilles-du-Gard

West of Arles, the N572 takes you through the drier parts of the Camargue. After crossing the Petit Rhône, you're in the **Petite Camargue**, in the *département* of the Gard, approaching **St-Gilles**, the only town for miles in any direction.

History

In medieval times and earlier, St-Gilles was a flourishing port, much nearer the sea than it is now. Remains have been found of a Phoenician merchant colony, and the Greek-Celtic *oppidum* that replaced it, but the place did not really blossom until the 11th century. The popes and the monks of Cluny, who owned it, conspired to make the resting place of Gilles, an obscure 8th-century Greek hermit, a major stop along the great pilgrim road to Compostela. The powerful counts of Toulouse helped too – the family originally came from St-Gilles. Soon pilgrims were pouring in from as far away as Germany and Poland, the port boomed with the onset of the Crusades, and both the Templars and Knights Hospitallers (who owned large tracts in the Camargue) built important commanderies. In 1116 the **abbey church of St-Gilles** was begun, one of the most ambitious projects ever undertaken in medieval Provence.

Tourist Information

Tourist office: Place Frédéric Mistral, t 04 66 87 33 75, f 04 66 87 16 28, *ot.st.gilles@ wanadoo.fr, www.ot-saint-gilles.fr*.

Market Days
Thursday and Sunday mornings.

Where to Stay and Eat

St-Gilles-du-Gard ✉ 30800
In the Middle Ages scores of pilgrims, sometimes thousands, would stay over at St-Gilles every night; try it now and the innkeepers themselves will wonder why.

★★★Heraclée, 30 Quai du Canal, t 04 66 87 44 10, f 04 66 87 13 65 (*inexpensive*). Not exciting but well run. *Closed Jan–Mar.*

★★Le Cours, 10 Allée F. Griffeuille, t 04 66 87 31 93, f 04 66 87 31 83, *hotel.le.cours@ wanadoo.fr, www.hotel-le-cours.com* (*inexpensive*). A typically traditional Logis de France residence, with a shady restaurant (*cheap*) terrace (try the Camargue pilaf and frog's legs). *Closed last 2 weeks in Feb.*

Destiny, however, soon began making it clear that this was not the place. As the delta gradually expanded, the canals silted up and St-Gilles could no longer function as a port (a major reason for the building of Aigues-Mortes; *see* below). The real disaster came with the Wars of Religion, when the town became a Protestant stronghold; the leaders of the Protestant army thought the church, that obsolete relic from the Age of Faith that took 200 years to build, would look much better as a fortress, and they demolished nearly all of it to that end. It was rebuilt, in a much smaller version, after 1650. What was left suffered more indignities during the Revolution – the loss of many of the figures' faces is nothing short of tragic – but it is a miracle that otherwise one of the greatest ensembles of medieval sculpture has survived more or less intact.

The Church Façade

This is the masterpiece of the Provençal school of 12th-century sculptors, the famous work that was copied, life-size, in the Cloisters Museum in New York. Created roughly at the same time as the façade of St-Trophime in Arles, it is likewise inspired by the ancient Roman triumphal arches. Instead of Roman worthies and battle scenes, the 12 Apostles hold place of honour between the Corinthian columns. This is a bold, confident sculpture, taking delight in naturalistic detail and elaborately folded draperies, with little of the conscious stylization that characterizes contemporary work in other parts of France. In this, too, the Romans were their masters. The scheme is complex, and worth describing in detail.

Left portal: tympanum of the Adoration of the Magi (1); beneath it, Jesus' entry into Jerusalem (2); flanking the door, a beautiful St Michael slaying the dragon (3); and on the right the first four Apostles, SS Matthew and Bartholomew, Thomas and James the Lesser (4–7).

Central portal: tympanum of Christ in Majesty (8), with symbols of the Evangelists; underneath, a long frieze that runs from one side portal across to the other: from left to right, Judas with his silver (9); Jesus expelling the money-changers from the

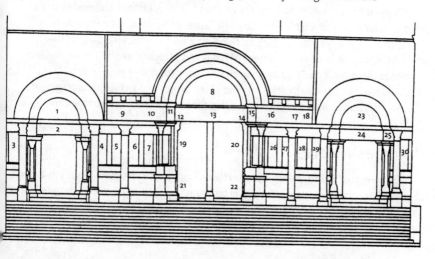

temple (10); the resurrection of Lazarus (11); Jesus prophesying the denial of Peter and the washing of the Apostles' feet (12); Last Supper (13); Kiss of Judas, a superb, intact work (14); Arrest of Christ (15); Christ before Pilate (16); Flagellation (17); Christ carrying the Cross (18). Left of the door, SS John and Peter (19); right of the door, SS James the Greater and Paul, with a soul-devouring Tarasque under his feet (20). Beneath these, at ground level, are small panels representing the sacrifices of Cain and Abel and the murder of Abel (21); a deer hunt and Balaam and his ass, and Samson and the Lion (22).

Right portal: tympanum of the Crucifixion (23); beneath it, two unusual scenes: the three Marys purchasing spices to anoint the body of Jesus, and the three Marys at the tomb. To the left of this, the Magdalen and Jesus (24); to the right, Jesus appearing to his disciples (25). Left of the door, four more unidentifiable Apostles (26–29; note how the 12 represented here are not the canonical list – better-known figures like John the Evangelist and Paul were commonly substituted for the more obscure of the original Apostles). To the right of the door, Archangels combat Satan (30).

The Vis de St-Gilles

The 17th-century interior of the rebuilt church holds little of interest, but underneath it the original, wide-vaulted **crypt** (*adm*) or lower church survives (so many pilgrims came to St-Gilles that upper and lower churches were built to hold them). Behind the church, you can see the ruins of the **choir and apse** of the original, which was much longer than the present structure. Here is the *vis* or 'screw' of St-Gilles, a spiral staircase of 50 steps that once led up one of the bell towers. Built about 1142, it is a tremendous *tour de force*. The stones are cut with amazing precision to make a self-supporting spiral vault; medieval masons always tried to make the St-Gilles pilgrimage just to see it. Its author, Master Mateo of Cluny, also worked on the church of Santiago de Compostela, where he is buried.

The Maison Romane

The rest of the town shows few traces of its former greatness. The medieval centre is unusually large, if a bit forlorn. Near the façade of the church, on Place de la République, is a fine 13th-century mansion, claimed to be the birthplace of Guy Folques, who became Pope Clement IV. Today this 'Maison Romane' houses St-Gilles' **Musée Lapidaire** (*t 04 66 87 40 42; open summer 9.30–12 and 3–7, winter 9–12 and 2–5, closed Jan and Sun; adm*), with a number of sculptures and architectural fragments from the church, and collections displaying the folk life and nature of the Camargue.

Aigues-Mortes

Every French history or geography textbook has a photo of Aigues-Mortes in it, and every Frenchman, most likely, carries in his mind the haunting picture – the great walls of the port where St Louis sailed off to the Crusades, now marooned in the muck of the advancing Rhône delta. It is as compelling a symbol of time and fate as any Roman ruin, and as evocative of medieval France as any Gothic cathedral.

Tourist Information

Tourist office: Porte de la Gardette, **t** 04 66 53 73 00, **f** 04 66 53 65 94, *ot-aiguesmortes@ wanadoo.fr; www.ot-aiguesmortes.fr*. They offer historical tours of the town, year round. *Open summer Mon–Fri 9–8, Sat and Sun 10–8; winter Mon–Fri 9–12 and 1–6, Sat and Sun 10–12 and 2–6.*

Parking: There are signs around all the entrances to the town forbidding cars; these you may ignore, just as everyone else does. There will be no problem driving around Aigues or finding parking, except perhaps in July and August.

Market Days

Wednesday and Sunday mornings, in Avenue F. Mistral; Saturday morning, flea market in Av F. Mistral.

Where to Stay and Eat

Aigues-Mortes ✉ 30220

★★★Le St-Louis, 10 Rue de l'Amiral Courbet, **t** 04 66 53 69 61, **f** 04 66 53 75 92, *hotel-saint-louis@wanadoo.fr* (*moderate*). Gracious and welcoming, in a distinguished and beautifully furnished 18th-century building just off Place St-Louis. Its popular restaurant, **L'Archère**, is the best in town for steaks and seafood, with good home-made desserts. *Closed Nov–Mar.*

Hermitage de St Antoine, 9 Bd Intérieur Nord, **t** 06 03 04 34 05, **f** 04 66 88 40 98 (*inexpensive*). A *chambres d'hôte* just inside the Porte St-Antoine in the medieval walls; only three rooms, all with en suite bathrooms. Added bonuses are a tranquil patio and a fantastic breakfast.

★La Tour de Constance, 1 Bd Diderot, **t** 04 66 53 83 50 (*cheap*). Another good choice for food, outside the northern wall. *Closed Nov–Feb.*

La Camargue, 19 Rue République, **t** 04 66 53 86 88 (*moderate*). The Gypsy Kings got their start here, but even in their absence this is the liveliest and most popular place in town, with flamenco guitars strumming in the background: try to eat in the garden in summer.

La Maguelone, 38 Rue République, **t** 04 66 53 74 60 (*moderate*). With a menu based on local ingredients: *matelote d'anguilles, bourride de lotte* and a *St-Marcel au chocolat croustillant aux coings.*

Activities and Entertainment

Like Saintes-Maries, Aigues-Mortes offers a wide selection of guided tours of flora and fauna:

Pescalune, **t** 04 66 53 79 47, and **Isle de Stel**, **t** 04 66 53 60 70, offer barge tours of the Petite Camargue; four-wheel-drive safari tours are run out of **Le Grau du Roi by Le Gitan**, **t** 04 66 53 04 99, and **Pierrot le Camarguais**, **t** 04 66 51 90 90.

Or save time and take a half-hour 3-D film tour of the Camargue at the **Cinéma 3-D Relief**, by the station at Place de Verdun (**t** 04 66 53 68 50; *open daily 3–7, July–Aug till 10pm; adm*).

History, Salt and Walls

In 1241 the Camargue was the only stretch of Mediterranean coast held by France. To solidify this precarious strip, Louis IX (St Louis) began construction of a new port and a town, laid out in an irregular grid, the better to stop the wind from racing up the streets. In 1248 the port was complete enough to hold the 1,500 ships that carried Louis and his knights to the Holy Land on the Seventh Crusade, which was to bring Louis disasters both at home and abroad (the town was the last he saw of France – he died in Tunis of the plague in 1270). His successor, Philip III, finished Aigues-Mortes and built its great walls. Being the only French Mediterranean port, by the late 13th century it was booming, with perhaps four times as many inhabitants as its present 4,800, its harbour filled with ships from as far away as Constantinople and Antioch.

Aigues-Mortes means 'dead waters', and it proved to be a prophetic name. The sea deserted Aigues and, despite efforts to keep the harbour dredged, the port went into decline after 1350. Attempts to revive it in the 1830s failed, ensuring Aigues' demise, but allowing the works of Louis and Philip to survive undisturbed. Forgotten and nearly empty a century ago, Aigues now makes its living from tourists, and from salt; half of France's supply is collected here, at the enormous **Salins-du-Midi** pans south of town in the Petite Camargue (*call* **t** *04 66 53 85 20 for organized visits in July and Aug, from Le Grau du Roi on Tues and Thurs, from Aigues-Mortes on Wed and Fri*).

Aigues-Mortes' **walls** are over a mile in length, streamlined and almost perfectly rectangular. The impressive **Tour de Constance** (*entry inside the walls on Rue Zola,* **t** *04 66 53 61 55; open daily 9.30–7 in summer; 10–5 in winter, last admission 4pm; adm*) is a huge cylindrical defence tower that guarded the northeastern land approach to the town. After the Crusades, the tower became a prison for Templars and later for Protestants. One of them, Marie Durand, spent 38 years here in unspeakable conditions. On her release in 1768, she left her credo, *register* ('resist' in Provençal), chiselled into the wall where it can still be seen. The tower to the south was used as a temporary mortuary in 1431, during the Hundred Years' War, when the Bourguignons, who held the city, were suddenly attacked and decimated by their archenemies, the Armagnacs. There were so many gruesome bodies that the Armagnacs simply stacked them in the tower, covering each with a layer of salt: hence the name, the Tower of the Salted Bourguignons.

Eight kilometres southwest of Aigues-Mortes, **Le Grau du Roi** doubles as France's most important fishing port (after Sète) and charmless if hyper beach resort; the Palais de la Mer, Av Palais de la Mer (*open May, June and Sept daily 9.30–8; July and Aug 10am–12 midnight; Jan–April and Oct–Dec daily 10–7; adm*), has a good aquarium, including tanks that pass right over your head, and a small museum on the town's history. Le Grau's **Port Camargue** is nothing less than Europe's largest marina, with 4,350 berths. South of this stretches the **Plage de l'Espiguette**, a remarkable stretch of natural sand dunes that go on and on and on, the only building in sight a lighthouse (the road ends there, by the *phare*, in an enormous car park).

Marseille and Metropolitan Provence

11

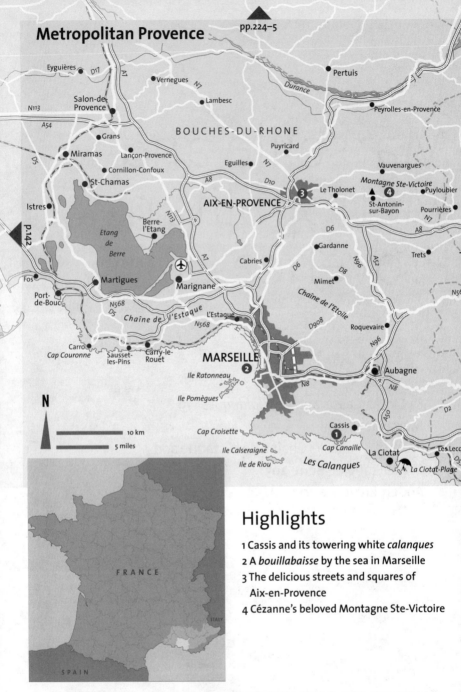

Metropolitan Provence

pp.224–5

Eyguières D17 A7 Verneques N7 Pertuis

Durance

Salon-de-Provence Lambesc

N113 A54 Peyrolles-en-Provence

Grans BOUCHES-DU-RHONE Puyricard

Miramas Lançon-Provence

Cornillon-Confoux Eguilles N7 Vauvenargues

D5 St-Chamas A8 D10 Montagne Ste-Victoire Puyloubier

Istres AIX-EN-PROVENCE 3 Le Tholonet 4 Pourrières

Berre-l'Etang St-Antonin-sur-Bayon N7

p.142

Etang de Berre N113 Cabries D6 Gardanne Trets

Fos A7 D6 N96 A52

Port-de-Bouc Martigues Marignane Mimet D8 N560

N568 Chaîne de l'Estaque L'Estaque Chaîne de l'Etoile

Carro N568 D908 Roquevaire

Cap Couronne Sausset-les-Pins Carry-le-Rouet MARSEILLE 2 N96 Aubagne

N Ile Ratonneau N8 N8 D2

Ile Pomègues A50

Cap Croisette Cassis 1

10 km Cap Canaille Les Lecqu

5 miles Ile Calseraigne La Ciotat D559

Ile de Riou Les Calanques La Ciotat-Plage

p.260

Highlights

1 Cassis and its towering white *calanques*
2 A *bouillabaisse* by the sea in Marseille
3 The delicious streets and squares of
  Aix-en-Provence
4 Cézanne's beloved Montagne Ste-Victoire

FRANCE

ITALY

SPAIN

Although this is the business end of Provence, the most densely populated, hurly-burly, industrial and everything-else-you've-come-to-get-away-from part of Provence, the region holds several trump cards: elegant and lively Aix-en-Provence,

Beaches

The beach at Cassis is pretty, with a dramatic backdrop of cliffs, but it gets crowded in summer.

Marseille possesses an artificial town beach, lively at all times of the year, but for more adventurous sand head into the *calanques*; boats run from Cassis and Marseille.

West of Marseille, La Côte Bleue is the playground of the Marseillais and gets crowded at weekends in summer. The beaches are mediocre; the best is at Carro. For real sand continue west, to the Camargue.

Best Beaches

Cassis, p.181: sand and cliffs.

Calanques: walk the cliff-top path and descend at will (*see* pp.181 and 200).

Marseille ('Plage du David'), p.200: soccer, kites, skateboards and windsurfers; an action beach, artificial pebbles.

Sausset-les-Pins, p.203: sand and caravans.

Carro, p.203: the furthest from Marseille, hence the quietest.

with its incredible markets and countryside synonymous with Cézanne; a tumultuous coastline ripped into the bones of the earth between La Ciotat and Marseille; and Marseille itself, every bit as good as its magnificent setting, as bad as any big port city, and as ugly as the fish in its heavenly *bouillabaisse*. Another plus: state-funded museums in the *département* of the Bouches du Rhône (and there are some good ones – only Paris has more than Marseille) charge only €1.52 admission.

La Ciotat, Cassis and the *Calanques*

Before settling down and creating the broad, smooth bay that permits the existence of Marseille, the Provençal coast bucks and rears with the fury of wild horses. La Ciotat, halfway between Toulon and Marseille, is a hard-nosed and gritty shipbuilding town, while chic, well-heeled Cassis is endowed with a dramatic setting, a bijou harbour and delicate wine.

La Ciotat: the World's First Film Set

A safe anchorage with fresh water and beaches, protected from the winds by a queerly eroded rock formation known as the Bec de l'Aigle ('eagle's beak'), La Ciotat has seen ancient Greeks, pirates, fishermen and, since the time of François I, shipbuilders – though instead of galleys to battle the Holy Roman Empire, the yards now produce vessels to transport liquefied gas. La Ciotat has also given the world two momentous pastimes. First, motion pictures, pioneered here in 1895, when Auguste and Louis Lumière filmed a train pulling into La Ciotat station (*L'Entrée d'un train en gare de La Ciotat*), a clip that made history's first film spectators jump out of their seats as the locomotive seemed to bear down upon them; the **Eden Théâtre**, where it was shown on 28 December 1895, is the oldest surviving cinema. The second is *pétanque*, that most Provençal of sports, which came into being here in 1907 when one old-timer's legs became paralysed and he could no longer take the regulation steps before a throw, as laid down in the laws of *boules*. The rules were changed for him and, as everyone enjoyed working up less of a sweat, they stuck.

Most visitors to La Ciotat keep to the beaches and marina around **La Ciotat-Plage** (with a monument to the Lumière brothers), but it's the business side of things,

Getting Around

La Ciotat is a main stop for **trains** between Marseille and Toulon; regular buses (t 04 42 08 90 90) cover the 3km from the station to the Vieux Port.

Cassis has less frequent services and its train station is just as far from the centre; if you're coming from Marseille, take one of the frequent coaches, which drop you off at Bd Anatole France, near the tourist office.

For **bike hire**, the best is Lleba Cycles, 3 bis Av Frédéric Mistral, t 04 42 83 60 30, in La Ciotat.

Tourist Information

La Ciotat ✉ 13600: Bd Anatole France, t 04 42 08 61 32, f 04 42 08 17 88, tourisme@free.fr. *Open Oct–May Mon–Sat 9–12 and 2.30–6, June–Sept Mon–Sat 9–8, plus Sun 10–1 April–Sept.*

Cassis ✉ 13260: Oustau Calendal, Quai des Moulins, t 04 42 01 71 17, f 04 42 01 28 31, omt-cassis@enprovence.com, www.visit provence.com. *Open summer Mon–Fri 9–7, Sat and Sun 9–1 and 3–7; spring Mon–Fri 9.30–6, Sat and Sun 10–12 and 2–5; autumn and winter Mon–Fri 9.30–12.30 and 2–5, Sat 10–12 and 2–5, Sun 10–12.*

Market Days

La Ciotat: Tuesday and Sunday mornings.
Cassis: Wednesday and Friday mornings.

Where to Stay and Eat

La Ciotat ✉ 13600

***Miramar, 3 Bd Beaurivage, t 04 42 83 09 54, f 04 42 83 33 79 (*expensive–moderate*). A classy, updated old hotel amid pine groves, by the beach; its restaurant, L'Orchidée, t 04 42 83 09 54, is the best in town.

**La Rotonde, 44 Bd de la République, t 04 42 08 67 50, f 04 42 08 45 21 (*inexpensive*). Your best bet near the Vieux Port.

*Beaurivage, 1 Av Beaurivage, t 04 42 98 04 34, f 04 42 71 88 80 (*inexpensive*). A good budget choice. *Closed Nov–Mar.*

Quai Stalingrad, near the shipyards, has the widest choice of restaurants with cheap menus, most – surprise, surprise – featuring seafood.

République Indépendante de Figuerolles, Calanque de Figuerolles, t 04 42 08 41 71,

---

around the **Vieux Port**, that affords the best loafing; in the evening, the shipyard cranes resemble luminous mutant insects from Mars. The **Musée Ciotaden** (*Quai Ganteaume, t 04 42 71 40 99; open mid-June–mid-Sept 4–7pm, mid-Sept–mid-June 3–6pm, closed Tues*) is dedicated to the history of La Ciotat and its shipyards. Beyond the latter, amid the wind-sculpted rocks and dishevelled Mediterranean flora of the Bec de l'Aigle, is the cliff-top **Parc du Mugel** (bus no.3 from the Vieux Port). Avenue de Figuerolles continues from here to the red pudding-stone walls and pebble beach of the **Calanque de Figuerolles**, with its hunchback monkish rock formation, once painted by Braque.

Floating offshore, the wee **Ile Verte** can be reached by boat from Quai Ganteaume; it has a restaurant and views back to the mainland that explain how the 'eagle's beak' got its name.

Route des Crêtes

If you can sneer at vertigo and laugh in the face of tenuous hairpin turns, ignore the main road between La Ciotat and Cassis, and twist and turn along the 17km **Corniche des Crêtes**. Alternatively, a footpath cuts through the road loops and takes about 4 hours. Your pains will be amply rewarded with plunging views from the highest cliffs in France: the **Falaises de Soubeyran**, or Grand Tête ('big head', 1,309ft), and craggy **Cap** f 04 42 71 93 39, *www.figuerolles.com* (moderate–inexpensive). A grand name for a *chambres d'hôte* (B&B) on the beach. It has a good restaurant (*moderate*) that becomes Russian Dec–May. *Closed Nov–mid-Dec.*

Cassis ✉ 13260

★★★★Les Roches Blanches, Av des Calanques, t 04 42 01 09 30, f 04 42 01 94 23, *hotel@roches.blanches-cassis.com, www.roches-blanches-cassis.com* (expensive). The most spectacular hotel in the area, perched on the promontory overlooking Cassis bay. Rooms are a tad small, but very comfortable; there's a private beach and sun terraces, and as usual half board is mandatory in season. *Closed mid-Nov–Feb.*

★★★Les Jardins de Cassis, Av Auguste Favier, t 04 42 01 84 85, f 04 42 01 32 38 (moderate). Set amid lemon groves and bougainvillaea, this is a lovely Provençal-style oasis, with a pool. *Closed Nov–Mar.*

★★★Le Royal Cottage, 6 Av du 11 Novembre, t 04 42 01 33 34, f 04 42 01 06 90, *info@royal-cottage.com, www.royal-cottage.com* (expensive). Just above the port, in a quiet park, with a pool, air conditioning and well-equipped rooms – but no restaurant. *Closed Christmas–New Year.*

★★Le Grand Jardin, 2 Rue Pierre Eydin, t 04 42 01 70 10, f 04 42 01 33 75 (inexpensive). Book months in advance.

★★Le Laurence, 8 Rue de l'Arène, t 04 42 01 88 78, f 04 42 01 81 04 (inexpensive). With a view up to the château. *Closed Nov–Jan.*

La Fontasse, Col de la Gardiole, t 04 42 01 02 72 (cheap). West of Cassis, in a magnificent setting overlooking the *calanques*, this is France's most remote youth hostel, a dusty drive or an hour's walk from town or the Marseille–Cassis bus stop *Les Calanques*. It's not for sissies – beds, lights and cold water are the only creature comforts (*bring your own food*). *Closed Jan–Feb.*

Chez César, 21 Quai des Baux, t 04 42 01 75 47. Reasonably priced food served in Marcel Pagnol décor. The local, rosy-pink sea urchins (*oursins*), often crop up on the menu. *Closed Mon eve, Tues and Jan.*

Nino, 1 Quai Barthélémy, t 04 42 01 74 32 (moderate). Tasty fish soup and grilled prawns on a summery seaside terrace. *Closed Sun eve and Mon.*

Canaille. From Pas de la Colle the road and path descend to the ancient Gallo-Roman Portus Carcisis, now known as Cassis.

Cassis and the *Calanques*

The old coral-fishing village of Cassis, with its fish-hook port, white cliffs, beaches and quaint houses spilling down steep alleyways, was a natural favourite of the Fauve painters. Since their day, the village has made the inevitable progression from fishing to artsy to chic, and is now beyond the purse of most fishermen and artists. The swanky, modern **Casino Municipal** does a roaring trade thanks to its proximity to the gambling-mad Marseillais, and in the summer so many tourists descend on the little port it's often elbow room only here and on the pebbly **Plage de Bestouan**. When they're not counting wads of banknotes, the Cassidans bestir themselves to make one of the most delicious, fragrant white wines of Provence.

Until 1990, Cassis had yet another profitable trade: exporting crystal-white stone, hewn from the sheer limestone cliffs that stand like a great jagged sea wall between Cassis and Marseille. Here and there the cliffs are pierced by startling tongues of lapis lazuli hue – mini-fjords known as *calanques*. The nearest *calanque*, **Port-Miou**, is accessible by car or foot (a 30min walk): its hard, white stone was cut for the Suez Canal. Another mile's hike will take you to **Port-Pin**, with a pretty beach, and another

Wine: Cassis AOC

In Cassis, they say their white wine obtained its divine quality when God came down the road from heaven and shed a tear at the plight of a family trying to scratch a living from the rocky amphitheatre overlooking the village. The divine tear fell on a vine and *voilà*, it gave birth to a dry wine of a pale green tint, with a bouquet of heather and rosemary.

The Cassis district is minute, but was one of the first to be granted AOC status (1936). Ugni blanc, marsanne, clairette and bourboulenc are the dominant grapes of this pale cocktail, popularized abroad by the late James Beard and considered by the Marseillais to be the only liquid worthy of washing down *bouillabaisse*, grilled red mullet and lobster. Try some in the vast, ancient cellars of **Clos Sainte-Magdeleine**, t 04 42 01 70 28, and **Château de Fontcreuse**, Route de La Ciotat, t 04 42 01 71 09, f 04 42 01 32 64, the district's only real château, which between the wars was the property of a retired English colonel who improved the stock and carved out new vineyards in the steep limestone hills.

hour to **En-Vau**, the most beautiful of them all, with a small skinny-dippers' beach tucked under the sheer cliffs, where daring human flies dangle from threads (you can also reach En-Vau with less toil from a car park on the Col de la Gardiole). Take a picnic and plenty of water. Serious walkers can continue along the GR98 all the way to Marseille (for details of further *calanques*, see pp.200–201).

Note, however, that after being ravaged by forest fires in 1990 the paths to the *calanques* are strictly **off limits** from the beginning of July to the second Saturday in September, when the only way to visit is by motor boat from Cassis port; excursions depart frequently throughout the day. If they let you disembark in the *calanques*, you are supposed to stick to the shore.

Marseille

Marseille isn't a city; it's a shock.
Marseille tourist office

Amid Provence's carefully nurtured image of lavender fields, rosé wine and *pétanque*, Marseille is the great anomaly, the second city of France (although Lyon is close) and the world's eighth largest port. Like New York, it has been the gateway to a new world for hundreds of thousands of immigrants – especially Corsicans, Armenians, Jews, Greeks, Turks, Italians, Spaniards and Algerians. Many have gone no further, creating in Marseille perhaps the most varied mix of cultures and religions in Europe, 'the meeting place of the entire world', as Alexandre Dumas called it. It is traditionally the great anti-Paris, ever defiant of central authority and bigwigs in any form, be they Julius Caesar, Louis XIV, Napoleon, Hitler or De Gaulle.

Unfortunately, Marseille also shares some of New York's less savoury traits: racial hostility towards whoever was the last off the boat, the petty crooks and hardened gangsters of the French mafia or *milieu*, heroin and prostitution rings, political and

Getting There and Around

By Air

Marseille's airport is to the northwest at Marignane; call t 04 42 14 14 14 for flight information (Air France, t 0802 802 802). A bus every 20 minutes (t 04 91 50 59 34) links the airport with the train station, Gare St-Charles, and takes 25 minutes.

By Train

Gare St-Charles, t 08 36 67 68 69, is the main train station, with its big stagey staircase straight out of a Busby Berkeley musical, draped with buxom statues representing Asia and Africa. At the time of writing, however, the station itself is being evicerated in a massive modernization programme. The developers promise, however, not to tamper with the great ironwork vault over the track, designed by Gustav Eiffel. There are connections with nearly every town in the south, and the TGV will get you to Paris in 4hrs 40mins.

By Boat

Ferries sail to Algeria (politics permitting), Corsica, Sardinia and Tunisia; contact SNCM, 61 Bd des Dames, reservations t 08 36 67 95 00; information t 08 36 64 00 95, f 04 91 56 35 86. On a smaller scale, you can take the pedestrian-only 'ferryboat' across the Vieux Port, immortalized by Marcel Pagnol and captained by Marseille characters who love to ham it up. For boats to the Château d'If and Frioul Islands, see p.201.

By Métro and Bus

Marseille runs an efficient bus network and two métro lines: the métro is safe, quick and highly efficient, but the buses can be an experience. Pick up the useful plan du réseau at the tourist office or at the RTM (Réseau de Transport Marseillais) information desk by the Bourse, 6–8 Rue des Fabres, t 04 91 91 92 10. Tickets are €1.40, valid for an hour, and transferable between bus and métro. At night buses (Fluobus) run from La Canebière across town. The gare routière, t 04 91 08 16 40, is behind the train station at 3 Place Victor Hugo; it has connections to Aix, Cassis, Nice, Arles, Avignon, Toulon and Cannes.

RTM also runs a bilingual tour bus, the Histobus, with 3-hour guided tours of historic Marseille (daily in summer, Sun in winter). It leaves at 2.30pm from the Vieux Port directly in front of the boats for the islands, and gives you half an hour to wander around Notre-Dame-de Garde.

By Taxi

We haven't tried them all, of course, but it would seem that Marseille's taxi drivers are maniacs to the man. If you need one, call t 04 9102 20 20, and make sure the meter is switched on at the start of your journey.

Car Hire

There are some car hire firms in the Gare St-Charles, including **Avis**, t 04 91 64 71 00. Others are **Hertz**, at 16 Bd Charles Nédelec (1er), t 04 91 14 04 24, and **Thrifty**, Place des Marseillaise (1er), t 04 91 95 00 00. Driving in central Marseille is not for the faint hearted, and if you park in the street, only leave things inside the car that you don't want any more.

Tourist Information

Tourist office: 4 La Canebière (1er), by the Vieux Port, t 04 91 13 89 00, f 04 91 13 89 20, accueil@marseille-tourisme.com, www.marseille-tourisme.com. Open July–Sept Mon–Sat 9–7.30, Sun 10–6; Oct–June Mon–Sat 9–7, Sun 10–5. There's also an office in the train station, t 04 91 50 59 18. Check at the La Canebière office for tours of the Opéra and the Vieux Port forts, and 'Taxi Tourisme' – four different set-price taxi tours of the city (€30–86), with an English cassette guide to explain what's what.

Post office: The central post office is at 1 Place de l'Hôtel des Postes (1er), t 04 91 15 47 00.

Emergencies: Hospital, 264 Rue St-Pierre (5e), t 04 91 38 56 65.

Special **Information Centres** exist for young people, at the very helpful CIJ, 96 La Canebière (1er), t 04 91 24 33 50; for disabled visitors, at the Office Municipal pour Handicapés et Inadaptés, at the Mairie, 128 Av du Prado (8e), t 04 91 81 58 80; and for **crime victims**, at AVAD, 7 Rue de la République (2e), t 04 96 11 68 80, which will help out if you're robbed.

Market Days

Daily old book, postcard and record market in Place A. et F. Carli (1er), near the Noailles métro; every other Sunday am, flea market in Cours Julien (6e; **ⓜ** Notre-Dame du Mont).

Shopping

Rue Saint-Ferréol, home of the Galeries Lafayette and Virgin Megastore, is the centre of the city's shopping district; parallel Rue Paradis has the upmarket boutiques, and Rue de Rome is a good place to look for fake leopardskin. Marseille holds a remarkable market of clay Christmas crib figures, the *Foire aux Santons*, from end Nov to Jan; at other times, you can find *santons* at **Marcel Carbonel**, near St-Victor at 47 Rue Neuve Ste-Catherine (7e), and even see them being made (*t 04 91 54 26 58; workshops open Tues and Thurs 2.30pm, closed Aug and Christmas; museum open all year Mon–Sat 9.30–12.30 and 2–7*). **Charles-Georges Bataille**, 18 Rue Fontange (6e), t 04 91 47 46 50, is the place for Provençal food and wine.

Sports and Activities

L'Olympique de Marseille (OM) is France's most enthusiastically supported football squad and tickets often sell out (Stade Vélodrome Municipal, Bd Michelet (8e), t 04 91 71 47 00). **Windsurf boards** can be hired at Pacific Palissades, Port de la Pointe Rouge, t 04 91 73 54 37, or neighbouring Sideral Times Club, t 04 91 25 00 90. On rainy days you can roll the rock or shoot some pool until 2am at Le Bowling Notre-Dame, 107 Bd Notre-Dame (6e), t 04 91 37 15 05.

Where to Stay

Marseille ✉ 13000

Marseille's top-notch hotels are the bastion of expense-account businessmen and -women, while its downmarket numbers attract working girls of a different kind. Be sure to book if you come in mid-September, when Marseille holds its fair and there are no hotel rooms for love or money.

Luxury

★★★★Le Petit Nice Passédat, Anse de Maldormé (7e), off Corniche Kennedy, t 04 91 59 25 92, f 04 91 59 28 08, *hotel@petitnice-passedat.com, www.petitnice-passedat. com*. Marseille's most refined, exclusive hotel is a former villa overlooking the Anse de Maldormé, with a fine restaurant, Le Passédat (*see* below).

Expensive

★★★Mercure Beauvau Vieux Port, 4 Rue Beauvau (1er), t 04 91 54 91 00, f 04 91 54 15 76, *H1293@accor-hotels.com*. Overlooking the Vieux Port and where Chopin and George Sand canoodled; wood-panelled and comfortable, with quiet, air-conditioned rooms (no restaurant).

★★Péron, 119 Corniche Kennedy (7e), t 04 91 31 01 41, f 04 91 59 42 01, *marseillehotelperon@minitel.net*. With an unusual cast-iron façade and good rooms.

Moderate

★★★New Hôtel Bompard, 2 Rue des Flots Bleus (7e), t 04 91 52 10 93, f 04 91 31 02 14, *marseillebompard@new-hotel.com*. Above the Corniche Kennedy (bus no.61 from **ⓜ** Joliette or St-Victor), this modern hotel seems remote from the city, set in its own peaceful grounds, with rooms overlooking a garden; the bungalows have kitchenettes.

Inexpensive

★★★Le Corbusier, 280 Bd Michelet (8e), t 04 91 16 78 00, f 04 91 16 78 28, *hotelcorbusier@wanadoo.fr*. A special treat for students of architecture is this hotel-restaurant incorporated into the Unité d'Habitation; reserve one of its 22 rooms as early as possible.

★★Azur, 24 Cours Roosevelt (1er), **ⓜ** Réformés, t 04 91 42 74 38, f 04 91 47 27 91, *www. azurhotel.fr*. Frills such as colour TV and garden views.

★★Le Richelieu, 52 Corniche Kennedy (7e), t 04 91 31 01 92, f 04 91 59 38 09, *hotelmer@club-internet.fr*. The best rooms here are Nos.28, 29 and 30.

★Little Palace, 39 Bd d'Athènes (1er), t 04 91 90 12 93, 04 91 90 72 03. The most benign choice near the Gare St-Charles, at the foot of the grand stair.

Cheap

**Moderne, 30 Rue Breteuil (6e), t 04 91 53 29 93, f 04 96 10 36 95. Nice rooms with showers and TV.

*Montgrand, 50 Rue Montgrand (6e), t 04 91 00 35 20, f 04 91 33 75 89. Another palatable budget choice.

Auberge de Jeunesse de Bois-Luzy, Allée des Primevères (12e), t/f 04 91 49 06 18. The best of Marseille's two youth hostels is in a 19th-century château overlooking the city (buses nos.6 or 8 from La Canebière, or bus K after dark; direction La Rose).

Eating Out

The Marseillais claim an ancient Greek – even divine – origin for their ballyhooed *bouillabaisse*: Aphrodite invented it to beguile her husband Hephaestos to sleep so that she could dally with her lover Ares – seafood and saffron being a legendary soporific. Good chefs prepare it just as seriously, and display like a doctor's diploma their *Charte de la Bouillabaisse* guaranteeing that their formula more or less subscribes to tradition: a saffron and garlic-flavoured soup cooked on a low boil (hence its name), based on *rascasse* (scorpion fish, the ugliest fish in the Med and always cooked with its leering head attached), which lives under the cliffs and has a bland taste that enhances the flavour of the other fish, especially *fielas* (conger eel), *grondin* (gurnard) and *saint-pierre* (John Dory). On menus you'll usually find three degrees of *bouillabaisse*: simple or *du pêcheur*, made from the day's catch with a few shellfish thrown in; *royale*, with half a lobster included; and, most expensive of all, *royale marseillaise*, the real McCoy, with all the right fish. When it's served, the fish is traditionally cut up before you and presented on a side dish of *aïoli* (*see* p.67) or *rouille*, a paste of Spanish peppers.

General Restaurants

Restaurant Michel, 6 Rue des Catalans (7e), t 04 91 52 30 63 (*luxury*). The best and certainly the swankiest *bouillabaisse* is served at this snooty joint: you'll be mixing with politicians and showbiz people. *Open daily, year round.*

Les Mets de Provence Chez Maurice Brun, Second Floor, 18 Quai de Rive Neuve (7e), t 04 91 33 35 38 (*expensive*). There's more than *bouillabaisse* in Marseille. For a genuine Provençal spread try this 50-year-old restaurant; it has an overwhelming four-course lunch menu that starts with eight different hors-d'œuvres and includes a *pichet* of Coteaux d'Aix. *Closed Sun and Mon lunch.*

Miramar, 12 Quai du Port (2e), t 04 91 91 10 40 (*expensive*). Reliable, traditional stuff. *Closed Sun, Mon lunch and Aug.*

Les Arcenaulx, 25 Cours Honoré d'Estienne d'Orves (1er), t 04 91 59 80 30 (*moderate*). Serves fresh market fare next to a bookshop full of art books. *Closed Sun.*

L'Atelier, 18 Place aux Huiles (1er), t 04 91 33 55 00 (*moderate*). Meals here are light, in order to leave room for the exquisite grand finales. *Closed Sat eve and Sun.*

Oscar, next door to Miramar, t 04 91 90 26 86 (*moderate*). Extremely popular and tasty *bouillabaisse*. *Closed Sun.*

Le Marseillois, Quai de Port (2e), t 04 91 90 72 52 (*cheap*). A sailing boat moored stern-on, with plenty of atmosphere.

International and Late-night Eating

Marseille's unique ethnic mix produces an unrivalled selection of inexpensive cuisines from around the world.

Au Roi du Couscous, 63 Rue de la République (2e), t 04 91 91 45 46. The best couscous in town. *Closed Mon.*

Shabu Shabu, 30 Rue de la Paix (1er), t 04 91 54 15 00 (*moderate*). Japanese cuisine. *Closed Sun, Mon lunch and Aug.*

Le Mas Lulli, 4 Rue Lulli (1er), by the Opéra, t 04 91 33 25 90 (*moderate*). Night owls can assuage their hunger pangs with good pasta dishes and grills. *Open daily until 6am; closed Aug.*

Au Stop, 16 Rue Saint-Saëns (1er), t 04 91 33 85 34. A popular, inexpensive, 24-hour institution with standard fill-ups.

Country Life, 14 Rue Venture (1er), t 04 96 11 28 00 (*cheap*). For those fed up with meat. *Open lunch times, Mon–Fri only.*

La Gentiane, 9 Rue des Trois Rois (6e), t 04 91 42 88 80 (*moderate*). Another suitable place for vegetarians. *Closed Sun and Mon.*

Along the Beaches and the *Calanques*

Le Passédat, Le Petit Nice Passédat hotel (*see above*), t 04 91 59 25 92 (*luxury*). Ravishing food in an exotic garden.

Chez Fonfon, Vallon des Auffes, t 04 91 52 14 38 (*expensive*). On the fishing port overlooking the Château d'If and Frioul islands you can feast on *bouillabaisse* from this charter member, which prides itself on the freshness of its fish. *Closed Sun, Mon lunch and Jan.*

L'Epuisette, Vallon des Auffes, t 04 91 52 17 82 (*expensive*). A Marseille institution for its seafood – try the *filet de roche poêlé aux aubergines confites à l'huile d'olive*. *Closed Sat, Sun eve and Mon lunch.*

Pizzeria Jeannot, Vallon des Auffes, t 04 91 52 11 28 (*moderate*). Fancy pizza. *Closed Sun eve and Mon.*

La Grotte, 1 Rue Pebrons, t 04 91 73 17 79 (*moderate*). A favourite for pizza by the sea.

Entertainment and Nightlife

Marseille may be going on 3,000 years, but the old girl's still kicking – sometimes in the wrong places, especially after 10 in the backstreets between the station and the Vieux Port, where British lorry drivers say you can get stabbed in the back and no one would notice. But you don't have to be a brawny sailor to have a good time: Marseille has lively after-dark pockets, especially around Place Thiars, Cours Estienne d'Orves and Cours Julien. You can find out what's happening in *Taktik* or *Atout Marseille*, distributed free by the tourist office, or in the pages of *La Marseillaise*, *Le Provençal* or the Wednesday edition of *Le Méridional*. Or try the book and record chain **FNAC**, in the Centre Bourse, t 04 91 39 94 00, which has information and sells tickets.

Theatre

Marseille has a vibrant theatre scene – and more seats per capita than Paris.

Théâtre National de la Criée, 32 Quai de Rive Neuve (7e), t 04 91 54 70 54. Since 1981, director Marcel Maréchal has put on performances to wide critical acclaim.

Théâtre les Bernardines, 15 Bd Garibaldi (1er), t 04 91 24 30 40. Experimental dance/theatre.

Théâtre du Merlan, Av Raimu (14e), t 04 91 11 19 30. More avant-garde stuff.

Cinemas

César, 4 Place Castellane (6e), t 04 91 37 12 80. New and cool, with first-run films in *v.o.*

Cinéma Alhambra, 2 Rue du Cinéma (16e), t 04 91 03 84 66. Old movies and art films in their original language (*v.o.*).

Les Variétés, 37 Rue Vincent Scotto (1er), t 04 96 11 61 61. Swish cinema with pretty neon, a wine bar and first-run films in *v.o.*

Classical Music

The city has always had a special affinity with music; in fact Berlioz claimed that Marseille understood Beethoven five years before Paris.

Opéra Municipal, Place Reyer (1er), t 04 91 55 14 99. The bill includes Italian opera and occasional ballets from the Ballet National de Marseille.

Ballet National de Marseille, 20 Bd Gabès (8e), t 04 91 32 72 72, f 04 91 71 51 12, *www.ballet-de-marseille.com*.

Abbaye de St-Victor, 3 Rue de l'Abbaye (7e), t 04 91 33 25 86. Hosts a chamber music festival from Oct to Dec.

Frioul Islands. Host a music festival every July.

Bars and Clubs

Nightlife in Marseille is concentrated in several zones. Place Jean-Jaurès/Cours Julien and around is perhaps the trendiest place.

Chocolat Théâtre, 59 Cours Julien (6e), t 04 91 42 19 29. Music, along with chocolates, pastries and *plats du jour* (*moderate*). *Closed Sun.*

Espace Julien, 39 Cours Julien (6e), t 04 96 12 23 40. Jazz, rock and reggae are all on offer; there's also a café with live music many nights of the week.

Platinum Café, 20 Rue Fortia (1er), t 04 91 54 03 03.

Trolleybus, 24 Quai de Rive Neuve (7e), t 04 91 54 30 45. A popular place for a drink or a dance.

There are also bars and Latin clubs along the sea at Plage de Borély (8e); there are a number of new places at Escale Borély, including the trendy **Café de la Plage**, 148 Av Pierre-Mendès-France, t 04 91 71 21 76, with karaoke nights.

financial scandals, and an international reputation propagated by films like *The French Connection*. Unemployment is disproportionately high (up to 30 per cent in some *arrondissements*) and xenophobia thrives. The National Front has generally picked up about a third of the vote here, although recent schisms (*see* pp.43–4) reduced their support and representation.

'These Marseillais make Marseilles hymns, and Marseilles vests, and Marseilles soap for all the world; but they never sing their hymns, or wear their vests, or wash with their soap themselves,' wrote Mark Twain. So what *do* they do? Marseille is a great unknown, a metropolis of 111 villages that in its 2,600 years has contributed precious little to Western civilization; it is the eternal capital of great expectations, 'a city that's been waiting for Godot', according to an editor in one of Marseille's young publishing houses. There are hints (in theatre, the plastic arts and research) that its long bottled-up juices are ripe and ready to flow. It has recently been declared a Ville d'Art, which translates, on a practical level, into state funds for restoration of its historic monuments (at the time of writing, some 2,000 façades are being cleaned up in the city centre), and the new RPR city government seems determined to make Marseille not only respectable but also welcoming to visitors; if nothing else, it comes as an unclogging shot of *pastis* to the blood after the Côte d'Azur.

History

The story goes that in 600 BC Greek colonists from the Ionian city of Phocaea, having obtained the approval of the gods, loaded their ship with olive saplings and sailed towards Gaul. They found a perfect bay, and their handsome leader, Protis, went to the local king to obtain permission to found a city. It just so happened that that very day the king was hosting a banquet for the young men of his land, after which, according to tradition, his daughter Gyptis would select her husband. Protis was invited to join and, thanks to his great beauty, was chosen by the princess. For his new wife's dowry, Protis asked for the land the Greeks coveted near the mouth of the Rhône, including the Lacydon (the Vieux Port). He named the new city Massalia.

Massalia boomed from the start. By 530 BC it had its own treasury at Delphi, and its own colonies, from Malaga to Nice; it traded for tin with Cornwall; and its great astronomer, Pytheas, explored the Baltic and in 350 BC became the first scientist to calculate latitudes accurately. As a commercial rival of Carthage, the city allied itself with Rome in the Punic Wars, and profited from the latter's conquests in Spain and Gaul. By the 2nd century BC, Massalia had a population of 50,000 and was ruled by a merchant oligarchy whose political astuteness was admired by Aristotle and Cicero. This astuteness failed them when they sided with Pompey, calling down the vengeance of Caesar, who conquered their city after a long siege and seized all of Massalia's colonies with the exception of Nice and Hyères. Yet even after the 2nd century AD, when Massalia adopted Roman law, it remained a city apart, the western-most enclave of Hellenism, with famous schools of Greek rhetoric and medicine.

As the Pax Romana crumbled, Marseille nearly went out of business, taking hard knocks from Goths, Franks, Saracens and then the Franks again in the 8th century

under Charles Martel. Plagued by pirates, business stayed bad until the 11th century, when the Crusaders showed up looking for transport to the Holy Land. This was the best get-rich-quick opportunity of the Middle Ages, and although Genoa and Venice grabbed the biggest trading concessions in the Levant, Marseille too grew fat on the proceeds. Briefly a republic, the city's real power soon passed to a merchant oligarchy; between 1178 and 1192 the big boss was the cultivated En Barral, patron of two of Provence's greatest troubadours, the mad Peire Vidal (*see* p.59) and Folquet of Marseille .

Trumped by Kings: Charles d'Anjou to Louis XIV

When Charles d'Anjou acquired Provence in 1252, he confiscated Marseille's entire fleet to make good his claim on Sicily. Thanks to the monumental arrogance of the Angevins, the ships were annihilated in the revolt of the Sicilian Vespers (1282). With its legitimate commerce undermined by its own rulers, Marseille became a den for pirates and went into such a decline that it became an easy target for the Angevins' rival, Alfonso V of Aragon, who destroyed as much of it as he could in 1423.

Coming under French rule in 1481 meant, for Marseille, tumbling headlong into the power-grasping scrum known as the Wars of Italy (1494–1559). The city's galleys went to war again, this time for François I, earning the fury of Emperor Charles V, who sent his henchman, the rebel Constable of Bourbon, to besiege the city. Marseille resisted heroically and François I showed his gratitude by giving the city the freedom to trade at will in the eastern Mediterranean. Once again the money rolled in, to be pumped into new industries, especially soap and sugar.

Marseille's longing to be left alone to mind its own affairs put her squarely at odds with Louis XIV; for 40 years the city thumbed its nose at his Solar Majesty while scrambling to retain its autonomy. By 1660, the King had had enough: he opened up a great breach in Marseille's walls and humiliated the city by turning its own cannons back on itself. The central authority that Louis forced on Marseille was dangerously lax when it came to issues crucial to the running of a good port – like quarantine. The result, in 1720, was a devastating plague that spread throughout Provence.

Tunes, Booms and Busts

Marseille buried its dead and went right back to business. New markets in the Middle East, North Africa and America made it Europe's greatest port in the 18th century. Its industries (soap, woollens, porcelain, tarot cards) blossomed – then withered away in the Revolution, which for 10 years bitterly divided workers and the oligarchy. The former did their share in upholding the Revolution; as 500 volunteers set off for Paris in July 1792, someone suggested singing the new battle song of the Army of the Rhine, recently composed by Rouget de l'Isle. It caught on, and as the Marseillais marched along they improved the rhythm and harmonies. By the time they reached Paris, the 'song of the Marseillais' was perfected and became the hit tune of the Revolution, and subsequently the most rousing and bloodcurdling of national anthems.

However, as the Revolution devolved into the Terror, Marseille was found so wanting in proper politics that it was known in Paris as the '*ville sans nom*'. Any building that had sheltered an anti-Revolutionary was demolished, including the famous monastery of St-Victor. The misery continued under Napoleon, who was added to the list of Marseille's bogeymen when he provoked the continental blockade by the British and ruined trade. Recovery came with the Second Empire, the conquest of Algeria in 1830 and the construction of the Suez Canal. Soon Marseille was more prosperous than ever, and more populous, with some 60,000 new immigrants every decade between 1850 and 1930 – Greeks and Armenians fleeing the Turks, Italians fleeing Fascism and, later, Spaniards fleeing Franco.

After becoming one of the first French cities to vote socialist (1890), Marseille's reputation took a nosedive. Corruption, rigged elections and an open link between the Hôtel de Ville and the bosses of the *milieu* were so rampant that in 1938 Paris dissolved the municipal government and ran the city at a distance. Yet the 1930s also saw the release of Marcel Pagnol's classic Marseillais film trilogy *Marius*, *Fanny* and *César*, which helped create throughout France an insatiable appetite for *opérette marseillaise*; even Joséphine Baker sang the tunes of Marseille's great songwriter Vincent Scotto.

In 1953, Marseille elected a socialist mayor – Gaston Deferre, the antagonist of De Gaulle, who reigned until his death in 1986. Deferre oversaw rapid and difficult changes: a sharp decline in trade when France lost its colonies, and a population that exploded from 660,000 in 1955 to 960,000 in 1975. To accommodate the new arrivals (mostly North Africans and French refugees from Algeria) the city infested itself with the shoddy high-rise housing that scars it to this day. Unemployment rose as the traditional soap and fat industries plummeted, while new projects, such as the steel-mills and port at Fos, failed to provide as many jobs as expected, fuelling the racial tensions and organized crime that still give the city a rough reputation.

Even when the city, or at least its revered soccer team, L'Olympique de Marseille, won the European championship in 1993, the team got itself banned from the 1994 European competition for match fixing and bribery. The team's flamboyant then-owner, maverick politician, businessman and Euro-deputy Bernard Tapie, served eight months in Marseille's most notorious jail for the offences.

Less well known than all the scandals is Marseille's reorientation, for the first time in its history, away from the Mediterranean and towards Europe. There's a new high-speed rail link with Paris, and a canal will link the Rhône with the Rhine by 2010. Marseille is now the most important research centre in France after Paris, home of a major science university, inventor of a new, fifth-generation computer language, and site of COMEX, the world's leading developer of underwater technologies.

Orientation

Marseille, with 111 neighbourhoods and 16 *arrondissements*, is one of Europe's largest cities, sprawling over twice as many acres as Paris. The northern neighbourhoods are the poorest, the first addresses of many new immigrants; the Panier (*see* below) and neighbourhoods around the station constitute the North African quarters, lively during the day but uncomfortable to wander in after dark. The southern neighbourhoods, with their parks and access to the beaches, are distinctly more monied and sanitized. A circle of hills divides the city from the mainland, physically and psychologically.

The Vieux Port, the heart of the city since its founding, is now used only for pleasure craft and boats out to the islets of Frioul and the Château d'If, while commercial port activities are concentrated to the north in the *Rade de Marseille*. To the south of the Vieux Port, the golden Virgin of Notre-Dame de la Garde towers high over her beloved city, while to the west the Parc du Pharo marks the start of a corniche road along the coast to Cap Croisette, lined with coves, beaches and restaurants, with a mountain, Marseilleveyre, that you can climb at the end for a view of all of the above.

The Vieux Port

Marseille the urban mangrove entwines its aquatic roots around the neat, rectangular Vieux Port, where people have lived continuously for the past 2,600 years. It's now a huge marina with over 10,000 berths; its cafés have fine views of the sunset, though in the morning the action and smells centre around the Quai des Belges and its boatside **fish market**, where the key ingredients of *bouillabaisse* are touted in a racy *patois* as thick as the soup itself. From the Quai des Belges, *vedettes* sail to the Château d'If and Frioul islands (*see* below), past the two bristling fortresses that still defend the harbour: to the north **St-Jean**, first built in the 12th century by the Knights of St John, and to the south **St-Nicolas**, built by Louis XIV to keep a close eye on Marseille rather than the sea.

A bronze marker in the Quai des Belges pinpoints the spot where the Greeks first set foot in Gaul. And yet Marseille concealed its age until the 20th century, when excavations for the glitzy new shopping mall, the Centre Bourse, revealed the eastern ramparts and gate of Massalia, dating back to the 3rd century BC, now enclosed in the **Jardin des Vestiges**. On the ground floor of the Centre Bourse, the **Musée d'Histoire de Marseille** (*t 04 91 90 42 22; open Mon–Sat 12–7; adm*) displays models, everyday items, mosaics and a 3rd-century BC wreck of a Roman ship, discovered in 1974. Built from 15 different kinds of pine, it had become so fragile that it had to be freeze-dried, like instant coffee, to prevent further deterioration and aid preservation.

Elaborate antique models of later ships that sailed into the Vieux Port and items related to Marseille's trading history are the main focus of the **Musée de la Marine et de l'Economie de Marseille** (*t 04 91 39 33 33; open daily 10–6; adm*). It's housed in the 1860 **Palais de la Bourse**, France's oldest stock exchange, built during the reign of Napoleon III to obliterate an unrepentant democratic quarter that spilled much blood in the Revolution of 1848. But this corner, stock exchange or not, remained a vortex for violence: a plaque on the Canebière side of the Bourse recalls that King Alexander of Yugoslavia was assassinated here in 1934.

Just up La Canebière from here, at No.11, the **Musée de la Mode** (*t 04 91 56 59 57; open Tues–Sun 12–7; adm*) has a wardrobe full of Chanel clothes and other pieces from the 1930s to the present, but they're not always on display. The emphasis is on changing exhibitions; a recent one followed the evolution of swimming costumes.

Le Panier

On sunny afternoons the Marseillais laze like contented cats in the cafés lining the north end of the Vieux Port, a custom probably as old as the city itself. Rising up behind them is the oldest part of the city, known rather oddly as the Panier (basket) after a popular 17th-century cabaret, although its irregular weave of winding narrow streets and stairs dates from the time of the ancient Greeks. When the well-to-do moved out in the 18th century, the Panier was given over to fishermen and a romanticized underworld; guides were published to its 'private' hotels and the hourly rates of their residents.

Before the war the Panier was a lively Corsican and Italian neighbourhood, and later its warren of secret ways absorbed hundreds of Jews and other refugees from the Nazis, hoping to escape to America (*see* box overleaf).

In January 1943, Hitler cottoned on to the leaks in Marseille and, in collusion with local property speculators, gave the order to dynamite everything between the Vieux Port and halfway up the hill, to the Grand'Rue/Rue Caisserie. Given one day to evacuate, the 20,000 departing residents were screened by French police and the Gestapo, who selected 3,500 for the concentration camps and sent them out of the city in a long line of tram cars. A monument in the quarter commemorates the destruction and deportees who never returned.

Two buildings were protected from the dynamite: the 17th-century **Hôtel de Ville** on the quay and, behind it, in Rue de la Prison, the **Maison Diamantée**, Marseille's 16th-century Mannerist masterpiece, named after the pyramidical points of its façade. It holds the **Musée du Vieux Marseille** (*t 04 91 55 28 68; open Tues–Sun 10–5; undergoing renovation from 2002*), a delightful attic where the city stashes its odds and ends: Provençal furniture; an extraordinary relief diorama made in 1850 by an iron merchant, depicting the uprising of 1848; 18th-century Neapolitan Christmas crib figures and *santons* made in Marseille; playing and tarot cards, long an important local industry; and poignant photos of the Panier before it was blown to smithereens. Some of the cheap housing thrown up after the war in Place du Mazeau has been demolished in turn to make way for a museum dedicated to the flamboyant sculptor and native Marseillais César.

The dynamite that blew up the lower Panier was responsible for revealing the contents of the **Musée des Docks Romains** (*2 Place Vivaux, t 04 91 91 24 62; open summer 11–6, winter 10–5, closed Mon; adm*), built over a stretch of the vast 1st-century AD Roman quay, where wine and grains were stored in *dolia*, or massive jars. Exhibits describe seafaring in the ancient Mediterranean.

One last survivor of the pre-war Panier is the oldest house in Marseille, the **Hôtel de Cabre** (1535), a Gothic-Renaissance confection on Grand'Rue. The city's oldest café, the 1903 **Café Parisien**, with colourful mosaics and stuccoes intact, is just up on Place Sadi-Carnot.

One Good Man

Many of those who did escape Marseille did so with little thanks to US officialdom. In the early 1940s, in spite of open visa quotas, the US Department of State, with its prejudiced, bury-its-head-in-the-sand bureaucracy, maintained a policy of turning back ships of refugees from Hitler. Consulates in Europe were advised, as one memo put it, 'to resort to various administrative devices which would postpone and postpone and postpone the granting of the visas'. In a particularly shameful episode, the US Vice Consul in Lyon denied visas to Jewish children because their parents might possibly be arrested, leaving their children to become public charges in the USA.

The one hero in the story is named Varian Fry. Two months after the Nazis occupied Marseille, the 32-year-old Fry, editor of a New York foreign policy review, arrived in the city as the representative of a privately funded group called the Emergency Rescue Committee. Although he had no previous experience in the field, and in spite of the considerable risks from the Gestapo and Vichy, and the opposition of his own government, Fry quickly made himself an expert in obtaining false papers, forging documents and organizing safe transport out of Marseille: among the 1,500 people he saved were Marcel Duchamp, Marc Chagall, Hannah Arendt, André Breton and Max Ernst.

Fry worked for 13 months before he was expelled from Marseille. On his return to the USA, he published an article on the systematic persecution of the Jews and the concentration camps – which made later pleas of official ignorance ring less than true.

Just before Varian Fry died in 1967, the French government awarded him the Legion of Honour. And in October 2000 a square next to the American consulate (on Boulevard Paul Peytral) was named in his honour, Place Varian Fry. Presiding over the dedication ceremony was the US ambassador to France, Felix Rohatyn, who as a child was spirited out of occupied Marseille, in all likelihood, by the good offices of Fry.

The Panier retains its original crusty character atop the well-worn steps of **Montée des Accoules** and around **Place de Lenche**, once the market or *agora* of the Greeks: lanky cats prowl, laundry flaps, cement mixers grind away, people sit on the sidewalk in kitchen chairs – it still feels more Greek than French, although that may soon change. A five-year programme to rehabilitate 1,700 of the Panier's 3,000 homes and flats has just begun, with the ground floors set aside for shops of 'touristic interest' (although it will probably be a few years before the *santon* and lavender oil shops really get cooking).

Signs point the way through the maze to the top of Rue du Petit-Puits and the elegant **Vieille-Charité**, designed by Pierre Puget, a student of Bernini and court architect to Louis XIV – and a native of the Panier. Built by the city fathers between 1671 and 1745 to take in homeless migrants from the countryside, this is one of the world's most palatial workhouses: three storeys of arcaded ambulatories in pale pink stone, overlooking a court with a sumptuous elliptical chapel crowned by an oval dome – a curvaceous Baroque work forced into a strait-laced neo-Corinthian façade in 1863. Although the complex became a barracks after the Revolution, it returned to its original purpose in 1860, housing families displaced first by the construction of the Bourse and later by the Nazis' destruction of the Panier. By 1962, the Charité was in so precarious a state that everyone was evacuated, and Le Corbusier, happening through, warned the city it was in danger of losing a masterpiece. A long restoration ensued and in 1985 it reopened – no longer a shelter for the homeless but for culture.

The Charité's middle gallery houses the excellent **Musée d'Archéologie Méditerranéenne** (*t 04 91 14 58 80; open summer 11–6, winter 10–5, closed Mon; adm*), featuring a collection of ancient Mediterranean artefacts. The remarkable collection of Egyptian art (second in France after the Louvre) has a range of fine art and sculpture to everyday bric-a-brac and cat, ibis and crocodile mummies; there are also beautiful works from ancient Cyprus, Susa, Mesopotamia, Greece (including a good section of vases), and pre-Roman and Roman Italy. Another section is devoted to the reconstructed Sanctuary of Roquepertuse from Velaux, near Aix. Built by a head-hunting Celto-Ligurian tribe called the Salians, the sanctuary has pillars pierced with holes to hold skulls, a lintel incised with the outline of four horse heads (these symbolically transported the dead soul), and Buddha-like figures sitting in the lotus position. Similar temples found in Entremont (*see* p.221) and Mouriès suggest a common religion, perhaps a chthonic cult in which warriors went to commune with the spirits of their dead heroes. The Charité also houses the **Musée d'Arts Africain, Océanien et Amérindien** (*open summer 11–6, winter 10–5, closed Mon; adm*), with a fascinating collection of ritual artefacts, especially those dealing with more recent cultures obsessed with human heads and skulls, as in the Amazon and Vanuatu (don't miss the Aztec skull intricately decorated with the teeniest tiniest turquoise tiles imaginable).

Just to the west, looming over the tankers and cargo ships drowsing in Marseille's outer harbour basin, are the two 'majors'. The striped neo-Byzantine, empty and unloved **Cathédrale de la Major** (*open Tues–Thurs 9–12 and 2–5.30, Fri 9–12 and 2–6.30, Sat and Sun 9–12 and 2.30–6*) was built in 1853 with the new money coming in from the conquest of Algeria – enough to make it the largest church built in France since the Middle Ages. Now utterly isolated by lanes of frantic traffic, the pile is held up by 444 marble columns; predictably, somehow, the monster is not only ugly but dangerous, and has to be encased in nets to keep the rare visitor from being brained by bits of falling stone.

The cathedral's Romanesque predecessor, the **Ancienne-Major**, is in better nick, in spite of having its transept brutally amputated for the new cathedral (note the poor angel, gesturing sadly without a hand). Inside, don't miss the Ancienne-Major's crossing, a fantasy in brick that sets an octagonal dome on four stepped conical squinches, a typically Provençal conceit. One chapel has a Descent from the Cross (early 16th century) by Nicolas della Robbia; the altar of SS. Lazarus, Martha and Mary Magdalene in Carrara marble (1475–81) is by Francesco Laurana and was considered by Anthony Blunt to be 'the earliest purely Italian work on French soil'. What you never get to see is the Ancienne-Major's old curiosity shop of relics: part of Jesus' cradle and one of His tears, St Peter's tooth and, best of all, the fishbones left over from the feast at the Sermon on the Mount.

South of the Vieux Port: Quai de Rive Neuve and St-Victor

In the last decade, this part of the Old Port has made a comeback: at lunch time and on summer evenings half of Marseille descends on its bars, restaurants, theatres and clubs on the quay, Rue Saint-Saëns and Place Thiars. The oldest cultural institution here is the **Opéra**, two blocks south of the port in Place Reyer, built in 1924 and graced with Art Deco Greek gods and a pure Art Deco interior (see the tourist office for tours). Two streets back, at 19 Rue Grignan, a *hôtel particulier* houses the **Musée Cantini** (*t 04 91 54 77 75; open summer 11–6, winter 10–5, closed Mon; adm*) and its modern art and frequent special exhibitions, which have included Picabia, Max Ernst, André Masson, Francis Bacon, Balthus, César, Arman and Ben. Permanent displays include Paul Signac's shimmering *Port de Marseille*, and the first Cubist views of L'Estaque that Dufy painted with Braque in 1908; the greater part of the Cantini's post-1960 works have been moved into the new Musée d'Art Contemporain (see p.200).

On **Quai de Rive Neuve** you'll find ship chandlers' shops, restaurants and the national theatre, **La Criée**, installed in a former fish auction house (see below). For better or worse, its presence has tamed the once salty Rive Neuve bars, including the **Bar de la Marine**, no longer recognizable as the set for the famous card-playing scene in Marcel Pagnol's *Marius*. Further along the *quai*, steps lead up to battlemented walls and towers good enough for a Hollywood castle, defending one of the oldest Christian shrines in Provence, the **Abbaye St-Victor**. St-Victor was founded in AD 416 by St Jean Cassien, formerly an anchorite in the Egyptian Thebaid. One account has it that he brought with him from Egypt the mummy of St Victor, though the more popular version says Victor was a Roman legionary who converted to Christianity and slew at least one sea serpent (see the relief over the door) before being ground to a pulp between a pair of millstones. In art he sometimes looks like Don Quixote, with a windmill.

St-Victor may be Marseille's oldest church, but it's no fuddy-duddy: like Broadway, it has an electronic sign at the entrance reeling off news, and the side aisles are equipped with TV screens so all the parishioners can view mass at the high altar – doings Jean Cassien never imagined 1,600 years ago when he excavated the first chapels into the flank of an ancient stone quarry near a Hellenistic necropolis, which he expanded for Christian use as a *martyrium* (rock-cut burial niches surrounding the tomb of a martyr). In the 11th century, when the monks of St-Victor adopted the Rule of St Benedict, they added the church on top, turning the old chapels into a labyrinthine **crypt** (*open daily 8–7.15; adm*). Although now well lit, this curious termitarium, with ceilings ranging from 6 to 60ft high, is suffused with ancient mystery – some of the beautifully sculpted sarcophagi date from the 3rd century AD and were found to contain seven or eight dead monks crowded like sardines, proof of the popularity of an abbey that founded 300 monastic houses in Provence and Sardinia. Then there's the 5th-century sarcophagus of St Jean Cassien, showing the saint preaching among the columns, and the cave-like 5th-century chapel, carved with a pair of weird old faces and stained green with moss, traditionally enshrining one of Marseille's three Black Virgins (supposedly Christian adaptations of Artemis, the patroness of Massalia). A primordial Candlemas rite begins here every 2 February: the archbishop comes to bless green candles before the Virgin, who gets to go out in a procession that ends at the abbey's bakery, where small loaves (*navettes*) are baked in the shape of boats – a similar custom, in the temples of Isis, once heralded the start of the navigation season. The faithful then take the green candles home to light at wakes as a symbol of rebirth.

Notre-Dame de la Garde

Below St-Victor is Louis XIV's **Fort St-Nicolas**, and beyond that the **Château du Pharo** (bus no.83 from the Vieux Port), built by Napoleon III as a gift for his wife, the Empress Eugénie, who never got around to seeing it. The gardens, with striking views over the port, are used for concerts and summer theatre under the stars; beyond are the *calanques* (*see* pp.200–201). The prize 360° view, however, is from Marseille's watchtower hill – an isolated limestone outcrop towering 530ft above the city, crowned by **Notre-Dame de la Garde** (*open daily summer 7am–8pm, winter 7am–7pm*), a neo-Byzantine/Romanesque pile with an unfortunate resemblance to a locomotive (a killer walk, and even fairly hair-raising to drive; let bus no.60 do the work from Place aux Huiles on Quai de Rive Neuve). This landmark supports France's largest golden mega-Madonna, 33ft high and shining like a beacon out to sea. In 1214 a monk of St-Victor built the first chapel here and over the decades it gained a reputation for the miracles performed by a statue of the Virgin, Marseille's 'Bonne Mère'. The chapel's florid Second Empire architecture attracted some real bombs when the Nazis made it their headquarters and last stand, and you can still see some of the dents. But besides the view, the main attraction is the basilica's great collection of *ex votos*, painted by fishermen and sailors.

La Canebière

Before La Canebière itself was laid out in Louis XIV's expansion scheme of 1666, this area was the ropemakers' quarter. The hemp they used has given its name to Marseille's most famous boulevard – *chanvre* in French, but in Provençal more like the Latin *cannabis* – a not entirely inappropriate allusion, for this was the high street of French *dolce far niente*, an essential ingredient of music-hall Marseille, which could swagger and boast that 'the Champs-Elysées is the Canebière of Paris'. In its day, La Canebière sported grand cafés, fancy shops and hotels where travellers of yore had their first thrills before sailing off to exotic lands, but these days La Canebière – or 'Can o' beer' as English sailors know it – has suffered the same fate as the Champs-Elysées: banks, airline offices and heavy traffic. Trees would do it a world of good.

Some of the Canebière's old pizzazz lingers in the lively streets to the south around 'Marseille's stomach', the **Marché des Capucins**, a grazer's heaven, where the air is filled with tempting, exotic smells and most of the shops are North African. Here, too, is Noailles station, the last resting place for the city's retired omnibuses and tramways (**La Galerie des Transports**, *t 04 91 54 15 15; open Wed–Sat 10–5*); Marseille's last working tram still has its terminus here. Behind this hurly-burly stretches the **Cours Julien**, a favourite promenade and *pétanque* court, lined with many antiques shops, galleries and several trendy restaurants.

North, and perpendicular to La Canebière, extends another tarnished grand boulevard, **Cours Belsunce**. Until 1964, No.54 was the site of the famous neo-Moorish/Art Nouveau music hall where Maurice Chevalier and Fernandel once starred, and where Tino Rossi and Yves Montand had their stage debuts. Now the Cours leads only to the **Porte d'Aix**, a fuzzy-minded Roman triumphal arch, vintage 1823, erected to Louis XVI or Liberty or both, and adorned with statues of virtues such as Resignation and Prudence, whose heads (much like Louis XVI's) suddenly fell off in 1937 and rolled down the street. This quarter, like the Panier, is now mostly North African: Marseille's mosque is just on the other side of the arch.

Palais Longchamp and Environs

In 1834, Marseille suffered a drought so severe that it dug a canal to bring in water from the Durance. This 80km feat of aquatic engineering ends with a heroic splash at the **Palais Longchamp**, a delightfully overblown nymphaeum and cascade, populated with stone felines, bulls and a buxom allegory of the Durance (Ⓜ Cinq-Avenues-Longchamp; bus no.80 from La Canebière). Behind the palace stretch the public gardens, an observatory (one of four in this city, which has been the home of many famous astronomers) and a little zoo; in the right wing of the palace itself, some of the creatures from it are embalmed in the **Muséum d'Histoire Naturelle**, sharing space with their fossilized ancestors (*t 04 91 14 59 50; open summer 11–6, winter 10–5, closed Mon; adm*).

The left wing of the Palais Longchamp houses the **Musée des Beaux-Arts** (*t 04 91 14 59 30; open summer 11–6, winter 10–5, closed Mon; adm*). Formed around art 'conquered' by Napoleon's army, it has some second-rate canvases by Italian masters such as Perugino, and stagey burlesques like Rubens' violent *Boar Hunt* (in which ladies daintily watch the spurting blood) or Louis Finson's *Samson and Delilah* (1600), with a nasty Delilah tugging the ear of a very dirty-footed Samson. The mood changes with Michel Serre's scrupulously dire *Scenes of the Marseille Plague of 1720*, where a large percentage of the plague's 40,000 victims are shown dropping like flies while healthy rich men in suits prance by on horseback, looking politely sympathetic.

These same gentlemen never dismounted to assist Marseille's native artists, either – even an establishment figure like Baroque sculptor, architect and painter Pierre Puget (1671–1745); the rooms devoted to him feature models for buildings and a lovely square that Marseille regrettably never built. Then there's Françoise Duparc, a follower of Chardin (1726–76), who worked most of her life in England; and the satirist Honoré Daumier (1808–97), who went to prison for his biting caricatures of Louis Philippe's toadies, here represented by *Spitting Image*-style satirical busts modelled after his drawings. Here, too, is Van Gogh's roving, bohemian precursor Adolphe Monticelli (1824–86), who sold his paint-encrusted canvases of fragmented colour for a day's food and drink in the cafés along La Canebière.

Also of note are paintings by Provençal pre-Impressionists, especially 18th-century scenes of Marseille's port by Joseph Vernet and sun-drenched landscapes by Paul Guigou.

Just across Boulevard Longchamp at No.140, the **Musée Grobet-Labadié** (*t 04 91 62 21 82; open summer 11–6, winter 10–5, closed Mon; adm*) contains a private collection as interesting for its eclecticism as for any individual painting, table, plate, instrument, tapestry or iron lock.

Heading South: Le Corbusier and Mazargues

The building that achieves speed will achieve success.
Le Corbusier

To pay your respects to Modular Man, take bus no.21 from the Bourse down wide Avenue du Prado and Boulevard Michelet (perfect for rollerblading, if you've brought your skates) and past the swish Vélodrome football stadium to the *Corbusier* stop. In 1945, at the height of Marseille's housing crisis, the French government commissioned Le Corbusier to build an experimental **Unité d'Habitation**, derived from his 1935 theory of 'La Cité Radieuse'. Le Corbusier thought the solution to urban *anomie* and transport and housing problems was to put living space, schools, shops and recreational facilities all under one roof, in a building designed according to the human proportions of Leonardo da Vinci's Renaissance man-in-a-circle, reborn as Le Corbusier's wiggly Modular Man symbol. You can see the Man in relief on the concrete *pilotis*, or stilts, the most revolutionary aspect of the building. Le Corbusier, who knew the future role of cars, intended that the ground level should be for parking.

For a city like Marseille, where people enjoy getting out and about at ground level, the building was a ghastly aberration, and was nicknamed the *casa de fada*, or 'house of the mentally deranged'. Plans for other *unités* were stifled and in 1952 the state sold the flats off as co-ops. But architects were entranced, and for the next 30 years thousands of buildings in every city in the world went up on *pilotis*, before everyone realized that the Marseillais were right all along: it is madness to deprive a building of its most important asset, a ground floor. The Unité's genuinely good points, unfortunately, had few imitators – each of its 337 flats is built on two levels and designed for maximum privacy, each with fine views over the mountains or sea. Of the original extras, only the school, the top-floor gym and the communal hotel for residents' guests (*see* 'Where to Stay', p.184) have survived.

Bus no.21 continues towards **Mazargues**, a once-fashionable *banlieue* under the Massif de Marseilleveyre, famous in the 19th century for its climate. When its residents died, at a ripe old age, they often chose to be remembered in the local cemetery by a mini-monument to their life's work – there are stone hedge-clippers, fishing boats, hoes and, on the tomb of an omnibus driver, a tramway.

Marseille's Corniche and Parc Borély

Why go to the Riviera when Marseille has one of its very own? From the Vieux Port, you can catch bus no.83 past the Parc du Pharo to **Corniche Kennedy**, a dramatic road overlooking a dramatic coast that must have reminded the ancient Greek colonists of home – now improved with artificial beaches, bars, restaurants, villas and nightclubs.

Amazingly, until the road was built in the 1850s, the first cove, the picture-postcard **Anse des Catalans**, was so isolated that the Catalan fisherfolk who lived there as squatters in the ruins of the old Lazaretto (quarantine station) could hardly speak French. This now has the most popular (and the only real) sandy beach. From the bus stop *Vallon des Auffes* you can walk down to the fishing village of **Anse des Auffes** ('of the rope-makers'), isolated from the corniche until after the Second World War and still determinedly intact.

Other typical quarters with still more piquant names lie further on: **Anse de Maldormé** and **Anse de la Fausse Monnaie**. As soon as the corniche was built, the wealthy families of Marseille planted grand villas along it: the Château Talabot is one of the most spectacular of these.

The corniche then descends to the artificial **Plage Gaston Deferre**, where a copy of Michelangelo's *David* holds court at the corner of Avenue du Prado, looking even more smugly ridiculous than he does in Florence. Beyond the big fellow opens the cool green expanse of **Parc Borély**, with a botanical garden, duck ponds and the **Château Borély**, an 18th-century palace built according to the strictest classical proportions for a wealthy merchant and unique for its surviving interior decoration. Behind it, Avenue de Hambourg leads into Sainte-Anne, another former village, where César's Giant Thumb emerges at the Avenue d'Haïfa, signalling the vast new **Musée d'Art Contemporain** at No.69 (*t 04 91 25 01 07; open summer 11–6, winter 10–5, closed Mon; adm*), with a large collection of post-war art (New Realists, Arte Povera, 'individual mythologies' and more).

The *Calanques* and Grotte Cosquer

To continue east along the coast from Parc Borély, you'll need to change to bus no.19, which passes by another beach and the **Musée de la Faïence**, in the 19th-century Château Pastré (*157 Av de Montredon, t 04 91 72 43 47; open summer 11–6, winter 10–5, closed Mon; adm*), with an exceptional collection of faïence from Neolithic times to the present, concentrating on the famous ware made in Marseille and Moustiers from the 17th century on.

Bus no.19 poops out just after Calanque du Mont Rose, Marseille's nudist beach. Bus no.20 from here continues to Cap Croisette, a miniature end-of-the-world at the base of the Massif de Marseilleveyre – which forms a backdrop to the fishing hamlet in the Calanque des Goudes – and the pebble beach at Calanque de Samena, facing the islets of Maïre and Tiboulen. The road gives out at the narrow Calanque de Callelongue, where the GR98 coastal path to Cassis begins (see pp.181–2). Another path from here leads in 2 hours to the summit of Marseilleveyre (1,417ft), with grand views over Marseille, its industrial rade and the islands.

In 1991 the next *calanque*, the beautiful, chalky, jagged **Calanque de Sormiou**, made national headlines when local diver Henri Cosquer discovered a hollow 130ft under the sea that hid the entrance to a tunnel. Cosquer swam up the tunnel and after 220 yards found himself in a subterranean cave above sea level, to his astonishment covered with paintings of running bison, horses, deer and the ancestors of the modern penguin. Along with the art, Cosquer found 'negative' handprints, made by blowing colour around a hand to create its outline on the wall. Similar 'artists' signatures' mark the famous painted caves in the Dordogne. Although first dismissed as a forgery, mainly because no similar works have ever been found in Provence, the Grotte Cosquer is now recognized by prehistorians as a contemporary of Lascaux (*c.* 27,000 BC). At the time, when much of the northern hemisphere's water was concentrated in Ice Age glaciers, the level of the Mediterranean was much lower, so that the entrance to the cave was on dry land. The climate of Provence was also considerably colder – hence the bison and penguins. To protect the art, the cave has been walled up, but reproductions are on display at the Exposition Grotte Henri Cosquer.

Sormiou and the more distant *calanques* are most painlessly reached from Marseille by boats which operate mid-June to mid-September from the Quai des Belges (Groupement des Armateurs Côtiers de Marseille, *t* 04 91 55 50 09). Alternatively, take bus no.21 from La Canebière to the end of the line (Luminy) and walk 40 minutes to Calanque de Morgiou, dotted with seaside cabanons, or to the wilder Calanque de Sugiton.

The Château d'If and Frioul Islands

'*If*' in French means yew, a tree associated with death, and an appropriately sinister name for this gloomy precursor of Alcatraz, the Château d'If (*t 04 91 59 02 30; open daily 9.30–6.30 except in rough seas; boats from the Quai des Belges, t 04 91 55 50 09; departures hourly 9–6 in summer; 9, 10.30, 12, 2, 3.30 and 5 in winter*), built by François I in 1524, originally to defend Marseille from Emperor Charles V. Even while Alexandre Dumas was still alive, visitors came to see the cell of the Count of Monte-Cristo, and a cell, complete with escape hole, was obligingly made to show to visitors. Real-life inmates included Mirabeau, imprisoned by his father-in-law for running up debts in Aix (*see* p.213); a Monsieur de Niozelles, condemned to six years in solitary confinement for not taking his hat off in front of Louis XIV; and, after the revocation of the Edict of Nantes, thousands of Protestants, who either died here or went on to die as galley slaves somewhere else.

The two other islands in the Archipel du Frioul, **Pomègues** and **Ratonneau**, are white as bones and nearly as dry, tortured into crags and lumps by the mistral. They were originally hunting and fishing reserves and witnessed, in 1516, one of the first rhinoceroses in Europe, who rambled here en route to Pope Leo X's menagerie in Rome. Later used as quarantine islands, they are now linked by a causeway at Port du Frioul, a marina designed by Le Corbusier's pupil, José-Luis Sert. Scores of swimming coves can be easily reached by foot, along paths lined with aromatic herbs and plants especially adapted to the extremely dry climate. A 20-minute path leads to the **Hôpital Caroline**, built in the 1820s on Ratonneau, where the winds blow the strongest – on the theory that they would help 'purify' infectious diseases. Now used for a summer festival, the hospital has excellent views of Marseille – as Marseille was meant to be seen, from the sea – that must have been heartbreaking to the imprisoned patients.

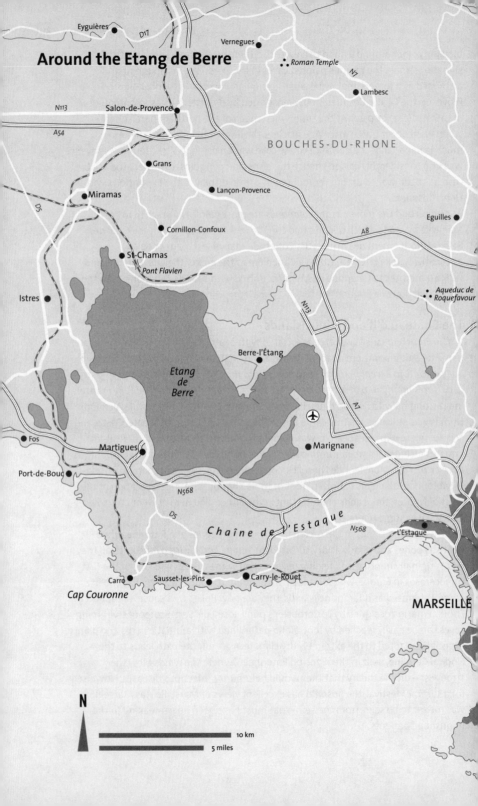

West of Marseille: Chaîne de l'Estaque and the Etang de Berre

Whatever personality of its own this region once had has been thoroughly chewed and swallowed by the metropolis next door. Once sheltering attractive, out-of-the-way retreats, the Estaque coast and the broad lagoon of Berre behind it have totally succumbed to creeping suburbia in the last three decades; isolated corners that once knew only hamlets of poor fishermen now suffer some of the biggest industrial complexes in France. Still, the 'Côte Bleue', as the tourist offices call the Estaque coast, is a very attractive piece of coastline. Especially in the east, the mountains plunge straight into the sea, with sheltered *calanques* between them; there is no road along the coast until Carry-le-Rouet.

L'Estaque to Sausset-les-Pins

Leaving Marseille on the N568, you'll pass the industrial suburb, docks and marinas of L'Estaque (bus no.35 from the Vieux Port) – a favourite subject of Cézanne, who came to paint here off and on for 15 years, and whose vision of a new, classical Provence transformed the town's smokestacks into Doric columns. He was followed by Braque, Dufy, Marquet and others; the Marseille tourist office has a brochure pinpointing the spots where they set up their easels, but don't expect to recognize too many of the scenes. The road then crosses over the Souterrain du Rove, the world's longest ship tunnel. A partial collapse closed it in the 1960s, and no one has found it worth repairing since. Tortuous side roads from the N568 will take you down to two pleasant enclaves harbouring old fishing villages, Niolon and Méjean.

The reputation of **Carry-le-Rouet**, the biggest town on the coast, is based on the two very odd-looking gifts it has bestowed on the world: the horse-faced actor Fernandel and prickly-stickly sea urchins; it celebrates the latter with a festival each February. There is a beach, often oversubscribed; Carry is fast being surrounded by the weekend villas of the Marseillais. **Sausset-les-Pins**, the next town, is much the same; however, if you press on further, there are popular, if often crowded, beaches around **Carro** and especially **Cap Couronne**, a favourite of the Marseillais.

Martigues

On the lagoon side of the Chaîne de l'Estaque, facing inland across the Etang de Berre, the distinguished old city of **Marignane** has been completely engulfed by Marseille's sprawl and airport. In the centre of the old town, you can visit its 14th-century château (now the *mairie*), an eccentric work with mythological frescoes. From here, making a clockwise tour around the Etang de Berre, the next stop is **Martigues**, a sweet little city full of salt air and sailboats, not a compelling place to visit but probably a wonderful place to live. If Carry-le-Rouet serves up sea urchins to visitors in February, Martigues can answer with its own speciality – fresh sardines – during its Sardine Festival in July and August.

Tourist Information

Carry-le-Rouet ✉ 13620: Av Aristide Briand,
t 04 42 13 20 36, **f** 04 42 44 52 03,
ot@carrylerouet@visitprovence.com,
www.carry-le-rouet.com. Open July–Aug
Mon–Sat 9–12 and 2–6, Sun 10–12; Sept–June
Tues –Sat 10–12 and 2–5.
Martigues ✉ 13500: 2 Quai Paul Doumer,
t 04 42 42 31 10, **f** 04 42 42 31 11,
www.martigues.com or www.martigues.org.
Open Mon–Sat 9–7, Sun and hols 9.30–12.30
and 3–7.
Salon ✉ 13300: 56 Cours Gimon, **t** 04 90 56
27 60, **f** 04 90 56 77 09, otsalon@visit
provence.com. Open summer daily 9–1 and
2–7, winter daily 9–12 and 2–6.30.

Market Days

Carry-le-Rouet: Tuesday and Friday.
Martigues: Thursday and Sunday mornings.
Salon: Wednesday mornings.

Where to Stay and Eat

Carry-le-Rouet ✉ 13620

Since most people here have villas or are on
a day trip from the city, accommodation is
scarce and functional.
★★La Tuilière, 53 Av Draïo-de-la-Mar, **t** 04 42
44 79 79, **f** 04 42 44 74 40 (inexpensive).
There's plenty of seafood along the
Promenade du Port.
L'Escale, **t** 04 42 45 00 47. Try the roast lobster
or sea bass grilled with spices on the attractive seaside terraces of L'Escale. Closed Sun
eve and Mon.
Le Calypso, Quai Vayssiere, **t** 04 42 45 10 64,
and **Le Madrigal**, Av G. Montus, **t** 04 42 44
58 63. Both places are moderately priced
and no more ordinary than L'Escale. Closed
Nov–Feb.

Martigues ✉ 13500

★★L'Eden, Bd Emile Zola, **t** 04 42 07 36 37,
f 04 42 07 10 55 (inexpensive). On the
outskirts of town.

Martigues sits astride the Canal de Caronte, which links the lagoon and the sea,
lending it a slight but much-trumpeted resemblance to Venice. According to legend,
the city was founded by and named after the Roman General Marius; the oldest part
of town is the Ile Brescon, at the head of the channel, with the Baroque church of the
Madeleine and a number of 17th- and 18th-century buildings. One of its prettiest
corners is a quay called the **Miroir des Oiseaux**, the 'mirror of birds'. On the mainland,
the **Musée Ziem** (Bd du 14 Juillet, **t** 04 42 80 66 06; open July and Aug Wed–Mon 10–12
and 2.30–6.30; Sept–June Wed–Sun 2.30–6.30; adm) has paintings left to Martigues by
landscape artist Félix Ziem, and works by Provençal painters Guigou, Monticelli and
Loubon, as well as archaeology exhibits.

Fos

The French, fascinated with technology, actually come to visit this gigantic industrial complex. Fos has an **information centre** on Av Jean Jaurès (**t** 04 42 47 71 96), and
there are guided tours. You too might consider a drive through – in its way, Fos is the
most astounding, unsettling sight in Provence. Before 1965, when France's
Mephistophelean economic planners commandeered it to replace the overcrowded
port of Marseille, this corner of the Camargue was pristine marshland. Today it is the
biggest oil port, and the biggest industrial complex, on the entire Mediterranean. In
area it is considerably larger than Marseille.

To a degree, it makes sense to concentrate unpleasant industry all in one place. But
when driving past the 19km of chemical plants, steel mills and power lines, rising out

Le Cigalon, 35 Bd 14 Juillet, **t 04 42 80 49 16, **f** 04 42 49 26 71, *www.lecigalon.fr* (*inexpensive; restaurant moderate*). In the centre. *Restaurant closed Mon lunch, Wed, Sun eve.*

Salon ✉ 13300

****Abbaye de Ste-Croix, Route du Val de Cuech (D16), **t** 04 90 56 24 55, **f** 04 90 56 31 12, *saintecroix@relaischateaux.fr* (*expensive*). If *force majeure* constrains you to spend a night in Salon, you can luxuriate at this Relais & Châteaux place, 5km out of town, with expensive and lovely rooms overlooking a medieval cloister. There's a swimming pool and horse-riding, an ultra-posh restaurant with shrimps flambéed in *pastis* and lamb in truffle sauce, and a big wine list. *Closed Nov to mid-Mar.*

****Le Mas du Soleil, 38 Chemin Saint Côme, **t** 04 90 56 06 53, **f** 04 90 56 21 52, *le.mas.du.soleil@wanadoo.fr* (*expensive*). Elegant, air-conditioned rooms, pool and terrace, and a traditional but not predictable restaurant, with beautifully

presented dishes including *civet de homard au Banyuls.*

Vendôme, 34 Rue du Maréchal Joffre, **t 04 90 56 01 96, **f** 04 90 56 48 78, *hotelvendome@ifrance.com* (*inexpensive*). Bright, pretty and old-fashioned.

Domaine de Roquerousse, north on the road to Avignon, **t 04 90 59 50 11, **f** 04 90 59 53 75, *reservation@domaine-de-roquebrune.com*, *www.domaine-de-roquebrune.com* (*inexpensive; restaurant cheap*). Pretty rooms in the individual buildings of a 19th-century *mas*, in a park, with a pool and tennis.

La Salle à Manger, 6 Rue du Maréchal Joffre, **t** 04 90 56 28 01 (*moderate*). Housed in an exuberantly floral 19th-century mansion and offering a delicious if rather extravagant choice of dishes (ostrich carpaccio, for instance, and 40 different puddings) to match the décor. *Closed Sun eve and Mon.*

La Brocherie des Cordeliers, 20 Rue d'Hozier, **t** 04 90 56 53 42 (*cheap*). Dine in the 13th-century chapel that once hosted Nostradamus' mortal remains. *Closed Sun eve and Mon.*

---

of the void like a mirage, the senses rebel. Economically, the 'ZIP' (*zone industrielle-portuaire*) is a failure; as planning, it is stupidly primitive, ecologically disastrous and demeaning to the people who live and work in it: the perfect marriage of corporate gigantism and bureaucratic simple-mindedness.

West and North of the Etang de Berre

Along the west shore there is more of the same, engulfing ancient villages like **St-Blaise**, which has a Romanesque church and a wealth of ruins currently being excavated, including a rare stretch of Greek wall. Of the two large towns, **Istres** has a Provençal Romanesque fortified church, Notre-Dame de Beauvoir, and a Musée Archéologique (**t** *04 42 55 50 08; open daily 2–6; adm*), filled with mostly Roman-era finds discovered by divers in the Golfe de Fos. **Miramas** is more attractive, with the ruins of its medieval predecessor nearby at Miramas-le-Vieux. There's also a railway museum (**t** *04 90 58 07 41*).

St-Chamas, to the southeast, has an impressive Baroque church. The Via Domitia passed this way, and over a small stream south of the village stands one of the finest and best-preserved Roman bridges anywhere, the **Pont Flavien**. Built in the 1st century AD, the single-arched span features a pair of very elegant triumphal arches at the approaches, decorated with Corinthian capitals, floral reliefs and stone lions. But life went on here even earlier than that, and there are troglodyte dwellings to prove it.

North of the Etang, towards Salon, lie three attractive villages: **Cornillon-Confoux**, on a steep hill with a wide view, **Grans** and **Lançon-Provence**, the latter being home of some of the most exquisite AOC Coteaux d'Aix-en-Provence wines (*see* p.220).

Salon-de-Provence

The home of Nostradamus should be a more interesting place. Aix-en-Provence's disagreeable little sister, Salon is quite well off from processing olive oil, making soap and being home to the French air force training school. The town seems aptly named: a little bourgeois parlour, smug and stuffy and neat as a pin. Its spirit is captured perfectly in the antiseptic, gentrified *vieille ville*, ruined by a hideous and insensitive restoration programme in the last few years. Even the antiseptic has its surprises, however: surely the snazziest tiled loos in France (underneath Place du Général de Gaulle), and L'Ecole des Bergers, France's national school for shepherds.

The old quarter, surrounded by a ring of boulevards, is entered by the 18th-century **Porte de l'Horloge**, with an ironwork clock tower. In the centre, at the highest point of Salon, is the **Château de l'Empéri**, parts of which go back to the 10th century. Long a possession of the Archbishops of Arles, it now houses the **Musée National de l'Empéri** (*t 04 90 56 22 36; open Wed–Mon 10–12 and 2.30–6; adm*), which contains a

---

Nostradamus

Salon's most famous citizen was born in St-Rémy in 1503, to a family of converted Jews. Trained as a doctor in Montpellier, young Michel de Nostredame made a name for himself by successfully treating plague victims in Lyon and Aix. In 1547 he married a girl from Salon and settled down there, practising medicine and pursuing a score of other interests besides – studying astrology, publishing almanacs and inventing new recipes for cosmetics and hair dyes. The first of his *Centuries*, ambiguous quatrains written in the future tense, were published in 1555, achieving celebrity for their author almost immediately.

Nostradamus himself said that his works came from 'natural instinct and poetic passion'; in form they are similar to some other poetry of the day, such as the *Visions* of Du Bellay. It may be that he had never really intended to become an occult super-star – but when the peasants start bringing you two-headed sheep asking for an explanation, and when the Queen Regent of France sends an invitation to court, what's a man to do? Nostradamus went to Paris, and later Charles IX and Catherine de' Medici came to visit him in Salon. The Salonnais didn't appreciate such notoriety; if it had not been for Nostradamus's royal favour, they might well have put him to the torch. Now they've made up, and you can visit the **Maison de Nostradamus,** just inside the Porte de l'Horloge (*11 Rue de Nostradamus, t 04 90 56 64 31; open Mon–Fri 9–12 and 2–6, Sat and Sun 2–6; adm*). On his death in 1566, Nostradamus was oddly buried inside the wall of the Cordeliers' church; tales spread that he was still alive in there, writing his final book of prophecies. After his tomb was desecrated in the Revolution, he was moved to the 14th-century Dominican church of St-Laurent, on Rue du Maréchal Joffre, where he rests today.

substantial hoard of weapons, bric-a-brac and epauletted mannequins on horseback, covering France's army from Louis XIV to 1918, with an emphasis on Napoleon.

The **Musée Grévin de la Provence** (*t 04 90 56 36 30; same hours as Maison de Nostradamus; adm*), run by the Parisian waxwork family Grévin, displays the history of Provence in 54 waxwork figures, from Marius' battle with the Barbarians, through a lifeless Napoleon, to Pagnol's *Manon des Sources*. If you can face yet another museum, there's the **Musée de Salon et de la Crau** (*Av Donnadieu, t 04 90 56 28 37; open Mon and Wed–Fri 10–12 and 2–6.30; Sat and Sun 2–6; adm*), with a dry, old-fashioned exhibition of costumes, furniture and paintings. East of Salon along the D572, the **Château de la Barben** once belonged to Napoleon's favourite sister, Pauline Borghese, and now has a little zoo in the grounds for the kids.

North of Salon on the D17, **Eyguières** is an archetypal Provençal village, with Celtic-Greek tombs above the ruins of a medieval castle; their contents may be seen in the **Dépôt Archéologique** (*t 04 90 57 90 64; open Sat am or by appointment; donation appreciated*). Also note the 10th-century Chapelle-St-Vérédème. **Vernègues**, in a forgotten corner of Provence (take the D16 northeast of Salon), has a ruined castle and, just east, the ruins of a 1st-century-BC Roman temple.

Aix-en-Provence

Elegant and honey-hued, the old capital of Provence is splashed by a score of fountains, a charming reminder that its very name comes from its waters, *Aquae Sextiae* – sweet water, mind you, with none of the saltiness and excesses of Marseille. For if tumultuous Marseille is the great anti-Paris, Aix-en-Provence is the stalwart anti-Marseille – bourgeois, cultured, aristocratic, urbane, slow-paced, convivial. Since 1948, Aix has hosted France's most elite festival of music and opera, while its 580-year-old university not only teaches the arts and humanities to the French but instructs foreign students in the fine arts of French civilization (the more 'practical' science departments are in Marseille). If a fifth of Aix's 150,000 souls are students, another large percentage are doctors, lawyers and professors, not to mention financial and underworld nabobs who commute to Marseille. But as cultured as it is, Aix can never quite live down having mocked and laughed at Cézanne, the one real genius it ever produced.

History

The first version of Aix, the *oppidum* of Entremont, was the capital of the Salyens, a Celto-Ligurian tribe who liked to decapitate their enemies and tie their heads to the tails of their horses. By 123 BC they had pulled this trick once too often on the Greeks of Massalia, who called in their Roman allies to teach them a lesson. Under Sextius Calvinus, the Romans did just that, and founded a camp by a nearby thermal spring which they named Aquae Sextiae Salluviorum.

Just 20 years later, in 102 BC, these Latin frontiersmen woke up one day to find 200,000 ferocious Teutones with covered wagons full of wives and children at their

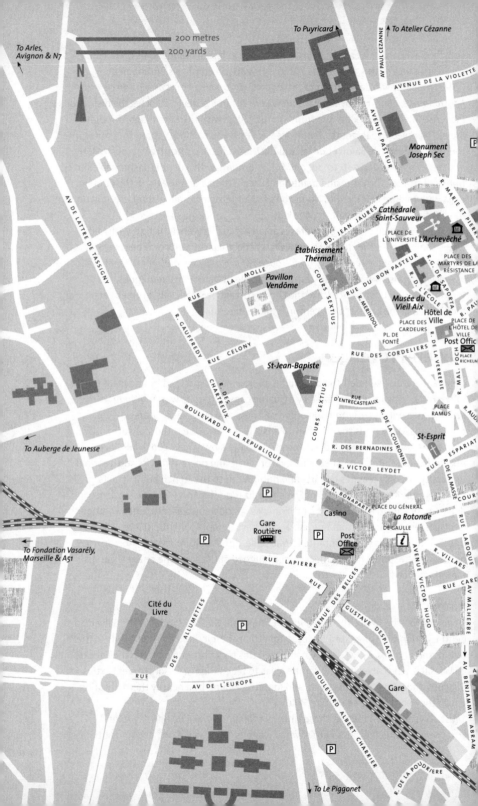

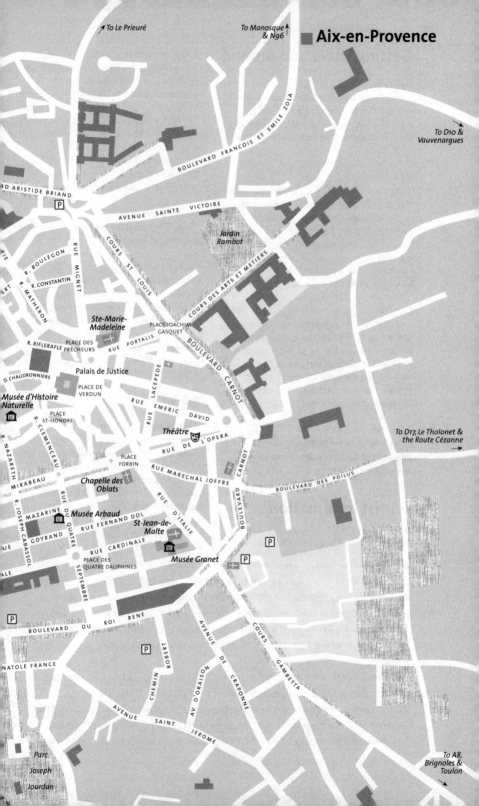

Getting There and Around

By Train

The station is on Rue G. Desplaces, at the end of Av Victor-Hugo; there are hourly connections to Marseille, and less frequently to Toulon. Central train reservations **t** 08 36 35 35 35.

By Bus

The hectic *gare routière* is in Av de l'Europe, **t** 04 42 91 26 80, with buses every 20–30mins to Marseille and direct to the airport, and others to Avignon, Cannes, Nice and Arles.

By Taxi

Av de l'Europe, **t** 04 42 27 71 11; at night call **t** 04 42 26 29 30.

Car Hire

You can rent a car at **Rent a Car**, 35 Rue de la Molle, **t** 04 42 38 58 29, and **ADA Location**, Av Henry-Mouret, **t** 04 42 52 36 36, as well as the big multinational companies. Parking isn't easy, especially on market days: try the car parks in Place des Cardeurs, Place Carnot, or by the coach station (behind the casino).

Bike Hire

Available at **La Route Bleue**, 5 Rue Lapierre, **t** 04 42 27 92 34, and **Cycles Zammit**, 27 Rue Mignet, **t** 04 42 23 19 53.

Tourist Information

Tourist office: Place du Général de Gaulle, **t** 04 42 16 11 61, **f** 04 42 16 11 62,

info@aixenprovencetourism.com *www.aixenprovencetourism.com*. Without doubt, one of the most pleasant tourist offices in the south of France. There's a host of circuits to navigate and explore: by yourself with a map or in guided groups; by foot, bus or car; in town or around the countryside; and whether your interest is in painting, architecture, history or just a good walk. *Open daily Mon–Sat 8.30-7, Sun 10–1 and 2–6, longer hours in season.*

Market Days

There's local produce every morning in Place Richelme, but Tuesdays, Thursdays and Saturdays are the days to come, when the centre of Aix overflows with good things: food in Place des Prêcheurs and Place de la Madeleine, flowers in Place de la Mairie, antiques and flea market bits in Place de Verdun, and clothes, fabrics and accessories along Rue Riflerafle; on Saturday nights in the summer the stands stay open late, all bustling and brightly lit, while the birds squawk indignantly in the trees above.

Festivals

Aix publishes a free monthly guide to events, *Le Mois à Aix*, which comes in especially handy during Aix's summer festivals. The headquarters and general booking office for these is the **Boutique du Festival**, 11 Rue Gaston de Saporta, **t** 04 42 17 34 34. The most famous is the **International Opera Festival**, featuring celebrity opera and classical music during the last three weeks of July. This highbrow (and *very* expensive) affair is supplemented with lively alternative performances

door, en route to Italy – looking not for a place to camp but for Lebensraum. The strategies of the great Roman general Marius caught them unawares, and in the battle that raged around Aix, so many Teutones were killed or committed suicide that for decades Aix enjoyed bumper crops thanks to soil enriched with corpses. The mountain where Marius' final triumph took place was renamed Montagne Sainte-Victoire.

Although by the next century Aquae Sextiae was a bustling town on the Aurelian Way, invaders in the Dark Ages destroyed it so thoroughly that little survived. Only in the 11th century did Aix begin to revive: the Bourg St-Sauveur grew up around the cathedral with such vigour that in the early 13th century the counts of Provence chose it as their capital. In 1409, Louis II d'Anjou endowed the university, and in the 1450s Aix in the streets and smaller theatres. It is preceded by a less formal **Rock Festival**, an umbrella title that includes jazz, big band music and chamber music during the second and third weeks of June, followed, in the first part of July, by the **International Dance Festival**, ranging from classical ballet to jazz and contemporary dance.

Shopping

The traditional souvenirs of Aix are its almond and glazed melon sweets, *calissons*, which have been made here since 1473; buy them at:

Béchard, 12 Cours Mirabeau, **t** 04 42 26 06 78.
Confiserie Brémond, 16 Rue d'Italie, **t** 04 42 38 01 70.

The better grocers sell the prize-winning *huile d'olive du pays d'Aix*: Aix calls itself 'the capital of the olive tree since the 18th century'. Buy local, world-renowned **pottery** at Terre du Soleil, 6 bis Rue Aude, **t** 04 42 93 04 54.

Where to Stay

Aix-en-Provence ✉ 13100

If you come in the summer during the festivals, you can't book early enough; Aix's less pricey hotels fill up especially fast (if you have a car, check where to stay around Aix as well, *see* p.219).

****Le Pigonnet, 5 Av du Pigonnet, **t** 04 42 59 02 90, **f** 04 42 59 47 77, *reservation@ hotelpigonnet.com* (*expensive*). A romantic old *bastide* on the outskirts, with rose arbours, pool, lovely rooms furnished with

antiques, an excellent restaurant and views out over the Aix countryside.
****Villa Gallici, Av de la Violette, **t** 04 42 23 29 23, **f** 04 42 96 30 45, *gallici@ relaischateaux.fr* (*luxury*). A member of the Relais & Châteaux group, just north of the centre, with all the warm atmosphere of an old Provençal *bastide*, charming rooms, garden, parking and pool.
***Grand Hôtel Nègre-Coste, 33 Cours Mirabeau, **t** 04 42 27 74 22, **f** 04 42 26 80 93 (*expensive–moderate*). A renovated, elegant 18th-century hotel which still hoists guests in its original elevator (*no restaurant*).
***Mercure Paul Cézanne, 40 Av Victor Hugo, **t** 04 42 91 11 11, **f** 04 42 91 11 10, *mercure.paulcezanne@free.fr* (*expensive*). An exceptional little hotel two blocks from the train station, furnished with antiques and serving delicious breakfasts.

Two of Aix's medieval religious houses have been converted into hotels:
***Des Augustins, 3 Rue de la Masse, just off Cours Mirabeau, **t** 04 42 27 28 59, **f** 04 42 26 74 87 (*expensive*). A 12th-century convent with soundproofed rooms.
***Le Manoir, 8 Rue d'Entrecasteaux, **t** 04 42 26 27 20, **f** 04 42 27 17 97, *msg@hotelmanoir. com* (*moderate*). Built around a 14th-century cloister. *Closed mid-Jan–Feb.*
Artea, 4 Bd de la République, **t 04 42 27 36 00, **f** 04 42 27 28 76, *artea-hotel@wanadoo. fr*, *www.hotel-artea.fr* (*moderate*). The former home of composer Darius Milhaud (who grew up in Aix) is now a comfortable hotel; don't expect any mementoes of the composer but do arrive after 8pm and get a discount out of season.

was the setting for the refined court of Good King René, fondly remembered, not for the way he squeezed every possible *sou* from his subjects, but for the artists he patronized, such as Francesco Laurana, Nicolas Froment and the Maître de l'Annonciation d'Aix, and the popular festivities he founded, especially the masquerades of the Fête-Dieu.

When René died at Aix in 1486, France absorbed his realm but maintained Aix's status as the capital of Provence, seat of the provincial Estates, the governor and the king-appointed *Parlement* – the latter institution so unpopular that it was counted as one of the three 'plagues' of Provence, along with the mistral and the Durance. In the 17th and 18th centuries, this unloved élite built themselves over 160 refined *hôtels particuliers* in golden stone, inspired by northern Italian Baroque architecture,

★★Le Prieuré, Route des Alpes, t 04 42 21 05 23, f 04 42 21 60 56 (*inexpensive*). Two kilometres north of the centre, this 17th-century building is charming, overlooking a garden designed by Le Nôtre.

★★De France, 63 Rue Espariat, t 04 42 27 90 15, f 04 42 26 11 47 (*inexpensive*). Cheaper, old-fashioned and in town.

★Paul, 10 Av Pasteur, t 04 42 23 23 89, f 04 42 63 17 80, hotel.paul@wanadoo.fr (*inexpensive*). Near the cathedral.

Auberge de Jeunesse, 3 Av Marcel Pagnol, Jas de Bouffan (bus nos.4 or 6), t 04 42 20 15 99, f 04 42 59 36 12.

Eating Out

Clos de la Violette, 10 Av de la Violette, t 04 42 23 30 71 (*expensive*). Under the masterful touch of Jean-Marc Banzo, who does wonderful things with seafood and Provençal herbs, this lovely restaurant has long been considered the best in Aix. *Closed Sun and Mon lunch.*

Le Bistro Latin, 18 Rue de la Couronne, t 04 42 38 22 88 (*moderate*). Features imaginative variations on local themes, such as leg of lamb with herbs, at refreshingly reasonable prices. *Closed Sun and Mon lunch.*

Chez Maxime, 12 Place Ramus, t 04 42 26 28 51 (*moderate*). Choose the shady terrace or cosy fireside for delicious meat or fish dishes, accompanied by a list of 500 wines. *Closed Sun and Mon lunch.*

Trattoria Chez Antoine, 3 Rue Clemenceau, t 04 42 38 27 10 (*moderate*). For fresh pasta and other Italian and Provençal dishes in an intimate, laid-back atmosphere.

Le Petit Verdot, 7 Rue d'Entrecasteaux, t 04 42 27 30 12 (*moderate*). More serious drinkers should head for this authentic evening bistro, where red wines by the glass are accompanied by ancient jazz records and simple dishes or charcuterie. *Closed Sun.*

La Vieille Auberge, 63 Rue Espariat, t 04 42 27 17 41 (*cheap*). A cosy, popular place serving tasty Provençal dishes at tasty prices.

L'Arbre à Pain, 12 Rue Constantin, t 04 42 96 99 95 (*cheap*). Reasonable vegetarian fare. *Closed Sun and Mon.*

L'Hacienda, 7 Rue Mérindol (near Place des Cardeurs), t 04 42 27 00 35 (*cheap*). Least expensive of all, L'Hacienda is eternally popular.

Entertainment and Nightlife

Mazarin, 6 Rue Laroque, t 08 36 68 72 70. A cinema showing films in their original language (*v.o.*).

Casino Municipal d'Aix Thermal, just off La Rotonde, t 04 42 26 30 33. *Open 10am–dawn.*

Bars and Clubs

Hot Brass, west of the centre on Chemin de la Plaine des Verguetiers, t 04 42 21 05 57. One of the many jazz clubs kept in business by the large student population of 'Sex-en-Provence', as they call it.

L'IPN, downstairs at 23 Cours Sextius, t 04 42 26 25 17.

Le Richelm, 24 Rue de la Verrerie, t 04 42 23 49 29.

Club 88, at La Petite Calade, north on the RN7, t 04 42 23 26 88.

bequeathing Aix a rich, harmonious urban fabric. Even the real plague of cholera in 1720 contributed to the city's embellishment when it contaminated the water supply; once new sources had been piped in, the city built its charming fountains to receive them.

In 1789 the tumultuous Count Mirabeau became a popular hero in Aix when he eloquently championed the people and condemned Provence's *Parlement* as unrepresentative; in 1800 the whole regional government was unceremoniously packed off to Marseille. Aix, the 'Athens of the Midi', has found enough to keep it busy without it, tending its university, making its sweets, hosting music festivals and, as of April 1997, inaugurating a brand new thermal spa for the spring that gave the city its name.

Cours Mirabeau

Canopied by its soaring plane trees, decked with fountains and flanked by cafés, banks, pâtisseries and *hôtels particuliers* from the 17th and 18th centuries, **Cours Mirabeau**, 'the most satisfying street in France', is the centre stage for Aixois society. Laid out in 1649 to replace the south walls, it begins in Place du Général de Gaulle, which takes the old roads from Marseille and Avignon and spins them around the pompous Second Empire fountain **La Rotonde**. Other fountains punctuate the Cours itself: the lumpy, mossy **Fontaine d'Eau Chaude**, oozing up its much esteemed 34°C water and, at the far end, the **Fontaine du Roi René**, with a fairy-tale statue of the good monarch holding up a bunch of the muscat grapes he introduced to Provence (along with the turkey and silkworm, discreetly omitted by the sculptor).

Of the fine *hôtels particuliers* on the Cours, No.12 is where Mirabeau wed the aristocratic Emilie de Covet-Marignane in 1772, after playing a dastardly trick on her. When the young lady refused his marriage proposal, Mirabeau sneaked into her house and appeared in the morning on her balcony, clad only in his nightshirt and socks, publicly compromising her virtue. In revenge, his new father-in-law refused the couple any money, and when Mirabeau ran up huge debts, he signed the order to have him imprisoned in the Château d'If. Mirabeau returned to Aix to plead in the subsequent divorce case, but despite his unparalleled eloquence he lost the appeal. Thus rebuked by his noble peers, he returned to Aix in 1789 as a member of the Third Estate and proceeded to attack their privileges – a trial run for his major role in igniting the Revolution in Paris.

Cézanne grew up at 55 Cours Mirabeau, the son of a hatter who later turned banker (on the façade you can still make out the sign of the *chapelier*). Nearby, at No.53, the elegant mirrored café **Les Deux Garçons** ('Les Deux G') has been Aix's smartest place to see and be seen since the Second World War, with a reputation and prices similar to Paris' café-citadels of artsy existentialist mumbo-jumbo; until recently, North Africans were not admitted to enjoy its rarefied air. It looks across towards the weighty façade of the 1647 **Hôtel Maurel de Pontevès** (No.38), the building that inspired Aix's secular Baroque – still supported after all these years by two muscle-bound stone giants, 'the only ones who do any work at all on the Cours', as the saying went in the days of Aix's parliament.

South of Cours Mirabeau, the straight lanes of the **Quartier Mazarin**, lined with *hôtels particuliers* and antiques shops, were laid out according to the rules of Renaissance urban design by the archbishop brother of the famous cardinal. At 2a Rue du Quatre Septembre, the **Musée Paul Arbaud** (*open 2–5, closed Sun and Jan; adm*) is the city's overflow tank for odds and ends, especially Provençal ceramics and a few hundred portraits of Mirabeau's overlarge pockmarked head.

Musée Granet

Place Saint Jean de Malte, t 04 42 38 14 70; open Wed–Mon 10–12 and 2–6; adm.

Walk two streets south of the Musée Arbaud and turn left at the Fountain of the Four Dolphins (unusually equipped with teeth and scales) for the more substantial archaeology and art collections of the **Musée Granet**, housed in the Priory of the Knights of Malta (1675), next to the **church of St-Jean-de-Malte**, where the counts of Provence lie buried. The museum's basement and ground floor are devoted to archaeology, especially to everyday items and sculptures from the Celto-Ligurian *oppidum* of Entremont. Appropriately enough for residents of the land that would invent the guillotine, the overall theme is cult decapitation. The remains of 15 embalmed heads were found in the sanctuary, and the sculptures on display here, like death masks, may have been carved to replace real heads that mouldered away; according to Tertullian, the Celts would spend nights with their dead ancestors, seeking oracular advice. The heads, singularly or in bunches, were once held as trophies by at least five statues of warriors; one has the same face as the famous gold mask of Agamemnon from Mycenae, another head resembles not so much a dead man as a resurrected youth. There are also finds from Roman Aquae Sextiae (note the fine sarcophagus depicting Leda and the swan, discovered in the cathedral), a superb statue of a Persian warrior (200 BC) of the Pergamon school, and Egyptian steles and cats.

Celtic head cults seem benign next to *Jupiter and Thetis* (1811), arguably Ingres' most objectionable canvas, holding court upstairs in a whole room of neoclassical mythologies inspired by Jacques-Louis David. But the real culprit behind this smirking art is Napoleon, whose totalitarian approach to statecraft opened a Pandora's box of kitsch: art like this is born when cloying sentiment and a cynical manipulation of the classical past are used to serve political ends. The expression on Jupiter's sublimely stupid face not only sums up a whole era, but looks ahead to the even more cynical kitsch-mongers of the 20th century, who make Napoleon look like Little Red Riding Hood.

There are other, more palatable works by Ingres, including the *Portrait of François Granet* (1775–1849), the artist from Aix after whom the museum is named, painted while the two sojourned at Rome's Villa Medici. Granet himself was capable of neoclassical folderol and received more than his share of commissions from the clergy, but he also painted Provençal landscapes in the same vein as Guigou, Loubon and Monticelli, who are also present.

There are 17th-century portraits of Aixois nobility, made fluffy and likeable by Largillière and Rigaud; Dutch and Flemish masters (Teniers, Brit, Neefs, Robert Campin, Rubens, and a sumptuous anonymous 15th-century triptych of the *Adoration of the Magi*); and the Italians (Alvise Vivarini, Previtali, Guercino, Preti, the mysterious, grave 15th-century Maître de l'Annonciation d'Aix, and from Carlo Portelli a bizarre 16th-century Counter-Reformation blast, the *Allegory of the Church Suffering, Militant, and Triumphant*).

But what of Cézanne, who took his first drawing classes in this very building? For years he was represented by three measly watercolours (no one in Aix would buy his works), until 1984, when the French government rectified the omission by depositing eight small canvases here that touch on the major themes of his work.

Vieil Aix

North of Cours Mirabeau, the narrow lanes and squares of Vieil Aix concentrate not only some of Provence's finest architecture, but the region's most delightful shopping, especially on market days (*see* above). Enter the casbah by way of Rue Espariat from Place du Général de Gaulle, and you'll come to a cast-iron Baroque campanile and the **church of St-Esprit**, where a 16th-century retable has portraits of 12 members of the first Provençal *Parlement* cast in the roles of the apostles. Further up, just beyond Aix's most elegant little square, the cobbled, fountained **Place d'Albertas**, you can pop into the lavish, Puget-inspired Hôtel Boyer d'Eguilles of 1675, now the **Muséum d'Histoire Naturelle** (*6 Rue Espariat, t 04 42 27 91 27; open 10–12 and 1–5; adm*) – well worth it for an impressive 17th-century interior, a grand stair and a clutch of petrified dinosaur eggs.

Rue Espariat ends at Place St-Honoré, just south of the neoclassical **Palais de Justice**, a dull building of the 1760s that hardly merited the demolition of a well-preserved Roman mausoleum and the medieval palace of the Counts of Provence.

Aix's flea market takes place in the adjacent Place de Verdun and **Place des Prêcheurs**, laid out in 1450 by King René for popular entertainments and executions of all sorts, including, in 1772, the burning in effigy of the Marquis de Sade and his valet after they were caught sodomizing prostitutes in Marseille. Here, the former Dominican **church of Ste-Marie-Madeleine** has a pleasant Second Empire façade, paintings by Rubens and Van Loo, and a gentle 13th-century polychrome statue of *Notre-Dame-de-Grâce* standing on a moon. However, the show-stopper is the central panel of the *Triptych of the Annunciation*, a luminous work of 1445 painted for a local draper – the two lateral panels are in Rotterdam and Brussels. Commonly attributed to Barthélémy d'Eyck, illuminator of King René's courtly allegories in the *Livre du Cœur d'Amour Epris* (now in Vienna's National Library), the central panel has provoked endless controversy over its singular, possibly heretical iconography: the angel Gabriel, winged with owl feathers (a bird of evil omen), kneels in the porch of a Gothic church, decorated with a bat and a dragon. From on high, an unconventional gesturing God the Father sends in a golden stream of breath a foetus bearing a cross, just missing a monkey's head; a vase of flowers holds poisonous belladonna.

The more orthodox blooms of Aix's flower market lend an intoxicating perfume to Place Hôtel de Ville (Place de la Mairie) in the very heart of Vieil Aix, a lovely square framed by the stately, perfectly proportioned **Hôtel de Ville** (1671), decorated with stone flowers and fruits and intricate iron grilles, and the flamboyant **Tour de l'Horloge** (1510), with clocks telling the hour and the phase of the moon and wooden statues that change with the season. Note, too, the former grain market in the same square (now the post office), crowned by a handsome allegory of a river and city, the latter dangling a dainty foot over the cornice.

From here, Rue Gaston de Saporta leads to the **Musée du Vieil Aix** (*No.17, t 04 42 21 43 55; open summer 10–12 and 2.30–6, winter 10–12 and 2–5, closed Mon; adm*), housed in another grand 17th-century *hôtel particulier* with another magnificent staircase. It stores some quaint paintings on velvet, a bevy of *santons* in a 'talking Christmas Crib' and marionettes made in the 19th century to represent the biblical, pagan and local personages who figured in King René's Fête-Dieu processions, beginning with a figure representing Moses and someone tossing a cat up and down, and ending with Death swinging his scythe.

Cathédrale St-Sauveur, the Tapestry Museum and Joseph Sec

Rue Gaston de Saporta continues north to Place de l'Université, once part of the forum of Roman Aix, and the **Cathédrale St-Sauveur**, a dignified patchwork of periods and styles crowned by an octagonal bell tower. The flamboyant Gothic west portal of 1340, decorated with scenes of the Transfiguration and the Apostles said to be by King René, was mutilated in the Revolution and partially restored in the 1830s; only the lovely Virgin on the central pillar was spared when someone popped a red cap of Liberty on her head and made Mary a Marianne. Fortunately, the Revolutionaries forgot to axe the doors; under their protective covers they have beautiful high reliefs of prophets and sibyls by Jean Guiramand of Toulon, sculpted 1508–10 (*open Tues 3–4*).

The interior has naves for every taste: from right to left, Romanesque, Gothic and Baroque. Tucked by the door inside the Romanesque nave, the octagonal **baptistry** dates from *c.* 375, when Aix was made a bishopric. The font is encircled by columns recycled from the temple of Apollo that once stood on this site in the forum.

The cathedral's most famous treasure, Nicolas Froment's *Triptyque du Buisson Ardent* (1476), is under restoration and can only be viewed between 3 and 4pm on Tuesdays. On the lateral panels are portraits of a well-fed King René, who commissioned the work, and his second wife, while the central scene depicts the vision of a monk of St-Victor of Marseille, who saw the Virgin and Child appear amidst the miraculous burning bush vouchsafed to Moses. The flaming green bush symbolizes her virginity (it burns without being consumed); the mirror held by the Child symbolizes his incarnation. The meticulously detailed castles in the background seem to have been inspired by Tarascon and Beaucaire.

On the same wall, from the same period, another triptych has scenes from the Passion with SS. Maximin and Mitre. Mitre, a 4th-century Greek slave serving a cruel master in Aix, was accused of sorcery and had his head chopped off by Roman soldiers. His trunk then picked up the head (already adorned with a halo) and carried it into the cathedral. The sight scared the children but made the Romans, who had a modern sense of humour, laugh until they cried, at least according to the 15th-century *Martyrdom of St Mitre*, perhaps on display in the chapel tucked behind the high altar, where the saint's 5th-century sarcophagus once emitted an ooze collected by the faithful to heal eye diseases.

The high altar itself is decorated with tapestries on the lives of Christ and the Virgin made in Brussels in 1510. These originally hung in Canterbury Cathedral, but were sold by the Commonwealth and purchased by a cathedral canon in Paris for next to nothing in 1656.

In the Baroque aisle is the striking **altar des Aygosi** (1470), formerly attributed to Francesco Laurana but now to Audinet Stephani, an itinerant sculptor from Cambrai. On top, the *Crucifixion* is surrounded by symbols: the sun and moon on either side represent universality; the skull of Adam set at the base of the Cross is purified by the blood from Christ's wounds, while above the pelican feeds her nestlings with her own blood, according to a popular medieval misconception. Below stand SS. Anne, Marcel and Marguerite, the latter emerging from the shoulders of an embarrassed-looking dragon who swallowed her whole. The guardian will on request also unlock the airy, twin-columned, 12th-century **cloister**, with capitals daintily carved, though in an awful state of repair.

To the right and back of the cathedral, the grand 17th–18th-century residence of Aix's archbishops, **L'Archevêché**, is the setting for the festival's operas. It also houses the **Musée des Tapisseries** (*t 04 42 23 09 91; open Wed–Mon 10–11.45 and 2–5.45; adm*), containing three sets of light-hearted Beauvais tapestries which were hidden under the roof during the Revolution and rediscovered only in the 1840s. The set known as the *Grotesques* (1689) features arabesques, animals, dancers and musicians; there are nine rococo scenes from the story of *Don Quixote* (1740s), and four on the subject of *Jeux Russiens* (1769–93), inspired by the rustic frolics that the court of Louis XVI got up to in the backwoods of Versailles.

Just north of the cathedral on Av Pasteur stands the 1792 **Monument Joseph Sec**, an eccentric discourse on the Revolution that spoiled those pampered bucolic daydreams. Sec, the builder, was a Jacobin who made his fortune floating timber down the Durance, and no one has ever satisfactorily explained the meaning behind the reliefs and statues of biblical characters, allegories and masonic symbols he chose for his monument 'dedicated to the municipality of a law-abiding town'. This obsession with law is continued in the inscriptions ('Risen from cruel slavery/ I have no master but myself/But of my freedom I desire no other use/than to obey the law') and presence of Moses (with horns) on top. Behind the monument are seven more statues in exedrae, including one of a woman driving a stake into a man's head, which must bemuse the Aixois who come to get their jabs in the adjacent vaccination centre.

Around Aix: Cézanne, the Pavillon de Vendôme and Cité du Livre

Paul Cézanne spent an idyllic childhood roaming Aix's countryside with his best friend, Emile Zola, and as adult painted those same landscapes in a way landscapes had never been painted before. The **Atelier Cézanne** (*9 Av Paul Cézanne, t 04 42 21 06 53; open summer 10–12 and 2.30–6, winter 10–12 and 2–5, closed Mon; adm*), the studio he built in 1897, half a kilometre north of the cathedral, has been rather grudgingly maintained as it was when the master died in 1906, with a few drawings, unfinished canvases, his smock, palette, pipe and some of the bottles and skulls used in his still-lifes. But for a better understanding of Cézanne's art, pick up the free *Circuit Cézanne* from the tourist office, a guide that points out the places he liked best to plant his easel around Aix.

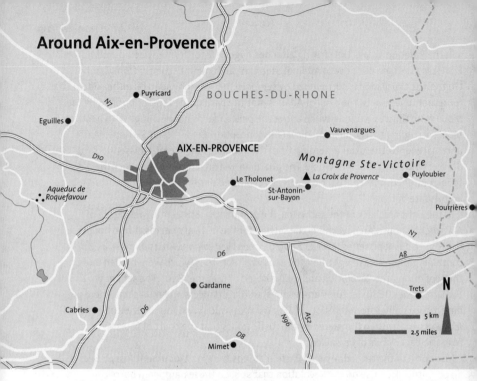

BOUCHES-DU-RHONE

Puyricard

Eguilles

N7

D10

AIX-EN-PROVENCE

Vauvenargues

Montagne Ste-Victoire

▲ *La Croix de Provence*

Puyloubier

Le Tholonet

St-Antonin-
sur-Bayon

Aqueduc de
Roquefavour

Pourrières

N7

D6

A8

Gardanne

Trets

N

Cabries

D6

N96

A52

5 km

2.5 miles

D8

Mimet

Cézanne's family home at Jas de Bouffan is now dominated by the irritating black and white cubic forms of the **Fondation Vasarély** (*t 04 42 20 01 09; open April–Oct Mon–Fri 10–1 and 2–7, Sat and Sun 10–7; Oct–Mar Mon–Fri 10–1 and 2–6, Sat and Sun 10–6; adm*), inaugurated in 1976 by the late op/geometric/kinetic artist at the height of his fame. The foundation is unpersuasively dedicated to promoting 'more human' urban development.

Along the boulevards west of Vieille Aix, in what was open country in 1665, a local cardinal built himself a lavish summer folly and park, the **Pavillon de Vendôme** (*32 Rue Célony, t 04 42 21 05 78; open April–Sept 10–12 and 2–6; Feb, March and Oct 10–12 and 1.30–5.30; Jan, Nov and Dec 10–12 and 1–5; closed Tues; adm*). The delightful exterior includes a pair of atlantes who, judging by their pained expressions, have just been staring into one of Vasarély's more fiendish optical illusions. Part of the interior décor is intact, complete with 17th- and 18th-century patrician furnishings and paintings.

Just to the south of the bus station at 8 Rue des Allumettes, the modern **Cité du Livre** collects several cultural entities under its roof, including the **Bibliothèque Méjanes** (*t 04 42 25 98 88; open Tues, Thurs and Fri 12–6, Wed and Sat 10–6*), with a rich collection of incunabula and illuminated manuscripts, some of which are usually on display; the **Fondation St-John Perse** (*t 04 42 25 98 85; open Tues–Fri 2–6*), a museum and study centre bequeathed to Aix by the French poet who won the Nobel Prize in 1960; and the **Vidéothèque Internationale d'Art Lyrique** (*t 04 42 37 70 89; open Tues–Fri 1–6, Sat 10–12 and 1–6*), where you can sit in a booth and take in a wide selection of celebrated operas and concerts filmed from 1950 to the present day.

Aix-urbia: East around Montagne Ste-Victoire

The rolling countryside around Aix is the quintessence of Provence for those who love Cézanne: the ochre soil, the dusty green cypresses – as still and classical as Van Gogh's are possessed and writhing – the simple geometry of the old *bastides* and villages and the pyramidal prow of the bluish-limestone Montagne Ste-Victoire. These landscapes are so inextricably a part of Cézanne's art that one can only wonder who created what. What if this grouchy, lonely genius had been born in Birmingham or New Jersey?

Along the south flank of the Montagne Ste-Victoire runs the **Route Cézanne** (D17), beginning at the wooded park and Italianate château of **Le Tholonet** (3km from Aix). Here Cézanne often painted the view towards the mountain, which haunts at least 60 of his canvases ('I am trying to get it right,' he explained). The château belongs to the local canal authority, while the park is used as a venue for Aix's music festival (take the bus from La Rotonde).

The entire 60km route around Montagne Ste-Victoire is striking and unspoiled; the mountain's wild shoulders are covered with maquis and holm oaks, growing back

Where to Stay and Eat

Le Tholonet ☒ 13100
La Petite Auberge du Tholonet, south of the centre on the D64E, **t** 04 42 66 84 24 (*moderate*). With views over Ste-Victoire and featuring local produce, good country fare and a number of vegetarian dishes. *Closed Sun eve, Mon and Tues.*

Beaurecueil ☒ 13100
★★★Relais Sainte-Victoire, 10km from Aix, off the N7, **t** 04 42 66 94 98, **f** 04 42 66 85 96, *relais-ste-victoire@wanadoo.fr* (*moderate*). A ravishing place to stay or eat, complete with a swimming pool, a gourmet restaurant (*expensive*) with a lovely veranda and, above all, tranquillity. Air-conditioned rooms with terraces; book early. *Closed Sun eve, Mon, Fri lunch in summer, all day Fri in winter and school hols.*

Puyloubier ☒ 13114
Relais de Saint-Ser, on the flanks of Ste-Victoire between Puyloubier and St-Antonin, **t** 04 42 66 37 26, **f** 04 42 66 33 91 (*inexpensive; restaurant moderate*). A small place for guests who want to get away from it all. *Closed Jan.*
Les Sarments, 4 Rue qui Monte, **t** 04 42 66 31 58 (*moderate*). Stop at this old country inn in the village, run by the family that runs the Relais Sainte-Victoire, for well-prepared *cuisine du terroir. Closed Jan and Mon.*

Vauvenargues ☒ 13126
Moulin de Provence, **t** 04 42 66 02 22, **f** 04 42 66 01 21, *www.lemoulindeprovence.com* (*inexpensive; restaurant moderate*). Twelve simple rooms and a breakfast terrace overlooking Picasso's castle.

Roquefavour ☒ 13122
★★Arquier, **t** 04 42 24 20 45, **f** 04 42 24 29 52, *arqui-hr@easynet.fr* (*inexpensive*). In the Arc valley, next to the aqueduct, the Arquier offers peaceful rooms immersed in trees, with a pleasant restaurant (*moderate*) and terrace along the river. *Closed Sun eve in season and Mon out of season.*

Gardanne ☒ 13320
★★★L'Etape Lani, Rte CD6, in Bouc Bel Air, **t** 04 42 22 61 90, **f** 04 42 22 68 67, *etapelani@worldonline.fr, www.lani.fr* (*inexpensive*). Comfortable, well-equipped and quiet rooms and a pool set in a pine wood 12km from Aix; the restaurant (*expensive–moderate*) features light, delicate and delicious seasonal dishes. *Closed Sat lunch, Sun eve, Mon and first 3 weeks in Aug.*

Wine: Coteaux d'Aix-en-Provence and La Palette

This relatively recent AOC district has begun to make a name for its red, rosé and white wines. Coteaux d'Aix-en-Provence originates in 50 communes in the highlands stretching from the Durance to Marignane, west to Salon and east to the flanks of Montagne Ste-Victoire, and consists of the region's traditional syrah, grenache, cinsault, mourvèdre and carignan grapes, enhanced in the past 20 years with the addition of cabernet sauvignon, a stock that has improved the wine's ageing ability. Coteaux d'Aix's sunny whites are made from sauvignon, grenache blanc and ugni – but never from René's sweet muscat grapes, although these now grow merrily in Roussillon.

Many growers welcome visitors, such as Puyricard's **Château du Seuil, t** 04 42 92 15 99, a handsomely restored 13th-century *bastide*, where the 1990 reds and whites are an excellent buy.

Or head further north, 20km from Aix, to Le Puy Ste-Réparade and the lush estate of **Château de Fonscolombe**, on the banks of the Durance, **t** 04 42 61 89 62, where James de Roany produces classic, fragrant red, rosé and white wines.

Further afield, another estate that welcomes visitors also supplies some of France's best restaurants: Jean Bonnet's 120-hectare **Château de Calissanne**, overlooking the Etang de Berre on the site of an ancient Celtic oppidum (on the D10, near Lançon-Provence), **t** 04 90 42 63 03. On the south bank of the lagoon, one of the sunniest corners of France, **Château St-Jean**, at Port de Bouc near Fos, **t** 04 42 44 70 14, produces prize-winning rosés (dominated by counoise, an old-fashioned stock, mixed with grenache and carignan) and reds full of old-fashioned finesse.

La Palette is a venerable, microscopic AOC region on a north-facing limestone scree east of Aix, on the left bank of the Arc; although fairly sheltered from the mistral, it has cooler summer and winter temperatures than its environs. La Palette's red, white and rosé nectar has been served at the royal fêtes of such diverse monarchs as King René and Edward VII, but only two estates still produce this rare fine wine of the south, aged in small casks: the celebrated 150-year-old **Château Simone**, at Meyreuil, off the pretty D58H, **t** 04 42 66 92 58, where dark, violet-scented reds are kept for three years in caves carved out by 16th-century Carmelites; and **Château Crémade, t** 04 42 66 92 66, a 17th-century *bastide* in Le Tholonet, which bottles magnificent, well-structured red wines and a fruity blanc de blancs.

after a devastating fire in 1989, or tamed with vineyards. The short detour up to **Beaurecueil** is repaid with lovely views, while further east **St-Antonin-sur-Bayon** is home to the **Maison de Ste-Victoire**, an information centre on the mountain; the GR9 begins nearby.

The ascent of **Montagne Ste-Victoire** takes about 2 hours (bring sturdy shoes, a hat and water) and there's a 17th-century stone *refuge* with water and a fireplace if you want to spend a night. Crowning the precipitous west face, the 55ft **Croix de Provence** (which Cézanne never painted) has been here, in one form or another, since the 16th century. Legend has it that Marius stood on the spot, watching his troops annihilate the Teutones, then, at the urging of his sibyl Marthe, had

300 defeated chieftains brought up and tossed into the **Garagaï**, Ste-Victoire's mighty chasm.

One legend claims the floor of the Garagaï is occupied by an enchanted lake and meadows, abode of the legendary Golden Goat of Provence; shepherds, they say, would lower their sick sheep and cows down on ropes to graze the therapeutic grass. Other stories claimed that the chasm was the entrance to hell, or linked to the Fountain of Vaucluse (*see* pp.246–7) – in fact, fluoride released here surfaced there three months later. In the 17th century, curiosity reached such a pitch that the *Parlement* in Aix offered a condemned man his freedom if he would agree to be lowered into the Garagaï and tell what he found. Carefully trussed, the man went down, but was strangled in the ropes before he reached the bottom.

Further east, the D17 passes through **Puyloubier**, a pleasant wine village, as is **Pourrières**, in spite of being named after *campi putridi*, the fields of putrefaction, where the unburied corpses of the Teutones rotted after Marius' victory; local farmers made vine trellises from their bones. A trophy was erected to Marius here, showing the victorious general carried shoulder-high on his shield by his soldiers. When it eroded away, parts of it were salvaged and reconstructed as a fountain. From Pourrières, the mountain circuit winds through the pines (D25), and at Le Puits-de-Rians veers back west towards Aix through the steep, forested Vallée de l'Infernet (D10).

Northerly approaches to the summit of Ste-Victoire begin at Les Cabassols or **Vauvenargues**. The 14th-century Château de Vauvenargues, strikingly set apart from the village, was the home of Luc de Clapiers (1715–47), author of the *Introduction à la connaissance de l'esprit humain*, in which he wrote that 'the highest perfection of the human soul is to make it capable of pleasure'. In 1958 the château was purchased by Picasso, who probably would have agreed with him; Picasso's grave is in the grounds, but off limits along with the rest of the château ('No admittance! Don't insist! The museum is in Paris!'). The idyllic D11 (parallel to the GR9) descends north of Vauvenargues for 13km to Jouques, sheltered in a cool, green valley.

Puyricard and the Arc Valley

Four kilometres to the north of Aix, overlooking the modern city, is the plateau where the city's story began, the Celto-Ligurian *Oppidum* of **Entremont**. For a place that lasted less than a century – it was founded in the 2nd century BC and destroyed by the Romans in 122 BC – it was an impressive achievement, its clusters of stone houses once sheltering some 5,000 souls. You can trace the foundations of the large public building that produced the sculptures that now reside in the Granet Museum (*bus no.20 from the BNP on Cours Sextius every half-hour; open Wed–Mon 9–12 and 2–6*).

The same bus continues north to Puyricard, and the **Chocolaterie Puyricard** (*420 Route du Puy Ste Réparade, t 04 42 96 11 21, f 04 42 21 47 10*), where some of the most delectable (and expensive) fresh chocolates you'll ever taste are made in the traditional pre-Willy Wonka manner; try the *clous de Cézanne*.

To the west of Aix, the D64 continues for 10km from the Fondation Vasarély to the three-tiered **Aqueduc de Roquefavour** (1847), twice as high as the Pont du Gard and built across the steep valley of the river Arc to bring the waters of the Durance to Marseille. The wooded setting is delightful – the Arc is the river where Cézanne painted his famous proto-Cubist scenes of bathers.

The edge of the Arc valley is dotted with old farms and *villages perchés* : **Eguilles**, north on the D543, with fine views from its William Morris-style medieval château (now the *mairie*); and south, off the busy Aix–Marseille routes, lofty **Cabriès** and **Mimet**. **Gardanne**, an old village often painted by Cézanne, has remained unchanged, defended by an ugly ring of industry and highways.

Northern Provence:
The Vaucluse

12

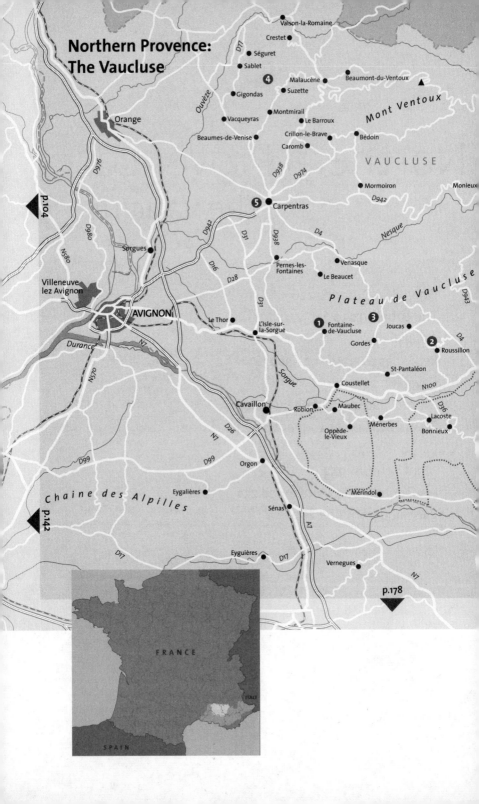

Northern Provence:
The Vaucluse

Valson-la-Romaine

Crestet

Séguret

Sablet

4

Malaucène
Suzette

Beaumont-du-Ventoux

Gigondas

Vacqueyras

Montmirail

Le Barroux

Beaumes-de-Venise

Crillon-le-Brave
Bédoin

Caromb

Mont Ventoux

VAUCLUSE

Orange

Ouvèze

D77

D938

D974

Mormoiron

Monieux

5 Carpentras

D942

Nesque

Sorgues

D942

D31

D938

D4

Pernes-les-
Fontaines

Venasque

Le Beaucet

Plateau de Vaucluse

D16

D28

D31

D943

Villeneuve
lez Avignon

Le Thor

AVIGNON

L'Isle-sur-
la-Sorgue

1 Fontaine-
de-Vaucluse

3

Joucas

Gordes

2 Roussillon

Durance

N7

Sorgue

St-Pantaléon

D4

N100

Cavaillon

Robion

Coustellet

D36

N570

Maubec

Ménerbes

Lacoste

Bonnieux

Oppède-
le-Vieux

D26

N7

Orgon

Eygalières

Mérindol

Chaîne des Alpilles

D99

D99

D17

Sénas

A7

Eyguières

D17

Vernegues

N7

p.178

D980

N580

D976

p.104

p.142

FRANCE

ITALY

SPAIN

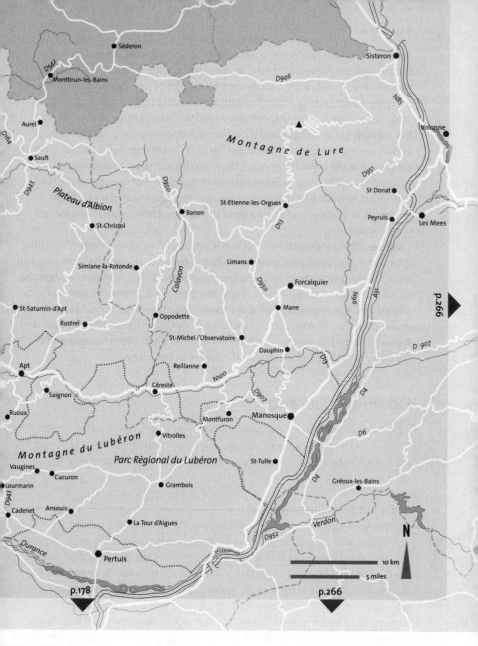

Highlights

1 The touristy but magical Fountaine-de-Vaucluse
2 Roussillon, a village built on ochre
3 The lavender-enveloped Abbaye de Sénanque
4 Vineyards under the lacy peaks of the Dentelles de Montmirail
5 The quirky old town of Carpentras

The 'Three Plagues of Provence', according to tradition, were the mistral, the Durance and the *Parlement* at Aix. The *Parlement* is ancient history, but the other two still serve to define the troublesome boundaries of this region: the long curve of the wicked, boat-sinking, valley-flooding river Durance to the south, and a line of long, ridge-like mountains, Mont Ventoux and the Montagne de Lure, to the north – folk wisdom has always credited these northern boundary-stones of Provence as the source of the terrible mistral. But the lands in between these natural prodigies are the eye of the hurricane, some of the most civilized countryside and loveliest villages in the Midi. They have not passed without notice, of course, and the rural Vaucluse is now what the Côte d'Azur was 40 years ago: the in-place for both the French and foreigners to find a bit of sun-splashed holiday paradise amongst the vineyards.

Not everything included in this section is actually in the *département* of Vaucluse (Manosque and Forcalquier are in Alpes-de-Haute-Provence); and the Vaucluse's two cities, Orange and Avignon, will be found in **Down the Rhône 1: Orange to Beaucaire**, pp.103–40. The remainder divides neatly into three areas: the mountainous Luberon, cradled in the Durance's arc, a *pays* of especially pretty villages; the old papal Comtat, nearer the Rhône, rich agricultural lands rightfully called the 'Garden of France'; and Provence's definitive northern wall, including the dramatic Mont Ventoux and the Dentelles de Montmirail, along with the Roman city of Vaison.

Down the Durance

The Durance was a major trade route in the Middle Ages, following the Roman Via Domitia, and religious centres grew up along it from the earliest times. These old priories, set in gentle rolling scenery, are the main attraction in this still fairly untouristed region.

St-Donat and Ganagobie

As you come down from Digne and the Provençal Alps, a startling landmark punctuates your entry into the Durance valley: **Les Mées** (a Provençal word for mile-stones), 2km of needle-like rock formations eroded into weird shapes, overlooking the D4. There is a bridge at the village of Les Mées, crossing over to **Peyruis** and its ruined castle. Up in the hills, 5km above Peyruis, the **church of St-Donat** enjoys a wonderful setting on a little wooded plateau. This graceful building, one of the earliest Romanesque monuments in Provence (11th century), was built for pilgrims visiting the relics of St Donat, a 5th-century holy man from Orléans who ended his life as a hermit here.

Of all the holy sites down the Durance, the one most worth visiting is the **Priory of Ganagobie**, just down the N96 south of Peyruis, in a setting as lovely as that of St-Donat (*t 04 92 68 00 04; open Tues–Sun 3–5*). Founded in the 9th century as a dependency of Cluny, the remarkable church was built some 200 years later. Its portal, though rebuilt in the 17th century, still has its original tympanum relief: a

Getting Around

The valley of the Durance is the main corridor for public transport. A **railway** line passes Manosque and continues along the bottom edge of the Luberon, serving Pertuis on its way to Aix and Marseille (five or six daily). Manosque is also the hub for **buses**, with several daily to Aix and Marseille, and also one or two a day to Forcalquier and to Digne, stopping in Les Mées.

Tourist Information

Forcalquier ✉ 04300: 13 Place du Bourguet, t 04 92 75 10 02, f 04 92 75 26 76, ot@forcalquier.com, www.forcalquier.com. Open mid-June–mid-Sept 9–12.30 and 2–7, Sun 10–1 (July–Aug Mon 9–7); mid-Sept–mid-June Mon–Sat 9–12 and 2–6.
Manosque ✉ 04100: Place Dr Joubert, t 04 92 72 16 00, f 04 92 72 58 98, www.ville-manosque.fr. Open mid-June–mid-Sept Mon–Sat 9–12.15 and 1.30–6.30, Sun 10–12; mid-Sept–mid-June Mon–Sat 9–12.15 and 1.30–6.

Market Days

Forcalquier: Monday morning.
Banon: Tuesday morning.
Manosque: Saturday morning.

Where to Stay and Eat

Dabisse-Les Mées ✉ 04190
Le Vieux Colombier, on the D4, t 04 92 34 32 32, f 04 92 34 34 26 (expensive–moderate). If at all possible, stop for lunch or dinner in this pleasant old farmhouse with a dovecot, appropriately specializing in succulent pigeon; superb cheese and desserts. Closed Wed, Sun eve and a week in Jan.

Forcalquier ✉ 04300
***Hostellerie des Deux Lions, 11 Place du Bourguet, t 04 92 75 25 30, f 04 92 75 06 41, hoteldeuxlions@aol.com (inexpensive). One

Christ in Majesty with the four Evangelists, one of the finest such works in Provence. Inside, another rare decoration: **mosaics** with geometric designs and peculiarly styled animals done in red, black and white. Discovered and restored in the 1960s, they were part of the church's original pavement.

Ganagobie used to have the relics of a certain St Transit; he is not found in any hagiography, and it seems that in the Middle Ages the habit of carrying holy relics in procession on a holiday (a *transit*) led to the invention of a new saint. Such things happened all the time in the Midi. (And there must have been some Provençaux colonists involved in a similar occurrence very much later, in New Orleans. The faithful in one parish there still beseech favours at the altar of St-Expédite. A statue of a female saint had arrived during the building of the church; no one knew who she was – but they found her name on the packing crate.) Ganagobie is still a monastery, but you can visit. Don't be confused by the roads – coming from the north, the village of Ganagobie is up a separate side road; you'll want the D30, about 3km further south. The lovely area around the priory is a great place for a picnic, or for some unambitious hiking along the old trails, with a few *bories* (see pp.46 and 245), medieval quarries and views over the valley.

Forcalquier, Mane and Around

Nowadays on the drowsy side, a bit too large and musty to attract the holiday-home-restoring crowd, **Forcalquier** only bestirs itself on Mondays for its market. Yet in the old days, in the 11th and 12th centuries, it was a miniature capital of a small-fry of the nicest places to stay, in the centre in a 17th-century posthouse with lovely rooms and a justifiedly popular restaurant, with menus that change daily and the best local cheeses and wines. *Closed Nov.*

Ferme du Bas-Chalus, 2km from Forcalquier, t 04 92 75 05 67, f 04 92 75 39 20, *amis@ wanadoo.fr* (*inexpensive*). A *ferme-auberge*. *Closed Jan–Feb.*

**Grand Hôtel, 10 Bd Latourette, t 04 92 75 00 35, f 04 92 75 06 32, *oti@forcalquier.com* (*inexpensive*). Not so grand but perfectly acceptable, with a garden out back.

**Le Colombier, Mas Les Dragons, t 04 92 75 03 71, f 04 92 75 14 30 (*moderate–inexpensive*). A nicely restored *mas* with a shady garden and pool out in the pretty countryside around Forcalquier, 3km south. *Closed Jan.*

**Auberge Charembeau, Route de Niozelles, t 04 92 70 91 70, f 04 92 70 91 83, *charembeau@provenceweb.fr* (*inexpensive*). In a Revolutionary-era farm 2.5km east, with a pool; there's no restaurant, but the rooms have kitchenettes. *Closed mid-Nov–mid-Feb.*

Manosque ✉ 04100

**Le Provence, Quart Durance, t 04 92 87 75 72, f 04 92 87 55 13 (*inexpensive*). Modern, pleasant, on the outskirts.

**François Ier, 18 Rue Guilhempierre, t 04 92 72 07 99, f 04 92 87 54 85 (*inexpensive*). Central and quiet.

Le Petit Pascal, 7 Promenade Aubert-Millot, near the Porte Saunerie, t 04 92 87 62 01 (*cheap*). A one-woman operation in a crowded hole-in-the-wall with no sign, with delicious, filling home-cooking. *Open for lunch only*

Valensole ✉ 04210

****Hostellerie de la Fuste, t 04 92 72 05 95, f 04 92 72 92 93, *lafuste@aol.com* (*expensive*). The only luxury hotel-restaurant in this area is across the Durance on the D4, near Oraison. The rooms are fine, in a restored *bastide* with a pool, but the real attraction is an elegant, highly rated restaurant. *Closed mid-Nov–first week of Dec and Jan; restaurant closed Sun eve and Mon.*

mountain state whose counts often made life difficult for the counts of Provence. Alphonse II managed to get it in 1209, by marriage, and later Provençal rulers like Raymond Bérenger V made Forcalquier a favoured residence during the 14th century. They left few traces: an obelisk in front of the stern Gothic cathedral commemorates Marguerite de Provence-Forcalquier, wife of St Louis; there's a Gothic fountain with the warrior angel and monkey faces in Place St-Michel; and also Europe's only listed cemetery (*open daily 9–5*), its ancient yew hedges trimmed to form the arcades of a cloister. A tower and other scanty remains of Forcalquier's citadel overlook the town, next to an octagonal chapel, crowned with a statue of the Virgin, honouring Pope Urban II, who came here to raise men and money for the First Crusade.

The well-restored 13th-century Couvent des Cordeliers (*t 04 92 75 10 02; guided tours mid-June–mid-Sept daily except Tues at 3.30; check with tourist office rest of the year; adm*), parts of which were originally the counts' palace, was given to the Franciscans by Raymond Bérenger V; it has medieval art, a Franciscan cloister garden and frequent exhibitions in summer. The Musée Municipal in the Hôtel de Ville (*t 04 92 70 00 19, call in advance for opening hours; adm*) has a small collection of antiquities, old furniture, ceramics from Moustiers and Apt, and items from daily life.

The lands around Forcalquier are some of the most beautiful in this part of Provence, full of oak forests and sheep meadows, rustic and peaceful and not yet as touristy as the Luberon to the south. Six kilometres west, in **Mane**, the 12th-century Benedictine Prieuré (Musée) de Salagon (*t 04 92 75 70 50; open May–Sept daily 10–12 and 2–7, Oct–Dec and Feb–April Sat and Sun only 2–6; adm*) was built on the site of a

Gallo-Roman farm and 5th-century Christian cemetery. Beautifully restored by the Conseil Général, the priory has medieval and medicinal gardens and houses the frequent exhibitions of the Alpes de Lumières, an organization dedicated to preserving and documenting local culture and customs. Mane's 18th-century Château de Sauvan (*t 04 92 75 05 64; guided tours July and Aug daily except Sat at 3.30; rest of the year Thurs, Sun and hols only at 3.30; adm*), owned by a friend of Marie Antoinette, is a fine example of French classicism, with period furnishings.

Twelve kilometres south of Forcalquier, the observatory near **St-Michel l'Observatoire** (*t 04 92 70 64 00; open April–Oct Wed 2–4, July and Aug Wed 10–2, rest of the year Wed 3pm; adm*) was attracted to the area by a study in the 1930s that found that the *pays de Forcalquier* had the cleanest, clearest air and the least fog of anywhere in France. There are guided tours, sadly only during the day, with films and a look at photos and the telescope.

This is also a region of *villages perchés*: **Dauphin**, just to the south, and **Oppedette**, to the west, overlooking the scenic canyon of the river Calavon. To the north, **Limans**, under brooding bald Montagne de Lure, is famous for its rather luxurious 16th-century *pigeonniers*, while **Banon** to the northwest is synonymous with Provence's most famous sheep's cheese. Most impressive of all, perhaps, is **Simiane-la-Rotonde**, set high on a small plateau. The '*rotonde*' is a peculiarly shaped 12th-century donjon dominating the village (*t 04 92 75 91 40; open April–mid-June and Sept Wed–Mon 3–5.30; mid-June–Aug Mon–Sat 10–12 and 3–7, Sun 3–7; Oct–March by reservation for groups only; adm*), with Romanesque carvings around what may have been a chapel – all that's left of a feudal castle. Simiane is by far the most chic of the villages in this area, with plenty of restored second homes; it's a charming place nevertheless, with a late Gothic church and an old covered market supported on stone pillars.

Manosque

By far the biggest town in this part of the Durance valley (pop. 20,000), Manosque is unavoidable. Nicknamed 'Manosque la Pudique' by François I after a beautiful girl from the village who disfigured herself rather than surrender to his unwanted advances, it was for centuries a drowsy place, with no other distinction than being the home town and lifetime abode of Jean Giono (1895–1970). Today it presents the spectacle of a Provençal village out of control. Acres of concrete suburban sprawl press against the hill-top medieval centre, and the traffic can be as ferocious as Marseille's. The culprit is Cadarache, France's national nuclear research centre, a huge complex to the south across the Durance, which was begun in 1959; most of its workers live around Manosque.

Manosque's tidy, teardrop-shaped centre, an oasis amidst the sprawling disorder, is entered through two 14th-century gates, the **Porte Saunerie** and the **Porte Soubeyran**, designed more for decoration than defence. Inside are two unremarkable churches on quietly lovely squares: **St-Sauveur**, made in bits and pieces from the 13th–18th centuries, but attractive nevertheless, and **Notre-Dame-de-Romigier**, with a Renaissance façade; the altar is an early Christian sarcophagus with reliefs of the Apostles.

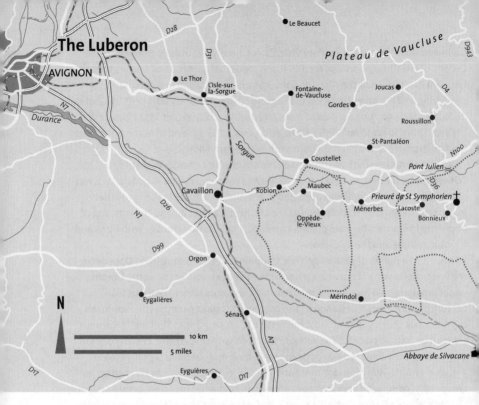

Manosque has a pair of newer attractions just outside the historic centre. A 19th-century *hôtel particulier* holds the **Centre Jean Giono**, just outside the Porte Saunerie (*1 Bd Elémir Bourges; open Tues–Sat 9–12 and 2–6; adm*). Dedicated to Manosque's literary lion, it holds an exhibition on his life and works, a library, and a *vidéothèque* with interviews and the films made from Giono's writings. A few doors down, the **Fondation Carzou**, in the neoclassical church at the Couvent de la Présentation, has frescoes by contemporary Armenian painter Jean Carzou based on the Apocalypse and New Jerusalem (*open Fri–Sun 10–12 and 2.30–6.30*).

The Luberon

As is the case with many a fair maiden, the Luberon's charms are proving to be her undoing. This is Peter Mayle country, the stage set for his surprise bestseller *A Year in Provence*. Yes, this is that magical place where the natives are endlessly warm and human, the vineyards ever-so-lovely in autumn, and the lunch in the little bistro worth writing about for pages and pages. All true, in fact – but everybody knows it, and the trickle of outsiders who began settling here in the 1950s, permanently or in holiday homes, has now become a flood, to the extent that the French have even dropped their accent – the Lubéron has become the Luberon, with a much-disputed change of pronunciation to go with it.

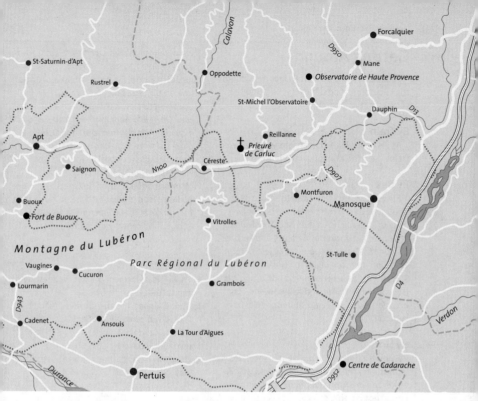

How you experience the Luberon will also depend on what time of year you come. Most of the year it's as quiet as a graveyard; in summer it can seem like St-Tropez-under-the-Poplars, with vast crowds of Brits, Yanks and Parisians milling about, waiting for lunch time. It's hard to imagine why anyone would want to come here in August; if you insist, make sure you have your hotel reservations months in advance.

The Regional Park

Like many parts of rural Provence, the Luberon presents a puzzling contrast – how these villages became such eminently civilized places, set amidst a landscape (and a population) that is more than a little rough around the edges. The real Luberon is a land of hunters stalking wild boar over Appalachian-like ridges, and weatherbeaten farmers in ancient Renaults full of rabbit cages and power tools. There are other regions of Provence, equally scenic and rustic, that merit being frozen into a nature preserve, but the Luberon was the one most in danger of being destroyed by a rash of outsiders and unplanned holiday villas.

The **Parc Régional du Luberon** was founded in 1977, a cooperative arrangement between the towns and villages that covers most of the territory between Manosque and Cavaillon, though quite a few places (often where the mayor is an estate agent or a notary) have decided not to participate at all. The Luberon is not an exceptional nature area like the Mercantour. Still, the park is doing God's work, protecting rare species like the long-legged Bonelli's eagle, a symbol of the Midi that needs plenty of

Getting Around

Public transport is woefully inconvenient in the Luberon; it is possible to get around the villages, but just barely.

By Train

Apt is on an SNCF branch line, with a few trains daily to Cavaillon and Avignon.

By Bus

Buses from Apt leave from the Place de la Bouquerie by the river; there are one or two daily to Roussillon, Avignon and Aix, stopping at Bonnieux, Lourmarin, Cadenet and Pertuis; also one to Digne, stopping at Céreste. From Cavaillon there are buses to L'Isle-sur-la-Sorgue, Pernes-les-Fontaines and Carpentras (several daily), to Apt and Avignon, and very occasionally to Bonnieux and other western Luberon villages.

By Horse

Finding a horse is no problem in most areas; in **Lauris**, try the Mas de Rocaute, t 04 90 08 29 58, and in **Lourmarin** phone the Centre Equestre, t 04 90 68 38 59.

Tourist Information

La Tour d'Aigues ✉ 84240: In the château, t 04 90 07 50 29, f 04 90 07 35 91, ot.valledaigues@free.fr. Open July–Aug daily 10–1 and 2.30–6.30; April–Oct Mon and Wed–Fri 9.30–12 and 2–6, Sat and Sun 2–6, Tues 9.30–12; Nov–Mar Mon and Wed–Fri 9.30–12 and 2–5, Sat and Sun 2–5 Tues 9.30–12.

Lourmarin ✉ 84160: Av Philippe de Girard, t/f 04 90 68 10 77, ot-lourmarin@axit.fr, www.lourmarin.com. Open Mon–Sat 9.30–1 and 3–7, Sun 9.30–12.

Cadenet ✉ 84160: Place du Tambour d'Arcole, t 04 90 68 38 21, f 04 90 68 24 49, ot-cadenet@axit.fr, www.provenceGuide.com. Open July–Sept Mon–Sat 9.30–12.30 and 3–7 (July–Aug also Sun 10–12.30); Oct–June Mon–Sat 9.30–12.30 and 2.15–6.15. Includes a shop for Cadenet's basket-weavers, the village's old craft speciality.

Park Information: Maison du Parc du Luberon, 60 Place Jean Jaurès, Apt, t 04 90 04 42 00, f 04 90 04 81 15, pnr.luberon@wanadoo.fr. Information centre with exhibitions, slide shows and a gift shop;

Market Days

Pertuis: Friday; farmers' market Wednesday and Saturday.

La Tour d'Aigues: Tuesday; farmers' market Thursday morning June–Sept.

Cucuron: Tuesday.

Lourmarin: Friday.

Cadenet: Monday; farmers' market Saturday May–Nov.

Where to Stay and Eat

Pertuis ✉ 84120

Le Boulevard, 50 Bd Pecout, t 04 90 09 69 31 (*moderate*). If you're passing through at lunch time, stop here for tasty and kindly priced Provençal classics. *Closed Tues eve, Sun eve and Wed.*

La Bastide-des-Jourdans ✉ 84240

*Auberge du Cheval Blanc, on the D27/D956 to La Tour d'Aigues, t 04 90 77 81 08, f 04 90 77 86 51 (*moderate*). A picture postcard hotel,

room to roam and is nearing extinction. Most of all, it is a reasonably effective legal barrier to keep the Luberon from being totally overwhelmed by the kind of building madness that wrecked the Côte d'Azur.

The Pays d'Aigues

The southern end of the Regional Park, the Pays d'Aigues, is the sleepier corner of the Luberon, a rolling stretch of good farmland sheltered by the Grand Luberon mountain to the north. **Pertuis**, a busy crossroads town along the D973, is the modest capital of the *pays*, with a bit of an aristocratic air; it earned the *fleur de lis* on its arms with a restaurant that specializes in game dishes and trout on an outdoor terrace. *Closed Feb; restaurant closed Thurs, Fri lunch in summer, Thurs & Fri lunch in winter.*

La Tour d'Aigues ✉ 84240

★★Les Fenouillets, just outside the village on the D956, **t** 04 90 07 48 22, **f** 04 90 07 34 26, *fenouillets@provence-luberon.net* (*moderate*). Rooms are simple, but there's a swimming pool nearby, and an inexpensive restaurant with outdoor tables that's the best bet for lunch.

Lourmarin ✉ 84160

Lourmarin, small as it is, has become the chic rendezvous in the southern Luberon.

★★★★Le Moulin, Rue du Temple, **t** 04 90 68 06 69, **f** 04 90 68 31 76, *moulin@provence-luberon.net* (*expensive*). A one-time olive mill on the western perimeter of the village with views over the château and nearby hills, this is one of the classiest establishments to open here in recent years. Provençal meets Art Nouveau in its tasteful decoration, while the restaurant serves attractive and delicious Provençal dishes. *Reserve early. Closed mid-Jan–Feb.*

★★★Hôtel de Guilles, Route de Vaugines, **t** 04 90 68 30 55, **f** 04 90 68 37 41, *guilles@provence-luberon.net* (*moderate*). An immaculately restored farmhouse just east of the village, beautifully decorated, with lots of antiques and all the amenities: tennis court, pool and gardens. *Closed Nov–mid-Mar.*

La Villa St Louis, 35 Rue Henri de Savournin, **t** 04 90 68 39 18, **f** 04 90 68 10 07, *villasaint louis@wanadoo.fr* (*moderate–inexpensive*). A charming *chambres d'hôte* in a 19th-century house on the edge of the village run by the warm and affable Mme Lassallette.

★★Le Paradou, Route d'Apt, **t** 04 90 68 04 05, **f** 04 90 08 54 94 , *paradou@provence-luberon.net* (*inexpensive; restaurant moderate*). In a dreamy setting north of Lourmarin on the D943, at the entrance to the Combe de Lourmarin. *Closed Thurs and Fri eve out of season.*

Lourmarin can also offer some of the best restaurants in the Luberon:

La Fenière, Rue du Grand Pré, **t** 04 90 68 11 79 (*expensive*). This restaurant in the centre combines expert, innovative cooking with old Provençal favourites: batter-fried courgette flowers and a hearty *daube. Closed Sun eve, Mon and Tues lunch.*

Le Bistrot, Av Raoul Dautry, **t** 04 90 68 29 74 (*moderate*). Overlooking the château and offering a choice of Provençal or Lyonnais cuisine. *Closed Thurs and last two weeks in Aug, and 20 Dec–mid-Jan.*

La Récré, 15 Rue Philippe de Girand, **t** 04 90 68 23 73 (*moderate*). Another good bet, with a terrace facing the château – fresh Provençal fare and good lamb dishes with garlic. *Closed Tues eve and Wed.*

Cadenet ✉ 84160

Cadenet, less expensive and touristy than Lourmarin, is a good alternative for a stay in this region.

★★Mas du Colombier, Route de Pertuis, **t** 04 90 68 29 00, **f** 04 90 68 36 77, *colombier@provence-luberon.net* (*moderate*). A newish, pleasant place with a pool, in an old vineyard. *Closed Feb and first 2 weeks in Nov.*

Stefáni, 35 Av Gambetta, **t** 04 90 68 07 14 (*cheap*). Delicious, simple fish and meat dishes are served on a panoramic terrace. *Closed Wed.*

for its loyalty to the French crown during the Wars of Religion. Prosperity in the 17th century has left it a number of fine buildings in the historic centre.

Of the smaller villages, a few stand out: **Grambois** to the northeast is a neatly rounded hill-top hamlet, a Saracen stronghold in the 8th–10th centuries and later one of the 12 citadels of Provence. Some walls remain, but the crenellated tower belongs to the church of Notre-Dame-et-St-Christophe. Both its patrons are represented in art inside: a good Renaissance altarpiece of the Virgin and an original 14th-century fresco of St Christopher, as well as, best of all, an anonymous 16th-century polyptych of John the Baptist, considered one of the masterpieces of the Provençal school. **Ansouis,** north of Pertuis on the D56, is a *village perché* built around the sumptuously furnished Château de Sabran (*t 04 90 09 82 70; open summer daily 2.30–6, Oct–Easter closed Tues; adm*), first mentioned in print in 961 and still in the hands of the original family. A Henry IV monumental stair leads to Flemish tapestries, Italian Renaissance furniture, portraits and later Bourbon bric-a-brac. The atmosphere is wonderfully snooty, but they let us in to visit just the same. The Musée Extraordinaire Georges Mazoyer (*t 04 90 09 82 64; open summer 2–7, winter 2–6, closed Tues; adm*) has some of this and some of that – sculptures, stained glass and other work by its namesake; also fossils and displays on underwater life.

For an airier, more pleasant castle without the bric-a-brac, try **La Tour d'Aigues**, just to the east. The château here, in fact, doesn't even have a roof. The Baron of Cental was still making repairs to damage caused by a fire in 1782 when the Revolution came, and the local peasantry torched the place for good. What's left is a thoroughly elegant Renaissance shell, begun in 1555 by an Italian architect, Ercole Nigra, imitating the styles then fashionable in Paris. The entrance, a massive triumphal arch carved with trophies, was inspired by the Roman arch at Orange. One of the château's side towers has been rebuilt, and the Conseil de Vaucluse, which now owns it, plans to restore the rest a little at a time as funds are available. There is a small museum in the cellar (*t 04 90 07 50 33; open July and Aug daily 10–1 and 2.30–6.30; Mar–Oct 9.30–12 and 2–6.30, closed Tues pm, Sat am and Sun am; Nov–Feb 9.30–12 and 2–5, closed as above; adm*), exhibiting both pottery and the history of Aigues. La Tour also has an unusual Romanesque church, Notre-Dame-de-Romegas, with an apse at either end – originally built facing the east, it was turned around in the 17th century when some clerical stickler for the rules had a second apse built.

Heading west, and still on the south flank of Montagne du Luberon, **Cucuron** was found perfect enough to be used as the set for *Le Hussard sur le toit* (*The Horseman on the Roof*), the film adaptation of a novel by Jean Giono; the view of the same roofs is especially pretty from the Donjon St-Michel. Cucuron's market takes place on the banks of its little lake, surrounded by ancient plane trees. The D56 leads on to **Vaugines**, a lovely little place (itself the setting for many scenes in *Manon des Sources* and *Jean de Florette*) and Lourmarin.

Lourmarin and Cadenet

Further west, into the heart of the Luberon, **Lourmarin** was the last home of Albert Camus. This is an unusual village, densely packed almost to the point of claustrophobia; many of its houses have tiny courtyards facing the street – too cute for its own good, as few villages, even in the Luberon, are so beset by tourists. Its landmark is a grand bell tower, so everyone always knows what time it is, and its main attraction is another 16th-century château (*t 04 90 68 15 23; open for guided tours May, June and Sept 10, 11, 2.30, 3.30, 4.30 and 5.30; July and Aug every 30mins 10–11.30 and 3–6; Oct–Dec and Feb–April at 11, 2.30, 3.30 and 4.30; Jan open Sat and Sun afternoons or by appointment; adm*). This was the residence of the counts of Agoult for three centuries; its last countess was the mother of Franz Liszt's three children, one of whom, Cosima, married Richard Wagner. Well restored, the 'Villa Medicis de Provence', as it's called, is now the property of the Académie of Aix, who use it for cultural programmes, concerts and exhibitions. The rooms have rare furnishings (don't miss the Aztec fireplace) and art, including a lovely *Lute Player* by the school of Leonardo da Vinci and a collection of engravings by Piranesi. If you are looking for the co-founder of existentialism, Albert Camus is buried on the left-hand side of the pretty cemetery, next to his wife.

Cadenet, a big village overlooking the rocky bed of the Durance, is only 5km away, but the difference is like day and night. An ancient place, Cadenet began as a pre-Celtic *oppidum*; even older are some of the cave dwellings that can be seen in the cliffs behind the village (others were refuges for persecuted Waldensian Protestants in the 16th century). It's also a very attractive village. On the Place du Tambour, one of the focal points of the Monday market, is a bronze statue of Cadenet's favourite son, André Estienne, a 15-year-old drummer boy who once managed a difficult river crossing for Napoleon's troops – wading right in and beating the charge under direct Austrian fire. The embarrassed soldiers could only follow. Have a peek inside the parish church, St-Etienne, on the northern edge of town. The baptismal font has well-preserved reliefs of a Bacchic orgy; scholars call it 3rd-century, but disagree over whether it was originally a sarcophagus or a bathtub. A new Musée de la Vannerie (*t 04 90 68 24 44; open April–Oct 10–12 and 2.30–6.30, closed Tues and Sun am; adm*) is dedicated to Cadenet's age-old occupation: wickerwork and basketry.

West of Cadenet, **Mérindol** isn't much to look at, but is worth a mention as a symbol of a very dark page of the Luberon's history. When plagues and war depopulated the region in the 14th century, immigrants from the Alps and from Italy came to work the land. Many were peaceful, hard-working Waldensian dissenters; when the Reformation began, the authorities could no longer tolerate them. In 1540, the Parlement of Aix oversaw the burning of 19 Waldensian villages in the Luberon, including Mérindol, and Lourmarin as well. Over 3,000 innocents were butchered, and hundreds more were sent off to the king's galleys. The ruins of Mérindol's castle house a Waldensian memorial; also note the curious onion-domed tower, called a 'Saracen bulb' in French.

Abbàye de Silvacane

t 04 42 50 41 69; open April–Sept daily 9–7; Oct–Mar Wed–Mon 10–1 and 2–5; adm.

Life as a medieval Cistercian was no picnic. Besides the strict discipline and a curious prejudice against heating, there was always the chance the Order might send you to somewhere in the middle of a swamp. They built this, the first of the 'Three Sisters of Provence', in just such a location because they meant to reclaim it – the 'forest of rushes' (*silva cana*), south of the Durance, 7km from Cadenet. It took a century or two, but they did the job, as you can see today from the fertile farmlands around Silvacane. A Benedictine community had already been established here when the Cistercians arrived in 1147. Work began on the present buildings soon after, partially financed by the barons of Les Baux, and Silvacane became quite prosperous. However, bad frosts in the 14th century killed all the olives and vines, starting

Silvacane on its long decline. When the government bought the complex to restore it in 1949, it was being used as a barn.

The church is as chastely fair as its younger sisters at Sénanque and Thoronet, and perhaps more austere and uncompromising still: even the apse is a plain rectangle. Of sculptural decoration there is hardly any (though scores of masons' marks on the columns and vaulting). The adjacent **cloister** now contains a herb garden, around a lovely broken fountain. Note the capitals on the arcades, carved, oddly, with maple leaves.

Northern Luberon: Along the N100 to Apt

Coming from Forcalquier, this route follows the northern slopes of the mountains, generally much more scenic country than the other side, with pretty villages like **Reillane**, almost deserted a century ago but now making a comeback, even attracting a few artists; and **Céreste**, with its Roman bridge, a village that grew up as a stopping point on the Via Domitia. Between the two, you can make an excursion to the **Prieuré de Carluc** (call **t** *04 42 54 22 70 to arrange guided tours, available July and Aug 3.30–7; adm*), with a 12th-century Romanesque chapel and unique ruins of the original early Christian priory, partly carved out of a rocky outcrop. Like Notre-Dame-du-Groseau on Mont Ventoux (*see* p.255), this was an ancient religious site built around a sacred spring; the ruins around the rock include a Gallo-Roman cemetery.

The narrow roads south of the N100 are some of the most beautiful in the Luberon, passing through **Vitrolles** or **Montfuron**, with its lofty ruined castle, on their way to the Pays d'Aigues. There are also several hiking trails, from Vitrolles or from **Saignon**, 5km southeast of Apt, leading up to the summit of the Grand Luberon, the **Mourre Nègre**, with views that take in all of the Vaucluse and beyond. Saignon itself is a beautiful *village perché* between two crags, boasting a well-preserved 12th-century church of Ste-Marie, with a curious lobed façade and a reliquary of the True Cross inside.

Apt

The capital of the Luberon (pop. 15,000 and growing) also claims to be the 'World Capital of Candied Fruits', with one big factory and plenty of smaller concerns that make these and every other sort of sweet. There is a certain stickiness about Apt; everyone in the Luberon comes here for the huge, animated Saturday market, but no one has ever admitted to liking the place, at least not in print. Roman Colonia Apta Julia, a colony refounded over a Celtic village, was the capital of the area even then. Despite languishing for a few dark centuries before being rebuilt in the 12th century, the streets still bear traces of a rectangular Roman plan, bent into kinks and curves through the ages.

The Cathedral and More Dubious Provençal Saints

We can guess that the **Rue des Marchands**, the main shopping street, roughly follows the course of its Roman predecessor. It leads to the **Tour de l'Horloge** (1567),

Tourist Information

Tourist office: 20 Av Philippe de Girard,
t 04 90 74 03 18, f 04 90 04 64 30,
tourisme.apt@pacwan.net.

Market Day

Saturday; Tuesday farmers' market in Cours
Lauze de Perret (May–Oct).

Where to Stay and Eat

Apt ✉ 84400

As rooms in the smaller villages are hard
to come by, you'll probably end up staying
in Apt.

★★★Auberge du Luberon, 17 Quai Léon Sagy,
on the river, t 04 90 74 12 50, f 04 90 04 79
49, *serge.peuzin@free.fr*, *www.auberge-
luberon-peuzin.com (moderate–inexpensive;
restaurant expensive–moderate)*. The
speciality here is rabbit with figs, and other
dishes with *confit d'Apt*. *Closed 2 weeks
in Nov.*

★★Le Palais, Place Gabriel-Péri, t 04 90 04
89 32 *(inexpensive)*. This hotel has a
pizzeria which serves other dishes too,

particularly a good ratatouille *(cheap)*.
Closed Oct–Mar.

Le Goût des Choses, Place du Septier, by the
hollow plane tree in Rue de la République,
t 04 90 74 27 97. For a simple lunch in central
Apt; tuck in to a choice of inexpensive pies
and salads.

★★Relais de Roquefure, on the N100, 4km
west, t 04 90 04 88 88, f 04 90 74 14 86,
*www.relaisderoquefure.com (moderate–
inexpensive)*. An old stone-built inn with a
pool and restaurant. *Closed Jan–mid-Feb
and Tues.*

Bernard Mathys, Gargas, 5km northwest,
t 04 90 04 84 64 *(expensive–moderate)*.
For a delightful meal with all the trimmings
(the vegetables are especially ravishing)
head for this lovely restaurant in an 18th-
century house. *Closed Tues and Wed,
mid-Jan–mid-Feb.*

Auberge du Presbytère, Place de la Fontaine,
Saignon, t 04 90 74 11 50, f 04 90 04 68 51
(moderate). Worth the detour: two 10th- and
11th-century buildings in the centre, with a
magnificent view over the Luberon,
charming homey rooms and a fine intimate
restaurant; *remember to book. Closed mid-
Nov–Jan.*

the bell tower of Apt's old **cathedral of Ste-Anne**. Begun in the late 12th century and
tinkered with incessantly until the 18th, the ungainly exterior conceals a wealth of
curiosities within. There is fine 14th-century stained glass in the apse, and an early
Christian sarcophagus and an odd golden painting of John the Baptist in two chapels
on the north side; also an interesting *trésor* with books of hours, reliquaries and some
Islamic ivories. Another trophy from the east is a linen banner, brought back from the
Crusades by a lord of Simiane; as its origin was forgotten, it came to be revered in Apt
as the **Veil of St Anne**.

Few regions of Europe had such a longing for relics as Provence in the Dark Ages.
Other peoples, the Germans and Venetians, had a kleptomanic urge to steal holy
bones when no one was looking; the Provençaux, showing less initiative but greater
imagination, simply invented them. We met St Transit at Ganagobie (*see* pp.226–7),
and the **crypt** here has two more. According to legend, the bones of St Anne, the
mother of Mary, were miraculously discovered in this crypt in the 8th century,
occasioning the building of the first cathedral. In those days, any early Christian
burial dug up was likely to be elevated to saint status; beyond that, scholars guess the
Anne invented for the occasion was less the biblical figure than a dim memory of the
primeval pan-European mother goddess, who was known as Ana, or Dana, to the
Celts, the Romans (*Anna Perenna*), and nearly everyone else. Next to her are the bones

of 'St Auspice', claimed to be Apt's first bishop – really the sacred auspices of pagan times (divination from bird flight or from the organs of sacrificed animals), another verbal confusion like St Transit.

Fruits and Fossils

Apt also has a good, well-laid-out **Musée d'Histoire et d'Archéologie** (*27 Rue de l'Amphithéâtre*, **t** *04 90 74 00 34; open June–Sept Wed, Thurs and Fri 10–12 and 2–5.30, Mon and Sat 10–12 and 2.30–5.30, Sun 2–6; Oct–May Mon 2.30–4.30, Wed, Thurs and Fri 2–5, Sat 10–12 and 2.30–5.30; adm*), with archaeological finds going back to the Palaeolithic period, late Roman sarcophagi, recent Roman and medieval finds from the centre of Apt, painted *ex votos* and a display of Apt's once-flourishing craft of faïence, which had its heyday in the 18th century.

The town's other attraction is the **Maison du Parc du Luberon** (*1 Place Jean Jaurès*, **t** *04 90 04 42 00; open Mon–Sat 9–12 and 1.30–6, to 7pm in summer*), the headquarters and information centre of the Regional Park; it has exhibits on the region's natural life, including a push-button Palaeontology Museum for the children, an interesting gift shop, and all the information you'll ever need on the wild areas of the Luberon.

Finally, you can take a tour of the **Apt-Union Factory**, west of town on the N100 (**t** *04 90 76 31 43*), where they make most of those crystallized fruits. It's an interesting process: they suck the water out of the fruit and replace it with a sugar solution – a bit like embalming.

Red Villages North of Apt

Technically, this isn't part of the Luberon, though it is within the boundaries of the Regional Park. Above Apt, on the southern slopes of the Plateau de Vaucluse, the geology changes abruptly. The plateau is mostly limestone, which erodes away to make caves and water tricks like the Fontaine-de-Vaucluse (*see* pp.246–7). This part has sandy deposits full of iron oxides – ochre, the material used in prehistoric times as skin-paint, and later to colour everything from soap to rugs. Centuries of mining have left some bizarre landscapes – cliffs and pits and peaks in what the locals claim are '17 shades of red', also yellow and cream and occasionally other hues besides.

Rustrel to Roussillon

Rustrel, northeast of Apt on the D22, was one of the mining towns until 1890. The huge, ruddy mess they left is called the **Colorado**; there are marked routes around it for tourists. From here, the D179 west takes you to **St-Saturnin-d'Apt** (St Saturnin is probably the Roman god Saturn). Inside a modern ring of bungalows, this old village had little to do with mining, but it has always grown nice red cherries; there are plenty of ruins, including a castle and bits of three different sets of walls (13th–16th centuries), a windmill for a landmark, and a simple Romanesque chapel from the 1050s. **Roussillon**, to the southwest, occupies a spectacular hill-top site, and well it should, for centuries of mining have removed nearly everything for miles around. The

Tourist Information

Roussillon ✉ 84220: Place de la Poste, **t** 04 90 05 60 25, **f** 04 90 05 63 31, *ot-roussillon@ axit.fr. Open April–Aug Mon–Sat 9.30–12 and 1.30–6.30, Sun 1.30–6.30; Sept–Oct Mon–Sat 10–12 and 2–6.30; Nov–Mar Mon–Sat 1.30–5.30.*

Bonnieux ✉ 84480: 7 Place Carnot, **t** 04 90 75 91 90, **f** 04 90 75 92 94, *ot-bonnieux@axit.fr. Open April–Oct 9.30–12.30 and 2–6.30.*

Market Days

Roussillon: Thursday, Place du Pasquier.
Bonnieux: Friday.
Lacoste: Tuesday.
Oppède: Saturday.

Where to Stay and Eat

St-Saturnin ✉ 84490

St-Saturnin is a friendly village, and though a bit out of the way, it is a good, reasonably priced choice for a base.

Hotel des Voyageurs, Place Gambetta, **t 04 90 75 42 08, **f** 04 90 75 50 58 (*inexpensive; restaurant moderate*). A delightfully old-fashioned Logis de France. *Closed end Jan–end Feb.*

Saint Hubert, Place de la Fraternité, **t** 04 90 75 42 02, **f** 04 90 75 49 90 (*inexpensive*). This has eight rooms and a restaurant with a pretty terrace; menus are posted daily on the chalkboard. *Closed Jan.* Note the 'wall-paper' in the bar.

Roussillon ✉ 84220

***Mas de Garrigon, **t** 04 90 05 63 22, **f** 04 90 05 70 01 (*expensive*). A well-restored farm-house with all the amenities, lovely rooms and a gourmet restaurant; both, unfortunately, are woefully overpriced. *Restaurant closed Dec.*

** Rêves d'Ocres, Route de Gordes, **t** 04 90 05 60 50, **f** 04 90 05 79 74 (*inexpensive*). Pleasant and lots cheaper, with convenient parking.

Le Val des Fées, Rue R. Casteau, **t** 04 90 05 64 99 (*moderate*). Lovely views over the ochre from the terrace.

Joucas ✉ 84220

****Le Phébus, **t** 04 90 05 78 83, **f** 04 90 05 73 61, *resphebus@wanadoo.fr, www. lephebus.com* (*expensive*). All done in exquisite taste, with views over the bizarre red hills of Roussillon, and a garden, pool, tennis and excellent restaurant, where the chef perks up his Provençal dishes with the freshest herbs. *Closed Nov–mid-Mar.*

Association Terre d'Ochres, an organization that wants to get the business going again, has an information centre in the village, and can direct you on a walk through the old quarries, known locally as the *Sables de Roussillon*. Samuel Beckett spent the war years exiled in Roussillon; rural peace and quiet gave him a nervous breakdown. Roussillon was the 'Peyrane' in the late Laurence Wylie's *Village in the Vaucluse;* the one place that readers will recognize from the 1950s is the Bar Castrum, with its old poster of the film *Marius* on the wall.

South of Roussillon, near the meeting of the N100 and D149 (south of the N100), is a well-preserved Roman bridge, the **Pont Julien**.

The little stone village of **Joucas**, just north of Roussillon, is quiet and uncommercial. North of here, at Murs, you can pick up the scenic D4 across the Plateau de Vaucluse and its gorges to **Venasque** (*see* p.250).

Villages of the Petit Luberon

West of Apt, and south of the N100, is a string of truly beautiful villages that have become the high-rent district of the Luberon, one of the poshest rural areas in France. Don't come here looking for that little place in the country to fix up; it's all been done,

****Le Mas des Herbes Blanches, t 04 90 05 79 79, f 04 90 05 71 96, *masherbes@ relaischateaux.fr* (*expensive*). A sumptuous Relais & Châteaux spread in an old *mas*, with a beautiful setting and all the fixings. *Closed Jan and Feb.*

Le Mas du Loriot, t 04 90 72 62 62, f 04 90 72 62 54 (*moderate*). More intimate and refined with just eight rooms in a new Provençal *mas* (*half board only*); it also has a pool. *Closed mid-Dec–Feb.*

**La Bergerie, t 04 90 05 78 73, f 04 90 05 73 41 (*inexpensive; restaurant moderate*). A country hotel-restaurant with 20 rooms and a pool.

Bonnieux ✉ 84480

***Hostellerie du Prieuré, t 04 90 75 80 78, f 04 90 75 96 00, *hotelprieur@hotmail.com* (*expensive*). A 17th-century priory in the village centre; the rooms have a view and there's a garden. *Closed Nov–Feb.*

**Hotel Le César, Place de la Liberté, t 04 90 75 96 35, f 04 90 75 86 38, *hotel.cesar@ waika9.com* (*inexpensive*). *Closed mid-Nov–mid-Mar.*

Le Pistou, Place de la Liberté, t 04 90 75 88 01 (*moderate*). Serves local produce on its imaginative menu.

Le Fournil, Place Carnot, t 04 90 75 83 62 (*moderate*). Excavated out of the cliff, serving light fresh fare. *Closed Mon and Jan.*

La Flambée, Place de la Liberté. A reasonable pizzeria.

Auberge des Seguins, Les Seguins (off the D113), t 04 90 74 16 37, f 04 90 74 03 26 (*moderate*). If you really want to get away from it all, there's this isolated hotel above Buoux (✉ 84480), near the Fort: simple rooms and home cooking in a memorable setting (*half board obligatory*).

Ménerbes ✉ 84560

***Le Roy Soleil, in an olive grove at Le Fort, along the Route des Beaumettes, t 04 90 72 25 61, f 04 90 72 36 55, *HRoysoleil@aol.com* (*expensive*). A 17th-century building overlooking Ménerbes, with a pool and tennis and excellent restaurant. *Closed Dec– mid-Mar.*

Oppède-le-Vieux ✉ 84580

**Le Mas des Capelans, on the N100, t 04 90 76 99 04, f 04 90 76 90 29 (*expensive*). Once a stable, now a pleasant country hotel, the Capelans has a pool, terrace and playground. *Closed mid-Nov–Dec.*

L'Oppidum, Place de la Croix, t 04 90 76 84 15 (*moderate*). Good-value local produce alongside local works of art beneath ruined medieval walls. *Open evenings only.*

as long as 40 years ago. The first to arrive were the Parisians, including many artists, intellectuals and eccentrics, giving the place a reputation as 'St-Germain-in-the Luberon'. Since the 1960s, a wave of outsiders looking for Provençal paradise, including many Americans, have transformed the place. None of this is readily apparent, apart from the infestations of swank villas on many hillsides outside the Regional Park boundaries. The villagers, a bit richer now, take it in their stride and carry on as they always have – separate worlds, existing side by side.

Biggest and busiest of the villages, **Bonnieux** is also one of the loveliest, a belvedere overlooking all the Petit Luberon. The ungainly modern church at the bottom of the village contains four colourful 16th-century wood paintings of the *Passion of Christ*; the other attraction, so to speak, is the Musée de la Boulangerie (*Rue de la République,* t 04 90 75 88 34; open June–Sept 10–12 and 3–6.30, closed Tues; April, May and Oct Sat and Sun and school hols only 10–12 and 3–6.30; adm), which as the name suggests will tell you everything you wanted to know about Provençal bread.

There are some wonderfully scenic excursions from here: take the D36/D943 south to Lourmarin. This is the only good road across the spine of the Luberon; it passes through a long and beautiful gorge called the **Combe de Lourmarin**. East of Bonnieux off the D943, a side road, the D113, takes you up into the mountains, passing the slender, elegant Romanesque bell tower of the **Prieuré de St Symphorien**, and up to the hamlet of **Buoux**; above it, the ruined medieval **Fort de Buoux** offers tremendous views over the heart of the Luberon. Nearby is the beginning of a **nature trail** marked out by the Regional Park, with informative placards on the Luberon's flora and fauna all along the way.

Lacoste, west of Bonnieux on the D109, is a trendy *village perché*, home to an American school run by the Cleveland Institute of Art. Overlooking the village is a gloomy ruined castle, the home of no less a personage than the Marquis de Sade (d. 1814). The French are a bit embarrassed by the author of *120 Journées de Sodome*, but he certainly wasn't insane, and he is a literary figure of some note, taking to extremes the urge for self-expression that came with the dawn of the Romantic movement. He did have his little weaknesses, which kept him in and out of the calaboose for decades, on charges such as pushing 'aphrodisiac bonbons' on servant girls, and worse. Scion of an old respectable Provençal family, he spent a lot of time here when Paris grew too hot for him. Oddly enough, the Marquis seems to have been a descendant of Petrarch's Laura – Laura de Sade (*see* Avignon, pp.120 and 127). The thought of it obsessed him for life and he saw her in visions in the castle here. The castle, burned in the Revolution, is currently undergoing a slow restoration and is closed to the public.

Continuing along the D109, you come to **Ménerbes**, honey-coloured, artsy and cuter than cute (with an attitude to match). As the former home of Peter Mayle – he's escaped to California – it now attracts fans of *A Year in Provence*, who come to pay homage and buy a postcard; there's not much else to do. Ménerbes is so narrow that from some angles it looks like a ship, cruising out of the Luberon toward Avignon; at the top is a small square, about 18ft across, with balconies on either side. The D188 from here takes you amongst waves of vines, to, fittingly, the world's first and only corkscrew museum, the **Musée du Tire-Bouchon**, at Domaine de la Citadelle

Wine: Côtes-du-Luberon

Between the mountains of the lower Durance and the Calavon Valley around Apt are the vineyards that produce AOC Côtes-du-Luberon – mostly young ruby wines made from grenache, syrah, cinsault, mourvèdre and carignan; the whites come from bourboulenc and clairette. This is produced in an extraordinary, high-tech works at the **Château Val-Joanis**, in Pertuis, **t** 04 90 79 20 77, **f** 04 90 09 69 52, where the red, with a high percentage of syrah (60 per cent), is both good and a good buy.

On the other hand, **Château de l'Isolette**, on the main road between Bonnieux and Apt, **t** 04 90 74 16 70, is run by the Pinatels, a family that has been making wine since the 16th century. Over the past decade the estate has won scores of medals, especially for its red wines aged in oak barrels, like the 1982 Grande Sélection; they also do a fine blanc de blancs and rosé.

In Bonnieux itself, look for **Château La Canorgue**, Route du Pont-Julien, **t** 04 90 75 81 01, a beautiful 16th-century château which won a gold medal at Blaye for its 1988 red, which has a bouquet of violets.

(**t** *04 90 72 41 58; open April–Oct 9–12 and 2–7, Nov–Mar 9–12 and 2–6, closed Sun; adm*), just to the west of Ménerbes. Created by a French film producer, the museum houses a collection of weird and wonderful bottle poppers, from 17th-century attempts to a bejewelled Cartier de luxe model, and an extensive display of porno-graphic corkscrews. From here the D188 continues through grand scenery almost to the top of the Petit Luberon, and **Oppède-le-Vieux**, with its even gloomier ruined castle, one that can be explored. Perhaps it has a curse on it; this was the home of the bloodthirsty Baron d'Oppède, leader of the genocide against the Waldensians in the 1540s. The road west of Oppède, by way of Maubec and Robion towards Cavaillon, is equally pretty; **Maubec**, with its Baroque church, may be the Luberon village of your dreams.

Cavaillon

Lacking anything more compelling, Cavaillon is famous for its melons. As one of the biggest agricultural market towns in France, it ships a million tonnes or so of these and all the other rich produce of the surrounding plains to Paris every year. Back in the 19th century, Alexandre Dumas loved the melons so much that he agreed to supply the local libraries with his books in exchange for a dozen melons a year.

Roman Cavaillon

Cavaillon is built under a steep hill overlooking the Durance, the **Colline St-Jacques**, where a Neolithic settlement has been uncovered next to a medieval chapel; it is a short climb up from central Place du Clos, with views on top stretching from Ventoux

to the Alpilles. Roman-era Cavaillon has left behind only a 1st-century AD **arch**, at the
foot of the hill. Unlike the arches of Carpentras and Orange, this one probably doesn't
mark any particular triumph; it is four-sided, a *quadroporticus* and, like the only
similar construction, the Arch of Janus in Rome, it probably was a simple decoration
for – appropriately enough – a marketplace. Its decorative reliefs, mostly fruits and
flowers, are now too eroded to be seen very clearly.

Cavaillon's other attractions include a small **Archaeological Museum**, in the chapel
of the Musée de l'Hôtel-Dieu on Cours Gambetta (*t 04 90 76 00 34; open mid-
April–mid-Sept 9.30–12.30 and 2.30–6.30, closed Tues and Wed; mid-Sept–mid-April
10–12 and 2–6.30, closed Tues, Sat and Sun; adm*); the odd-shaped, rather forbidding
Romanesque **cathedral of Notre-Dame et St-Véran**, with a tatterdemalion 17th-
century interior and a pretty cloister; and an ornate 18th-century **synagogue**, similar
to the one in Carpentras, with a small museum, on Rue Hébraïque (*same hours as
museum*). Before the Revolution, Cavaillon had the biggest Jewish population
in the papal enclave; among them were the ancestors of the composer Darius
Milhaud. Segregated in a tiny ghetto around the synagogue, the community prospered despite occasional gusts of papal persecution; after the Revolution most of
Cavaillon's Jews moved to the larger cities of Provence, and there are none living in
the town today.

On the Plateau de Vaucluse

The Plateau de Vaucluse is the high ground that runs between the Luberon and
Mont Ventoux to the north. Beware that both Gordes and Fontaine-de-Vaucluse can
get crowded by the heaving coachloads in the summer.

Gordes

The first thing you'll notice about this striking *village perché* is that it has a rock
problem. They have it under control; the vast surplus has been put to use in houses
and sheds, and also for the hundreds of thick stone walls that make Gordes seem
more like a south Italian village than one in Provence. The stones made agriculture
a bad bet here, so the Gordiens planted olives instead, and became famous for them –
at least until the terrible frost of 1976 killed off most of the trees. But without ever
asking for it, Gordes has found something easier and more profitable: art tourism,
with exhibitions and concerts in the summer.

Gordes was a fierce Resistance stronghold in the war and suffered for it, with
wholesale massacres of citizens and the destruction of much of the village; after the
war the village was awarded the Croix de Guerre. All the damage the Nazis did has
been repaired; the village centre, all steep, cobbled streets and arches, is extremely
attractive. At the centre, you may see flocks of well-scrubbed art students lounging
on the steps of the imposing château built by the lords of Simiane in the 1520s.
They are making their pilgrimage to an avant-garde that no longer exists. Even the
rearguard – a 'didactic museum' of the works of the late Hungarian op art/poster

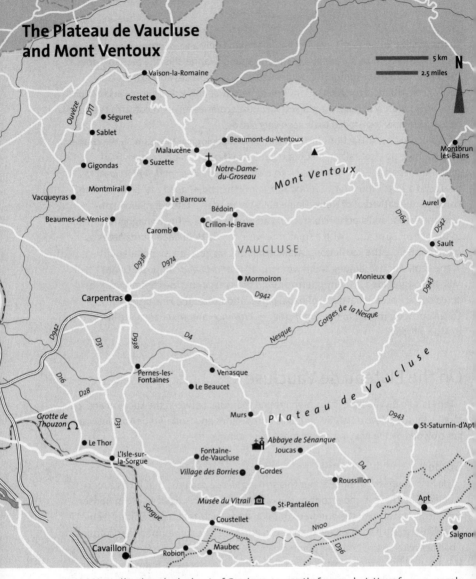

The Plateau de Vaucluse and Mont Ventoux

artist Vasarély – has ducked out of Gordes, apparently for good, victim of an unseemly quarrel over money between Vasarély's heirs and the management. If you're disappointed, the **Galerie Pascal Lainé** in Place du Château has a permanent exhibit of his works.

To see what real art's all about, walk over to Gordes' parish **church of St-Fermin**, with a memorable 18th-century interior of purple, pink and gilded jiggumabobs, a lodge brother's fantasy seraglio. A statue of the Magdalen on the right looks down on it with a jaundiced eye. The **château** itself (*open 10–12 and 2–6; adm*) has a superb Renaissance fireplace, the second largest in France, and a hodgepodge of art in the Musée Pol Mara up on the second and third floors.

Around Gordes: Les Bories and Another Bore

Across the Midi they are called *bories*, or *garriotes*, or *capitelles*, or a dozen other local names. In Provence, there are some 3,000 of them, but the largest collection in one place is the **Village des Bories**, south of Gordes off the D2 (*t 04 90 72 03 48; open daily 9–sunset; adm*). A *borie* is a small dry-stone hut, usually with a well-made corbelled dome or vault for a ceiling. Because of their resemblance to Neolithic works (like the *nuraghi* of Sardinia) they have always intrigued scholars. Recently it has been established, however, that though the method of building goes way back, none of the *bories* you see today is older than the 1600s. Elsewhere they are usually shepherds' huts, but these are believed to have been a refuge for the villagers in times of plague. This group of 12 *bories* has been restored as a rural museum. You'll see other *bories* all around Gordes; some have been restored as holiday homes, and one has even become an expensive restaurant. Determined *borie*-hunters should also tour the large concentrations in the countryside around Bonnieux, Apt, Buoux, St-Saturnin and Saumane, north of Fontaine-de-Vaucluse.

South of Gordes, there is a beautiful, simple Romanesque church in the hamlet of **St-Pantaléon**. West of that, watch out for the well-publicized Musée du Vitrail

Tourist Information

Gordes ✉ 84220: Le Château, **t** 04 90 72 02 75, **f** 04 90 72 02 26, *office.gordes@wanadoo.fr*. *Open June–Sept Mon–Sat 9–12.30 and 2–6.30, Sun 10–12.30 and 2–6; Oct–May Mon–Sat 9–12 and 2–6, Sun 10–12 and 2–6.*

Fontaine-de-Vaucluse ✉ 84800: Chemin de la Fontaine, **t** 04 90 20 32 22, **f** 04 90 20 21 37, *officetourisme.vaucluse@wanadoo.fr. Open Mon–Sat 9–7.*

Market Days

Gordes: Tuesday.

Where to Stay and Eat

Gordes ✉ 84220

Gordes is big business; several fancy villa-hotels have sprung up on the outskirts, but the whole Gordes scene is expensive, over the top and a bit exploitative of the credulous, who want it and deserve it. The tourist office has a list of the many *chambres d'hôtes* in the area.

★★Auberge de Carcarille, southwest of town on the D2, **t** 04 90 72 02 63, **f** 04 90 72 05 74, *carcaril@club-internet.fr (moderate–inexpensive)*. An honest establishment outside the village, this is a carefully restored *mas* with pretty rooms, some with balconies, and a reasonable restaurant specializing in fish and game. *Closed mid-Nov–Dec except 27 Dec–31 Dec.*

Restaurant Tante Yvonne, Place du Château, **t** 04 90 72 02 54 *(moderate)*. A solid choice for lunch, with a few unusual specialities. *Closed Sun eve and Wed.*

Fontaine-de-Vaucluse ✉ 84800

Fontaine-de-Vaucluse, in spite of its touristic vocation, is a quite pleasant place in which to stay or dine.

★★Le Parc, near the river and centre at Les Bourgades, **t** 04 90 20 31 57, **f** 04 90 20 27 03 *(inexpensive)*. A simple, pretty hotel wrapped in roses; its restaurant *(moderate)* serves some of the best Italian food in Provence. *Closed Jan–mid-Feb and Wed.*

Hostellerie Le Château, in Fontaine's old *mairie*, **t** 04 90 20 31 54, **f** 04 90 20 28 02 *(cheap)*. With an outdoor terrace overlooking the Sorgue (behind glass, so you won't get splashed by the water wheel in front). Excellent cooking *(moderate)* includes delicate sautéed frogs' legs and *rouget à la tapenade*); also five nice rooms.

Philip, Chemin de la Fontaine, **t** 04 90 20 31 81 *(moderate)*. The closest restaurant to the spring, serving mostly fish, with an outside terrace by the river. *Closed Nov–Easter.*

(stained glass) and **Musée du Moulin des Bouillons** (*t 04 90 72 22 11; open summer 10–12 and 2–6, closed winter; adm*), where another little Vasarély has set up shop near the oldest intact olive oil press in France. There are indeed exhibits on the history of stained glass, and others on Marseille soap, but their only purpose is to suck you into the adjacent gallery to look at the high-priced and gruesome work of Duran and others. Further south still, at **Coustellet**, the Musée de la Lavande (*t 04 90 76 91 23; open daily summer 10–12 and 2–9, winter 10–12 and 2–6; adm*) reveals all you have ever wanted to know about lavender, and more.

Abbaye de Sénanque

The loveliest of the Cistercian 'Three Sisters' lies 4km north of Gordes on the D177. The church may be almost a double of the one at Thoronet (*see* pp.295–6), but built in the warm golden stone of the Vaucluse and set among lavender fields and oak groves, it makes quite an impression. Now it is in the hands of the same cultural association that controls the abbey at St-Maximin-la-Ste-Baume; oddly enough they use the place for studies of Saharan nomads, and there is a room of exhibits on the subject. The Benedictine monks of Ile St-Honorat, who hold the title, seem interested in occupying it again, so Sénanque's status is uncertain. Meanwhile, it is a favourite venue for summer concerts, often of medieval music.

The **church** (*t 04 90 72 05 72; open Feb–Oct Mon–Sat 10–12 and 2–6, Sun 2–6; Nov–Jan Mon–Fri 2–5, Sat and Sun 2–6; adm*), begun about 1160, shows the same early Cistercian seriousness as Thoronet and Silvacane, and has been changed little over the centuries; even the original altar is present. Most of the monastic buildings have also survived, including a lovely **cloister**, the *chauffoir*, the only heated room, where the monks transcribed books, and a refectory with displays giving a fascinating introduction to Sénanque and the Cistercians.

Fontaine-de-Vaucluse

Over a century ago, explorers found the source of the Nile. They're still looking for the source of the little Vaucluse river called the Sorgue. It's underground; the best spelunkers in France have been combing the region's caves for decades without success, and in 1983 a tiny, specially made submarine probe (the *Sorguonaute*) sent back data from some 820ft below the surface of the **Fontaine-de-Vaucluse**, where the Sorgue makes its daylight debut through a dramatic gaping hole in a cliff in the beautiful narrow valley the Romans called Vallis Clausa – the origin of Vaucluse. A second probe, *Sorguonaute II*, was sent down in 1984, and imploded soon after immersion; finally, in 1985, a sophisticated device usually used in oil exploration – the *Modexa 350* – plunged to a sandy bed 1,024ft below the surface, though the passages that carry the stream into this remain unexplored.

Medieval legends record St Véran, patron of Cavaillon, dispatching a dragon near the source – a sure sign this was an ancient holy place, given the close connection between underground water and mythological serpents everywhere in Europe. The more prosaic Romans channelled the water into an aqueduct, remains of which can still be seen along the D24 towards Cavaillon. In later times, among those attracted by Provence's greatest natural wonder was Petrarch, who beginning in 1327 spent many seasons in a villa by the river bank writing his *De Vita Solitaria*, until 1353, when a band of brigands sacked the village and frightened him back to Italy.

The Fontaine is still an exquisite place, but the 540 or so residents of the town of Fontaine-de-Vaucluse have not been able to keep the place from being transformed into one of Provence's more garish tourist traps. To reach it, from the car park next to the church you'll have to walk a noisy 2km gauntlet of commerciality – everything from *frites* stands to a museum of authentic Provençal *santons* and a museum of medieval torture instruments. Incredibly, many of the attractions are worthwhile.

There is **Norbert Castaret's Musée de Spéléologie (Ecomusée du Gouffre)** (*t 04 90 20 34 13; open 10–12 and 2–6, closed Tues and Christmas–Feb; adm*), a 'subterranean world' museum of underground rarities and informational exhibits overseen by France's best-known cave explorer, and **Vallis Clausa** (*t 04 90 20 34 14; open 9–12.30 and 2–7; guided tours and sales*), an art gallery containing a paper-mill powered by old wooden wheels in the river that keeps up an old craft tradition on the Sorgue, making paper the 15th-century way for art books and stationery.

Most surprising of all, in a sharp modern building, is the **Musée Histoire Appel de la Liberté** (*t 04 90 20 24 00; open 10–12 and 2–6, closed Tues and Oct–Feb; adm*), a government-sponsored institution that opened in 1990 and recaptures the wartime years vividly with two floors of explanatory displays, vignettes of daily life under the Nazis, newsreels and magazines, weapons and other relics. As at Gordes, Resistance life around Fontaine-de-Vaucluse was no joke; among the exhibits is a tribute to Fontaine's own mayor, Robert Garcin, whose aid to the *maquis* earned him a one-way ticket to Buchenwald in 1944.

Finally, there is the spring itself, well worth the trouble even in its off-season. In the spring, and occasionally in winter, it pours out at a rate of as much as 200 cubic metres per second, forming a small, intensely green lake under the cliff. From the late spring until autumn it is greatly diminished, and often stops overflowing altogether (the water appears slightly further down the cliff); its unpredictability is as much a mystery as its source. It is a beautiful spot; if you're ambitious, it is also the beginning of two excellent hiking trails (GR6 and GR97), leading up into some of the most scenic parts of the Plateau de Vaucluse. More easily, you can climb up to the romantically ruined 13th-century **château** overlooking the spring, once owned by Petrarch's friend Philippe de Cabassole.

Before you leave, have a look at the village church, **Ste-Marie-et-St-Véran**. Begun in 1134, this lovely Romanesque building incorporates Roman and Carolingian fragments, including some bits of floral arabesques and the columns and capitals around the altar. The cornice outside is decorated with winsome rows of human and animal faces. Inside, there is the 6th-century Merovingian tomb of St Véran, and a good painted altarpiece of the *Crucifixion*, donated in 1654 by the village's *confrérie* of paper-makers. Also on the way out, peek in at the **Musée Pétrarque** (*t 04 90 20 37 20; open 10–12 and 2–6, closed Tues and Oct–Feb; adm*), a subdued look at the life and times of the poet during his stay in the town. Note the column, erected in 1804 by the Athenaeum Valclusianum to celebrate the 500th anniversary of his birth.

From Cavaillon to Carpentras

Until the Revolution, the western Vaucluse plains from Cavaillon north to Vaison-la-Romaine were known as the Comtat Venaissin, a county that was a part of the papal dominions in France, though legally separate from Avignon. St Louis had stolen the territory from the counts of Toulouse in 1229, part of the French Crown's share of the booty after the Albigensian crusade, and Philip III passed it along to the popes in 1274 to settle an old dispute. It was a worthy prize – medieval irrigation schemes had already made the rich lands of the Comtat the 'Garden of France', an honorific it holds today as the most productive agricultural region in the country. Besides Cavaillon's

Tourist Information

L'Isle-sur-la-Sorgue ✉ 84800: Place de la Liberté, t 04 90 38 04 78, f 04 90 38 35 43, office-tourisme.islesur-sorgue@wanadoo.fr. Open Mon–Sat 9–1 and 2.30–6.30, Sun 9–12; shorter hours in winter.

Le Thor ✉ 84250: Place du 11 Novembre, t 04 90 33 92 31, ot-lethor@axit.fr. Open Mon 2–6, Tues–Fri 10–12 and 2–6, Sat 2–6.

Pernes-les-Fontaines ✉ 84210: Place Gabriel Moutte, t 04 90 61 31 04, f 04 90 61 33 23, ot-pernes@axit.fr, www.ville-pernes-les-fontaines.fr. Open mid-June–mid-Sept Mon–Fri 9–12 and 2.30–7, Sat 9–12 and 2.30–6, Sun 10–12; mid-Sept–mid-June Mon–Fri 9–12 and 2–5.30, Sat 9–12 and 2–5.

Market Days

L'Isle-sur-la-Sorgue: Thursday and Sunday. Antiques market Sunday, year round.
Le Thor: Saturday.
Pernes-les-Fontaines: Saturday.

Where to Stay and Eat

L'Isle-sur-la-Sorgue ✉ 84800

L'Isle-sur-la-Sorgue can be a delightful place for a stay when not being ravaged by summer tour buses, and its accommodation is fine.

***Mas de Cure Bourse, Route de Caumont, Velorgues, 2km south of town on the D938, t 04 90 38 16 58, f 04 90 38 52 31 (moderate). A restored inn from the 18th century, with a pool and extensive gardens, 13 rooms and a restaurant where the poêlé de faisan mariné '1,000 choux' is a treat. Restaurant closed first 2 weeks in Jan, and Mon and Tues lunch.

**La Gueulardière, Route d'Apt, right in the centre of town, t 04 90 38 10 52, f 04 90 20 83 70 (inexpensive). Cosy rooms and a garden terrace for dining; specialities of the house include gâteau d'aubergines aux foies de volaille (moderate). Closed Dec; restaurant closed Tues lunch and Wed.

Le Vivier de la Sorgue, Cours Fernande-Peyre, t 04 90 38 52 80 (moderate). Fish in a number of tasty forms is served on the lovely terrace over the river. Closed Sat lunch and Sun eve.

Le Carré d'Herbes, 13 Av des Quatre-Otages, t 04 90 38 62 95 (moderate). Serves Provençal specialities with an exotic touch in a dining room full of antiques. Closed Tues eve and Wed.

Pernes-les-Fontaines ✉ 84210

***L'Hermitage, Route de Carpentras, t 04 90 66 51 41, f 04 90 61 36 41 (moderate). Open year round.

**Prato Plage, Route de Carpentras, t 04 90 61 31 72, f 04 90 61 33 34 (inexpensive; restaurant cheap). With 20 rooms, slightly less expensive than its competitor. Open year round.

Le Palépoli, Route de Carpentras, t 04 90 61 34 00 (moderate). Get a table here for some of the best Italian food in Provence – spaghetti alle vongole, carpaccio, tiramisù. Closed Sat lunch.

Venasque ✉ 84210

Auberge de la Fontaine, Place de la Fontaine, t 04 90 66 02 79, f 04 90 66 66 67 (expensive). With five pricey suites and the best food in the village: eat upstairs in the charming dining room (moderate). Closed mid-Nov–mid-Dec.

famous melons, this small area has 5 per cent of all France's vineyards, including its best table grapes, and still finds room to grow tonnes of cherries, asparagus, apples and everything else a Frenchman could desire. All this intensive agriculture doesn't do the scenery any harm, and passing through it you'll find some fat, contented villages that make the trip worthwhile.

L'Isle-sur-la-Sorgue and Le Thor

The Sorgue, that singular river that jumps out of the ground at Fontaine-de-Vaucluse and makes fly fishermen happy all the way to the suburbs of Avignon (it's one of France's best trout streams), has one more trick to play before it reaches the Rhône. At L'Isle-sur-la-Sorgue, it briefly splits into two channels to make this Provençal Venice, a charming town of 17,000 souls, an island indeed. In the Middle Ages, as a scrappy semi-independent commune, L'Isle-sur-la-Sorgue dug two more channels and put the water to work running mills and textile factories; when trouble came, as during the Wars of Religion, the town knew how to keep out invaders by flooding the surrounding plains and making itself even more of an island.

Today, L'Isle-sur-la-Sorgue still makes fabrics and carpets, but it is best known as the antiques centre of Provence, with a number of permanent shops on the southern edge of town, around Avenue des Quatre Otages, and a big 'Antiques Village' by the train station, open on Sundays (*some booths also open Sat and Mon*). Circumnavigating the town is a pleasant diversion; you pass a number of old canals and wooden **mills**, some still in use, and houses with little front terraces built over the rushing water. There are two mills along Rue Jean Théophile, a street that will also take you to the 18th-century **Hôtel-Dieu** (hospital), with a sumptuous chapel and a perfectly preserved pharmacy of that era that can be visited, an ensemble of Moustiers faïence and ornate carved wood. There are frequent art exhibitions in an 18th-century palace, the **Musée Donadéï Campredon** (*20 Rue Dr Tallet, t 04 90 38 17 41; open July–Oct 10–1 and 3–6.30, Nov–June 9.30–12 and 2–6, closed Mon; adm*). And finally, right in the centre, is the town's beached whale of a church, 17th-century **Notre-Dame-des-Anges** (*open Tues–Sat 10–12 and 3–6*), sprawling across Place de l'Eglise. Even in a region full of marvellously awful churches, this one is a jewel, a mouldering imitation of Roman Baroque outside and gilt everything within. Opposite the façade, note the old firm of Fauques-Beyret, the prettiest drapery shop in Provence, with a fine Art Nouveau front; inside and out, nothing seems to have changed since about 1900.

West of L'Isle-sur-la-Sorgue, the N100 leads to **Le Thor**, with one of the best Romanesque churches in Provence, carrying the intriguing name of Notre-Dame-du-Lac. Begun about 1200, it is a work of transition, the Provençal Romanesque giving way to Gothic influences, as seen in the pointed vaulting of the nave. The sculptural decoration is spare but elegant, emphasizing the perfect symmetry of one of the last great medieval buildings in this region.

Some 3km north of Le Thor on the D16 is the **Grotte de Thouzon** (*t 04 90 33 93 65; open April–June and Sept–Oct daily 10–12 and 2–6, July and Aug daily 9.30–7, Nov–Mar Sun and bank hols 2–6; adm*). Of all the caves in Provence, this may be the one most worth seeing – weird and colourful, with rare needle-slender stalactites hanging down as much as 10ft.

Pernes-les-Fontaines

L'Isle-sur-la-Sorgue's tiny neighbour to the north, Pernes-les-Fontaines, has only a single drowsy stream passing through it, the Nesque. In the 18th century, perhaps out of jealousy, the Pernois took it into their heads to build decorative fountains instead. They got a bit carried away and now there are 37 of them, or one for every 190 inhabitants. The fountains contribute a lot to making Pernes one of the most delightful towns in the Vaucluse. It is an introspective place, still turning its back on the world, sheltering inside a circuit of walls that was demolished a hundred years ago, to be replaced by a ring of boulevards. Pernes is for walking; the Pernois have used the centuries to make their town an integrated work of art, looking exactly the way they want it to look; there's a surprise around every corner – or at least a fountain.

Starting from the centre, the old **bridge** over the Nesque is embellished at both ends, with the 16th-century Porte de Notre-Dame, the Cormorant Fountain and the small chapel of Notre-Dame-des-Grâces, from the same era. Behind it, the 12th-century **church of Notre-Dame-de-Nazareth** includes some Gothic chapels and reliefs of Old Testament scenes. The relative simplicity of its interior, in contrast with so many other Provençal churches, is a reminder of Pernes' earnest Catholicism through the centuries (one of its current economic mainstays, incidentally, is making the communion hosts for all the churches of France). Note the **Tour de l'Horloge**, once the keep of the castle of the counts of Toulouse, now crowned with a pussycat weather vane (*you can climb up Mar–Sept daily 9–6.30, Oct–Feb daily 10–5*). Ask at the tourist office for a guide to take you around to the **Tour Ferrande**, on Rue Gambetta. This unassuming medieval tower, next to a fountain with carved grotesques, contains some of the oldest frescoes in France (*c.* 1275): vigorous, primitive scriptural scenes, Charles of Anjou in Sicily, St Sebastian and St Christopher, and a certain Count William of Orange battling against a giant.

East of Pernes-les-Fontaines is a very odd place, **Le Beaucet** (on the D39 south of St-Didier), where the people used to live in cave houses, some of which can still be seen, along with a ruined castle. Above it, in the mountains, a spring similar to Fontaine-de-Vaucluse has given rise to one of the biggest pilgrimage sites in Provence, a well-decorated chapel dedicated to the 12th-century **St-Gens**, a rain-maker and tamer of wolves.

Venasque, further east, was the old capital of the Comtat Venaissin, and gave the county its name. Though a pretty village, and lately fashionable, nothing is left of its former distinction but the usual ruined fortifications and a venerable baptistry, really a 6th-century Merovingian funeral chapel reworked in the 12th century.

The twisting D4, connecting Carpentras and Apt, was the main road of the Vaucluse in medieval times; it is still an exceptionally lovely route, passing southeast from Venasque through the **Forêt de Venasque** and some rocky gorges on the edge of the Plateau de Vaucluse.

Carpentras

The average French town of 30,000 or so, unless it has some great historical importance or major monument, is likely to be a rather anonymous place. Carpentras isn't. Perhaps because of its long isolation from the rest of France, under papal rule but really run by its own bishops, Carpentras has character and a subtle but distinct sense of place. A bit unkempt, and unconcerned about it, immune to progress and to any sudden urges for urban renewal, it is nevertheless an interesting place to visit. There are some cockeyed monuments, and some surprises. The rest of Provence pays Carpentras little mind; ask anyone, and they'll probably remember only that the town is famous for caramels, mint-flavoured ones called *berlingots*.

Into the Centre

As in so many other French towns, you'll have to cross a sort of motorway to get into the centre: a ring road of boulevards that was created when the town walls were knocked down in the 19th century (it's one-way and very fast – miss a turn and you'll have to go all the way around again; the French find these very entertaining). One part of the fortifications remains, the towering 14th-century **Porte d'Orange**, built in the 1360s under Pope Innocent IV. If you can get in, you'll find an amiable and lively town, especially when the gorgeous produce of the Comtat farmers rolls in for the Friday market. The stands fill half the town, but the centre is Rue des Halles, with the

Getting There and Around

Carpentras is the node for what little there is of **bus** transport in the northern Vaucluse, with good connections to Avignon (some going by way of Pernes-les-Fontaines and L'Isle-sur-la-Sorgue) and Orange, one a day to Marseille, and one or two a day to Vaison-la-Romaine and some villages of the Dentelles de Montmirail, including Beaumes-de-Venise and Gigondas. Almost all buses stop at Place Aristide-Briand, on the ring boulevard.

There are also several daily SNCF **trains** to Orange and Avignon.

Tourist Information

Tourist office: 170 Allée Jean-Jaurès, **t** 04 90 63 00 78, **f** 04 90 60 41 02, *tourist.carpentras@ axit.fr, www.provenceGuide.com* or *www.tourisme.fr/carpentras. Open July–Oct Mon–Sat 9–7, Sun 9.30–1; Sept–May Mon–Sat 9–12.30 and 2–6.30.*

Market Day

Friday morning (with truffles Nov–Mar).

Where to Stay and Eat

Carpentras ✉ **84200**

Carpentras somehow manages to be left out of the annual tourist visitations, and accommodation here is limited.

Le Fiacre, 153 Rue Vigne, **t 04 90 63 03 15, **f** 04 90 60 49 73 (*inexpensive*). An elegant old hotel in an 18th-century building near the tourist office.

*Hôtel du Théâtre, 7 Av Albin Durand, **t** 04 90 63 02 90 (*inexpensive*). The budget choice is on the ring boulevard; the friendly proprietor may try to corner you into a game of chess. *Closed Christmas and New Year.*

Le Vert Galant, Rue de Clapiès, **t** 04 90 67 15 50 (*moderate*). For original cooking and strictly fresh seafood. *Closed Sat lunch, Sun eve and Mon lunch.*

Le Marijo, 73 Rue Raspail, **t** 04 90 60 42 65 (*moderate*). Serving traditional Provençal food, along with well-cooked trout. *Closed Jan, all day Sun in winter, Sun eve in summer.*

Passage Boyer, an imposing glass-roofed arcade built by Carpentras' unemployed in the national public works programme started after the 1848 revolution.

Cathédrale St-Siffrein

Open 10–12 and 2–6, closed Sun pm.

Undoubtedly, this is one of the most absurd cathedrals in Christendom. So many architects, in so many periods, and no one has ever been able to get it finished and get it right. Worst of all is the mongrel façade – Baroque on the bottom, a bit of Gothic and who knows what else above – like a mutt with a spot around its eye, likeable somehow, the kind that follows you home and you end up keeping him. Begun in the 15th century, remodellings and restorations proceeded in fits and starts until 1902. Some of the original intentions can be seen in the fine Flamboyant Gothic portal on the southern side, called the **Porte Juive** because Jewish converts were taken through it, in suitably humiliating ceremonies, to be baptized. Just above the centre of the arch is Carpentras' famous curio, the small sculpted *Boule aux Rats* – a globe covered with rats. The usual explanation is that this has something to do with the Jews, or heretics. But bigotry was never really fashionable among 15th-century artists, and more likely this is a joke on an old fanciful etymology of the town's name: *carpet ras*, or 'the rat nibbles'.

The interior, richly decorated in dubious taste, includes some stained glass of the 16th century (much restored) and an early 15th-century golden triptych (left of the high altar) by the school of Enguerrand Quarton, an island of calm among so much busyness. The sacred treasures are in a chapel on the left: the relics of St Siffrein, one of the most obscure of all saints, not even mentioned in any early hagiographies; and the *Saint-Mors*, the 'holy bridle bit', said to have been made by St Helen out of two nails of the Cross as a present for her son, the Emperor Constantine.

Next to the cathedral, the **Palais de Justice** (1640) is the former Archbishops' Palace, occupying the site of an earlier palace, which, for the brief periods that popes like Innocent IV chose to stay in Carpentras, was the centre of the Christian world. The present building, modelled after the Farnese Palace in Rome, contains some interesting frescoes from the 17th and 18th centuries, including mythological scenes, and also views of Comtat villages and towns (ask the concierge to show you around).

The Triumphal Arch and the Secret Cathedral

Everyone knows that if you walk around a church widdershins (against the sun: counter-clockwise), you'll end up in fairyland, like Childe Harolde. Try it in Carpentras, and you'll find some strange business. The 28ft Roman **Triumphal Arch**, tucked in a corner between the cathedral and the Palais de Justice, was built about the same time as that of Orange, in the early 1st century AD. Anyone who hasn't seen Orange's would hardly guess this one was Roman. Of all the ancient Provençal monuments, this shows the bizarre Celtic quality of Gallo-Roman art at its most stylized extreme, with its reliefs of enchained captives and trophies. In the 14th century, the arch was incorporated into the now-lost Episcopal Palace. By 1640, when it was cleared, it was serving an inglorious role separating the archbishop's kitchens from his prisons. Originally, it must have connected the palace with the earlier Romanesque cathedral.

Now, look at the clumsily built exterior wall of the present cathedral, opposite the arch. There are two large gaps, through which you can have a peek at something that few books mention, and that even the Carpentrassiens themselves seem to have forgotten: the **crossing and cupola** of the 12th-century cathedral, used in the rebuilt church to support a bell tower (later demolished) and neglected for centuries. In its time this must have been one of the greatest buildings of Provence, done in an ambitious, classicizing style – perhaps too ambitious, since its partial collapse in 1399 necessitated the rebuilding. The sculpted decoration, vine and acanthus-leaf patterns, along with winged creatures and scriptural scenes, is excellent work; some of it has been moved to the town museum.

The Synagogue and Museums

Behind the cathedral and palace, two streets north up Rue Barret, is the broad Place de l'Hôtel de Ville, marking the site of Carpentras' Jewish Ghetto. Before the Revolution, over 2,000 Jews were forced to live here in unspeakable conditions, walled in and obliged to pay a fee any time they wanted to leave. A small population remains; one that is only just recovering from the trauma of a brutish desecration incident in the local Jewish cemetery. The crime went unsolved for years and stirred up passions, rumours and bitterness on a national scale until March 1997, when a few local skinheads finally confessed, and apologized in court. All that remains of the old ghetto is the **Synagogue** at the end of the square (*open Mon–Thurs 10–12 and 3–5, Fri 10–12 and 3–4*). Built in 1741, it has a glorious decorated interior in the best 18th-century secular taste.

Other attractions in town include the **Hôtel-Dieu** on Place Aristide Briand (*open Mon, Wed and Thurs 9–11.30*), an 18th-century hospital with a well-preserved pharmacy and an attractive chapel containing the tomb of Carpentras' famous bishop and civic benefactor, the Monseigneur d'Inguimbert (1735–73). This hospital is his monument, along with the important library he left to the town and the beginning of the collections in the **Musée Comtadin-Duplessis** on the ring road (*Bd Albin-Durand, t 04 90 63 04 92; open April–Oct 10–12 and 2–6, Nov–Mar 10–12 and 2–4, closed Tues; adm*). Here are displayed artefacts and clutter from Carpentras' history, old views of the town, and 16th- and 17th-century paintings, many by local artists.

Between Carpentras and Mont Ventoux; the Gorges de la Nesque

Heading north for Mont Ventoux and Vaison-la-Romaine, you might consider a slight detour to the east, along the D974. Towards the village of **Bédoin**, a small resort below Mont Ventoux famous for its enormous forest, you will pass Carpentras' **aqueduct** – not Roman but a 17th-century work, impressive nevertheless. **Crillon-le-Brave**, just west, was the birthplace of Henri IV's companion-at-arms and has a belvedere with splendid views on to Mont Ventoux. **Caromb**, west of the D974 on the D55, is an attractive village that has kept parts of its medieval fortifications, as well as

Where to Stay and Eat

Le Barroux ✉ 84330
★★★**Hostellerie François Joseph**, Chemin des Rabassières, **t** 04 90 62 52 78, **f** 04 90 62 33 54, *hotel-f-joseph@wanadoo.fr* (*expensive–moderate*). Just below the monastery, surrounded by flowerbeds and acres of woods, it is so quiet here that guests awaken to birdsong. There's a pool, and the bright rooms are all well equipped with TV and mini-bar; many have kitchenettes as well. *Closed mid-Nov–Mar.*

Le Four à Chaux, by the crossroads for Caromb, **t** 04 90 62 40 10 (*moderate*). Dine well on refined, traditional dishes. *Closed Mon and Tues.*

Crillon-le-Brave ✉ 84410
★★★★**Hostellerie de Crillon-le-Brave**, **t** 04 90 65 61 61, **f** 04 90 65 62 86, *crillonlebrave@relaischateaux.fr* (*expensive*). A sunny, sumptuous hotel in an old manor house, run by a Canadian infatuated with Provence. Glorious views of Mont Ventoux are supplemented with the hotel's helpful guide to walks in the area. *Closed Jan–mid-Mar; restaurant closed lunch Mon–Fri.*

a surprisingly grand church, Notre-Dame-et-St-Maurice, with a wealth of Renaissance decoration inside. From here the skyline is dominated by **Le Barroux**, a dramatically perched village built around a 13th-century château (*open for tours in the summer*) that belonged to the Seigneurs of Baux. Follow the signs in the village up to the lofty Benedictine monastery of Ste-Madeleine, set in a geometrical lavender garden, a fine example of Provençal Romanesque – built in the late 1970s. Come at 9.30am (10 on Sundays) to hear the 50 monks sing Gregorian chant for an uncanny journey straight back to the days when Romanesque was spanking new.

Or take a tour through the centre of the Plateau de Vaucluse, on the D942 almost as far as Sault, then return on the D1. Few ever take it, though those who don't miss the most spectacular scenery the Vaucluse has to offer: the dry, rugged **Gorges de la Nesque**, leading to Sault and the Plateau d'Albion (*see* below). **Monieux**, at the eastern end of the Gorges, is a strange and isolated village that seems to have grown out of the rocky cliffs. There are caves and underground streams in the neighbourhood; experiments with dyeing the water have suggested that one of the sources of the Fontaine-de-Vaucluse may be here.

Mont Ventoux

You can pick it out from almost anywhere on the plains around Carpentras, a commanding presence on the northern horizon. **Mont Ventoux**, a bald, massive humpbacked massif over 12 miles across, is the northern boundary stone of Provence, and it has always loomed large in the Provençal consciousness. For the Celts, as for the peoples who came before them, it was a holy place, the Home of the Winds; excavations in the early 20th century at its summit brought to light hundreds of small terracotta trumpets, a sort of *ex voto* that has never been completely explained. Winds, in Provence, inevitably suggest the mistral, and as the source of that chilling blast, Mont Ventoux has always had a somewhat evil reputation among the people; medieval Christians sought to exorcize it, perhaps, with the string of simple chapels that mark its slopes.

Mountain climbers will find a special interest in Mont Ventoux, if only because the sport was invented here. Petrarch, that admirably modern soul, went up with his brother in 1336 – this, according to historian Jacob Burckhardt, was the first recorded instance of anyone doing such an odd thing simply for pleasure. The experience had an unexpected effect on the poet. Reading a passage from his *Confessions of St Augustine* at the summit, he was seized with a vision of the folly of his past life and resolved to return to Italy: '…and men go forth, and admire lofty mountains and broad seas, and roaring torrents, and the course of the stars, and forget their own selves in doing so.' For us the trip will be easier, if perhaps less profound; Edouard Daladier, the Carpentrassien who became French prime minister in the 1930s, had a road built to the top (the D974).

Malaucène and the Fountain of Groseau

The base for visiting the mountain is **Malaucène**, an open, friendly village on the road from Carpentras to Vaison. Piled under a little conical nib of a hill, its landmark is the enormous church-cum-fortress of St-Michel-et-St-Pierre, built in 1309 by Pope Clement V. From here, the D153 was the ancient route around Mont Ventoux, passing a pair of medieval chapels and a ruined defence tower around the village of **Beaumont-du-Ventoux** (it now peters out into a hiking trail, the GR4).

The D974, into the heart of the massif, passes a pre-Celtic site dedicated not to wind, but water. **Notre-Dame-du-Groseau**, an unusual 11th-century octagonal chapel, marks the spot today. Originally, this was part of a large monastery, now completely disappeared. Pope Clement V used it as his summer home, and his escutcheon can be seen painted inside (the *curé* at Malaucène has the key). But this was also a holy spot in remotest antiquity; the iron cross outside the chapel is planted on a stone believed to have been a Celtic altar. *Groseau* comes from *Groselos*, a Celtic god of springs; the object of veneration is a short distance up the road, the **Source du Groseau**, pouring out of a cliff face. The Romans, as at Fontaine-de-Vaucluse, channelled the spring into an aqueduct, here for the city of Vaison; fragments of this can still be seen.

Wine: Côtes-du-Ventoux

The vineyards of this little known AOC region are situated on the lower slopes of Mont Ventoux. The area is known principally for its reds, which are similar in style to the Côtes-du-Rhone AOC. The best estates, such as the **Domaine des Anges**, make wines with a high proportion of syrah in the blend giving them depth and structure.

A 15th-century glassworks, **Domaine de la Verrière**, at Goult, **t** 04 90 72 20 88, **f** 04 90 72 40 33, has been transformed into another of the area's best sources of wine. M. Maubert produces a wine of unusual concentration, full of broad, spicy flavours which complement the local dishes perfectly. The Perrin brothers, famous for producing one of the finest and most sought-after Châteauneuf-du-Pape wines at Château de Beaucastel, also make a very fine Côtes-du-Ventoux at their purpose-built winery on the outskirts of Orange, **La Vieille Ferme, t** 04 90 34 64 25.

Tourist Information

Malaucène ✉ 84340: Place de la Mairie,
t 04 90 65 22 59, *ot-malaucene@axit.fr. Open
summer Mon–Sat 9.30–12.30 and 3–6; winter
Mon–Sat 10–12 and 3–5.*
Sault ✉ 84390: Av de la Promenade,
t 04 90 64 01 21, f 04 90 64 15 03,
*ot-sault@axit.fr. Open April–June and Sept
daily 9–12 and 2–6; July–Aug daily 9–1 and
2–7; Nov–Mar Mon–Thurs 9–12 and 2–6, Fri
and Sat 10–12 and 2.30–4.30.*

Market Days

Malaucène: Wednesday.
Sault: Wednesday.

Where to Stay and Eat

Malaucène ✉ 84340

Malaucène makes a good base for Ventoux
and the Dentelles de Montmirail.
Hostellerie La Chevalerie, Place de l'Eglise, Les
Remparts, t 04 90 65 11 19, f 04 90 12 69 22
(*moderate*). By St-Michel; peaceful, with the
most comfortable rooms in town; the
restaurant has a charming terrace. *Closed
Wed and Tues eve out of season.*
**L'Origan, Cours des Isnards, t 04 90 65 27
08, f 04 90 65 12 92 (*inexpensive*). Clean,
shipshape and in the centre; dishes such as
guinea fowl with *morilles* (*moderate*). *Closed
Oct–mid-Mar and Mon.*

**Le Venaissin, Cours des Isnards, t 04 90 65
20 31, f 04 90 65 18 03 (*inexpensive*). Similar
to L'Origan.
La Maison, Hameau de Piolon, outside
Beaumont-du-Ventoux, t 04 90 65 15 50
(*moderate*). For the best cooking in the area.
There's only one menu, though it has a wide
selection of dishes, many with a touch of the
southwest; try the *pintadeau en croûte.*
*Closed Mon lunch, Tues lunch and Wed lunch,
and Oct–Easter.*

Around Mont Ventoux: Sault and Aurel ✉ 84390

***Hostellerie du Val de Sault, Ancien
Chemin d'Aurel, Sault, t 04 90 64 01 41,
f 04 90 64 12 74, *valdesault@aol.com*
(*expensive*). A handsome new hotel 2,494ft
up and facing Mont Ventoux, with only 11
rooms and five suites surrounded by trees
and gardens; equipped with a pool, gym,
salle de pétanque and good restaurant
(*expensive–moderate*). *Closed Nov–Mar.*
*Relais du Mont Ventoux, Aurel, t 04 90 64
00 62, f 04 90 64 12 88 (*inexpensive*). Plain
but comfortable rooms and a restaurant
(*cheap*) with no surprises. *Closed mid-
Nov–mid-Mar.*
Chalet-Reynard, east of the summit of
Ventoux, at the corner of the D164 and
D974, t 04 90 61 84 55 (*moderate–cheap*).
The only restaurant for miles, a cosy, wood-
lined bar where the local lumberjacks tuck
into boar and a *pichet de rouge* at lunch
time. *Closed Tues.*

Further up the mountain, the almost permanent winds make themselves known
and vegetation becomes more scarce (despite big reforestation programmes). The
D974's big day comes, almost every summer, when the Tour de France puffs over it,
probably the most tortuous part of the race; it was here that the English World
Champion Tommy Simpson collapsed and died in 1967. The top of Ventoux (6,200ft) is
a gravelly wasteland, embellished with communications towers and a meteorological
observatory. Coming down the eastern side of the mountain takes you into one of the
least-visited backwaters of Provence, a land of shepherds, boar and *cèpes.*

There are a few attractive villages: **Sault**, on its outcrop, surrounded by bucolic landscapes, forests and lavender fields, with a quirky Musée Municipal (*t 04 90 64 02 30;
open July–Aug Mon–Sat 3–6*) of fossils, village curios and archaeology (even a
mummy); and further north, two medieval *villages perchés*, **Aurel** and **Montbrun-les-
Bains**. South of Sault, the lonely **Plateau d'Albion** takes its name (like the English

Albion, the Alps and the Provençal village of Aups) from an ancient Indo-European root meaning white – from the odd limestone mountains around it, that seem to be covered in snow. The landscape can be a bit eerie, even more so when you consider that much of this territory, around the village of St-Christol, has been taken over for a complex of bases where France keeps most of its nuclear missiles.

Les Dentelles de Montmirail

Montmirail's 'lace' is a small crown of dolomitic limestone mountains, opposite Mont Ventoux on the other side of Malaucène. Eroded by the wind into a lace-like fantasy of thick columns and spikes, the peaks form an ever-changing pattern as you circle around them. This is superb walking country, and superb wine country.

Wine and Antiques

The ideal overview of the Dentelles is along the D90 from Malaucène to Beaumes-de-Venise, passing by way of **Suzette**, a cluster of sunbleached stone houses and a bar-pizzeria enjoying a dream-like vision of the mountains at their most fantastical. If you're in no hurry, steep semi-paved roads from Suzette plunge into the heart of the mountains for more of the same, towards Séguret to the west (*see* below), or north to **Crestet**, a half-abandoned, half-restored *village perché* with a castle, more fabulous views and an art centre with changing and usually quirky exhibitions.

The D90 takes you into Côtes-du-Rhône country (*see* below), beginning with **Beaumes-de-Venise**, the metropolis of the Dentelles, where the worthies sit out on the wall sunning themselves like fat cats. There's a ruined castle to explore, and a small archaeological museum. Don't expect any canals: the name Beaumes comes from the Provençal word for cave, and the Venise from a corruption of Comtat Venaissin – the papal county.

North along the D81, the Romanesque chapel of **Notre-Dame-d'Aubune** overlooks the Comtat plain, with a lofty bell tower decorated with classical pilasters. A track leads up the *Côte balméenne*, where terraces were settled by the Celto-Ligurians, Greeks, Romans and Saracens. Since the archaeologists had their way with it in the 1980s, the terraces have been replanted with olive, almond and fruit trees.

Vacqueyras, a dusty little crossroads devoted entirely to wine, has a by-road up to **Montmirail**, a spa once famous for its purgative waters. It was sold off after the Second World War: a Greek shipping tycoon now owns the grand Victorian villa, while the rest of the spa is now a hotel (*see* 'Where to Stay'). A few kilometres north of Vacqueyras, **Gigondas**, like so many wine villages in the south, is much smaller than its fame: sweet and small, overlooking the immaculate vineyards and full of shops to *déguster* the eponymous red nectar. The château on top of the village has been turned into a modest outdoor sculpture garden. The extremely helpful tourist office sells maps of the paths through the Dentelles: the GR4 passes nearby, and steep white roads lead back to Beaumes or to the Col du Cayron and Lafare (south of Suzette) for more lovely Dentelles scenery.

Tourist Information

Beaumes-de-Venise ✉ 84190: Maison des Dentelles, Place du Marché, **t** 04 90 62 93 25, **f** 04 90 62 94 31, *ot-beaumes@wanadoo.fr*. *Open Mon–Sat 9–12 and 2.30–6.30, shorter hours in winter.* There's also an office on Cours Jean-Jaurès. *Open Mon–Sat 9–12 and 2.30–6.30 (plus Sun 9–12 June–Aug).*
Gigondas ✉ 84190: Rue du Portail, **t** 04 90 65 85 46, **f** 04 90 65 88 42, *ot-gigondas@axit.fr*, *www.begond.fr/village/gigondas.html.*

Market Day

Beaumes-de-Venise: Tuesday.

Where to Stay and Eat

Beaumes-de-Venise ✉ 84190

Auberge St-Roch, Av Jules Ferry, **t** 04 90 65 08 21 (*cheap*). Has a modest restaurant with seafood and local dishes. Closed Dec.

Vacqueyras ✉ 84190

★★★**Hôtel Montmirail**, **t** 04 90 65 84 01, **f** 04 90 65 81 50, *hotel.montmirail@wanadoo.fr* (*moderate*). Once part of the spa, with pool, garden and restaurant.
★★**Le Pradet**, Route de Vaison, **t** 04 90 65 81 00, **f** 04 90 65 80 27 (*inexpensive; restaurant moderate*). A quiet, new complex on the edge of the village. *Closed mid-Oct–mid-Mar; restaurant closed Thurs and Sat lunch.*
★**Hôtel Restaurant des Dentelles**, **t** 04 90 65 86 21, **f** 04 90 65 89 89 (*inexpensive*). Offers modern two-star comfort (at two-star prices), and so-so food in the restaurant.

Gigondas ✉ 84190

★★**Les Florets**, Route des Dentelles, **t** 04 90 65 85 01, **f** 04 90 65 83 80 (*moderate*). Simple rustic rooms and plenty of peace and quiet in the middle of a vineyard. *Closed Jan–Feb.*
L'Oustalet, Place Gabrielle Andéol, **t** 04 90 65 85 30 (*moderate*). Good beef in wine in a neoclassical building. *Closed Sun and Mon, but open for Sun lunch in Jan.*
Le Mas de Bouvau, Route de Cairanne, Violès (✉ 84150), just west of Gigondas, **t** 04 90 70 94 08, **f** 04 90 70 95 99 (*inexpensive*). A charming family-run hotel-cum-restaurant in the vines, serving specialities from south-east France: duck *confit*, *magret*, foie gras, pigeon and rabbit (*moderate*). *Closed mid-Dec–Jan, Sun eve and Mon.*
La Farigoule, Le Plan de Dieu, Violès (✉ 84150), **t** 04 90 70 91 78 (*inexpensive*). Bed and breakfast in a pleasant old farmhouse; they also rent bikes. *Closed Nov–Mar.*

Séguret ✉ 84110

★★★**Domaine de Cabasse**, on the D23 towards Sablet, **t** 04 90 46 91 12, **f** 04 90 46 94 01, *info@domaine-de-cabasse.fr, www.domaine-de-cabasse.fr* (*moderate*). Part of a Côtes-du-Rhône estate; a few comfortable rooms with terraces, a pool and an excellent restaurant that has truffles in season and other rather extravagant dishes year round. *Closed Nov–Mar.*
★★★**La Table du Comtat**, in the village, **t** 04 90 46 91 49, **f** 04 90 46 94 27 (*expensive*). Well known for refined dishes such as *julienne de truffe en coque d'œuf. Closed Oct–June Tues eve and Wed.*
Le Mesclun, in the village, **t** 04 90 46 93 43 (*moderate*). Simpler local fare à la carte. *Closed Mon.*

Sablet, north of Gigondas, is another pretty, hard-working wine village packed on a hill, with old covered lanes to explore. Most of the passing tourists home in on **Séguret**, built on a terrace over the vine-striped Ouvèze plain. It bears the burden of being 'One of the Most Beautiful Villages in France' with a fair amount of grace: there's no room for cars, and none more than a handful of artists and *santonniers*. Note the funny weathered faces on the 14th-century Fontaine des Mascarons. Séguret is a good base for hiking; there are two trails (GR4 and GR7) and one village track that passes through a gap in the Dentelles to the eastern side. The back road to Vaison-la-Romaine is steep but beautiful.

Wine: Côtes-du-Rhône Sud

Wines called Côtes-du-Rhône originate in 263 communes within the 200km between Vienne and Avignon. Because of the diversity of growing conditions in such a vast area, from hot rocky plains to steep green slopes, the district is a crazy-quilt of local varieties, which as a general rule are better than wines merely labelled Côtes-du-Rhône. You may find any mix of 13 varieties of grapes in a bottle of southern Côtes-du-Rhône, but the dominant forces are grenache, which gives it tannin and its famous sturdy quality, while cinsault counterbalances with its delicacy and finesse, and syrah contributes fragrance and ability to age.

The star of the Dentelles is Gigondas, its very name derived from 'joy', or Jocunditas, a holiday camp for Roman soldiers. Part of their delight, according to Pliny, was in the wine, one of the most subtle, noble, dark and fragrant of all Côtes-du-Rhônes, the perfect match for pheasant, partridge, wild rabbit or truffles. Two excellent wines to buy and keep around are the Signature 1990 and Pavillon de Beaumirail 1988, aged in oak barrels at the **Cave des Vignerons de Gigondas, t** 04 90 65 86 27, **f** 04 90 65 80 13, responsible for 20 per cent of the total Gigondas production.

As usual, for the finest wines, one has to go to the individual estates, where the best wine-makers can concentrate on producing small quantities of wine from the very best vineyard sites. Jean-Marc Autran, the young superstar of Gigondas, makes elegant Gigondas and rich Sablet at the **Domaine de Piaugier**, Sablet, **t** 04 90 46 96 49, **f** 04 90 46 99 48. The **Domaine les Pallières**, in Gigondas, **t** 04 90 65 85 07, is currently run by the Brunier family. The **Domaine Les Goubert, t** 04 90 65 86 38, **f** 04 90 65 81 52, also in Gigondas, offers the remarkably dense Cuvée Florence 1990 and, more unusual for the Dentelles, a Sablet Blanc, a fine white wine from ancient clairette vines.

Vacqueyras, the minute region just to the south of Gigondas, produces sober and full-bodied wines; some of the finest used to be made by a Provençal-speaking Pole named Jocelyn Chudzikiewicz at the **Domaine des Amouriers**, Les Garrigues, Sarrians, **t** 04 90 65 83 22, **f** 04 90 65 84 13 (the 1987 has a fine truffle perfume and the 1988 is so dense it's almost black). Chudzikiewicz died tragically aged 46 in 1997 in a motor-bike accident; the estate is run on behalf of his heirs by Patrick Gras. Try the **Château de Montmirail**, in Vacqueyras, **t** 04 90 65 85 12, **f** 04 90 65 81 31, a long-established family vineyard which also does a delightfully mellow Gigondas.

The small appellation of Beaumes-de-Venise produces good reds, but is rightly famous for its rich sweet white wine made from the muscat grape. The wine is made by partially fermenting very ripe grapes and arresting the fermentation by the addition of alcohol, which kills off the yeasts, leaving much of the sugar and giving the wine an extra potency. The locals find the rather eccentric English habit of treating it as a dessert wine highly amusing: they drink it as an aperitif. The local cooperative makes a very good example.

The two leading estates are **Domaine de Durban**, which is owned by M. Leydier, **t** 04 90 62 94 26, **f** 04 90 65 01 85, and the Perrin brothers of **La Vieille Ferme, t** 04 90 34 64 25, on the outskirts of Orange.

Vaison-la-Romaine

Vaison, in all its 2,400 years, has never been able to make up its mind which side of the river Ouvèze it wanted to be on. Locals have always been wary of the river's mighty potential for destruction, and the town's peregrinations from bank to bank have left behind a host of monuments, including extensive Roman ruins. Such circumspection was proved justified in 1992 when, on the night of 22 September, the Ouvèze burst its banks and swept away houses, caravans, bridges and roads, drowning 30 people in one of the worst French floods of the century. The town's riverside is still being rebuilt, and the scars of the tragedy are yet to heal.

Yet, as the tourist office proclaims, the best way to support Vaison is to continue to visit. The Roman ruins were untouched, and life goes on: Vaison is a pleasant and beautiful place (with a good market if you are staying locally), and despite the summer crowds, if you're interested in the Romans or the Middle Ages it will be a mandatory stop on your Provençal agenda.

The Vaison Festivals draw large crowds from July to September, when theatre groups, choirs and musicians from France and around the world gather for performances in venues ranging from the Roman amphitheatre to the town's car parks. For information contact the tourist office.

Tourist Information

Tourist office: Place du Chanoine Sautel, t 04 90 36 02 11, f 04 90 28 76 04, ot-vaison@axit.fr, www.vaison-la-romaine.com. There is a vast car park across the street for visitors. *Open Sept–mid Oct and April–June Mon–Sat 9–12 and 2–5.45, Sun 9–12; July–Aug daily 9–12 and 2–6.45; mid-Oct–Mar Mon–Sat 9–12 and 2–5.45.*

Market Day

Tuesday, in the lower town. Farmers' market, Tuesday, Thursday and Saturday in summer.

Where to Stay and Eat

Vaison-la-Romaine ✉ 84110

Vaison has plenty of room, and in the crowded summer months you might end up here even if you preferred to be in one of the villages of the Dentelles.

★★Hôtel Les Auric, west of Vaison on the D977, t 04 90 36 03 15 (*inexpensive*). A modernized old farmhouse with a pool. *Closed mid-Nov–Mar, and Sun out of season.*

Staying up in the Haute-Ville is not entirely convenient, but it can be very gratifying.

★★★Le Beffroi, Rue de l'Evêché, t 04 90 36 04 71, f 04 90 36 24 78, beffroi@wanadoo.fr (*expensive–moderate*). A picturesque 16th-century house, furnished to match. It's a bargain for its category. *Closed Feb and Mar.*

★★Le Burrhus, 1 Place Montfort, t 04 90 36 00 11, f 04 90 36 39 05 (*inexpensive*). Comfortable rooms with an Art Deco touch, and a shady terrace. *Closed mid-Nov to mid-Dec.*

Le Brin d'Olivier, 4 Rue du Ventoux, t 04 90 28 74 79 (*moderate*). Vaison was something of a gastronomic desert until 1995, when young Olivia and Didier Rogne opened Le Brin d'Olivier, an intimate, romantic hotel with an inner courtyard. It's the ideal place to feast on Olivia's fresh, imaginative Provençal cuisine, in which fresh herbs hold pride of place (*expensive*). *Closed Wed, lunch daily July–Sept, and Sat lunch out of season.*

La Fête en Provence, Place du Vieux Marché, t 04 90 36 36 43 (*moderate*). Serves its own *foie gras de canard*, followed by a *magret* of lamb with olives. *Closed mid-Nov–mid-March, and Wed.*

History

Vaison began on the heights south of the Ouvèze as a Celtic *oppidum*. In the late 2nd century BC, the Romans took control and refounded it as Vasio Vocontiorum, a typical colony on the gentler slopes to the north of the river. For an out-of-the-way site, Vasio prospered spectacularly for the next five centuries, an *urbs opulentissima* with a large number of wealthy villas and as many inhabitants as it has today (about 6,000).

Vaison survived the age of invasions better than many of its neighbours; church councils were held here in the 6th century, a time when the city could afford to begin its imposing cathedral. In the following centuries, bishops ruled in Vaison as the city gradually declined. Perhaps in the 8th century, the counts of Toulouse acquired the site of the old Celtic *oppidum* and built a castle on it. They carried on a chronic quarrel with the bishops; meanwhile, most of the people were abandoning the Roman town (and the bishops) for the freedom and safety of the heights, the beginnings of what is now the Haute-Ville. In the 14th century, Vaison fell into the hands of the pope, along with the rest of the Comtat Venaissin, and did not become part of France until the Revolution.

In the 19th century, on the move once more, the Vaisonnais were abandoning the Haute-Ville for the river bank. In 1840 the first excavations were undertaken in the Roman city. Vaison nevertheless had to wait for a local abbot, the Chanoine Sautel, to do the job seriously. He dug from 1907 until 1955, financed mostly by a local businessman.

The Ruins

Open Mar–May and Oct daily 10–12 and 2–6, June–Sept daily 9.30–12.30 and 2–7, Nov–Feb Wed–Mon 10–12 and 2–4.30; Site Puymin open July and Aug 9.30–7; same adm for both, also includes cathedral cloister.

The canon uncovered almost 11 hectares of Roman Vaison's foundations, while the modern town grew up around the digs. There are two separate areas, the **Quartier de la Villasse** and the **Site Puymin**; their entrances are on either side of the central Place du Chanoine-Sautel, by the tourist information pavilion. Vaison's ruins are an argument for leaving the archaeologists alone; with everything sanitized and tidy, interspersed with gardens and playgrounds, there is the unmistakable air of an archaeological theme park. The Villasse is the smaller of the two areas; from the entrance, a Roman street takes you past the city's **baths** (the best parts are still hidden under Vaison's post office) and the **Maison au Buste d'Argent**, a truly posh villa with two *atria* and some mosaic floors. It has its own baths, as does the adjacent **Maison au Dauphin**; beyond this is a short stretch of a **colonnaded street**, a status embellishment in the most prosperous Roman towns.

The Puymin quarter has more of the same: another villa, the **Maison des Messii**, is near the entrance. Beyond that, however, is an *insula*, or block of flats for the common folk, as well as a large, partially excavated quadrangle called the **Portique de Pompée**, an enclosed public garden with statuary that was probably attached to a temple. On the opposite side of the *insula* is a largely ruined *nymphaeum*, or monumental fountain. From here you can walk uphill to the **theatre**, restored and used for concerts in the summer, and the **museum**, displaying the best of the finds from the excavations. You'll learn more about Roman Vaison here than from the bare foundations around it; there is a model of one of the villas as it may have looked. All the items a Roman museum must have are present: restored mosaics and fragments of wall paintings, some lead pipes, inscriptions, hairpins and bracelets, and of course statuary: municipal notables of Vaison, a wonderful monster *acroterion* (roof ornament) from a mausoleum, and a few marble gods and emperors – including a startling family portrait with the Emperor Hadrian completely naked and evidently proud of it, next to his demurely clothed Empress Sabina, smiling wanly.

The Cathedral of Notre-Dame-de-Nazareth

The French, with their incurable adoration of anything Roman, go on forever about the ruins and neglect Vaison's real attraction, one of the most fascinating medieval monuments of the Midi. A treasure house of oddities, it is a reminder that there is more to the art and religion of the Middle Ages than meets the eye, and much of significance that is lost to us forever. It stands half a kilometre west of the ruins, on Avenue Jules Ferry.

The church was begun in the 6th century. Its **apse** is the oldest part; looking at it from the outside, you'll see where excavations have uncovered the dressed Roman stones and drums of columns that were recycled to serve as a foundation. The rest of the structure dates from a rebuilding that began in the 12th century, including some handsome sculptural decoration around the portals, cornices and bell tower. The first clues to the mystery of this church can be seen near the top of the façade: a rectangular **maze**, and a triangular figure that may be a mystic representation of the Sun. Even with this, the exterior is subdued, and the muscular perfection of the columns and vaults inside comes as a surprise.

The 12th-century nave is Romanesque at its best, but still the eye is drawn down it to the magnificent, arcaded interior of the apse. There is nothing like this apse in France; it is a place to muse on time and fate – the last surviving work of Roman Provence, the wistful farewell of a civilization that can be heard across the centuries. Almost incredibly, the 6th-century marble **altar** is still present, carved in a beautiful wave-like pattern. Also here are the original bishop's throne, and benches set around the semicircle of the apse where the monks would sit: the earliest form of a choir, as in the churches of Ravenna.

In the medieval nave, some of the decoration is as provocative as that on the façade. At the rear, near a column that survives from the original basilica, you'll notice the figure of an unidentifiable 'hairy person', extending a hand in a gesture of benediction. Elaborate masons' marks are everywhere. Odd figures of the Evangelists embellish the squinches of the fine octagonal cupola; behind one of them, high up, on the second column on the right side of the nave, is what appears to be a little devil. You'll meet his big brother in the cloister.

The Cloister

Look around as you enter. Grinning over the ticket-booth to the cloister is Vaison's most famous citizen – Old Nick himself, with horns and goatee, carved into the stone as big as life. This is not a personage one usually sees portrayed in cathedral cloisters, and no one has ever come up with an explanation for his presence here – one unlikely guess is that it's really Jesus, superimposed over a crescent moon. This is a small but graceful cloister from the 12th century, with finely carved capitals (one with a pair of entwined serpents) and architectural fragments displayed around the walls.

And if you think the Devil and all the other curiosities were simply fanciful decoration, look up from the cloister at the Latin verse inscription, running the entire length of the church's southern cornice:

I exhort you, brothers, to triumph over the party of Aquilon [the north],
faithfully maintaining the rule of the cloister, for thus will you arrive at
the south, in order that the divine triple fire shall not neglect to illuminate
the quadrangular abode in such a way as to bring to life the arched
stones, to the number of two times six. Peace to this house.

The medieval Latin is in parts obscure enough for other interpretations to be possible, but these tend to be even stranger. The 12 stones seem to be pillars of the cloister, the 'quadrangular abode'. The rest is lost in arcane, erudite medieval mysticism, wrapped up with the architecture and unique embellishments, and undoubtedly with a monastic community that was up to something not entirely orthodox. Like most medieval secrets, this one will never be completely understood.

Chapelle St-Quenin

A bit of a climb to the north, on Avenue de St-Quenin, you can continue in this same vein of medieval peculiarity. St-Quenin, a chapel dedicated to a 6th-century bishop who became Vaison's patron saint, fooled people for centuries into thinking it a Roman building. Its apse, unique in France, is triangular instead of the usual semi-circle, and crowned with a cornice that includes fragments from Roman buildings as well as primitive reliefs that may date from Merovingian times. It is difficult to ascribe any special significance to this odd form. Probably built in the 11th or 12th centuries, it may be simply an architectural experiment, typical of the creative freedom of the early Romanesque. On the front of the chapel is a Merovingian-era relief of two vine shoots emerging from a vase, a piece of early Christian symbolism that has become the symbol of Vaison.

The Haute-Ville

From Roman and modern Vaison, the medieval version of the town is a splendid sight atop its cliff, a honey-coloured skyline of stone houses under the castle of the counts of Toulouse. Almost abandoned at the turn of the last century, the Haute-Ville is becoming quite chic now, with restorations everywhere and more than a few artists' studios. You reach it by crossing the Ouvèze on a **Roman bridge**, still in good nick after 18 centuries of service (although it had to be repaired after the last floods;

note the plaque, in Latin), then climb up to the gate of the 14th-century fortifications, next to the **Tour Beffroi**, the clock tower which is the most prominent sight of the Haute-Ville's silhouette. The cobbled streets and the shady **Place du Vieux-Marché**, with its fountain, are lovely; trails lead higher up to the 12th–14th-century **castle**, half-ruined but offering a view.

The Provençal Alps

13

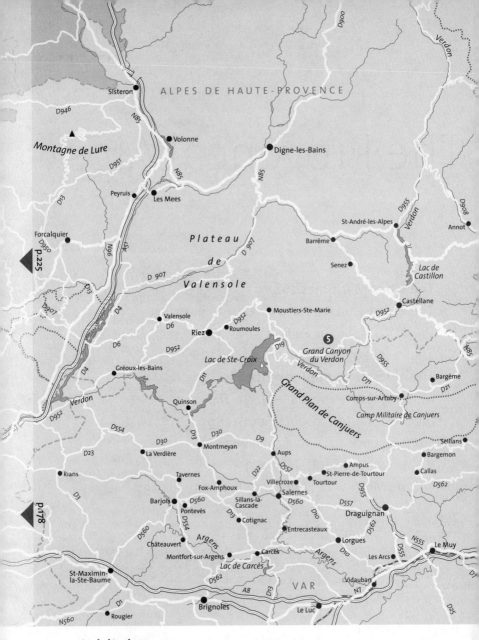

Highlights

1 Alpine heights and wild flowers in the Parc Mercantour
2 Enigmatic prehistoric engravings of the Vallée des Merveilles
3 Notre-Dame-des-Fontaines, the 'Sistine Chapel' of the Alpes-Maritimes
4 The mountain-climbing Train des Pignes, from Nice to Digne
5 The Grand Canyon de Verdun, France's answer to Arizona's

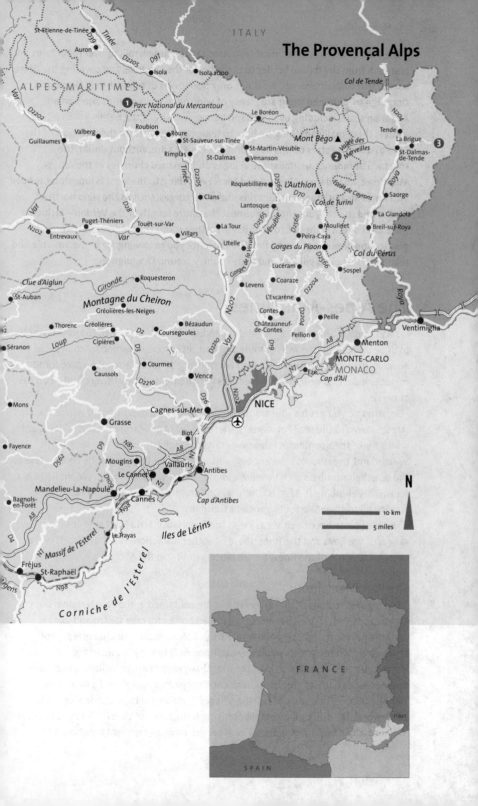

The Côte d'Azur has an admirably spacious back garden, rolling over mountains and plateaux from the Italian border to the valley of the Durance, and covering the better part of three *départements*. Yet it has only two towns of any size in it, Digne and Draguignan. Between them are plenty of wide open spaces, landscapes on an Arizonan scale, including even a Grand Canyon worthy of the name.

But is there really anything up here to tempt you away from the fleshpots of the Côte d'Azur? The stars of this huge and diverse area are, without doubt, the spectacular mountains, Italianate villages and frescoed churches of the Alpes-Maritimes, inland from Monaco and Nice. Everything to the west is limestone, eroded into fantastically shaped mountains and deep gorges, such as the *clues* north of Grasse and the canyons that run almost the entire length of the Verdon – including the Grand one, a sight not to be missed. Further south the landscapes become gentler and greener; you may find the Provence you're looking for in the amiable and relatively unspoiled villages and wine country around Draguignan.

The Alpes-Maritimes

'*Lacet*' means a shoelace, or a hairpin bend. It's a word you'll need to know if you try to drive up here, on the worst mountain roads in Europe, designed for mules and never improved. When you see a sign announcing '20 *lacets* ahead', prepare for 10 minutes in second gear, close encounters with demented lorry drivers, and a bad case of nerves.

So, what do you get for your trouble in this corrugated *département* where the Alps stretch down to the sea? For starters, these are real Alps – arrogant crystalline giants, which make their contempt felt as we crawl through the valleys beneath. Up in Switzerland, they would have enough altitude to make the geography books. Close to the sea, their numbers aren't overwhelming – but if you think 9,197ft Mont Bégo is a foothill, try climbing it. Bégo is a holy mountain, an Ararat or a Mount Meru, a pre-historic pilgrimage site for the ancient Ligurians.

The best parts have been set aside as the Parc National du Mercantour. In the valleys of the Roya and the Tinée, there's another attraction – all those *lacets* will also take you to some of the finest Renaissance painting in the Midi.

The Parc Mercantour

The highest regions of this *département* are contained in the Parc National du Mercantour, which stretches along the Italian border for over 128km and joins with the adjacent Argentera National Park in Italy to make a unique preserve of alpine and Mediterranean wildlife. Established only in 1979, it consists of a central 'protected zone', a narrow strip of the most inaccessible areas, including the Vallée des Merveilles with its prehistoric rock carvings (*see* pp.272–3), and a much larger 'peripheral zone' that includes all the villages from Sospel to St-Etienne-de-Tinée and beyond. There are many excellent hiking trails, some of which allow you to cross over into Italy. The park rangers, all local people, have an excellent reputation for

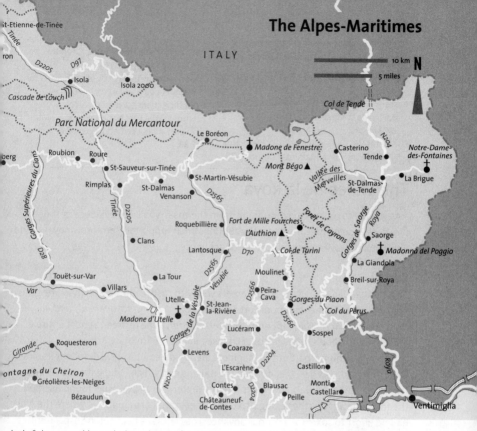

helpfulness and knowledge. They enforce some strict rules in the protected zone: no tents, dogs or fires, no motor vehicles (though all-terrain vehicles have recently been allowed on trails only, as an experiment), and no collecting flowers, insects or anything else.

The most spectacular alpine fauna, and the sort you're most likely to see, are the birds of prey: golden eagles, falcons and vultures. A recent addition, reintroduced from the Balkans after becoming extinct here, is the mighty *gypaète barbu* (lammergeyer), a 'bearded' vulture with a bizarre face, orange-red feathers, black wings and a reputation for carrying off lambs and children. On the ground, there's the ubiquitous stoat or ermine, popping out of the snow in his white winter coat and looking entirely too cute to be made into royal coat linings. There's also his bulkier cousin, the marmot, and plenty of boars, foxes, *mouflons* (wild mountain sheep), chamois and, in the more inaccessible places, *bouquetins* (ibex). All of these have been rapidly increasing in number since the establishment of the park.

As for wild flowers, the symbol of the park is the spiky *saxifrage multiflora*, one of 25 species found nowhere but here. Edelweiss exists in the park, but is as elusive as anywhere else. Beyond these exotic blooms, there is a tremendous wealth of everything that grows. Blue gentians and anemones are everywhere, plus hundreds of other species, in microclimates that range from Mediterranean to alpine. Half the flowers of the whole of France are represented here.

Park Information Centres

Tende ✉ 06430: Gare de St-Dalmas, **t** 04 93 04 67 00.
Castérino (Vallée des Merveilles) ✉ 06430: Maison de la Minière, **t** 04 93 04 68 66. *Summer only.*
St-Martin-Vésubie ✉ 06450: Rue Kellermann Sérurier, Place de la Mairie, **t** 04 93 16 78 88.

St-Sauveur-sur-Tinée ✉ 06420: on the D2205, **t** 04 93 02 01 63.
St-Etienne-de-Tinée ✉ 06660: Quartier de l'Ardon, **t** 04 93 02 42 27.
  In **Nice**, there is a helpful information centre for the Parc National du Mercantour at 23 Rue d'Italie, ✉ 06000, **t** 04 93 16 78 88.

The Vallée de la Roya

As you climb up into the mountains from the coast, you'll see evidence of the prosperous peasant culture these mountains once supported. Terraced vineyards and fields line the lower slopes, most no longer in use.

Sospel

Along the road from Nice, Sospel greets you with rusty cannons and machine guns, pointing out over the road from **Fort St-Roch** (*t 04 93 04 00 70; open July and Aug Tues–Sun 2–6; April, May, Sept and Oct weekends only*). The fortress, almost entirely underground, shows only a few blockhouses, in a sort of military Art Deco; it dates from a 1930s counterpart of the Maginot Line. Inside, exhibits give details of its short career. The fort was designed to keep the Italians out, which it did with ease until the French surrender in 1940. Four years later, in September 1944, Sospel found itself on the front line again – the vexing *sitzkrieg* of the Provençal mountains, where the Allies had no effort to spare for a serious advance. The Germans held out in Sospel until almost the end of the war.

Through all that, the town suffered considerable damage, now entirely, and lovingly, restored, including Sospel's landmark, the **Pont Vieux**, the base of which dates back to the 10th century. The tiny tower in the middle of the bridge was the toll on the **salt road**; in the Middle Ages, salt from the flats of Toulon and Hyères was taken by boat to Nice, and from there by convoys of mules to Piedmont and Lombardy. Now the toll bridge houses the tourist information office.

The **cathedral of St-Michel**, in a handsome arcaded square, retains its original 12th-century bell tower, but the rest has been Baroqued with charming tastelessness inside and out, including a wonderful circus-tent baldachin over the altar, dripping with gilt and tassels. A chapel to the left discreetly hides a fine *Annunciation* by Ludovico Brea, as well as another retable of the Virgin in a Gothic frame, possibly also by Brea or one of his followers. Don't miss a wander around the narrow winding streets of the rest of the old town, and another arcaded square, **Place St-Nicolas**, with a 15th-century fountain, on the other side of the bridge.

Breil and Saorge

To the north, the D2204 is the best route into the Vallée de la Roya, with only a few dozen *lacets* and one mountain pass; the other route, following the D93 and the N204, is slightly shorter, but it passes two border crossings in and out of Italy.

Breil-sur-Roya, the first town in the French part of the valley, has two peculiar attractions: the unidentifiable black pseudo-turkeys who live in the river Roya under the bridge, and the 18th-century church of Sancta-Maria-in-Albis, with large cracks in its ill-formed walls that seem ready to bring the place down around the ears of the faithful. Inside is another retable attributed to Brea, though not a very good one. Further north, the village of **La Giandola** sits among the olive groves that once were the valley's only resource, and beyond that come the **Gorges de Saorge**.

After the gorge, the village of **Saorge** is a magnificent sight – neat rows of Italian slate-roofed, green-shuttered houses, perched on a height like some remote Byzantine monastery and punctuated by church steeples with cupolas of coloured tiles. Saorge guards the Roya valley, and the Piedmontese made it a key border stronghold. You won't see more than the ruins of their fort today – it was destroyed after a young commander named Bonaparte took it during the wars of the Revolution. The town suffered during the Second World War, when its inhabitants were evacuated and forced to spend the duration in Antibes.

Saorge is just as attractive from close up, an ancient border village with customs and a dialect all its own, a little bit Occitan and a little bit Ligurian Italian; instead of *rue* or *via* on the street signs, you'll see *caréra* or *chu* or *ciassa*. The streets, stairways

Getting Around

Of all the hinterlands of Provence, this is the region most difficult to navigate by car, and the most convenient for public transport.

By Train

One of the best ways to see the Vallée de la Roya is from that alpine rarity – a train. The railway line from Nice that runs to Cuneoin Italy offers spectacular scenery and serves L'Escarène, Sospel, Breil, St-Dalmas and Tende (five daily). One train a day goes on to Turin. Don't miss the historic train cars parked at Sospel station, including an old Orient Express.

By Bus

Sospel has four daily buses (no.910) to and from Menton, which take 30 minutes. There are regular bus services from Nice to L'Escarène and Contes (some five a day) and Lucéram (five a day), and a range of buses from Sospel into the smaller valleys (t 04 93 04 01 24 or t 04 93 04 01 40).

Tourist Information

Sospel ✉ 06380: on the Pont Vieux, t 04 93 04 15 80, f 04 93 04 19 96, *adtrb@cote-dazur.*

com, wwwroyabevera.com. Open July–Aug daily 9–12.30 and 1–7; Sept–June Mon–Sat 9–12 and 2.30–5.30, Sun 9.30–12.30.

Breil-sur-Roya ✉ 06540: at the *mairie*, 17 Place Biancheri, t/f 04 93 04 99 76. Open Mon–Sat 9–12 and 1.30–5.50, Sun 9–12.

Tende ✉ 06430: Av du 16 Sept 1847, t 04 93 04 73 71, f 04 93 04 35 09, *info@tendemerveilles. com.* Open summer daily 9–12 and 2–6; winter Mon–Sat 9–12 and 2–6.

Market Days

Sospel: Thursday all day; Sunday morning farmers' market.

Breil: Tuesday and Saturday all day, Marché Provençal.

Tende: Wednesday.

Where to Stay and Eat

Sospel ✉ 06380

There's little choice between its five hotels.

★★Des Etrangers, 7 Av de Verdun, t 04 93 04 00 09, f 04 93 04 12 31, *sospel@france.com*, *www.sospel.net* (*inexpensive*). With a pool. Closed Nov–Feb.

★★L'Auberge Provençale, Route de Menton, t 04 93 04 00 31, f 04 93 04 24 45, *aubpro@aol.com* (*moderate*). Almost 2km

more often than not, climb and dive and duck under arches. The sights require a kilometre's hike to the outskirts: the 18th-century Franciscan Monastery, in elegant
Piedmontese Baroque, and beyond that the 11th-century chapel of the Madonna del
Poggio, with Renaissance frescoes, including a Marriage of the Virgin. West of Saorge,
you can penetrate into the southernmost corner of the Mercantour National Park, up
the narrow D40 into the Forêt de Caïros (or **Cayrons**).

Vallée des Merveilles

Before going further, understand that the Roya is a cul-de-sac; there's no way out
except by retracing your steps or continuing through the Tende tunnel to Cuneo, Italy.
After Saorge, the mountains close in immediately, with the **Gorges de Bergue et
de Paganin**; these end at the village of **St-Dalmas-de-Tende**, once the border post
between France and Italy and now the gateway to the **Vallée des Merveilles**.

From about 1800 BC onwards, the Ligurian natives of these mountains began
scratching pictures and symbols on the rocks here. They kept at it for the next 800
years, until over 100,000 inscriptions decorated the valley: human figures, religious
symbols (plenty of bulls, horns and serpents), weapons and tools. Most defy any
conclusive interpretation – circles, spirals and ladders or chequerboard patterns of the

---

from Sospel, this inn has a *terrasse* with a
magnificent view over Sospel. *Closed Thurs
mid-Nov–mid-Dec.*
Domaine du Paraïs, t 04 93 04 15 78
(*inexpensive*). This *chambre d'hôte* outside
Sospel, off the D2566 towards Moulinet
at La Vesta (you will need a car), was a
villa taken over by officers during the war,
now proudly restored by its owners.
Book ahead.
L'Escargot d'Or, 3 Bd de Verdun, t 04 93 04
00 43 (*moderate*). The best place to eat in
Sospel, specializing in meat fondues. Ring to
reserve, and to check that they're open out
of season.

Breil-sur-Roya ☑ 06540
★★Castel du Roy, Route de Tende, t 04 93 04
43 66, f 04 93 04 91 83 (*moderate–inexpensive*). Modern, comfortable, and spread out
among several buildings near the river,
with a pool and a highly rated restaurant.
Closed Nov–Mar.
★★Le Roya, t 04 93 04 48 10, f 04 93 04 92 70
(*inexpensive*). A functional place in the
village square.
L'Etoile, 19 Bd Rouvier, t 04 93 04 41 61 (*cheap*).
Ravioli, rabbit and trout at reasonable prices.
Closed Wed.

Saorge ☑ 06540
Le Bellevue, 5 Rue L-Périssol, t 04 93 04 51 37
(*moderate*). *Closed Tues eve and Wed.*
Lou Pountin, Rue Revelli, t 04 93 04 54 90.
Excellent pizzas for lunch (*cheap*).
Closed Wed.

La Brigue ☑ 06430
★★Le Mirval, Rue St-Vincent Ferrier, at the west
end of the village, t 04 93 04 63 71, f 04 93 04
79 81 (*inexpensive*). The best of the three
hotels here; some rooms have good views
and the management can arrange a trip
(*expensive*) into the Vallée des Merveilles.
Closed Nov–Mar.

Castérino ☑ 06430
If you're doing the Merveilles on your own,
it's convenient to start from Castérino, a
hamlet at the end of the D91.
★Les Melèzes, t 04 93 04 95 95, f 04 93 04
95 96 (*inexpensive*). Small but comfortable
rooms and a good restaurant (*moderate*).
*Restaurant closed Tues eve and Wed out of
season.*
Santa Maria Maddalena, t 04 93 04 65 93, f 04
93 04 77 65 (*cheap, half board obligatory in
season*). Also has a restaurant; try the
smoked trout. *Closed Nov–Dec and April.*

kind found all over the Mediterranean (the Val Camonica in northern Italy has even more carvings, from the same era). Why they were made is an open question; one very appealing hypothesis is that this valley, beneath Mont Bégo, was a holy place and a pilgrimage site, and that the carvings can be taken as *ex votos* made by the pilgrims.

The presence of these symbols has brought the valley some notoriety – superstition gave the surroundings place names like Cime du Diable (Devil's Peak) and Valmasque (*masco*, mask, was an old local word for sorcerer). The first person to study the site systematically was an Englishman, Clarence Bicknell, in the early part of the 20th century. As the prime attraction of the Parc Mercantour, the valley gets its share of visitors these days. Besides the carvings, the landscape itself is worth the hike, including a score of mountain lakes, mostly above the tree line, all in the shadow of the rugged, uncanny **Mont Bégo**, highest of the peaks around the Roya; the mountain's name, as far as anyone can tell, comes from an Etruscan god of storms.

Don't just wander up here like some fool tourist, looking for Neolithic etchings. Plan the trip out beforehand, with advice from the park information offices. They will probably recommend a guided tour; the symbols are plentiful, but nonetheless inconspicuous and hard to find. Outside the summer months, many will be covered in snow. To tour the valley is *at least* a 20km round-trip trek from the *refuge* at Les Mesches, at the end of the road west from St-Dalmas. There are hotels in nearby **Castérino** (*see* p.272) and *refuges* within the park if you want to stay over; make arrangements at the park office. Jeep-taxis can also take you around (expensively) from St-Dalmas.

La Brigue and Notre-Dame-des-Fontaines

Vittorio Emanuele II, the last king of Piedmont-Sardinia and the first of unified Italy, may have been utterly useless at his job, but as a hunter few crowned heads could match him. When he arranged to give away the County of Nice in 1860, he stipulated only that the Upper Roya, above St-Dalmas-de-Tende, be left for him as a hunting reserve (to add to a few others he had, strung out across Italy, including the famous Isle of Montecristo). The few inhabitants had already voted (under French supervision) on union with France; suspiciously, 73 per cent of the electorate abstained. So this had to wait until 1947, when another plebiscite was held and the valley became France's latest territorial acquisition.

Tende, a dour, slate-roofed *bourg*, is the only town. No longer a dead end since the road tunnel through to Italy was built, it has become a busy place by local standards. It has the ruined castle of the Lascaris, long-time feudal lords of the Roya, and a late Gothic church, Ste-Marie-des-Bois, with a pretty sculpted Renaissance portal, and painted façade and ceiling. Don't miss its cemetery, built on steps for lack of space. On Avenue du 16 Septembre 1847, the **Musée des Merveilles** (*t 04 93 04 32 50; open May–mid-Oct 10.30–6.30, to 9pm Sat; mid-Oct–April 10.30–5; closed Tues; adm*) has copies and photos of the rock engravings, as well as ethnographic exhibits on life in the valley from prehistoric times up to the 18th century.

East of St-Dalmas-de-Tende, the D143 takes you into La Brigue, a minute region (partly in Italy) that grows apples and pears and raises trout. **La Brigue**, the tiny capital, has some fine paintings in its church of St-Martin, another late Gothic work of the 15th century: three altarpieces by Ludovico Brea and his followers, along with Italian paintings from the 17th and 18th centuries. The people who live in La Brigue seem to have an elevated opinion of tourists, since the only ones who pass through have come a long way to see their paintings and, more importantly, those by Giovanni Canavesio at **Notre-Dame-des-Fontaines**, 4km from the village of La Brigue. The name comes from seven intermittent local springs, miniature versions of the Fontaine-de-Vaucluse (*see* pp.246–7), gushing out of the rock or stopping according to pressure and the water table; these can still be seen, though now they are on the Italian side of the border.

The Upper Roya may not have been much of an economic or strategic gain for France, but artistically it was a real prize – the country's total number of good Renaissance frescoes went up considerably. Giovanni Canavesio, from Piedmont, is not well known outside his own region, but he was a painter in the best north Italian Renaissance tradition: bright colours, exquisite, stylized draughtsmanship and an ability to put a genuine religious feeling into his frescoes that recalls Fra Angelico. His works in this rural chapel, done in the 1490s, include 26 large scenes of the *Passion of Christ* in the nave, and on one of the side walls a tremendous *Last Judgement*, a gentle reminder that God wasn't joking. All the tortures of the damned are portrayed in intricate detail, as the devils sweep them into the gaping Mouth of Hell. Around the choir, on the triumphal arch, he painted scenes from the Life of Mary, from the *Birth of Mary* at the upper left to the *Presentation at the Temple* at the bottom right.

The frescoes in the choir itself are by another hand, Giovanni Baleison. Done in the 1470s, in a more old-fashioned style that still shows the influence of Byzantium, these include the *Four Evangelists* on the vaulted ceiling, the four *Doctors of the Church* (Ambrose, Jerome, Gregory and Augustine) under the arch, and more scenes from the Life of Mary, including an *Assumption* on the back wall, over the *Reproach of Thomas* and the *Visit to the Tomb*.

West of Sospel: the Paillon Valley

There is some painting here too, in the rugged mountains between Sospel and the valley of the Var. The Italian influence shows itself in another way – the road map looks like a plate of spaghetti, with more twists and bends than anywhere in the *département*. Lacking a mule, you'll need to return to Sospel to get out of the Roya.

L'Escarène

The D2204 west will take you to L'Escarène, a lovely Italianate village that served as a posting station between Turin and Nice. From the bridge you can see the houses overhanging the river, and you can visit the **Chapelle des Pénitents-Blancs**, with spectacular rococo stucco decoration. There are some peculiar landscapes to the south: stone quarries on the road to Nice that have carved out a huge, nearly perfect

Getting Around

All the villages in the Paillon are served by at least two buses a day from Nice.

Tourist Information

Coaraze ⊠ 06390: Place Ste-Catherine, at the village entrance, **t** 04 93 79 37 47.
Contes ⊠ 06390: Place Albert-Ollivier, **t** 04 93 79 13 99, **f** 04 93 79 26 30. *Open Mon–Fri 2–5.*

Where to Stay and Eat

Chic sophistication goes only as far as the foothills. In these mountains, so close to Nice and Monte Carlo, both food and accommodation are surprisingly basic and humble.

Lucéram ⊠ 06440

Trois Vallées, Moulinet, **t 04 93 91 57 21, **f** 04 93 79 53 62, *troisvallees@villages-passion.com* (*moderate–inexpensive; restaurant moderate*). At the top of Col de Turini, you can stop for the view and lunch on roast boar and such at this handsome chalet in the woods.
La Bocca Fina, Lucéram, **t** 04 93 79 51 54 (*moderate–cheap*).

Coaraze ⊠ 06390

Coaraze, with its sundials and restored houses, seems to get more visitors than the other villages, perhaps because of the most attractive mountain hideaway in the area:
Auberge du Soleil, **t** 04 93 79 08 11, **f** 04 93 79 37 79 (*moderate*). In a dreamy location at the top of the village, with a pool and a fine restaurant with a memorable view from the terrace. This end of the village is closed to traffic – call ahead if you need help with your baggage. The restaurant has an excellent menu. *Closed Nov–mid-Feb.*

Contes ⊠ 06390

Auberge le Cellier, 3 Bd Charles-Alunni, **t/f** 04 93 79 00 64 (*cheap*). With only five rooms and a simple but nourishing restaurant (*moderate*). *Hotel closed Christmas–New Year; restaurant closed Sun.*

ziggurat (perhaps the Médecins of Nice could tunnel inside and make it their family tomb); the road is sometimes closed in the mornings for blasting. In the hills above, around Blausasc, 19th-century deforestation has left a lunar wasteland of bare rock; the government is currently building water channels to keep the erosion from spreading.

Lucéram

North of L'Escarène, Lucéram is an old shoe of a village, well worn and a bit out at the toes. Full of arches and tunnels like Saorge, it has some remains of walls and towers on the mountainside, a steep but pleasant excursion if you want to circumnavigate them. The church of **Ste-Marguerite** is second only to Notre-Dame-des-Fontaines as an artistic attraction. Amidst the gaudy Baroque stucco of the interior, the altarpieces of the Nice school seem uncomfortably out of place. The best, with an innocence and spirituality matched by few other saintly portraits, is the *Retable de Ste-Marguerite* over the main altar, attributed to Ludovico Brea. Marguerite, a martyr of Antioch, is another popular Provençal dragon-slayer, often confused with St Martha (*see* p.134). Brea made her exceedingly lovely; the Tarasque-like demon at her feet obviously never stood a chance.

The other retables around the church include *SS. Peter and Paul* (with the keys and sword), *St Claude, St Lawrence* (with his gridiron, upon which he was barbecued) and *St Bernard*, all by unknown 15th-century artists; Giovanni Baleison contributed a good one of *St Anthony of Padua* (1480) in the Chapelle du Trésor. It keeps company with a **Trésor** of awful clutter: reliquaries, monstrances and statuettes, including a silver image containing relics of St Marguerite. Outside the church, the **Chapelle St-Jean** was built by the Knights of St John – the Knights of Malta, who had a commandery here. Its beautiful exterior is painted to imitate precious marble (though the inside is full of electricity generators).

If you have the time, there are some worthwhile digressions into the mountains around Lucéram, beginning just outside the village with two more chapels with frescoes by Giovanni Baleison, similar to his work at Notre-Dame-des-Fontaines: **St-Grat** (on the road towards L'Escarène) and **Notre-Dame-de-Bon-Cœur** (on the road for Coaraze); the sacristan in Lucéram has the keys for both. East of Lucéram, a half-hour climb up into the hills, there is a wild spot with a huge circular prehistoric wall, the site of a fortified village from the time of the inscriptions in the Vallée des Merveilles – a logical place for such a settlement, with a fine view of holy Mont Bégo.

North of Lucéram, the D21 and D2566 take you past Peïra-Cava, a resort for the French military and their families, to the Forêt de Turini, centred around a 4,987ft mountain pass, the **Col de Turini**, at the tip of three river valleys. Up above the pass are several old forts, near the summit of Mont l'Authion, an eyrie that commands almost all the Alpes-Maritimes. These were one of the Germans' last redoubts in the war; signs of the battle are still evident, especially around the **Fort des Mille Fourches**, damaged, incredibly, by bombardment from the sea in 1945.

The Devil's Tail and Other Tales

A long tour on the D2566/D15 west from Lucéram (7km for the crow, 19 for you) will take you with some difficulty to **Coaraze**, a village that is a magnet for attracting stories. One is its name, *Caude Rase* in medieval times, or the 'cut tail' of the Devil. The villagers back then somehow trapped Old Nick, who had to give up his tail like a lizard to get away. Coaraze has also attracted its share of artists lately; one has given the village centre a lizard mosaic to commemorate the event. Other artists, including Cocteau, have contributed a number of colourful ceramic sundials around the village.

Another legend deals with the abandoned village of **Roccasparvière**, an hour's walk from Coaraze in the mountains. Queen Jeanne of Provence, the story goes, once took refuge from her enemies here. The plot differs in every version, but in most of them someone in the village kills Jeanne's twin sons and serves them up for dinner. '*Roc, méchant roc,*' Jeanne cursed. '*Un jour viendra où plus ne chantera ni poule ni coq.*' No chickens indeed are singing in Roccasparvière today, but spoilsport historians say it was because the village well dried up.

Another tortuous 10km south of here on the D15, **Contes** has its stories too. One fine day in 1508, the village was attacked by a horde of caterpillars. Apparently it was not the first time; the area has a colourful species the French call *chenilles procession-naires*, who enjoy a promenade in town every now and then. This time, the Contois had had enough; they called in the Bishop of Nice, who brought inquisitors and exorcists, and made anathemas and proclamations until the caterpillars finally grew uncomfortable and went home. Such affairs were not uncommon, especially in old

France. Animals, too, were considered subject to God's law; horses and dogs occasionally went on trial for their indiscretions when times were dull. Contes has another altarpiece in the Brea manner in its church, and down by the river a well-preserved forge with a water-powered hammer, near the communal olive oil press. Here, and in many villages in the mountains, the oil presses are still in use. Across the river, and 9km up in the Ferion mountains, there is another abandoned village to explore, 2km outside **Châteauneuf-de-Contes** (*note: the road is open weekends and holidays only*).

The Valleys of the Vésubie and the Tinée

The extensive valley of the river Vésubie is almost completely isolated from the regions to the east; from Lucéram the only ways across are the D21/D2566/D70 through the Col de Turini, or the miserable D2566/D73 directly over the mountains. There's an equally tortuous route from Contes – the D815/D19.

Levens to Lantosque

The Vésubie flows into the Var near **Levens**, a big walled village high on a small plain, with a big church and a scattering of small private art galleries. Beneath it, the main road up the valley, the D2565, follows the scenic **Gorges de la Vésubie**. From St-Jean-la-Rivière, at the end of the gorge, a winding 15km detour leads to the sanctuary of the **Madone d'Utelle**, one of the most popular pilgrimage sites in Provence, with a chapel full of naïve *ex votos* to Notre-Dame-des-Miracles, many from sailors, and a spectacular view as far as the sea. **Lantosque**, the next village up the valley from St-Jean, is a humble place, regularly shaken by landslides and earthquakes. Lantosque was occupied by the Austrians in the Revolution. One of them must have been *un bon coq*, as the French say; it's a joke in the other villages that you can always find someone in Lantosque named Otto.

St-Martin-Vésubie

At the top of the valley, St-Martin is the only town for a great distance in any direction, and a base for tackling the upper part of the Mercantour. It's as unaffectedly cute as a town can be, and once it was a spa of some repute. In the delightful and shady town square is an old fountain where the mineral waters used to flow, with inscriptions testifying to their 'organoleptic properties'. The medieval centre is traversed by a lovely street (Rue Dr Cagnoli) with a mountain spring flowing down a narrow channel in the middle, as in a garden of the Alhambra. On this street you'll see an impressive Gothic mansion, the **Maison des Contes de Gubernatis**, and the parish church, housing an altarpiece attributed to Brea and a polychrome wooden statue of the Virgin from the 14th century.

In the vicinity, **Venanson** is a beautiful village up in the mountains above St-Martin, with a small church full of frescoes by Giovanni Baleison. To the east, up into the Parc Mercantour on the D94, the **Sanctuaire de la Madone de Fenestre** was an ancient holy site near the present Italian border; the name comes from a natural window in a

Getting Around

There are no trains in either the Vésubie or the Tinée valleys, and the coach service is sketchy.

St-Martin-Vésubie can be reached by **bus** from the *gare routière* in Nice (Cars TRAM, **t** 04 93 89 47 14); buses for St-Sauveur and St-Etienne in the Tinée also leave from here.

Roads in this area are as difficult as those to the east; service stations are few so keep your tank full.

Tourist Information

Levens ✉ 06670: **t** 04 93 79 71 00, **f** 04 93 91 61 17.
St-Martin-Vésubie ✉ 06450: Place Félix Faure, **t/f** 04 93 03 21 28. *Open summer 9–12.30 and 3–7; winter 10–12 and 2.30–5.30.*

Market Days

Levens: Country show, first Saturday in June.
St-Martin-Vésubie: Tuesday, Thursday, Saturday and Sunday in summer.

Where to Stay and Eat

Levens ✉ 06450

La Vigneraie, on the Nice road below the village, **t** 04 93 79 70 46, **f** 04 93 79 84 35 (*cheap*). A real bargain. Comfortable rooms in this friendly *auberge* are inexpensive, but it would be madness not to take full board at a hostelry that locals travel miles to visit just for Sunday lunch. Lunch alone is possible if you're not staying (*moderate; book early*) – but you'll wish you had a room to sleep in afterwards. *Closed Oct–Jan.*

Lantosque ✉ 06450

★★★Hostellerie de l'Ancienne Gendarmerie, **t** 04 93 03 00 65, **f** 04 93 03 06 31 (*moderate*). This 'former police station' occupies a pretty hillside site on the way up to the Parc Mercantour, with garden-side rooms and a pool. The restaurant specializes in sea fish and *escargots* (*expensive*). *Closed Nov–mid-Mar*

St-Martin-Vésubie ✉ 06450

★★La Bonne Auberge, Allés de Verdun, **t** 04 93 03 20 49, **f** 04 93 03 20 69 (*inexpensive*). As good as its name – a welcoming and pretty place with nice rooms and a cosy cellar restaurant with a boar's head over the chimneypiece, serving grilled chops, *escargots*, *civet de lapin* and profiteroles (*moderate*). *Closed mid-Nov–Jan.*

★Les Alpes, Place Félix Faure, **t** 04 93 03 21 06 (*cheap*). If the *auberge* is full, settle for this modern place across the square.

La Trappa, Place du Marché, **t** 04 93 03 21 50 (*moderate*). Mountain fare and heady house wine. *Closed Sun eve and Mon.*

La Treille, Rue Dr Cagnoli, **t** 04 93 03 30 85 (*moderate*). Some of the best pizza this side of the border, baked in a proper pizza oven; also pasta and more ambitious dishes. *Weekends only in winter.*

Le Cavalet, Le Boréon, **t** 04 93 03 21 46, **f** 04 93 03 34 34 (*moderate*). A simple abode in a dreamy lakeside setting outside St-Martin, at the forest edge. The restaurant is excellent; half board is required for hotel guests. *Closed Nov–Mar.*

Le Bella Vista, Venanson, **t** 04 93 03 25 11 (*inexpensive; restaurant moderate*). A simple place outside St-Martin (half board compulsory in season). *Closed Nov–Mar.*

The Tinée Valley

Don't expect anything out of the ordinary in the sparsely populated, little-visited Tinée valley: simple country inns with restaurants are the rule.

Auberge St-Jean, Clans ✉ 06420, **t** 04 93 02 90 21. Half board compulsory in the summer.

Chalet du Val de Blore, Valdeblore ✉ 06420, **t** 04 93 02 83 29, **f** 04 93 02 83 06 (*inexpensive; 7 night minimum stay in summer*). A family hotel on the D2565 west of St-Dalmas; 35 very simple rooms in a modern chalet with Italian-Niçoise home cooking. *Closed Nov.*

When in the mountains, look out for locally made liqueurs, an Alpine speciality: *myrtille* (bilberry), pear or something called *genépi Meunier*, made from an Alpine herb that is closely related to absinthe.

nearby mountain peak. The chapel has burned four times. In the Middle Ages the Templars held the site; they were massacred in the 14th century and their ghosts were often seen in the neighbourhood. Hiking trails from here can take you on a very scenic route to the Vallée des Merveilles. Another road from St-Martin, the D89, leads northwest up a valley between the peaks of Mont Archas and Cime du Piagu to the resort village of **Le Boréon**; this is a lovely area, with many hiking trails, a waterfall (near the village) and some mountain lakes near the Italian border.

The Valley of the Tinée

There's nothing splashy or spectacular about the Tinée. People who love the Mercantour follow the slow D2205 along its length, from the N202 out of Nice up to the protected zone of the park. Skiers flock in winter to the modern resorts of Isola 2000 and Valberg. But outside their punctual visitations, there is a sort of pious hush in this valley, which is serenely beautiful even by alpine standards. In the lower part of the valley, the scenery is as much indoors as out; prosperity in the 15th and 16th centuries allowed the villages of the Lower Tinée to decorate their modest churches with fine Renaissance frescoes by artists of the Nice school.

The river flows into the Var with a climax at the **gorges**, across the mountains from Utelle. To the northeast, **La Tour** has frescoes from 1491 in its Chapelle des Pénitents-Blancs. The traditional subjects are represented: the *Passion* and a colourful *Last Judgement*, with Christ sitting on a rainbow and allegorical figures of the Seven Deadly Sins riding on fantastical animals, accompanying the damned to hell.

The next paintings are at **Clans**, in two chapels just outside the village. St-Antoine offers more Sins, from an unknown, late 15th-century hand; they accompany some 20 rather peculiar scenes from the *Life of St Anthony* – cooking eggs and exorcizing female demons. St-Michel has frescoes by an Italian named Andrea de Cella, *c.* 1515, including St Michael 'fishing for souls', an odd conceit that goes back to Byzantine art. The parish church in the centre of the village has pictures too: surprisingly, a rare late medieval hunting scene. Next up the valley, there is a pleasant detour on the D2565 through Valdeblore, the only reasonable road through to the Vésubie. It begins at **Rimplas**, and the nearby **Chapelle de la Madeleine**, a conspicuous landmark occupying a gorgeous site overlooking the valley, and continues through **St-Dalmas-Valdeblore**, where there is a large and sophisticated Romanesque church, the Eglise de l'Invention de la Sainte-Croix, with fragments of its original frescoes.

Continuing up the Tinée, the next stop is **St-Sauveur-sur-Tinée**, throbbing metropolis of the valley, with its 496 souls. From here the D130 follows the Vionène valley west through the rugged and lovely villages of **Roure** and **Roubion**. The former, set amidst the biggest larch forest in Europe, has more painting: a Brea (attributed) altarpiece in the church of St-Laurent, and unusual frescoes of the lives of St Sebastian and St Bernard in the chapel outside the village – all these chapels outside villages, incidentally, are a regional peculiarity, set outside the gates as if to avert evil influences, and often dedicated to plague saints like Sebastian. Roubion has a Sebastian chapel too, with another frescoed set of Deadly Sins. Continuing in this direction, the next town is the modern ski resort of **Valberg**. There is alpine scenery in these parts, but little else; the best of it is in the long, lonely canyons stretching south off the D30/D28: the **Gorges Supérieures du Cians** and the **Gorges de Daluis**.

The uppermost part of the Tinée, following the D2205, runs through the northern half of the Parc Mercantour, never more than a few kilometres from the Italian border. After St-Sauveur come the **Gorges de Valabres**, decorated with an EDF electric plant that somehow managed to sneak inside the park borders.

Isola, on the other side of the river, has some more appealing sights, both just off the D2205: a magnificently tall waterfall, the **Cascade de Louche**, and an impressive Romanesque bell tower, the only survival from an abbey washed away by a flood 300 years ago. A good road takes you up to the Italian border and **Isola 2000**, a British-built, modern, concrete ski resort that does good business due to its proximity to the coast. Everywhere else to the north is at ski level, and almost all the villages have learned to bend their lives and habits to the seasonal invasions of the ski-bunnies.

If you haven't yet had enough Renaissance frescoes, you may want to follow the Tinée to its source. In **Auron**, the 12th-century church of St-Erige has a sequence of paintings of that obscure Provençal saint, along with the Parisian St Denis, a stranger in these parts. **St-Etienne-de-Tinée** has two painted rural chapels: St-Sébastien, with a cycle of works by Canavesio and Baleison, in very bad shape, and the chapel of the Couvent des Trinitaires, where the subject is, of all things, the great naval victory of the Venetians and Spaniards over the Turks at Lepanto in 1571.

The Alpes de Haute-Provence

Clearly we find ourselves in a place that is out of the ordinary.
You need a strong character, and a little bit of soul.
Jean Giono

There is something of the Wild West in this *département*, complete with lofty plateaux and canyons; it even has a Grand Canyon of its own. Provence's wide open spaces are full of lavender fields and fresh air, a place to white-water raft, hang-glide, ride, climb or hike. The **Maison des Alpes de Haute-Provence** (*19 Rue Docteur Honnorat*, ✉ *04005 Digne-les-Bains*, **t** *04 92 31 57 29*, **f** *04 92 32 12 46*), publishes a free, and extremely useful, practical guide (*Sports and Leisure Activities in the Open Air*) on how and where to indulge in your favourite sport.

Alpes de Haute-Provence North

Villars to Entrevaux along the N202

The N202 is the east–west traffic chute, following the upper Var, and the only convenient way to get through the mountains north of Grasse. It isn't scenic, though the gravelly, impossibly blue Var makes a refreshing sight alongside; it may, however, be an antidote to claustrophobia after traversing too many gorges. The trip begins

Getting Around

Buses are so rare they aren't worth the trouble, but it can be fun seeing this region by the scenic, recently modernized, narrow-gauge **rail line** from Nice to Digne, familiarly called the *Train des Pignes*.

It follows the Var, and a few trains – five a day at the most – stop at villages along the way: Villars, Puget-Théniers, Entrevaux and Annot. This is not the SNCF, but a separate line called Chemin de Fer de Provence (in Digne, call **t** 04 92 31 01 58 for details).

Tourist Information

Puget-Théniers ✉ 06260: **t** 04 93 05 05 05, **f** 04 93 05 17 22, *info@provence-val-dazur.com, www.provence-val-dazur.com. Open daily 9–12.30 and 2.30–7.*
Entrevaux ✉ 04320: at the Porte Royale du Pont Levis, **t** 04 93 05 46 73, **f** 04 93 05 40 71, *sivomentrevaux@wanadoo.fr, www.netprovence.com/sivomentrevaux. Open Feb–June 9–12 and 1–5.30 (Feb–April Mon–Fri, April–June daily); July–Aug daily 9–7; Sept–Nov 9–12 and 1.30–6 (Oct–Nov until 5.30).*

Where to Stay and Eat

Being the only good road across this region, the N202 has the best selection of places to stay and eat along it, with a few that are rather better than the average *routier*.

Touët-sur-Var ✉ 06710

Restaurant des Chasseurs, **t** 04 93 05 71 11 (*moderate*). Has a few rooms, but does most of its business serving fish and game to appreciative locals; ravioli and rabbit stew figure. *Closed eves.*

Puget-Théniers ✉ 06260

★★Alizé, Rue Alexandre Barety, **t/f** 04 93 05 06 20, *hotel.alize@wanadoo.fr* (*inexpensive; restaurant moderate*).
★★Langier, Place A. Conil, **t/f** 04 93 05 01 00 (*inexpensive*). Picturesque, but has a noisy bar and uncomfortable beds. *Closed Nov–Mar.*
Les Acacias, Le Planet, **t** 04 93 05 05 25 (*moderate*). For dining, you won't do better than this place, which features duck, pigeon and rabbit prepared in imaginative ways. *Closed Wed.*

Entrevaux ✉ 04320

Vauban, **t** 04 93 05 42 40, **f** 04 93 05 48 38 (*inexpensive; restaurant moderate*). Surprisingly, the only hotel in Entrevaux. *Closed Jan; restaurant closed Mon.*
Chambre d'hôtes, Mme Gaydon, **t** 04 93 05 06 91 (*inexpensive*). *Open all year.*
L'Echauguette, Place de la Mairie, **t** 04 93 05 49 60 (*moderate*). Outside tables and menus including some seafood and, for starters, a salad served with the local speciality, a beef sausage called *secca*.
Le Pont Levis, Place Louis Moreau, **t** 04 93 05 40 12 (*moderate*). Good cuisine; great view of fort, village and valley. *Closed Fri.*

with a local novelty – wine – at **Villars-sur-Var**. The centre of the only, tiny AOC wine region in the mountains, Villars was almost abandoned before the awarding of the *dénomination* in the 1970s. Production has vastly increased since then, and you'll occasionally see this variety of Côtes-de-Provence in trendy restaurants on the coast – perhaps more for its curiosity value than for anything else. The village church has a few Renaissance pieces: a retable of *St John the Baptist* and an Italian fresco of the *Annunciation*, both anonymous works of the early 16th century.

Next comes a postcard shot: **Touët-sur-Var**, seemingly pasted up on the side of a cliff, with much of its medieval defences still intact in case anyone tries to storm the place. **Puget-Théniers**, the biggest village on this stretch of the Var, is more open and welcoming, a shady oasis after the stark mountain landscapes, where you may stop for lunch and look at more pictures. There are two genuine jewels among a number of altarpieces in the parish church: Antoine Ronzen's *Notre-Dame du Secours* and

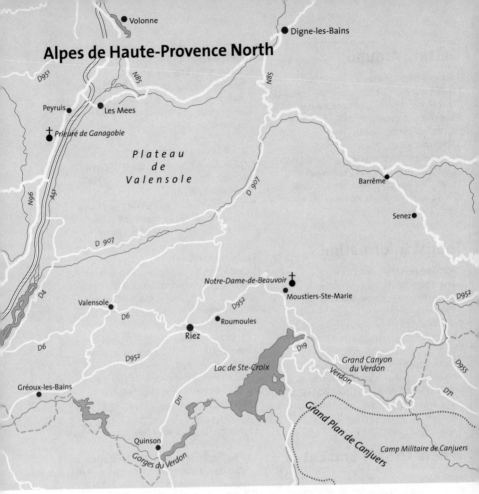

Mathieu d'Anvers' *Passion*, both done about 1525. A monument by Aristide Maillol in the town square commemorates Puget's pride: a local boy named Auguste Blanqui, who became a journalist and one of the leaders of the Paris Commune in 1870, for which he paid by spending 36 years in prison.

Under the sweeping twist of its cliffs, **Entrevaux** is the strategic key to the valley. There has been a fort of some kind here since Roman times, and its present incarnation is particularly impressive – the work of Louis XIV's celebrated engineer Vauban, high above the village, complete with Second World War additions. At the time it was built, the French-Piedmontese border was only a few miles away (it is now the departmental boundary between Var and Alpes-Maritimes). The entrance is a fortified bridge, rebuilt by Vauban on medieval foundations. Around the village, vestiges of its old garrison days can be seen: barracks and powder-houses, and an ancient drawbridge, still in working order, behind the 17th-century cathedral.

There's a honeycomb of buildings and narrow alleys where people live; if you wander through the smelly damp alleys there are flowers high up in the windows,

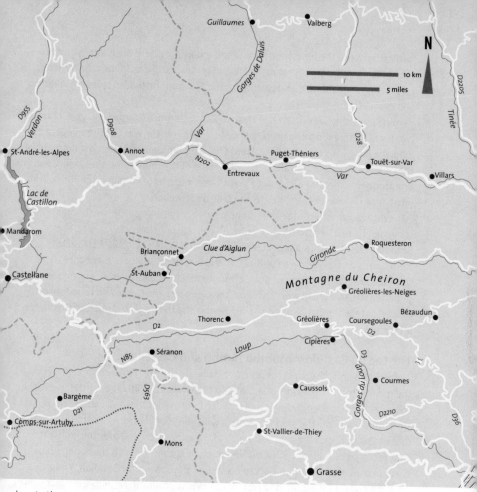

duvets thrown over the sills in the mornings. The serious part of the fort is a hard 15-minute climb if you're fit; take water, a sunhat, some historical imagination and some coins for the turnstile and you're on your own to explore the derelict tunnels and dungeons – once deliciously dangerous, now undergoing restoration to make them safe. The landscape below, with the little *Train des Pignes*, is as unlikely as an alpine train set. Try to get up there before 9am, when the first of the coaches are beginning to fit themselves in below. (Check out the barking dog behind the hotel just across the road from the gate; it's a parrot.) Harley fans will enjoy Entrevaux's Musée de la Moto (*t 04 93 79 12 70; open April–Sept 10–12 and 2–7*), a collection of motorcycles from 1901 to 1967.

The Clues and the Esteron Valley

South of the Var is a grim and lonely region; you can see Nice and Cannes from the summit of the **Montagne du Cheiron** in its centre, but from here the Riviera beaches seem a world away. A *clue*, or more properly *cluse*, is a transverse valley, formed between the limestone folds of the mountains; here the name is given to the many narrow gorges that make life and communications in the area difficult. Local villages are humble and crumbling and few, and the roads across are winding and exasperating.

From Puget, the D2211A/D17 takes you to **Roquesteron**, a fortified village divided into two parts (before 1860 one was Piedmontese, one French). West of the village, a bad road, the D10, leads off into the isolated **Clue d'Aiglun**, perhaps the most dramatic of the *clues*, with a big waterfall. On the other side of the mountains, the D2211A leads to **Briançonnet**, a spectral village with great views and bits of Roman inscriptions built into the old houses; beyond here is the **Clue de St-Auban**.

The more southerly route – with a choice of roads running east–west, some conveniently reached from Vence or Nice – passes some lovely *villages perchés*: **Bézaudun-les-Alpes**, **Coursegoules**, **Gréolières** and **Cipières** (follow D1/D8/D2 from Carros on the Var, north of Nice), all starting to be colonized by people from the Riviera. Gréolières, under the Montagne du Cheiron, has an enormous ruined castle; from here you can follow the D603 into the **Gorges du Loup** towards Grasse, or take the D2/D802 on to the Cheiron and the new ski station of **Gréolières-les-Neiges**.

The Lac du Castillon, Mumbo Jumbo and Castellane

After Entrevaux, the Var turns northwards, while the main road continues west, past the modest mountain resort of **Annot** and the **Gorges du Galange**. Further west, the country becomes even stranger and lonelier; long monotonous stretches lull you to sleep until suddenly the road sinks into a wild gorge, or confronts a patch of striated mountains that look like gigantic *millefeuille* pastries tumbled over the landscape. Grey is the predominant colour, making a startling contrast with the opaque blue sheet of the **Lac de Castillon**, backed up behind the Barrage de Castillon, a mighty 292ft concrete dam begun in 1942 under the Vichy government, with a distinctly grim, wartime look about it. **St-André-des-Alpes**, on the north end of the lake, is France's hang-gliding capital.

And what is that warped theme park on the west shore? Why, that's **Mandarom Shambhasalem**, the centre of Aumism, a fruit cake of a cult that half-bakes bits of every religion into its batter. You can visit most afternoons (road up from Castellane): the cult statues of the world's religious elite are enough to make the average *santon* look like a Michelangelo.

Castellane, south of the lake, has become the capital of the Grand Canyon and the base for visiting one of the greatest natural wonders in Europe. It's centred round a pretty square of plane trees (the grilles surrounding the trees are worked in the shapes of plane leaves) where people play *boules* and amiably hang about. But its edges are deep in up-to-the-minute sports shops supplying slick whizz-gimmickry for any sport you could or couldn't conceive (such as bungee jumping). There is a pretty *mairie* and a church, where the 597ft ascent up Castellane's landmark square rock begins: pick up the key for the chapel on top from outside the *curé*'s house, or collect it on your way up from the last person coming down. Castellane's motto 'Napoleon

Tourist Information

Castellane ✉ 04120: Rue Nationale,
t 04 92 83 61 14, f 04 92 83 76 89,
office@castellane.org, www.castellane.org.
Ask about the guided tours organized by
the office. *Open summer Mon–Sat 9–12 and
2–7, Sun 10–1; shorter hours in winter.*
Riez ✉ 04500: 4 Allée Louis Gardiol,
t 04 92 77 99 09, f 04 92 77 99 07. *15 June–
Sept Mon–Sat 9–7 and Sun 9–1; shorter hours
in winter.*
Moustiers-Ste-Marie ✉ 04360: Rue de la
Bourgade, t 04 92 74 67 84, f 04 92 74 60 65,
*moustiers@wanadoo.fr, www.ville-moustiers-
sainte-marie.fr.*
Digne ✉ 04000: Place du Tampinet, t 04 92 36
62 62, f 04 92 32 27 24, *info@ot-dignesles
bains.fr, www.ot-dignelesbains.fr. Open
July–Aug daily 8.45–12.30 and 1.30–6.30;
Sept–June Mon–Sat 8.45–12 and 2–6, Sun
10.30–12.30.*

Market Days

Castellane: Wednesday and Saturday.
Riez: Wednesday and Saturday.
Moustiers: Friday.
Digne: Wednesday and Saturday.

Where to Stay and Eat

Castellane ✉ 04120
★★★Nouvel Hôtel du Commerce, Place de
l'Eglise, t 04 92 83 61 00, f 04 92 83 72 82
(*moderate*). Friendly and comfortable.
*Closed mid-Oct–Feb; restaurant closed Tues,
and Wed lunch.*
★★Ma Petite Auberge, 8 Bd de la République,
t 04 92 83 62 06, f 04 92 83 68 49,
*mapetite-auberge@libertysurf.fr (inexpen-
sive; restaurant moderate).* Acceptable for a
short stay. *Closed mid-Nov–mid-March, Wed
and Thurs lunch.*
★★Hôtel La Forge, at the foot of the rock next
to the church, t 04 92 83 62 61, f 04 92 83 65
81, *http://perso.wanadoo.fr/forge (inexpensive; restaurant cheap).* With a terrace from
which to view the village and the walkers
going up and down the *roc. Closed mid-
Dec–mid-Jan; restaurant closed Sat.*
★★Grand Canyon, Falaise des Cavaliers, t 04 94
76 91 31, f 04 94 76 92 29, *hotel.gd.canyon.
verdon@wanadoo.fr (inexpensive).* The best
way to see the Canyon is from the glassed-in
restaurant (*moderate*) terrace, 14km east of
the village of Aiguines, which looks 984ft

stopped here. Why don't you?' comes from its spot on the **Route Napoléon**, the road
taken by the emperor on his return from the island of Elba, now a tourist trail starting
from his landing point at Golfe Juan and ending at his destination, Grenoble.

The Grand Canyon of the Verdon

The most surprising thing about the Grand Canyon du Verdon is that it was not
'discovered' until 1905. That the most spectacular canyon on the continent could be so
overlooked speaks volumes about the French – their long-held aversion to nature,
which they are now working so enthusiastically to correct, and the traditional disdain
of Parisian authorities for the Midi. The locals always knew about it, of course; agriculturally useless and almost inaccessible, the 21km canyon had an evil reputation for
centuries as a haunt of devils and 'wild men'. Even after a famous speleologist named
Martel brought it to the world's attention at the beginning of the century, many
Frenchmen weren't impressed. In the 1950s the government decided to flood the
whole thing for another dam (the tunnels they dug are still visible in many places at
the bottom); when the plan was finally abandoned, it was for reasons of cost, not
natural preservation.

The name 'Grand Canyon' was a modern idea; when the French became aware of its
existence, comparisons with that grand-daddy of all canyons in Arizona were

down on to the Verdon. *Closed Oct–Mar; restaurant closed Mon eve and Tues.*

Moustiers-Ste-Marie ✉ 04360

****La Bastide de Moustiers,** just outside the village at La Grisolière, t 04 92 70 47 47, f 04 92 70 47 48, *contact@bastide.moustiers. com, www.bastide-moustiers.com (expensive).* Sleep in comfort and splurge for a memorable dinner at celeb-chef Alain Ducasse's 17th-century hotel, with 12 individually fashioned rooms, Jacuzzi, pool, riding stable, etc. The food is predominantly local, picked fresh from the kitchen garden, and innovative – herb and vegetable tart, spit-roasted baron of lamb followed by cherries baked in batter. *Restaurant closed Wed and Thurs from mid-Dec–Feb.*

Belvédère, t 04 92 74 66 04, **f** 04 92 74 62 31 (*inexpensive; restaurant cheap*). Up in the village and rather more affordable. *Restaurant closed Mon out of season and Dec.*

Les Santons, Place de l'Eglise, **t** 04 92 74 66 48 (*expensive*). Enjoys a gorgeous setting on top of the village overlooking the torrent; the refined Provençal cooking matches the views. *Closed Mon eve and Dec–Jan; book ahead.*

Quinson ✉ 04500

****Relais Notre Dame, t** 04 92 74 40 01, **f** 04 92 74 02 10, *www.relais-notre-dame.com (inexpensive).* In the middle of the Gorges du Verdon, the Relais Notre Dame has a garden and swimming pool, but most importantly a real, warm welcome and very good food (*moderate*). *Closed mid-Dec–Jan; restaurant closed Mon eve, and Tues out of season.*

Digne ✉ 04000

*****Du Grand Paris,** 19 Bd Thiers, **t** 04 92 31 11 15, **f** 04 92 32 32 82, *grandparis@ wanadoo.fr (moderate).* A distinguished hotel in a restored 17th-century monastery, with an excellent restaurant (*expensive*) featuring classic cuisine with truffles. *Closed Dec–Feb.*

De Provence, 17 Bd Thiers, **t** 04 92 31 32 19, **f** 04 92 31 48 39 (*inexpensive*). Central and comfortable, with a good restaurant.

Hôtel du Petit St-Jean, 14 Cours des Arès, **t** 04 92 31 30 04, **f** 04 92 36 05 80 (*cheap*). This might look quaint but the air is tainted with the whiff of chip oil from the neighbouring restaurant. If you stay here, eat elsewhere. *Closed 24 Dec–5 Jan.*

---

inevitable. It does put on a grand show: sheer limestone cliffs as much as half a kilometre apart, snaking back and forth to follow the meandering course of the Verdon; in many places there are vast panoramas down the length of it. There are roads along both sides, though not for the entire distance. Most of the best views are from the so-called **Corniche Sublime** (D71) on the southern side; if you want to explore the bottom, ask about trails and the best way to approach them (it's a long trek) at the tourist information office in Castellane.

The lands south of the canyon are some of the most desolate in France; you will find them either romantic or tiresome depending on your mood. But either mood will be definitively broken when columns of tanks and missile-carriers come rattling up the road. The army has appropriated almost all of this area, the **Grand Plan de Canjuers,** for manœuvres and target practice; you'll see their base camp on the D955 towards Draguignan.

Directly west of the canyon, a less spectacular section of the Verdon has indeed been dammed up, forming the enormous **Lac de Ste-Croix.** There is yet another dam further downstream, and the next 40km of the river valley are underwater too: the **Gorges du Verdon,** in parts as good as the Grand Canyon, but sacrificed forever to the beaverish Paris planners. It's wild country on both sides, and access is limited since the roads are few. Beyond the dam, on the way to Manosque and the Luberon,

Gréoux-les-Bains, with its above-average number of launderettes and poodles, is quite a favourite with the rheumatic set, who regularly treat their aching bones to a jolt of sulphurous, radioactive water at the baths. Les Bains is a clinical, eerie, hairdresser-smelling place, with New Age oddities on sale as if by money-changers at the temple. Gréoux was a fashionable resort in the early 19th century, when Napoleon's tearaway sister Pauline Borghese dropped by, but that's about it. The village turns its back on the shabby castle, built in the 12th century by the Templars, which is occasionally used as a theatre (*open Wed for guided tours only, at 2.30pm most of year, 4pm July and Aug*).

Riez and Moustiers

The **Plateau de Valensole**, north of the Verdon and the Lac de Ste-Croix, is a hot, dry plain of olive and almond trees, and one of the big lavender-growing areas of Provence – come in July to see it in full bloom. **Riez**, in the middle, is an old centre for lavender distilling, now adapted to tourism. Ruined medieval houses have been restored, and artists and potters have moved in. It's pretty but bustling, a good place to dawdle in. Riez was an important Celtic religious site, though it isn't clear exactly which deity it honoured. Testimonies to later piety can be seen at the western edge of town, thought to have been the centre of Roman-era Riez: four standing columns of a Roman Temple of Apollo, and a 6th-century Baptistry that is one of the few surviving monuments in France from the Merovingian era. Octagonal, like most early Christian baptistries, it has eight recycled Roman columns and capitals; all the rest was heavily restored in the 19th century. Inside is a small museum of archaeological finds, including an altar with bull horns (*t 04 92 77 99 09; open mid-June–mid-Sept Mon, Fri and Sat 3–7; mid–end Sept Tues, Fri and Sat 3–7; otherwise by appointment only; adm*).

Inside the medieval gates of the town are two pretty fountains recycled from Roman remains, and a number of modest palaces and chapels that recall Riez's prosperity in the 16th to 18th centuries. Fourteen kilometres west of Riez, introspective, overlooked **Valensole** is an ancient village built over the ruins of its Roman predecessor.

To the east, some 15km on the D952, **Moustiers-Ste-Marie** gets all the attention, spectacularly hanging on the west cliffs of the Grand Canyon du Verdon. Like Castellane on the other side, it is a popular base for visiting the canyon, and busy in summer. The town will be familiar to anyone who haunts the museums of the Midi, as Moustiers in the old days was Provence's famous centre for painted ceramics. The blue and yellow faïences, usually painted with country scenes or floral designs, were often works of art in their own right; first popular in the time of Louis XIV, they were made here as late as the 1870s. Today, a large number of potters, some talented and some pretty awful, clutter the village streets, capitalizing on the perfect clay of the region (and on the tourists). You can compare their efforts with the originals at the Musée de la Faïence, a small collection on Place du Presbytère (*t 04 92 74 61 64; open April–Oct Wed–Mon 9–12 and 2–6, July and Aug to 7pm; school hols Mon and Wed–Fri 2–5; closed Jan; adm*).

In the middle of the village is the deep-set 12th-century parish church, with a kink in it. Moustiers' other distinction, as everyone in Provence knows, is the **Cadeno de**

Moustié, a 783ft chain suspended between the tops of two peaks overlooking the village. A knight of the local Blacas family, while a prisoner of the Saracens during the Crusades, made a vow to put it up if he ever saw home again; the star in the middle comes from his coat of arms. The original (thought to be solid silver, but really plated) was stolen in the Wars of Religion and a replacement didn't appear until 1957. A climb up under the chain will take you to the Chapelle Notre-Dame-de-Beauvoir, where a notice piously requests that pilgrims do not write on the walls but inscribe their names on the heart of the Virgin instead.

Also Worthy of Your Attention...

Digne means 'worthy', and one suspects a degree of deliberate etymological mutation in the gradual name change from the local Gaulish tribe, the Bodiontici, whose capital this was, to Roman Dinia, and finally to Digne. The capital of *département* number 04 (Alpes de Haute-Provence), and the only city in a long stretch of mountains between Orange and Turin, over in Italy, Digne has one thriving boulevard of cafés and touristic knick-knackery mixed with smart shoe shops, posh chocolates and more than one bookshop. It has recently rediscovered its role as a spa, and you will be given a glossy pamphlet in the tourist office consisting entirely of pictures of people smiling in the thermal baths. In the minuscule medieval centre is the crumbling, down-at-heel, 15th-century **Cathédrale de St-Jérome**; this and its surrounding brightly painted houses stand shoulder to shoulder with some daring grey municipal buildings.

Out of town is something entirely unexpected: the **Fondation Alexandra David-Néel** (*27 Av du Maréchal Juin,* **t** *04 92 31 32 38, neel@alexandra-david-neel.org, www.alexandra-david-nel.org; guided tours with her former secretary, July–Sept daily at 10.30, 2, 3.30 and 5; otherwise at 10.30, 2 and 4*), the former home of a truly remarkable Frenchwoman who settled here in her 'Himalayas in miniature' after a lifetime exploring in Tibet. Ms David-Néel called this house *Samten Dzong*, the 'castle of meditation', and Tibetan Buddhist monks attended her when she died here in 1969 at the age of 101. The Dalai Lama has since come twice to visit. There are exhibits of Tibetan art and culture, photographs and Tibetan crafts on sale. In summer, there are up to 40 people crammed into this tiny museum, so be prepared to wait in the garden. Staff will be happy to play the commentary in English if you ask.

At Place Paradis in an old bunker in the hillside is the **Museum of the Second World War** (*t 04 92 31 54 80; open May, June and Sept–mid-Oct Wed 2–5; July and Aug Mon–Thurs 2–6, Fri 2–5.30; mid-Oct–April by appointment only, to groups of 3 or more*).

At St-Benoit, the **Geology Centre** (*t 04 92 36 70 70; open April–Oct 9–12 and 2–5.30, to 4.30pm Fri; Nov–Mar closed Sat and Sun*) houses the largest geology collection in Europe, including an impressive wall of ammonites. Follow Boulevard Gassendi to the eastern edge of town, passing the peculiar neoclassical **Grande Fontaine** (1829), and you will find Digne's former cathedral, **Notre-Dame-du-Bourg**, a large Lombard-style Romanesque building of the 12th century, complete with a bell tower of that date, a deep-set Romanesque arch below a beautiful rose window, and fresco fragments.

Alpes de Haute-Provence South

If you get off the motorway, the route across the Var from Grasse to Aix-en-Provence takes you through some charming villages, and some not so charming. Within an hour it can show you lush green landscapes, as well as lonely steel-grey plateaus where only dolmens and army bases grow. The greener parts are wine-growing country too, falling within the largest AOC region in France, Côtes-de-Provence.

From Fayence to Draguignan

This first leg of the journey is close enough to the coast to have become thoroughly colonized by the holiday-home set.

Fayence, a large village of moderate cuteness, has plenty of Englishmen and estate agents. Built on a steep hillside like Grasse, its road winds back and forth up to the centre, which is pleasant enough: there is a *mairie* perched on an arch over the main street, a forgotten 18th-century church and a view not to be missed from the Tour de l'Horloge at the very top of the village. Check the view you see against the ceramic panoramas painted and baked into tiles under your hands. North of Fayence, there is some lovely, wild countryside; off the D37, **Roche Taillée** has a Roman aqueduct still in use – but don't expect the Pont du Gard. This one is entirely carved out of the rock, along a steady descent of some 5km. Also from the D37, you'll see the towers of an impressive 17th-century castle, the **Château de Beauregard**, a private home.

Further north, **Mons** is a beautiful and strange village of narrow streets overhung with arches. The language of its inhabitants still conserves some Ligurian Italian words; the people of Mons were totally wiped out in the Black Death of 1348, and colonists from the area around Genoa and Ventimiglia were brought in to replace

Getting Around

By Train

The main Provençal railway follows the motorway from Aix and Marseille to Cannes; for Draguignan you'll usually have to change at Les Arcs.

Draguignan and Brignoles are well served, unlike almost everywhere else.

By Bus

Draguignan is also the hub for village buses, though as always these are few and generally inconvenient. There are several buses daily to Grasse, stopping at Bargemon, Seillans and Fayence along the way, and several daily in the other direction, to Tourtour and Aups, with at best one or two to the other villages.

By Car and Bike

Driving in this southern half of the Provençal mountains will prove much less trouble than the areas to the north and east; roads are better and service facilities more common.

You can take the A8/E80 motorway straight across and miss everything, but the villages to the east and west of Draguignan offer some of the most delightful opportunities for casual touring in Provence; it's good bicycling country too.

Two possible itineraries for you: from Fayence (west of Grasse on the D562) to Le Muy, through the lovely villages along the D19 and D25 (the latter is the wine route); or from Draguignan, west on the D557, dipping into the mountains on the D77 for Aups, then the D22 for Sillans-la-Cascade and Cotignac, and west again (D32) to Fox-Amphoux or Barjols.

them. There are a large numbers of **dolmens** in the area; some are inaccessibly located on the base of the Canjuers army camp, the borders of which are only 2km away.

West of Fayence, the farmhouses may now all be bijoux holiday homes, but the scenery is delicious; the main road, the D562 to Draguignan, is fine, but even better is the winding D19/D25, passing through three pretty villages.

Seillans has been occupied since the time of the Ligurians, giving it some two and a half millennia to perfect its charm, with cobbled streets leading up to the restored castle. It's one of the most beautiful villages in France and, like the others, it's got a plaque to prove it. The village lives on flowers, and was the last home of Max Ernst. **Bargemon**, further west, is just as old; behind its medieval gates are several fountains and a 15th-century church with a Flamboyant portal and heads sculpted by Pierre Puget.

From here you can take a detour north through the thoroughly depressing Canjuers military zone to **Bargème**, the highest village in the Var (3,589ft), still encircled by its walls and ruined castle, although only two people live there year-round to enjoy it.

Last before you reach Draguignan is **Callas**, which lies beneath a ruined castle. The D25 south of Callas, as far as Le Muy, is a beautiful drive through forests, with the **Gorges de Pennafort** and a waterfall along the way; it is also one of the best wine

Alpes de Haute-Provence South

roads in the region, with a few places to stop and sample Côtes-de-Provence along the way (*see* pp.300–301).

Draguignan

Draguignan gets a bad press, especially from the timid English: ugly, depraved, full of soldiers; *avoid it if you can*... We watched a young fellow on the Boulevard de Maréchal Joffre being run in by a pair of municipal policemen – clean-shaven, brutishly intelligent, all dressed up military-style in black and silver like American cops. Beautiful women waltzed by, swinging their handbags and smiling at the unfortunate; flaccid shopkeepers squinted furtively through immaculately clean windows.

After the Casino at Monte Carlo, there's no better free theatre in Provence. Tough, sharp-edged Draguignan is not French so much as French Colonial. The Army owns it – it's the biggest base in France – and its dusty, palm-shaded boulevards (laid out in 1849 by Baron Haussmann, *préfet* of the Var, who treated the town to a trial run of his urban planning efforts in Paris) pass the national schools of artillery and military science. Draguignan's symbol is the *drac* – yet another Provençal dragon, chased out by an early bishop, though its fire-spitting image can still be seen everywhere. Draguignan could be Saigon or Algiers or Dakar, a cinematic fantasy in a wreath of *Gauloise* smoke, waiting for the Warner Bros cameras to capture Bogart, Lorre and Greenstreet conspiring in some tawdry nightclub.

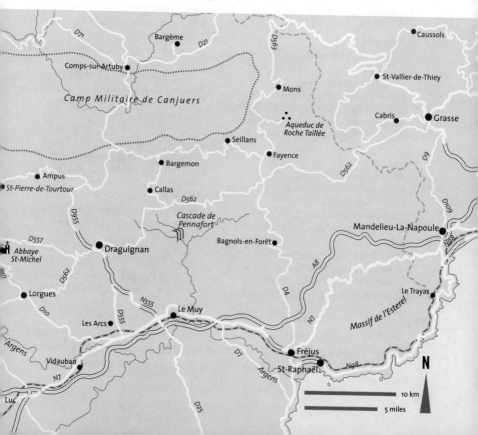

Tourist Information

Fayence ✉ 83440: Place Léon Roux, **t** 04 94 76 20 08, **f** 04 94 34 15 96, *ot.fayence@ wanadoo.fr. Open summer Mon–Sat 9.15–12.15 and 2–6.30, Sun 9.30–12; winter Mon–Sat 9–12 and 2–6.*

Seillans ✉ 83440: Le Valat, **t** 04 94 76 85 91, **f** 04 94 39 13 53, *ot.seillans@wanadoo.fr, www.seillans-var.com. Open Mon–Sat 9.30–12.30 and 2.30–6 (June–Sept to 6.30; plus Sun Aug–Sept). Guided tours all year (also in English) Thurs am.*

Draguignan ✉ 83300: 2 Av Carnot, **t** 04 98 10 51 05, **f** 04 98 10 51 10, *contact@cœurde provence.com, www.cœurdeprovence.com. Open July–Aug Mon–Sat 9–7 and Sun 9–1; Sept–June Mon–Sat 9–6, Sun 10–12.*

Market Days

Fayence: Tuesday, Thursday and Saturday.
Draguignan: Wednesday all day and Saturday.

Where to Stay and Eat

Fayence ✉ 83440

★★★**Moulin de la Camandoule**, Chemin Notre-Dame-des-Cyprès, **t/f** 04 94 76 00 84, *moulin.camandoule@wanadoo.fr (expensive–moderate).* A lovely old olive-oil mill, prettily restored (by a British couple) with all the amenities – pool, garden, etc. – and a restaurant *(expensive). Half board obligatory Mar–Oct. Restaurant closed Jan.*

La Sousto, 4 Rue du Paty, **t** 04 94 76 02 16 *(inexpensive).* Small and starless, this has charming rooms equipped with kitchenettes overlooking the valley.

★★**Auberge de la Fontaine**, Route de Fréjus, **t/f** 04 94 76 07 59 *(cheap; restaurant moderate).*

Le Castellaras, Route de Seillans, **t** 04 94 76 13 80 *(expensive).* For refined, sunny cuisine, head out here. Try the courgette flowers stuffed with ratatouille; it's got a great wine list too. *Closed Tues.*

Seillans ✉ 83440

★★★**Des Deux Rocs**, Place Font d'Amont, **t** 04 94 76 87 32, **f** 04 94 76 88 68 *(moderate).* Much lauded and offering a matriarchal welcome as well as the odd bomb from the army firing range. Near-perfect food, crowned with sublime desserts: a favourite with Americans. *Closed Dec–Mar, Tues lunch and Thurs lunch out of season.*

★★★**De France Clariond**, Place du Thouron, **t** 04 94 76 96 10, **f** 04 94 76 89 20 *(moderate).* Not as quaint as the Deux Rocs, but busy; its swimming pool overlooks the valley. *Closed Nov–Jan.*

La Chirane, Rue de l'Hospice, **t** 04 94 76 96 20. A converted stable underneath the houses halfway up the hill, painted jolly blue and with tables outside looking down over the lower village. There's live jazz monthly; *reserve on Saturday nights.* Specialities include chicken in garlic, ham from the bone and home-baked bread. *Closed Dec–Mar, and Wed lunch.*

Bargemon ✉ 83620

Bargemon is a good place to rest without breaking the bank.

★★**Auberge des Arcades**, Av Pasteur, **t** 04 94 76 60 36, **f** 04 94 76 68 33 *(inexpensive; restaurant moderate). Closed Tues and Jan.*

Restaurant Pierrot, Place Chauvier, **t** 04 94 76 62 19 *(moderate).* A fine restaurant with an outside terrace.

Draguignan ✉ 83300

★★**Les Etoiles de l'Ange**, on the D557 towards Lorgues, **t/f** 04 94 68 23 01, *ange.provence. hotel@wanadoo.fr (moderate).* The only really decent place in the area, this is outside town, clean, modern and colourless – but with a view. *Closed Nov–one week before Easter.*

Le Galoubet, 23 Bd Jean-Jaurès, **t** 04 94 68 08 50 *(moderate).* Serves good seafood; try the *filet de St-Pierre* with leeks. *Closed Mon and Sun eves and the last fortnight in Aug.*

Anyhow, have your papers in order and try not to exceed the speed limits. Touring in Provence you'll be bound to pass through here once or twice, and it's a pleasant stop, really. The Saturday market is especially good, and there are a few things to see:

the 17th-century **Tour de l'Horloge**, Draguignan's architectural pride; and a small **Musée Municipal** on Rue de la République (*t 04 94 47 28 80; open 9–12 and 2–6, closed Sun and hols*) with a picture gallery (including *Child Blowing a Soap Bubble*, by Rembrandt, a portrait by Camille Claudel and faïences from Moustiers, along with porcelain from China).

The **Musée des Arts et Traditions Populaires** (*15 Rue Joseph Roumanille, t 04 94 47 05 72; open 10–12 and 2–6, closed Sun morning and Mon; adm*) is a complete, didactic overview of everything you'll never see in the real Provence any more – from mules to silk culture, along with reconstructions of country life, including kitchens, barns, festivals and, naturally, some antique *boules* and *tambourins*; a pretty old merry-go-round with painted horses steals the show.

There's a large **American War Cemetery** and Memorial on Boulevard John Kennedy, with a bronze map tracing the route of the 150,000 men of the 7th army who disembarked in the south of France in the two weeks following D-Day. And just outside town, on the D955 towards the Verdon Canyon, is one of the biggest and most spectacular dolmens in Provence, the **Pierre de la Fée**; the table stone weighs over 20 tonnes.

Villages of the Central Var

Heading west from Draguignan, there are two choices. If aesthetics are a bigger consideration than time, don't bother with the A8 motorway or the parallel road through Brignoles and St-Maximin (for which, *see* below); instead, take the D557 or D562 directly west for a leisurely tour through some of Provence's loveliest and most typical landscapes.

Though this area gets its share of foreign and Parisian summer folk, it isn't quite chic – compared with similar but totally colonized places like the Luberon. But there's enough lavender and blowing cypresses, plenty of wine, and a dozen relentlessly charming villages that won't trouble you with any strenuous sightseeing.

From Lorgues to Aups

Lorgues is the first village, with a complete ensemble of 18th-century municipal decorations, proof that the *ancien régime* wasn't quite so useless after all: a fountain, the huge, dignified church of St-Martin, and the inevitable avenue of venerable plane trees, one of the longest and fairest in Provence. To the north, along the D10, you'll pass the **monastery of St-Michel**, a recently refounded Russian Orthodox community; its handmade wooden chapel, a replica of a Russian church, may be visited.

Further north, there are a number of pretty villages around the valley of the Nartuby: **Ampus**, **Tourtour**, over-restored but up on a height with views down to the sea, and **Villecroze**, with its vaulted lanes. At the edge of the Plan de Canjuers, Villecroze is built up against a tufa cliff; there is an unusual park at the base of it, with a small waterfall and a cave-house dug into the rock in the 16th century.

Tourist Information

Aups ✉ 83630: Place Frédéric Mistral, **t** 04 94 70 00 80, **f** 04 94 84 00 69. *Open Mon 2.30–5.30, Tues and Thurs–Sat 9–12 and 2.30–5.30, Wed 9–12.*

Barjols ✉ 83670: Bd Grisolle, **t** 04 94 77 20 01, **f** 04 94 77 08 41, *ot-barjols@free.fr, www.ville-barjols.fr. Open summer daily 9–12 and 2–7; shorter hours in winter.*

Market Days

Aups: Wednesday and Saturday. Truffle market on Thursdays in winter.
Barjols: Saturday morning.

Where to Stay and Eat

Lorgues ✉ 83510

Lorgues, 13km from Draguignan, is a more pleasant place to stop over if you're passing through the area.
Hôtel du Parc, 25 Bd Clemenceau, **t** 04 94 73 70 01, **f** 04 94 67 68 46 (*inexpensive*). A venerable, classy hotel in the centre, a bit down on its luck but still comfortable, with a restaurant. *Closed Nov; restaurant closed Sun eve in winter.*

Brasserie du Parc, next door to the Hôtel du Parc. Does a great *café au lait. Closed Nov.*

Chez Bruno, Le Plan, **t** 04 94 85 93 93, **f** 04 94 85 93 99 (*expensive*). For something extra special; three luxurious rooms and one suite, at prices that extend into the ozone layer, in an old *mas* where the chef does wonderful things with truffles (*luxury*). *Closed Sun eve and Mon.*

Tourtour ✉ 83690

Easily the poshest of the villages in this region, Tourtour also has the most luxurious accommodation.

****Bastide de Tourtour, Montée St Denis, **t** 04 98 10 54 20, **f** 04 94 70 54 90, *bastide@verdon.net, www.verdon.net* (*expensive*). A modern, Relais & Châteaux complex with pool, tennis and all the amenities, including a highly reputed restaurant with a blend of Provençal cooking and classic French. *Restaurant closed lunch Mon–Sat except July–Aug.*

***Le Mas des Collines, Route de Villecroze, **t** 04 94 70 59 30, **f** 04 94 70 57 62 (*moderate*). A charming little hotel offering tranquillity, air-conditioned rooms and a pretty pool overlooking the valley below Tourtour. *Restaurant closed Nov–Mar.*

Aups was a Ligurian settlement and a Roman town; its name comes from the same ancient root as Alps. It has a reputation for being different; a monument in the town square records Aups' finest hour, when the citizens put up a doomed republican resistance to Louis Napoleon's coup of 1851. The village is known in the region for its Thursday truffle market, held through the winter months. The village church is oddly below surface level; the ground level around it was raised to avoid the frequent flooding of the old days. Aups, like the other villages, has not completely escaped Riviera modernism. The **Musée Simon Segal** (*Av Albert Ier,* **t** *04 94 70 01 95; open mid-June–mid-Sept daily 10–12 and 4–7; adm*), founded by an eponymous Russian artist, contains his and other 20th-century works.

Salernes, south of Aups, has been known for over 200 years as a manufacturer of tiles: the small, hexagonal terracotta floor-tiles called *tomettes* that are as much a trademark of Provence as lavender. They still make them, and in a day when French factory-made tiles all come in insipid beige, they are at a premium. Lately Salernes' factories and individual artisans have been expanding into coloured ceramics and pottery; there are a few shops in the village and factory showrooms on the outskirts. Despite such a workmanlike background, the village itself is rather drab, with a medieval fountain and a simple 13th-century church in the centre.

*Les Chênes Verts, 2km on the Route de Villecroze, t 04 94 70 55 06, f 04 94 70 59 35 (*expensive*). With just three pricey rooms, but the wonderful food is the strongest magnet – classical and featuring lobster, seafood, truffles, and game in season, prepared to perfection. *Closed Tues, Wed and June.*

***Auberge St-Pierre, St-Pierre-de-Tourtour, t 04 94 70 57 17, f 04 94 70 59 04 (*moderate*). Three kilometres east, this is a find – an up-to-date working farm built around a hotel; exceptional rooms in an 18th-century house and a fine restaurant, with authentic Provençal food – largely the farm's own produce. It also offers a swimming pool, gym, tennis, archery and fishing. Beware of the hostess when she is tired. *Closed mid-Oct–Mar; restaurant closed Wed.*

Salernes ✉ 83690

*Hôtel Allègre, 20 Rue Rousseau, t 04 94 70 60 30, f 04 94 70 78 84 (*inexpensive*). An old establishment with a bit of faded grandeur and some of its 1920s décor intact. The cooking's a bit faded too. *Closed mid-Nov–mid-Mar; restaurant closed Mon out of season.*

La Fontaine, Place du 8 Mai 1945, t 04 94 70 64 51 (*moderate*). Sample a simple *maigret* or stewed rabbit at outside tables. *Closed Sun eve, Mon and Jan.*

Sillans ✉ 83690

Hôtel-Restaurant des Pins, right on the D32, t 04 94 04 63 26, f 04 94 04 72 71 (*inexpensive; restaurant moderate*). A very popular restaurant in an old stone house, serving grilled meats with shrimps for openers . It also has a few rooms, but book way ahead in the summer. *Closed mid-Jan–Feb, and Wed eve and Thurs out of season.*

Fox-Amphoux ✉ 83670

***Auberge du Vieux Fox, t 04 94 80 71 69, f 04 94 80 78 38 (*moderate*). One of the most pleasant village inns in Provence, with rooms overlooking the Place de l'Eglise and a delightful restaurant. Try the *carré d'agneau*.

Cotignac ✉ 83570

***Lou Calen , 1 Cours Gambetta, t 04 94 04 60 40, f 04 94 04 76 64 (*expensive–moderate*). An unexpectedly stylish hotel-restaurant in the centre of the village, newly refurbished and with a lovely garden and pool. Only eight rooms, and as many (more expensive) suites; also a somewhat unex-citing restaurant (*moderate*). *Half board obligatory in season.*

Further west, **Sillans** has lately been calling itself Sillans-la-Cascade, to draw attention to the 118ft waterfall just south of the village (it dries up in summer). Beyond that, **Fox-Amphoux** is worth a visit just to hear the locals pronounce the name; this minuscule and well-restored village of stepped medieval alleys sits on a defensible height. There is a ruined castle and, on the trail to the hamlet of Amphoux, an odd cave-chapel, Notre-Dame-du-Secours, hung with *ex votos*, many from sailors.

Thoronet Abbey

South of Salernes, **Entrecasteaux** is dominated by a 17th-century castle, completely restored in the 1970s by a Scotsman named McGarvie-Munn; visitors are admitted, but there's nothing to see and the fee is exorbitant. Further south, the artificial **Lac de Carcès** has been a favourite with fishermen since the dam was built in the 1930s. To the east are the biggest bauxite mines in France, which are playing hell with one of the most impressive medieval abbeys in Provence.

The **Abbaye du Thoronet** (*t 04 94 60 43 90; open April–Sept Mon–Sat 9–7, Sun 2–7; Oct–Mar Mon–Sat 10–1 and 2–5, Sun 10–12 and 2–5; adm*) was the first Cistercian foundation in Provence, built on land donated by Count Raymond Bérenger of

Toulouse in 1136; the present buildings were begun about 1160. Like most Cistercian houses, it was in utter decay by the 15th century; and like so many other medieval monuments in the Midi, it owes its restoration to Prosper Mérimée, Romantic novelist (*Carmen*, among others) and State Inspector of Historic Monuments under Napoleon III. He chanced upon it in 1873, when most of the roof was gone, the galleries were overgrown with bushes and the only beings dining in the refectory were cows.

It often seems as if the restoration is still under way; you may find it full of props, scaffolding and concrete piers, as its keepers experiment desperately to save Thoronet from being shaken to pieces by the bauxite lorries rumbling past on the D79. The mines themselves (nearby, but screened by trees) have caused some subsidence and cracks are opening in the walls. Nevertheless, this purest and plainest of the Cistercian 'Three Sisters' of Provence (along with Silvacane, pp.235–6, and Sénanque, p.246) is worth a detour. Following the stern austerity of Bernard of Clairvaux, it displays sophisticated Romanesque architecture stripped to its bare essentials, with no worldly splendour to distract a monkish mind, only grace of form and proportion. The elegant stone bell tower would have been forbidden in any other Cistercian house (to keep local barons from commandeering them for defence towers), but those in Provence got a special dispensation – thanks to the mistral, which would have blown a wooden one down with ease. There are no such compromises in the blank façade, but behind it is a marvellously elegant interior; note the slight point of the arches, a hint of the dawning Gothic – Thoronet was begun in the same year as France's first Gothic churches, in the north at St-Denis and Sens.

The **cloister**, with its heavy arcades, is equally good, enclosing a delightful stone fountain-house. There's a cellar to visit, too, to see how the monks fared, and a modern chapel where people pray and visitors gawp and take photographs over the sign clearly requesting that they do not.

If you like fine rosé wine, visit the nearby **Domaine de l'Abbaye**, where wine-grower Franc Petit makes some of the best. His secret? Hand-picking the grapes by moonlight, when temperatures are cooler and the grapes avoid the shock of coming in from the hot sun into the cool of the *pressoir*. The grapes supposedly keep more of their strength, and the wine is bottled in a distinctive sky blue bottle to protect it from the light.

Cotignac and Barjols

Its inhabitants might be unaware of it, but **Cotignac** is one of the cutest of the cute, a Sunday supplement-quality Provençal village where everything is just right. There are no sights, but one looming peculiarity: the tufa cliffs that hang dramatically over it. In former times these were hollowed out for wine cellars, stables or even habitations; today there are trails up to them for anyone who wants to explore. At the base of the cliffs there is a meadow where Cotignac holds its summer music festival.

Westwards on the D13/D560, the landscapes are delicious and drowsy; **Pontevès** will startle you awake again, a castle with a remarkable setting atop a steep conical hill. Long the stronghold of the Pontevès family, feudal rulers of most of this region, the apparition loses some of its romantic charm after the climb up; there's nothing inside but a few houses, *La Poste* and a food shop.

Three kilometres further on, **Barjols** has little cuteness but much more character. This metropolis of 2,000 souls owes its existence to leather tanning, an important industry here for the last 300 years. There is still one shoe factory left, but Barjols is now little more than a market town, although it retains an urban and somewhat sombre air: elegant rectangular squares of the 18th century, and moss-covered fountains and *lavoirs* similar to the ones in Aix – hence its nickname 'the Tivoli of Provence'. If you stop in at the tourist office, you can get a *circuit des fontaines* to guide you round all 42 of them.

To see Barjols at its best, come on 16–17 January, the feast of St Marcel (Marcellus, the 4th-century pope), whose gaudy relics, stolen in the Middle Ages from a Provençal monastery, can be seen in the 16th-century parish church. There'll be a bit of dancing (*la danse des tripettes*) and, equally unusual for Provence, the essentially pagan slaughter and roasting of an ox, accomplished to the sound of flutes and *tambourins*.

Off the Motorway: From Draguignan to Aix

With the Var's rocky coast, and the mountains behind it, the only easy route across the *département* is a narrow corridor through Brignoles and St-Maximin-la-Ste-Baume. The French have obligingly plonked down a motorway across it, successor to the Via Aurelia and the St-Maximin pilgrims' route as the great high road of Provence.

Les Arcs and Le Luc

Picking up the D555 south of Draguignan, you'll pass through **Les Arcs**, a well-exploited village of stepped streets, pink stone and ivy. Next comes **Le Luc**, practically strangled by the motorway and parallel national routes, but a game town nevertheless, with another steep medieval centre, a castle on top and a restored Romanesque church flanked by an unusual hexagonal tower dating from the 16th century.

To entertain the hordes of coast-bound tourists there's a Musée Régional du Timbre, housed in a 17th-century château on Place de la Convention (*t 04 94 47 96 16; open June–Aug Wed and Thurs 2.30–6, Fri–Sun 10–12 and 2.30–6; Oct–May Wed and Thurs 2.30–5.30, Fri–Sun 10–12 and 2.30–5.30; closed Sept*), and another small museum in a 16th-century church, the Musée Historique du Centre Var (*24 Rue Victor Hugo, t 04 94 60 70 20; open mid-May to mid-Oct Mon–Sat 3–6*), with a collection ranging from fossils and Neolithic finds to medieval art.

Brignoles

The biggest date in Brignoles' history, perhaps, is 25 September 1973, when several thousand dead toads rained down from the sky, an event that does not seem to be commemorated in any way. Little else has ever happened here. This gritty but

Tourist Information

Brignoles ✉ 83170: Hôtel de Clavier Rue du Palais, **t** 04 94 69 27 51, **f** 04 94 69 44 08. *Open Mon–Fri 9–12 and 1.30–6.30; longer hours in summer.* There's also an office at Carrefour de l'Europe, **t** 04 94 72 04 21, **f** 04 94 72 04 22, *contact@la-provence-verte.org, www.la-provence-verte.org. Open Mon–Sat 9–12.30 and 2–7.30, Sun 10–12 and 2.30–6.30 (closed Sun in winter).*

St-Maximin-la-Ste-Baume ✉ 83470: Hôtel de Ville, **t** 04 94 59 84 59, **f** 04 94 59 82 92, *office.tourisme.stmaximin@ wanadoo.fr, www.la-provence-verte.org. Open July–Aug daily 9–12.30 and 2–6, Sept–June 9–12.30 and 2–6.*

Market Days

Brignoles: Saturday.
St-Maximin: Wednesday.

Where to Stay and Eat

Les Arcs ✉ 83460

★★★Le Logis du Guetteur, Place du Château, **t** 04 94 99 51 10, **f** 04 94 99 51 29, *le.logis.du.guetteur@wanadoo.fr, www.logisduguetteur.com (expensive).* Les Arcs, strategically located on the road to the Côte d'Azur, has spawned one exceptional hotel-restaurant. Le Logis du Guetteur is located at the top of the old town, a lavishly restored castle dating in parts from the 11th century, with a garden and pool; some rooms have wonderful views. The restaurant serves ambitious *haute cuisine*: smoked salmon, stuffed sole and elaborate desserts. *Closed mid-Jan–Feb.*

Brignoles ✉ 83170

★★La Grillade au Feu de Bois, on the N7 in the village of Flassans-sur-Issole (✉ 83340), **t** 04 94 69 71 20, **f** 04 94 59 66 11 (*expensive– moderate; half board compulsory in summer*). Brignoles has plenty of inexpensive hotels, most of them dives. A little further east is this gracious and friendly farm hotel, with 16 rooms and a restaurant serving admirable home cooking.

Saigon, Square St-Louis, **t** 04 94 59 14 51 (*moderate–cheap*). A good Vietnamese restaurant.

Le Relais des Templiers, Place G. Péri, Montfort-sur-Argens, **t** 04 94 59 55 06, **f** 04 94 59 78 76 (*moderate*). Six kilometres north of Brignoles, this is a peaceful place for an intimate meal: it has only a handful of tables and a *table d'hôte. Closed Tues and Nov.*

St-Maximin ✉ 83470

★★Hôtel Le Plaisance, 20 Place Malherbe, **t** 04 94 78 16 74, **f** 04 94 78 18 39 (*inexpensive*). If you are compelled to stay in St-Maximin, head for the wild orange shutters of the Plaisance. Dining in this town is an adventure; the local speciality is limp pizza, and finding anything else can be difficult.

somehow likeable place earns its living mining bauxite. It has an attractive medieval centre, and a museum to remember.

Le Musée du Pays Brignolais (Regional Museum)

Place du Palais des Comtes de Provence; open May–Oct Wed–Sun 9–12 and 2.30–5, Nov–April Wed–Sun 9–12 and 3–5; adm.

Situated at the top of the old town, in a palace that was the summer residence of the counts of Provence, Brignoles' incredible curiosity shop has grown to fill the whole building since a local doctor began the collection in 1947. Over two big floors packed full of oil presses, fossils, cannon balls, reliquaries and roof tiles, you'll see some things you never dreamed existed.

In the place of honour, near the entrance, is the original model of a great invention by Brignoles' own Joseph Lambot (1814–87): the **steel-reinforced concrete canoe**.

Contemporary accounts on display suggest the thing floated, though the idea somehow never caught on. Lambot probably never collected a *sou* for his revolutionary new construction technique, since found to be better adapted to skyscrapers.

Admittedly a hard act to follow, but just across the room is a provocative **sarcophagus**, dated *c.* AD 175–225, that is nothing less than the earliest Christian monument in France. Well sculpted and well preserved, the imagery is a remarkable testament to religious transition. The centre shows a familiar classical scene, a seated god receiving a soul into the underworld – but whether the god is Hades, Jesus or another remains a mystery. Also present are Jesus as the 'Good Shepherd' (the most common early Christian symbol), a figure that may be St Peter (fishing, figuratively, for souls), another that seems to be a deified Sun, and another early Christian symbol, an anchor. The sarcophagus is believed to be Greek, possibly made in Antioch or Smyrna; how it got here no one knows.

Nearby is a rare but badly worn Merovingian tombstone, and a part of the counts' palace, the **chapel of St-Louis-d'Anjou**, a Provençal bishop who may be better known in California – the town of San Luis Obispo is named after him. The chapel houses a hoard of gaudy church clutter, with Louis' chasuble and rows of wax saints under glass. After that, you may inspect a **reconstructed Provençal farm kitchen**, and a **reconstructed mine tunnel**. Other prizes await on the second floor: a **plywood model of Milan Cathedral** by a local madman, a stuffed weasel and large collections of owls and moths. Local painters are exhaustively represented: some of the finest works are 19th-century *ex votos* in the French tradition, with the Virgin Mary blessing people falling off wagons and out of windows. Even after all this, Gaston Huffman's *Allegory of Voluptuous Folly* takes the cake, a medieval conceit in a modern style, with a delicious lady in a little boat enjoying the caresses of a cigar-smoking pig. Rue des Lanciers, the spine of old Brignoles, begins opposite the museum's front door, passing the 13th-century **Maison des Lanciers**, where the counts' guards stayed when they were visiting.

West of Brignoles, there are two sights of some interest off the main road, both of which you'll need to talk your way in to visit: first the half-ruined **Abbaye de la Celle**, an ancient foundation (started in the 6th century) that made a reputation for itself due to the open licentiousness of its nuns, and which was dissolved in 1770; the buildings are now part of a farm. Second, also on a farm, off the D205 6km east of Tourves, is the **Chapelle de la Gayole**, an early Romanesque cemetery chapel in the shape of a Greek cross (built in 1029, though parts of it go back to the 700s).

St-Maximin-la-Ste-Baume

For proof that Provençal sunlight softens the Anglo-Saxon brain, consider St-Maximin. 'Considerable charm', gushes one guidebook; 'another pretty Provençal village', yawns another. Prosper Mérimée, back in 1834, got it right: 'St-Maximin is a miserable hole between Aix and Draguignan.' It hasn't changed. The general atmosphere of bricks and litter is reminiscent of some burnt-out inner-city in the Midlands or Midwest. It is hard to imagine a place remaining in such a state of total,

Wine: Côtes-de-Provence – La Vie en Rose

Half of all French rosés originate in the Republic's largest AOC region, the 18,000-hectare Côtes-de-Provence. The growing area stretches from St-Raphaël to Hyères, with separate patches around La Ciotat and Villars-sur-Var, and a wide swathe south and west of Aix. Based on grenache, mourvèdre, cinsault, tibouren, cabernet and syrah grapes, Côtes-de-Provence rosé is a dry, fruity, and elegant summer wine that doesn't have to worry about travelling well: more than enough eager oenophiles travel to it every holiday season. Unfortunately, its price in the past couple of years has travelled too, and there are no prizes for guessing which way. It is, however, possible to find good inexpensive alternatives since some estates produce a vin de pays. This is often as good as wines with full appellation contrôlée status.

An excellent example is **Château d'Astros**, at Vidauban, t 04 94 73 00 25, f 04 94 73 00 18, which produces a wonderful range of Vin de Pays des Maures: red, white and rosé. The property is run by M. Galliano. A visit to this grand rambling house and estate in the forest is great fun. One can also buy *en vrac* – either supply your own containers or buy one from the owner.

Côtes-de-Provence reds (20 per cent of the production) are much finer today than the rough plonk Caesar issued to his legions, most notably the special cuvées put out by the better estates. The whites, of clairette and ugni blanc grapes, are scarcer still, and account for only 5 per cent of the AOC label. With 57 cooperatives and 350 private cellars, Côtes-de-Provence wine is easily sampled, especially along the signposted 400km Route des Vins, which you can pick up at Le Luc or Le Muy from the A8 or N7, or at Fréjus, Les Arcs and Puget-sur-Argens.

lackadaisical decrepitude in the midst of a prosperous region, without some effort of will on the part of its inhabitants.

But once upon a time, the Miserable Hole was a goal for the pious from all over France. According to legend, the site was the burial place of the Magdalen (*see* Stes-Maries-de-la-Mer, p.168) and her companions St Maximin, the martyred first bishop of Aix, and St Sidonius. Their bodies, supposedly hidden from Saracen raiders in a crypt, had disappeared and were conveniently 'rediscovered' in 1279 by the efforts of Charles II of Anjou, Count of Provence. Inconveniently, the body of the Magdalen was already on display at the famous church of Vézelay, in Burgundy. Nevertheless, an ambitious basilica and abbey complex was begun, and eventually the pope was convinced or bribed into declaring St Maximin's relics the real McCoy. The pilgrim trade made St-Maximin into a town; among the visitors were several kings of France, the last being Louis XIV.

There were wild times during the Revolution; St-Maximin renamed itself 'Marathon', and was briefly under the command of Lucien Bonaparte, who was calling himself 'Brutus'. This most devoutly revolutionary of Bonapartes saved the basilica from a sacking. As the local legend tells it, an official from Paris came down to oversee its liquidation, but Brutus had him greeted with the *Marseillaise*, played all stops out on the church's great organ.

Two of the best-known producers are at Trets, on the D56 east of Aix: Château Ferry-Lacombe, **t** 04 42 29 40 04, where the vines are planted on ancient Roman terraces (along with the pink stuff, you can find the excellent Cuvée Lou Cascaï); and the 1610 **Château Grand'Boise**, **t** 04 42 29 22 95, where the subtle red Cuvée Mazarine and a flowery blanc des blancs are grown amid a large forest.

Near Le Luc, Hervé Goudard's **Domaine de St-Baillon**, on the N7 at Flassans-sur-Issole, **t** 04 94 69 74 60, **f** 04 94 69 80 29, mixes syrah and cabernet bordelais to produce its truffle-scented Cuvée du Roudaï. Just under the landmark cliffs of Montagne Ste-Victoire, **Domaine Richeaume**, at Puyloubier, **t** 04 42 66 31 27, is run by Sylvain Hoesch in Provence's most modern and efficient cave, producing along with rosés an interesting selection of red wines, one of pure syrah and another of pure cabernet-sauvignon. At La Londe-les-Maures (west of Bormes-les-Mimosas), **Domaines Ott**, Clos Mireille, Route de Brégançon, **t** 04 94 01 53 53, offers one of the appellation's top white wines, of ugni and sémillon grapes aged in wooden barrels.

A much higher percentage of red wine is produced in the cooler, drier Coteaux Varois, a region of 28 communes around Brignoles in the central Var, beginning a few miles north of the Bandol district and extending north as far as Tavernes. This old vin de pays has recently been elevated to the ranks of VDQS, and all the vintners along the N7 and the other roads outside Brignoles hang out signs to lure you in.

You can try a good (and completely organic) Coteaux Varois at the **Domaine de Bos Deffens**, on the Cotignac road just east of Barjols. Or sample both Côtes-de-Provence and Coteaux Varois (especially the 1990 reds) at **Château Thuerry**, set in a magnificent wooded landscape at Villecroze, **t** 04 94 70 63 02, **f** 04 94 70 67 03.

Basilica Ste-Marie-Madeleine

After its ramshackle, unfinished façade, on a desolate square decorated only by a faded Dubonnet sign, the interior seems an apparition: the only significant Gothic building in Provence. Despite the prevailing gloom and the hosts of awful, neglected 18th- and 19th-century chapels and altars, the tall arches of the nave and the lovely apse, with its stained glass, leave an impression of dignity and grace.

The original decoration is spare: coats of arms and effigies of Charles of Anjou and Queen Jeanne on some of its capitals. Among the later additions, the most impressive is the enormous, aforementioned **organ**, almost 3,000 pipes and all the work of one man, a Dominican monk named Isnard (1773). Another Dominican, Vincent Funel, was responsible for the lovely choir screen (1691).

To the left of the high altar, don't miss the retable of the *Passion of Christ* (1520) by an obscure Renaissance Fleming named Ronzen, 22 panels of the familiar scenes with some surprising backgrounds: the Papal Palace in Avignon, the Colosseum and Venice's Piazzetta San Marco. Stairs lead down to the **crypt**, a funeral vault from the 4th or 5th century AD, where the holy sarcophagi lie with a host of eerie reliquaries.

The Couvent Royal

The monastery attached to Ste-Marie-Madeleine was a 'royal' convent because the kings of France were its titular priors. After losing it in the Revolution, the Dominican Order bought back the monastery and church in 1859. Apparently St-Maximin proved too depressing even for Dominicans; they bolted for Toulouse in 1957, leaving the vast complex in a terrible state.

Restorations have been going on fitfully since the 1960s. The buildings include the imposing **hospice** from the 1750s (now the town hall), to the left of the basilica's façade; the rest, behind it, now houses an institute for cultural exchanges. The best part is the **cloister**, with Lebanon cedars and a charming subtropical garden in the centre. One of the arcades is a Gothic original of 1295. (*Guided tours of the cloister and basilica available; open all year 9–6; adm*).

The Massif de la Ste-Baume

If you're heading towards Marseille or the coast from here, you might consider a detour into this small but remarkable patch of mountains. Rising as high as 3,199ft, and offering views over the sea and as far north as Mont Ventoux, the massif shelters a small forested plateau called the **Plan d'Aups**. This is a northern-style forest, including maple, beech and sycamore, as well as scores of species of wild flowers and other plants not often seen around the Mediterranean. They have remained in their primeval state because the massif is holy ground, the site of the **cave** (*Sainte-Baume*, or holy grotto) where, according to legend, the Magdalen spent the last years of her life as a hermit. The cave, furnished as a chapel, was part of the pilgrimage to St-Maximin from the Middle Ages on, and can be seen today along the D80. Monastic communities grew up around the site, and you may visit the 13th-century Cistercian **Abbaye de St-Pons**, near the loveliest part of the forests (the Parc de St-Pons).

Beaches on the Côte d'Azur

14

The beaches of the eastern Riviera are not renowned for their beauty. From Menton to Antibes the shore is rocky – beaches are shingle, or in some cases artificial pebble. Lack of sand is more than compensated for by the spectacular settings, backed by 200m cliffs, palm trees and some of the world's most expensive real estate. But purists should head as far as Antibes, where the sand starts in earnest. There are two public beaches in Antibes: the best lie south of the town centre, just before the cape.

Juan-les-Pins, blessed with fine sand, is also cursed with countless private beach clubs. Public beaches exist here – try further west towards Golfe-Juan. Cannes has even more snooty beach clubs, but here, too, there is a public beach, right in front of the Palais des Festivals. Further west towards Mandelieu the beach is sandy, and free.

The western Côte d'Azur region contains some of the most enticing beaches in France. From Cannes to St-Tropez the dramatic corniche road offers glimpses down to small sandy coves hiding between jagged rocks. This is above all a place to take your time, stopping where fancy dictates. The beaches of St-Tropez are actually 5km south of the town – Plage de Tahiti is the most infamous, Plage de Pampelonne the least spoiled. True aficionados head south to Plage de l'Escalet and round Cap Lardier to Gigaro. The footpath east of Gigaro takes you to a well-patronized nudist beach.

From St-Trop to Toulon the road climbs and falls along the Corniche des Maures. Some of the most revered beaches in Europe lie offshore – those on the Ile de Porquerolles have national park status and offer unrivalled sand (catch a ferry from Hyères). West of Toulon, Sanary and Bandol have thin strips of beach, but these get very crowded in summer.

If you fancy a day-trip to a beach during your stay in Provence, here is a selection of the best, from Monaco on the eastern end of the Côte to Bandol and La Ciotat in the west. On p.179 you can find a list of the best beaches in the Marseille area.

Monaco Chic and sharp; safe swimming.
Beaulieu (Plage des Fourmis) Backed by palms, view across to Cap Ferrat.
Villefranche-sur-Mer Fashionable, shingled and safe for children.
St-Jean-Cap-Ferrat (Plage du Passable) Views to Villefranche.
Antibes Port and south of centre on the D2559.
Cannes Palais des Festivals and west to Mandelieu.
St-Aygulf Long sand, lots of space, but crowded in summer.
Les Issambres As above.
Port Grimaud Long beach backing onto Spoerry's *Cité Lacustre*.
St-Tropez Plage de Tahiti, Plage de Pampelonne, Plage de l'Escalet.
Gigaro Long beach, a favourite with families.
Cavalaire-sur-Mer The long sandy beach of the bay, popular with families.
St-Clair Just outside Le Lavandou; views across to the islands.
Cap de Bregançon Wilder coves, off the beaten track.
Ile de Porquerolles Plage de Notre Dame, or any of the northern coastal beaches.
Ile du Levant Héliopolis, premier nudist beach.
Hyères Large town beach.
Bandol/Sanary/La Ciotat Thin beaches; crowded in summer, restful off-season.

Language

Everywhere in France the same level of politeness is expected: use *monsieur, madame* or *mademoiselle* when speaking to everyone (and never *garçon* in restaurants!), from your first *bonjour* to your last *au revoir*.

See pp.70–76 for menu vocabulary.

Pronunciation
Vowels
a, à, â between *a* in 'bat' and 'part'
é, er, ez at end of word as *a* in 'plate' but a bit shorter
e, è, ê as *e* in 'bet'
e at end of word not pronounced
e at end of syllable or in one-syllable word pronounced weakly, like *er* in 'mother'
i as *ee* in 'bee'
o as *o* in 'pot'
ô as *o* in 'go'
u, û between *oo* in 'boot' and *ee* in 'bee'

Vowel Combinations
ai as *a* in 'plate'
aî as *e* in 'bet'
ail as *i* in 'kite'
au, eau as *o* in 'go'
ei as *e* in 'bet'
eu, œu as *er* in 'mother'
oi between *wa* in 'swam' and *wu* in 'swum'
oy as 'why'
ui as *wee* in 'twee'

Nasal Vowels
Vowels followed by an **n** or **m** have a nasal sound.
an, en as *o* in 'pot' + nasal sound
ain, ein, in as *a* in 'bat' + nasal sound
on as *aw* in 'paw' + nasal sound
un as *u* in 'nut' + nasal sound

Consonants
Many French consonants are pronounced as in English, but there are some exceptions:

c followed by *e, i* or *y*, and *ç* as *s* in 'sit'
c followed by *a, o, u* as *c* in 'cat'
g followed by *e, i* or *y* as *s* in 'pleasure'
g followed by *a, o, u* as *g* in 'good'
gn as *ni* in 'opinion'
j as *s* in 'pleasure'
ll as *y* in 'yes'
qu as *k* in 'kite'
s between vowels as *z* in 'zebra'
s otherwise as *s* in 'sit'
w except in English words as *v* in 'vest'
x at end of word as *s* in 'sit'
x otherwise as *x* in 'six'

Stress
The stress usually falls on the last syllable except when the word ends with an unaccented *e*.

Vocabulary

General
hello *bonjour*
good evening *bonsoir*
good night *bonne nuit*
goodbye *au revoir*
please *s'il vous plaît*
thank you (very much) *merci (beaucoup)*
yes *oui*
no *non*
good *bon (bonne)*
bad *mauvais*
excuse me *pardon, excusez-moi*
My name is... *Je m'appelle...*
What is your name? *Comment t'appelles-tu?* (informal), *Comment vous appelez-vous?* (formal)
How are you? *Comment allez-vous?*
Fine *Ça va bien*

I don't understand *Je ne comprend pas*
I don't know *Je ne sais pas*

Could you speak more slowly? *Pourriez-vous parler plus lentement?*
Can you help me? *Pourriez-vous m'aider?*
How do you say ... in French? *Comment dit-on ... en français?*
Help! *Au secours!*

WC *les toilettes*
men *hommes*
ladies *dames* or *femmes*
drinking water *eau potable*
non-drinking water *eau non potable*

doctor *le médecin*
hospital *un hôpital*
emergency room *la salle des urgences*
police station *le commissariat de police*
tourist information office *l'office de tourisme*

No Smoking *Défense de fumer*

Shopping and Sightseeing

Do you have...? *Est-ce que vous avez...?*
I would like... *J'aimerais...*
Where is/are...? *Où est/sont...*
How much is it? *C'est combien?*
It's too expensive *C'est trop cher*

entrance *l'entrée*
exit *la sortie*
open *ouvert*
closed *fermé*
push *poussez*
pull *tirez*

bank *une banque*
money *l'argent*
traveller's cheque *un chèque de voyage*
post office *la poste*
stamp *un timbre*
phone card *la télécarte*
postcard *une carte postale*
public phone *une cabine téléphonique*
Do you have any change? *Avez-vous de la monnaie?*

shop *un magasin*
covered food market *les halles*
tobacconist *un tabac*
pharmacy *la pharmacie*
aspirin *l'aspirine*
condoms *les préservatifs*

insect repellent *crème anti-insecte*
sun cream *la crème solaire*
tampons *les tampons hygiéniques*

beach *la plage*
booking/box office *le bureau de location*
church *l'église*
museum *le musée*
sea *la mer*
theatre *le théâtre*

Accommodation

Do you have a room? *Avez-vous une chambre?*
Can I look at the room? *Puis-je voir la chambre?*
How much is the room per day/week? *La chambre coûte combien par jour/semaine?*
single room *une chambre pour une personne*
twin room *une chambre à deux lits*
double room *une chambre pour deux personnes*
... with a shower/bath *... avec douche/salle de bains*
... for one night/one week *... pour une nuit/une semaine*

bed *un lit*
blanket *une couverture*
cot (child's bed) *un lit d'enfant*
pillow *un oreiller*
soap *du savon*
towel *une serviette*

Directions

Where is...? *Où se trouve...?*
left *à gauche*
right *à droite*
straight on *tout droit*

here *ici*
there *là*
close *proche* or *près*
far *loin*
forwards *en avant*
backwards *en arrière*
up *en haut*
down *en bas*
corner *le coin*
square *la place*
street *la rue*

Transport

I want to go to... *Je voudrais aller à...*
How can I get to...? *Comment puis-je aller à...?*
When is the next...? *Quel est le prochain...?*
What time does it leave (arrive)? *A quelle heure part-il (arrive-t-il)?*
From where does it leave? *D'où part-il?*
Do you stop at...? *Passez-vous par...?*
How long does the trip take? *Combien de temps dure le voyage?*

A (single/return) ticket to... *un aller or aller simple/aller et retour) pour...*
How much is the fare? *Combien coûte le billet?*
Have a good trip! *Bon voyage!*

airport *l'aéroport*
aeroplane *l'avion*
berth *la couchette*
bicycle *la bicyclette/le vélo*
mountain bike *le vélo tout terrain, VTT*
bus *l'autobus*
bus stop *l'arrêt d'autobus*
car *la voiture*
coach *l'autocar*
coach station *la gare routière*
flight *le vol*
on foot *à pied*
port *le port*
railway station *la gare*
ship *le bateau*
subway *le métro*
taxi *le taxi*
train *le train*

delayed *en retard*
on time *à l'heure*
platform *le quai*
date-stamp machine *le composteur*
timetable *l'horaire*
left-luggage locker *la consigne automatique*
ticket office *le guichet*
ticket *le billet*
customs *la douane*
seat *la place*

Driving

breakdown *la panne*
car *la voiture*
danger *le danger*
diesel *gazole/gasoil*

driver *le chauffeur*
entrance *l'entrée*
exit *la sortie*
give way/yield *céder le passage*
hire *louer*
(international) driving licence *un permis de conduire (international)*
motorbike/moped *la moto/le vélomoteur*
no parking *stationnement interdit*
petrol (unleaded) *l'essence (sans plomb)*
road *la route*
road works *les travaux*

This doesn't work *Ça ne marche pas*
Is the road good? *Est-ce que la route est bonne?*

Months

January *janvier*
February *février*
March *mars*
April *avril*
May *mai*
June *juin*
July *juillet*
August *août*
September *septembre*
October *octobre*
November *novembre*
December *décembre*

Days

Monday *lundi*
Tuesday *mardi*
Wednesday *mercredi*
Thursday *jeudi*
Friday *vendredi*
Saturday *samedi*
Sunday *dimanche*

Numbers

quarter *un quart*
half *une moitié or un demi*
one *un*
two *deux*
three *trois*
four *quatre*
five *cinq*
six *six*

seven *sept*
eight *huit*
nine *neuf*
ten *dix*
eleven *onze*
twelve *douze*
thirteen *treize*
fourteen *quatorze*
fifteen *quinze*
sixteen *seize*
seventeen *dix-sept*
eighteen *dix-huit*
nineteen *dix-neuf*
twenty *vingt*
twenty-one *vingt et un*
twenty-two *vingt-deux*
thirty *trente*
forty *quarante*
fifty *cinquante*
sixty *soixante*
seventy *soixante-dix*
seventy-one *soixante et onze*
eighty *quatre-vingts*
eighty-one *quatre-vingt-un*
ninety *quatre-vingt-dix*
one hundred *cent*
two hundred *deux cents*
one thousand *mille*

Time

What time is it? *Quelle heure est-il?*
It's 2 o'clock (am/pm) *Il est deux heures
    (du matin/de l'après-midi)*
... half past 2 ...*deux heures et demie*
... a quarter past 2 ...*deux heures et quart*
... a quarter to 3 ...*trois heures moins le
    quart*
it is early *il est tôt*
it is late *il est tard*

month *un mois*
fortnight *une quinzaine*
week *une semaine*
day *un jour/une journée*
morning *le matin*
afternoon *l'après-midi*
evening *le soir*
night *la nuit*
today *aujourd'hui*
yesterday *hier*
tomorrow *demain*
day before yesterday *avant-hier*
day after tomorrow *après-demain*
soon *bientôt*

Glossary

Abbaye: abbey

Anse: cove

Arrondissement: a city district.

Auberge: inn

Aven: natural well

Bastide: taller, more elaborate version of a *mas*, with balconies, wrought-ironwork, reliefs, etc; also a medieval new town, fortified and laid out in a grid.

Beffroi: tower with a town's bell

Borie: dry-stone shepherd's hut with a corbelled roof

Buffet d'eau: in French gardens, a fountain built into a wall with water falling through levels of urns or basins

Cabane: simple weekend or holiday retreat, usually near the sea; a *cabane de gardian* is a thatched cowboy's abode in the Camargue

Calanque: narrow coastal creek, like a miniature fjord

Capitelles: the name for *bories* in Languedoc

Cardo: the main north–south street in a Roman *castrum* or town

Caryatid: column or pillar carved in the figure of a woman

Castrum: rectangular Roman army camp, which often grew into a permanent settlement

Causse: rocky, arid limestone plateaus, north of Hérault and in the lower Languedoc

Cave: (wine) cellar

Château: mansion, manor house or castle

Chemin: path

Chevet: eastern end of a church, including the apse

Cirque: round natural depression created by erosion at the loop of a river

Cloître: cloister

Clue: rocky cleft or transverse valley

Col: mountain pass

Commune: in the Middle Ages, the government of a free town or city; today, the smallest unit of local government, encompassing a town or village

Côte: coast; on wine labels, *côtes, coteaux* and *costières* mean 'hills' or 'slopes'

Cours: wide main street, like an elongated main square

Couvent: convent or monastery

Crèche: Christmas crib with *santons*

Donjon: castle keep

Ecluse: canal lock

Eglise: church

Etang: lagoon or swamp

Félibre: member of the movement to bring back the use of the Provençal language

Ferrade: cattle branding

Gardian: a cowboy of the Camargue

Gare: train station (SNCF)

Gare routière: coach station

Garrigues: irregular limestone hills pitted with caves, especially those north of Nîmes and Montpellier

Gisant: sculpted prone effigy on a tomb

Gîte: shelter

Gîte d'etape: basic shelter for walkers

Grande Randonnée (GR): long-distance hiking path

Grau: a narrowing, either of a canyon or a river

Halles: covered market

Hôtel: originally the town residence of the nobility; by the 18th century the word became more generally used for any large, private residence

Hôtel de Ville: city hall.

Lavoir: communal fountain, usually covered, for the washing of clothes

Mairie: town hall

Manade: a *gardian*'s farm in the Camargue

Maquis: Mediterranean scrub. Also used as a term for the French Resistance during the Second World War

Marché: market

Mas: a farmhouse and its outbuildings

Mascaron: ornamental mask, usually one carved on the keystone of an arch

Modillon: stone projecting from the cornice of a church, carved with a face or animal figure

Motte: hammock, or a raised area in a swamp

Oppidum: pre-Roman fortified settlement

Parlement: French juridical body, with members appointed by the king; by the late *ancien régime, parlements* exercised a great deal of influence over political affairs

Pays: region or village

Pont: bridge

Porte: gateway

Predella: small paintings beneath the main subject of a retable

Presqu'île: peninsula

Puy: hill

Restanques: vine or olive terraces

Retable: carved or painted altarpiece, often consisting of a number of scenes or sculpted ensembles

Rez-de-chaussée (RC): ground floor

Santon: figure in a Christmas nativity scene, usually made of terracotta and dressed in 18th-century Provençal costume

Source: spring

Tour: tower

Transi: on a tomb, a relief of the decomposing cadaver

Tympanum: sculpted semicircular panel over a church door

Vieille ville: historic, old quarter of town

Village perché: hill-top village

Chronology

BC

c. 1,000,000 First human presence, near Menton; use of bone as a tool

c. 400,000 Discovery of fire, as at Terra Amata in Nice

c. 60,000 Neanderthal hunters on the Riviera and around Ganges

c. 40,000 Advent of *Homo sapiens*; invention of art

c. 8000 Invention of the bow

c. 3500 Development of Neolithic culture; first villages built

c. 2000 First metallurgy; copper and tin at Vence and Caussols

c. 1800–1000 Worship on Mont Bégo, at Tende, incisions made in the Vallée des Merveilles

c. 600 Greek traders found Marseille

c. 380 Celtic invasions in Provence

218 Hannibal and elephants pass through region on the way to Italy

125 Roman legions attack Celto-Ligurian tribes that threaten Marseille

122 Founding of Aquae Sextiae (Aix)

118 Founding of Narbonne and Provincia, the first Roman province in Gaul

102 Marius and his legionaries defeat the Teutones

49 Marius' nephew, Julius Caesar, punishes Marseille for supporting Pompey

14 Augustus defeats Ligurian tribes in the Alpes-Maritimes

AD

46 Arrival of the Boat of Bethany at Stes-Maries-de-la-Mer (trad.)

310 Emperor Maximilian captured at Marseille by son-in-law Constantine

314 Constantine calls Church Council at Arles

413 Visigoths conquer Languedoc

476 Formal end of Western Roman Empire

535 Provence and Languedoc ceded to the Franks

719 Arab invasions in Languedoc

737 Charles Martel defeats Arabs and crushes anti-Frank rebellions in Arles, Avignon and Marseille

759 Pépin the Short adds region to his Frankish empire

855 Creation of the kingdom of Provence for Charles the Bald

879 Duke Viennois Boson proclaims himself king of Provence

c. 890 More Arab raids and invasions

924 Magyars (Hungarians) sack Nîmes

949 Conrad of Burgundy inherits Provence and divides it into four feudal counties

979 Count William defeats Saracens at La Garde-Freinet, proclaims himself marquis of Provence

1002 First written text in Occitan

1032 Death of Rudolph II, king of Burgundy and Provence; lands bequeathed to Holy Roman Emperor Conrad II

1095 Occitans join First Crusade under Raymond of St-Gilles, count of Toulouse and marquis of Provence; William of Aquitaine writes first troubadour poetry

1112 Marriage of Douce, duchess of Provence, with Raymond-Berenger III, count of Barcelona

1125 Provence divided between the houses of Barcelona and Toulouse

1176 Pierre Valdo of Lyon founds Waldensian (Vaudois) sect

1186 Counts of Provence make Aix their capital

1187 Discovery of relics of St Martha at Tarascon

1246 Charles I of Anjou weds Béatrice, heiress of Provence, beginning the Angevin dynasty

1248 St Louis embarks on Seventh Crusade from Aigues-Mortes

1266 Battle of Benevento gives Charles of Anjou the Kingdom of Naples

1272 Narbonne Cathedral begun

1274 Papacy acquires Comtat Venaissin

1280 Relics of Mary Magdalene 'discovered' at St-Maximin-la-Ste-Baume

1286 First meeting of the Etats de Provence

1295 The death of the 'last troubadour', Guiraut Riquier

1297 Francesco Grimaldi the Spiteful, merchant-prince of Genoa, conquers Monaco (but is forced to abandon it in 1301)

1303 Boniface VIII founds University of Avignon

1309 Papacy moves to Avignon

1327 Petrarch first sees Laura

1340s Siennese painters bring International Gothic style to Avignon

1348 Jeanne of Naples and Provence sells Avignon to the pope; the Black Death strikes the south

1349 Jews expelled from France and take refuge in the Comtat Venaissin

c. 1350 First paper mills in the Comtat Venaissin

1362 Election of abbot of St-Victor as Pope Urban V

1360s The Grandes Compagnies ravage the countryside

1363 The Grimaldis recover Monaco and hold it still

1377 Papacy returns to Rome

1380 Louis I d'Anjou adopted by Jeanne of Naples

1388 Regions of Nice, Barcelonnette and Puget-Théniers secede from Provence and join county of Savoy

1464 Founding of the Fair of Beaucaire

1481 Count of Provence leaves Provence to the king of France

1501 French create *Parlement* of Aix to oversee Provence

1524 Provence invaded by the imperial troops of Charles V

1525 Jews in the Comtat Venaissin compelled to wear yellow hats

1539 Edict of Villars-Cotterêts forces use of French as official language

1540 *Parlement* of Aix orders massacre of Waldensians in the Luberon

1559 Completion of the canal between the Durance and Salon

1562 Beginning of Wars of Religion: Protestant assembly at Mérindol

1577 First soap factory (Prunemoyr) founded in Marseille

1590–2 Carlo Emanuele of Savoy invades Provence

1598 Edict of Nantes ends the Wars of Religion

1603 Royal college founded at Aix

1639 Last meeting of the Etats de Provence before the Revolution

1646 Jews confined to ghettos

1680 Louis XIV enters rebellious Marseille

1685 Louis XIV revokes Edict of Nantes

1702–4 The War of the Camisards

1720–1 100,000 die of plague, mostly in Marseille

1731 Principality of Orange incorporated into France

1752 Last Protestant persecutions

1779 Roman mausoleum and palace of the counts demolished, at Aix

1784 Hot air balloon goes up in Marseille

1787 The Edict of Tolerance

1790 France divided into *départements*

1791 France annexes Comtat Venaissin

1792 Volunteers from Marseille sing La Marseillaise to Paris

1793 Revolutionary tribunal in Marseille; Siege of Toulon makes Bonaparte famous

1795 Massacres in Marseille and Tarascon

1800 Marseille population around 100,000

1815 Napoleon escapes Elba

1830 Revolution brings Louis Philippe to power

1831 Lord Brougham begins the vogue for wintering in Cannes

1839 Inauguration of Marseille–Sète railroad; birth of Cézanne

1840–8 Prime Ministry of Guizot, Protestant liberal from Nîmes

1851 Louis Napoleon's coup ends Second Republic; armed resistance in the south

1854 Founding of the Félibrige at the Château de Fontségugne

1859 Mistral publishes *Miréio*

1860 Plebiscite in county of Nice votes for union with France

1865 Silkworm industry destroyed by disease

1868–90 Phylloxera epidemic devastates vines

1869 Opening of Suez Canal brings boom times to Marseille

1888 Stephen Liégeard gives the Côte d'Azur its name

1888–90 Van Gogh in Provence

1900 Population reaches 500,000 in Marseille, 20% of which is Italian

1904 Frédéric Mistral wins the Nobel Prize for Literature

1906 Colonial Exposition at Marseille

1924–5 Scott and Zelda Fitzgerald raise hell on the Riviera

1928 Creation of the Camargue Regional Park

1930s Marcel Pagnol films his *Marius, Fanny* and *César* trilogy in Marseille

1939 Founding of the Cannes Film Festival

1942 Sinking of the fleet at Toulon

1943 Formation of the Maquis resistance cells

1944 American and French landings around St-Tropez; Provence liberated in two weeks

1945 Creation of the Institut d'Etudes Occitanes

1962 Independence of Algeria: tens of thousands of French North Africans (*pieds-noirs*) settle in the south

1965 Last silk weaving company closed

1966 Steelworks founded at Fos

1970 Completion of Paris–Lyon–Marseille *autoroute*

1982 Regional governments created

1992 30 die in Vaison-la-Romaine floods

2001 High-speed rail link between Paris and Marseille opened

Further Reading

Ardagh, John, *France Today* (Penguin, 1987). One in Penguin's informative paperback series on contemporary Europe.

Barr, Alfred, *Henri Matisse: his Art and his Public* (Museum of Modern Art, New York, 1951).

Bishop, Morris, *Petrarch and His World* (Chatto & Windus, 1964).

Bonner, Anthony, *Songs of the Troubadours* (Allen & Unwin, 1973). An excellent introduction to the life and times of the troubadours, with translations of the best-known verses.

Cézanne, Paul, *Letters* (London, 1941).

Cook, Theodore A., *Old Provence* (London, 1905). A classic traveller's account of the region, out of print and hard to find.

Daudet, Alphonse, *Letters from my Windmill* (Penguin, 1982). Bittersweet 19th-century tales of Midi nostalgia by Van Gogh's favourite novelist.

Dumas, Alexandre, *The Count of Monte Cristo*, many editions; romantic fantastical tale of revenge, much of it set in Marseille and the Château d'If.

Durrell, Lawrence, *The Avignon Quintet* (Faber, 1974–85); lush wartime sagas that take place in Avignon and around.

Fitzgerald, F. Scott, *Tender is the Night*, many editions. 1920s Riviera decadence based on personal research.

Ford, Ford Madox, *Provence: From Minstrels to the Machine* (Allen & Unwin, 1935). A lyrical pre-war view of the region.

Fortescue, Winifred, *Perfume from Provence* (1935). Poor, intolerable Lady Fortescue's misadventures with the garlicky peasants near Nice.

Giono, Jean, *To the Slaughterhouse, Two Riders of the Storm* (Peter Owen, 1988). Giono is a major 20th-century novelist of Provence, whose deep pessimism contrasts with the sunnier views of his contemporary Pagnol.

Goldring, Douglas, *The South of France* (Macdonald, 1952). Travels and comments by another English resident.

Gramont, Sanche de, *The French: Portrait of a People* (Putnam, New York, 1969). One of the funnier attempts at the favourite French intellectual pastime: national self-analysis.

Greene, Graham, *J'Accuse: The Dark Side of Nice* (Bodley Head, 1982). The late Graham Greene, resident of Antibes, discovers the mafia connections and graft in the government of discredited mayor Jacques Médecin.

Hugo, Victor, *Les Misérables*, many editions. Injustice among the galley-slaves and basis for the hit musical.

Ladurie, Emmanuel Leroi, *Love, Death and Money in the Pays d'Oc* (Scolar, 1982).

de Larrabeiti, Michael, *The Provençal Tales* (Pavilion, 1988). Troubadours' tales, legends and stories told by shepherds around the camp fire.

Lyall, Archibald, *Companion Guide to the South of France* (Collins, 1978). Personal, well-written but dated guide to the entire Mediterranean coast.

Mayle, Peter, *A Year in Provence* and *Toujours Provence* (Sinclair Stevenson/Pan, 1989 and 1991). The entertaining bestsellers on ex-pat life in the Luberon.

Mistral, Frédéric, *Miréio* and *Poème du Rhône*, epic poems by the Nobel Prize-winning Félibre, widely available in French or Provençal.

More, Carey and Julian, *A Taste of Provence* (Pavilion, 1987). Father and daughter team up to evoke the countryside and gastronomy of Provence in words and photographs.

Morris, Edwin T., *Fragrance: The Story of Perfume from Cleopatra to Chanel* (Charles Scribner & Sons, 1984).

Pagnol, Marcel, *Jean de Florette* and *Manon of the Springs. The Days were too Short* (Picador, 1960). Autobiography by Provence's most beloved writer.

Petrarch, Francesco, *Songs and Sonnets from Laura's Lifetime* (Anvil Press, 1985).

Pope Hennessy, James, *Aspects of Provence* (Penguin, 1952). A fussy but lyrical view of the region in the 1940s and 50s.

Smollett, Tobias, *Travels through France and Italy* (London, 1766). The irrepressible, grouchy Tobias 'Smelfungus' makes modern travel writing look like advertising copy.

Stendhal, *Travels through the South of France* (London, 1971).

Süskind, Patrick, *Perfume* (Penguin, 1989). Thrilling and fragrant murder in the 18th-century perfume industry in Grasse.

Van Gogh, Vincent, *Collected Letters of Vincent Van Gogh* (New York, 1978).

Vergé, Roger, *Cuisine of the Sun* (London, 1979). The owner of the Moulin de Mougins tells some of his secrets of nouvelle Provençal cooking.

Whitfield, Sarah, *Fauvism* (Thames and Hudson, 1991). A good introduction to the movement that changed art history.

Worwood, Valerie, *Aromantics* (Pan, 1987). An amusing look at aromatherapy.

Wylie, L., *Village in the Vaucluse* (Harvard University Press, 1971). The third edition of a very readable sociologist's classic based on the village of Roussillon.

Zeldin, Theodore, *France 1845–1945* (Oxford University Press, 1980). Five well-written volumes on all aspects of the period.

Index

Main page references are in **bold**. Page references to maps are in *italics*.

Also available from Cadogan Guides in our European series...

Italy

Italy
Italy: The Bay of Naples and Southern Italy
Italy: Lombardy and the Italian Lakes
Italy: Tuscany, Umbria and the Marches
Italy: Tuscany
Italy: Umbria
Italy: Northeast Italy
Italy: Italian Riviera
Italy: Bologna and Emilia Romagna
Italy: Rome and the Heart of Italy
Sardinia
Sicily
Rome, Florence, Venice
Florence, Siena, Pisa & Lucca
Venice

Spain

Spain
Spain: Andalucía
Spain: Northern Spain
Spain: Bilbao and the Basque Lands
Granada, Seville, Cordoba
Madrid, Barcelona, Seville

Greece

Greece: The Peloponnese
Greek Islands
Greek Islands By Air
Corfu & the Ionian Islands
Mykonos, Santorini & the Cyclades
Rhodes & the Dodecanese
Crete

France

France
France: Dordogne & the Lot
France: Gascony & the Pyrenees
France: Brittany
France: Loire

France: The South of France
France: Provence
France: Côte d'Azur
Corsica
Short Breaks in Northern France

The UK and Ireland

London–Amsterdam
London–Edinburgh
London–Paris
London–Brussels

Scotland
Scotland: Highlands and Islands
Edinburgh

Ireland
Ireland: Southwest Ireland
Ireland: Northern Ireland

Other Europe

Portugal
Portugal: The Algarve
Madeira & Porto Santo

Malta
Germany: Bavaria
Holland

The City Guide Series

Amsterdam
Brussels
Paris
Rome
Barcelona
Madrid
London
Florence
Prague
Bruges
Sydney

Cadogan Guides are available from good bookshops, or via **Grantham Book Services,** Isaac Newton Way, Alma Park Industrial Estate, Grantham NG31 9SD, **t** (01476) 541 080, **f** (01476) 541 061; and **The Globe Pequot Press,** 246 Goose Lane, PO Box 480, Guilford, Connecticut 06437–0480, **t** 800 458 4500/**f** (203) 458 4500, **t** (203) 458 4603.

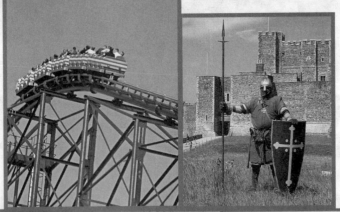

'Everything you need to know about going on holiday with your children.'
The Express

CADOGANguides
well travelled well read

Provence touring atlas

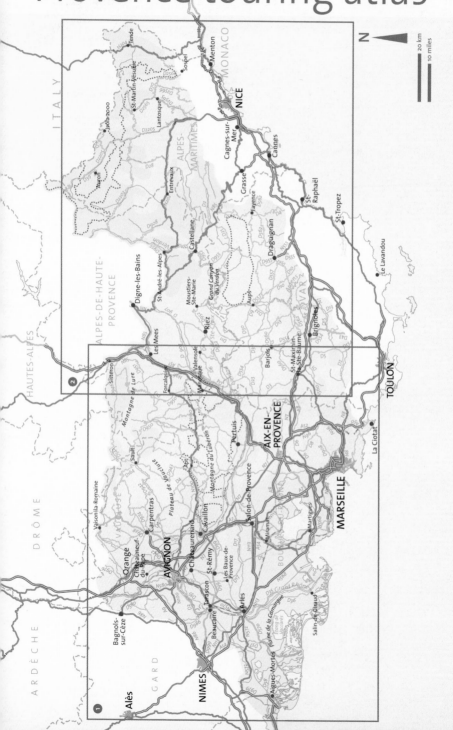

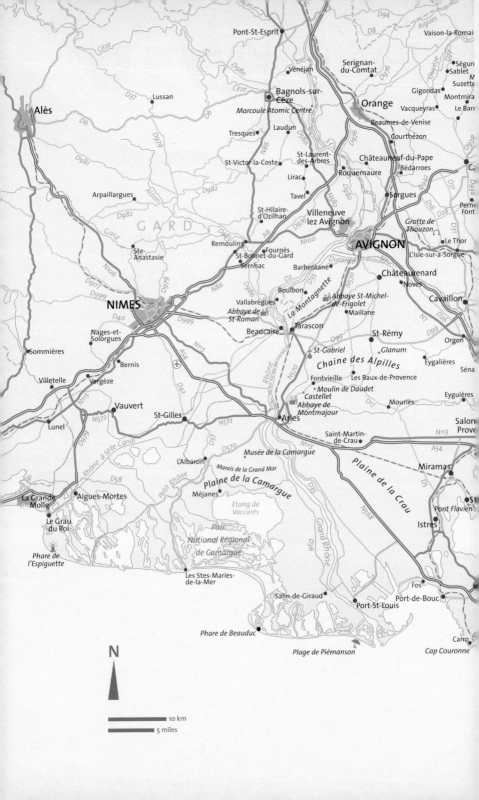

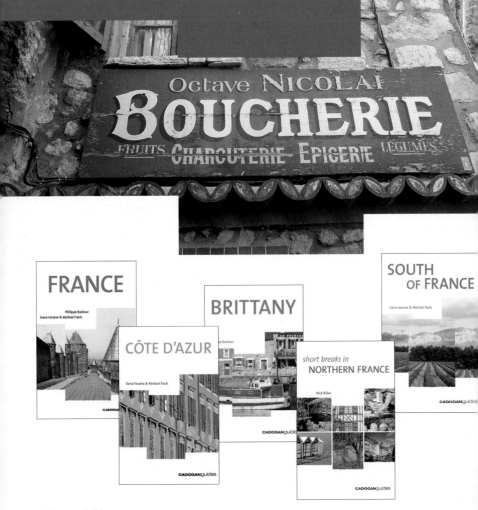

'veritable page-turners...
excellently written,
bursting with character'
Holiday Which

FRANCE

CÔTE D'AZUR

BRITTANY

short breaks in
NORTHERN FRANCE

SOUTH
OF FRANCE

Also available:
Corsica
Dordogne and the Lot
Gascony and the Pyrenees
The Loire
Take the Kids Paris

CADOGANguides
www.cadoganguides.com

Shorten your drive

lengthen your holiday

Don't spend your holiday driving hundreds of miles through France, when we can take you and your car closer to your holiday destination. Not only that, we offer the best choice of routes and the finest on-board experience, all for less than you'd expect.

Reservations & Bookings
0870 908 1286

Brittany Ferries